T0323046

Constructing Organizational Life

Constructing Organizational Life

How Social-Symbolic Work Shapes Selves, Organizations, and Institutions

Thomas B. Lawrence and Nelson Phillips

OXFORD
UNIVERSITY PRESS

OXFORD
UNIVERSITY PRESS

Great Clarendon Street, Oxford, OX2 6DP,
United Kingdom

Oxford University Press is a department of the University of Oxford.
It furthers the University's objective of excellence in research, scholarship,
and education by publishing worldwide. Oxford is a registered trade mark of
Oxford University Press in the UK and in certain other countries

First Edition published in 2019

Published in the United States of America by Oxford University Press
198 Madison Avenue, New York, NY 10016, United States of America

British Library Cataloguing in Publication Data
Data available

Library of Congress Control Number: 2019937244

ISBN 978-0-19-884002-2

Printed and bound by
CPI Group (UK) Ltd, Croydon, CR0 4YY

For our parents, who taught us the importance of work
and the value of love

Preface

We entered academe at the time the Soviet Union and apartheid collapsed. Just as we were starting our doctorates in organizational analysis at the University of Alberta, these seemingly immutable structures that had occupied such a central cultural and political position since the Second World War (and for our entire lives), simply disappeared. Our seminar discussions, and, perhaps more importantly, endless informal conversations in Java U (our favorite campus coffee shop) and the Power Plant (the graduate student bar), were energized and shaped by these fundamental social changes. We argued for hours about the usefulness of existing theories of society and organization in understanding these events, whether this mattered, and what to do about it. Our entire PhD experience was shaped by the challenge of figuring out what these kinds of events meant for social theory.

We were especially moved by the images of citizens with sledgehammers breaking down the Berlin Wall and eventually distilled our concerns into a question: we wanted to know why, if social structures that seemed as enduring as these could be changed by people working together, were purposeful agents so absent from the social theory that we were studying? The world was evidently not just mutable and changing, it was changeable by the purposeful acts of common citizens! This was an exciting idea that we spent many hours discussing, and eventually writing about.

The second thing that affected how we think about the social world was the appearance of a new version of the "end of history" argument. Many philosophers and social scientists over the last 200 years have written about the idea that at some point a particularly enduring economic, social, and political system would appear that would signal the end of socioeconomic evolution (think, for example, of Marx and his writings on the final communist system).

In 1989, Francis Fukuyama published an essay entitled "The end of history?" in which he argued that, with the fall of the Soviet Union, we were witnessing not just the end of a regime, but the end of history. From his perspective, the fall of the Soviet Union was not just the fall of a great nation state, it marked disappearance of the engine of history. The grand arc carved out by the clash of capitalism and communism that characterized the twentieth century was over. As he argued (Fukuyama, 1989: 4):

> What we may be witnessing is not just the end of the Cold War, or the passing of a particular period of post-war history, but the end of history as such: that is, the end point of mankind's ideological evolution and the universalization of Western liberal democracy as the final form of human government.

But this raised a second important question for us: how should we think about and investigate this new, post-historical world? Without the clash of great ideologies, what would be the engine of change? Or was change just a characteristic of social systems and no engine was needed? For two budding social theorists, this led to the substitution of the modernist ideas of Marx, Weber, and Durkheim with the postmodernism of Foucault, Lyotard, and Baudrillard. The collision of totalizing ideologies and the resulting structuring of the world was replaced with the idea that change was driven by much smaller-scale actions, and the chaos and uncertainty that this often entails. This also meant, however, that we needed a better theory of how local action leads to social structure, something that led us to new and exciting theoretical areas such as social constructionism and poststructuralism.

Our supervisors and professors were somewhat bemused by where we were going with all of this. Their feelings can best be summarized by a comment from a faculty member visiting the University of Alberta from the University of Illinois who, following a particularly combative seminar when one of us tried to present some of these ideas, said: "This is probably all true but why do you have to say it? There are perfectly good existing theories to explain these things." We didn't agree.

In combination, these events and trends provided the motivation and context that have fueled almost three decades of work and eventually led to this book. We wanted to explore the role of actors in the construction of the social world and communicate the exciting ramifications of what we found. At the same time, we wanted to understand the limits of intentional local action and try to define the point at which the social becomes unmanageable as larger forces take over. In doing so, we hoped to provide a roadmap for studying and analyzing people's purposeful efforts to shape the social world. We believe this represents an exciting project and hope you find it as interesting and hopeful as we do.

Of course, in developing this project, we have had help from a number of people and groups that we would like to thank here. First, we would like to thank the following people for their comments on draft material and presentations: Sally Maitlis, Emilio Marti, Eva Schlindwein, Gloria Kutscher, Rene Weidner, Pedro Monteiro, Gerry McGivern, participants in our EGOS sub-themes in Copenhagen and Tallin, Write Club members at the University of Oxford, seminar participants at Warwick Business School, the University of Arizona, Tilburg University, and the 5th Austrian Early Scholars Workshop in Management.

We also want to thank Stephanie Creary for the joy and insight she brought to co-convening with us a series of EGOS sub-themes on social-symbolic work—qualities we believe may have rubbed off in the better parts of the book. We want to thank our editor at OUP, Adam Swallow, for his guidance and patience, as well as the anonymous reviewers who helped us clarify our direction in the early stages of the book's development. We also want to thank two professors at the University of Alberta who taught us then and continue to inspire us today—Bob Hinings and Royston Greenwood deserve much of the credit for any academic value this book might deliver (but of course none of the blame for what we got wrong).

More generally, in writing this book we have benefited from conversations with a great many people about our developing ideas about organizations, institutions, selves, and work. These conversations have helped us immeasurably as we have developed the ideas that populate this book. There are far too many of you to list here, but we want to shout out to a few without whom this book would look nothing like it does, and likely not exist at all: John Amis, Stephanie Bertels, Graham Dover, Bruno Dyck, Bryan Gallagher, Bob Gephart, Christian Hampel, Cynthia Hardy, Paul Hirsch, Dev Jennings, Matt Kraatz, Bernard Leca, Mike Lounsbury, Steve Maguire, Michael Mauws, Kamal Munir, Christine Oliver, Cliff Oswick, Markus Perkmann, Davide Ravasi, Masoud Shadnam, Roy Suddaby, Paul Tracey, Charlene Zietsma, and Tammar Zilber. We know we are missing many others, but you know who you are, and we thank you.

Finally, we want to thank our partners and families who make the work both possible and meaningful. Nelson would like to thank Cristina for her patience and support when it must have seemed like it might never end. Tom would like to thank Sally, Evan, Claire, Alice, and Nina—it's done.

Table of Contents

Detailed Table of Contents

Part III

List of Figures

List of Tables

Part I

1

Introduction to Constructing Organizational Life

At the head office of a large insurance company in the American Midwest, Roberta de Pina looked at the clock in the corner of her computer screen and sighed. She only had two hours until the Executive Committee meeting where she would present her new proposal to strengthen the company's diversity and inclusion policy. As the Chief Diversity Officer, she was deeply committed to improving the way LGBTQ+ staff were treated. At the same time, she knew that the discussion of her proposal would be tricky, and that the members of the Executive Committee were in very different places in terms of their thinking on gender and sexuality. It would be a challenge to get them to agree to support her forward-looking proposal, perhaps especially the formation of an LGBT corporate network and mentorship program. Yet, Roberta felt strongly that change was necessary if the organization was to really support diversity and she was excited by the opportunity to make a real difference. Now if she could just convince the committee!

At around the same time, Peter Spicer looked out of the window of his flat in London's East End. The setting sun cast a warm light on the Victorian houses that lined the street, but Peter hardly noticed. He was deep in thought, mulling over how to ensure his demanding clients were well taken care of while he was on his upcoming paternity leave. Becoming a dad was something that he was really looking forward to, but it came with significant challenges, especially as he was the first partner in his firm to take paternity leave. And, as one of the youngest partners, he was aware that he still had much to prove in the eyes of some of the senior partners. But Peter was also committed to participating fully in bringing up his daughter. He felt strongly that taking the leave would help him to start building the sort of bond he wanted to have with her. But he knew he would need to find a way to be both a successful partner and an engaged parent if he was to make a success of the next year.

Back across the Atlantic, Marie Tremblant was addressing a meeting of CLASSE, a student activist group at a large university in Montreal, Canada. Marie was sketching out the arrangements that had been made for representatives of CLASSE to join a province-wide planning committee to agree on the plan for an upcoming student protest against university fees in Quebec. One of the members raised her hand to ask about the goal of the protest. Marie explained that the goals were twofold. First, to put pressure on the government to commit to reversing the recent decision to raise tuition fees and, second, to change the way people in Quebec thought about the right of young people to an affordable education. This second goal was the one that really animated Marie. Her excitement about changing societal attitudes toward free university education showed in her voice and body language as she explained more about this second goal and enthusiastically pitched her view of the possibilities for the future.

* * *

Roberta, Peter, and Marie are constructing organizational life, including the rules and routines that shape and enable organizational activity, the identities of people who occupy organizations, and the societal norms and assumptions that provide the context for organizational action. We use the term "constructing" to emphasize the ways in which people and groups engage in purposeful, reflexive efforts rooted in an awareness of organizational life as constructed and therefore changeable. This kind of purposeful action is the focus of increasing scholarly attention across management and organizational research, with growing streams of research developing in areas like strategy work, boundary work, identity work, institutional work, and many others.

These disparate streams of research share an appreciation of the importance of purposeful, reflexive efforts in shaping organizational life. Missing from these conversations, however, is a recognition of the underlying similarities among the actions of an insurance company executive revamping her organization's policies and routines, a lawyer negotiating a new identity as both a parent and a professional, and a student leader influencing the societal conversation on access to higher education. Also missing is recognition of how these forms of action interact: scholars have largely focused on the efforts of people to shape organizational routines *or* personal identities *or* societal assumptions, while the ways in which these efforts and their impacts are interwoven and interdependent has been largely overlooked.

Our aim in this book is to develop a perspective that can overcome these limitations and provide a basis for scholars to explore people's efforts to shape the social world of organizations, not as isolated forms of action, but as a broad family of activities with essential commonalities as well as important differences. What connects these forms of action is their common focus on shaping what we refer to as "social-symbolic objects"—combinations of discursive, relational, and material elements that constitute meaningful patterns in social systems. In organizational life, social-symbolic objects include elements of the organization such as strategies, boundaries, and technologies, as well as the identities, emotions, and careers of members, and the beliefs, assumptions, and categories that populate an organization's institutional context. Because people's efforts to change the social world are focused on social-symbolic objects, we refer to these efforts as "social-symbolic work," which we define as purposeful, reflexive efforts intended to shape or maintain social-symbolic objects in organizational life.

In this book, we develop a social-symbolic work perspective on analyzing and understanding the social world, and see it as complementary to existing structural and processual approaches. Our focus is on the efforts of interested actors working to affect the social and symbolic world around them. This involves a shift from examining the role of social structures in shaping social action or the processes that underpin social life, to examining the actors and actions that shape those structures and processes, transforming them as well as holding them in place. We argue that by examining the intentional efforts of people and groups to shape the social world *in addition to* these more conventional approaches, we can come to a richer understanding of the social world, how it came to be the way it is, how it is held in place, how it changes, and perhaps most importantly, who it is that makes these things happen in the first place (see Box 1.1 for an illustration of the differences between structural, process, and work perspectives).

The Intellectual Foundations of Our Book

The intellectual roots of this book are both old—our arguments draw on ideas about the nature of language that were first suggested more than a century ago—and new—they build on recent scholarship in the social sciences that has focused on understanding the heterogeneous relationship between agency and social structure. As a prelude to the chapters that lay out our arguments and explore the concepts we are proposing, we will discuss some of these ideas and how they underpin our framework.

The Intellectual Roots of Social-Symbolic Objects

The concept of a social-symbolic object arises out of the long arc of increasing interest in, and appreciation for, the role of language in social life. This "linguistic turn" (Rorty, 1967) reflects a growing recognition that language is

---

Box 1.1. STRUCTURE/PROCESS/WORK VIEWS

"It's not personal, Sonny. It's strictly business." (Michael Corleone, *The Godfather*)

In the 1972 crime drama *The Godfather*, Al Pacino plays Michael Corleone, a recent Ivy League graduate who must unexpectedly take over from his father as the Don of a New York crime family. The movie chronicles Michael's transformation from reluctant outsider to terrifyingly effective crime boss following the attempted murder of his father. The story provides a useful example to consider how social phenomenon can be analyzed from the three perspectives we have discussed in this chapter in order to highlight the underlying assumptions and contribution of each perspective.

Structural perspective. First, from a structural perspective, the story can be understood as one where the patterned social arrangements in place in American society, and in the social milieu of the Corleone family, inescapably shape Michael and turn an Ivy League graduate heading for a conventional job in a company into the don of one of the biggest crime families in America. Michael's initial desire to avoid entering the dark world of the Mafia is irrelevant in the face of the pressures that are created by the social structures in which he is embedded and that inexorably draw him into the role he has always avoided. These structures work "behind the actor's back" to shape Michael's actions and interests in ways that lead to an all too predictable outcome. The important contribution of a structural perspective is that it highlights the larger social forces that are at work and focuses on explaining the predictable patterns in outcome that occur in social systems.

Process perspective. A process perspective, on the other hand, is not about predicting the outcome but rather revealing the ongoing movement and flux that characterize social systems. From this perspective, the social world is not a set of structures that require identification, but rather a complex process that needs to be described. It is not, therefore, the larger structures that are of interest but rather the patterns in the changes that occur and the mechanisms that are driving these changes. In the case of Michael, it is the process through which he undergoes this transformation and the mechanisms that drive it. The attempted murder of his father and the resulting chaos in his family become triggering events for a transformation in how he thinks about himself and his role in the family. The incompetence of his brothers and the lack of leadership they display add to the complex process that reshapes Michael. From this perspective, flow replaces stability, as the focus of attention moves to understanding the sequence of events that occur through time and the patterns of change in a particular social world.

Social-symbolic work perspective. Finally, a work perspective changes the focus once again. Rather than attending to outcome or process, a work perspective focuses our attention on Michael's efforts to change himself and the Corleone crime syndicate. In the film, we see Michael perform a number of different kinds of work as he fashions a new identity for himself as don of the Corleone empire and as he works at the organizational level to maintain and strengthen aspects of the organization that he believes to be important while also working to remove practices and change boundaries where appropriate. From this perspective, the purposeful efforts of Michael to change or maintain his identity, the organization and its boundaries, and the relation between the organization and the broader social environment become the focus of attention.

not simply a tool for communicating information, but that it plays an active role in constituting social reality. From this perspective, words do not describe a pre-existing world that we have discovered; instead, the world that we encounter is constituted by the concepts that are available in language to divide it up and make sense of it. This view of language as being more than a "mirror of nature" began in philosophy with writers like de Saussure (1983) and Wittgenstein (2009), and went on to profoundly influence work first in the humanities and, somewhat later, in the social sciences. This shift in our understanding of the role of language in constituting social reality has led to a fundamental change in how scholars working from this perspective think about and study social phenomena.

Along this influential arc, two contributions have particularly inspired our approach to conceptualizing social-symbolic objects. The first was the publication of Berger and Luckmann's (1966) *The social construction of reality*. We inherit from Berger and Luckmann an interest in understanding how people, through language, interaction, and reflection, assemble social reality from their direct experiences and their inherited histories. Two aspects of Berger and Luckmann's argument are of particular importance to the perspective we are developing. The first is institutionalization, which, for Berger and Luckmann, describes the process through which meaning is assigned to sets of habits and routines. The second is legitimation, which involves the construction of explanations that justify institutions to new generations of participants in social arenas. For us, these two processes are central to understanding the construction and maintenance of social-symbolic objects and are thus central to the aims of this book.

The second source of inspiration comes from the work of Michel Foucault, who in a series of monographs including *The birth of the clinic*, *Madness and civilization*, and *The archaeology of knowledge*, established an approach to understanding the origins and evolution of social-symbolic objects that has profoundly influenced a generation of scholars, demonstrating not only that reality is socially constructed, but that the processes through which that construction occurs are infused with heterogeneous forms of power, some of which may be tied to conflict but others distinctly not so.

In this book, the impact of Foucault's writing can be clearly seen in our own attempts to understand the historical evolution of the social-symbolic objects on which we focus. Before exploring the social-symbolic work associated with particular objects, we first examine the history of those objects, developing our own short "archaeologies" that help explain how and in what ways the social-symbolic objects have become the targets of social-symbolic work. Our specific approach to this question is informed by writers who have emphasized the distinctive historical shifts associated with modernity and postmodernity (Bauman, 2000; Giddens, 1991; Harvey, 1989; Jameson, 1991; Lyotard, 1984).

For each of the main social-symbolic objects we discuss, we explore how they were transformed in the transitions to modernity and postmodernity, and how these transformations made possible new kinds of social-symbolic work.

To illustrate the idea of a social-symbolic object, consider the concept of an endangered species. This idea is now widely accepted, it appears commonly in everyday speech, and lists of endangered species can be found on various websites. But the idea of an "endangered species" is not simply a descriptor denoting that only a few members of a species exist. Instead, it brings with it an inescapable sense that for a species to be endangered is a bad thing that demands action. This moral imperative has, in some countries, been translated into laws that specify the actions that must be taken to protect species identified as endangered. The term emerged from work done over more than a century by a vast array of conservationists, hunting organizations, government agencies, and scientists. In the United States, the term was eventually codified in a series of legislative acts, culminating in the 1973 Endangered Species Act. Consequently, "endangered species" is now a social-symbolic object that brings with it ideas about how to recognize a species as endangered as well as a moral imperative for action once one is identified.

The first important aspect of this example involves the relationship between "endangered species" as a social-symbolic object and the world it describes. At this point in history, the concept of endangered species exists as part of a set of interrelated concepts that make up a particular view of the natural environment and allow forms of action not possible without these concepts. Endangered species can be identified in the world and action taken to protect them (or not). Endangered species are real in the sense that they are part of social reality, rather than imagined, fictional, or unreal in some other way. At the same time, endangered species were not something out there waiting to be found, but were constructed through more or less intentional human activity. There were no "endangered species" until lawmakers, scientists, environmental activists, and others engaged in work that made this concept meaningful—that is, performed the social-symbolic work that made it real. Prior to the introduction and widespread acceptance of this term, there were populations of animals of which only a few remained; but there were no "endangered species" that deserved protection. This concept was socially constructed and in coming into being allowed particular groups of animals to be identified as endangered species and treated as such.

The Intellectual Roots of Social-Symbolic Work

While the broader literature on social construction focuses primarily on how social reality is constructed and the nature of the social-symbolic objects produced, more recent streams of literature have brought increased attention to the role of actors working purposefully to shape processes of social construction. Questions about the relationship between agency and social structure have long occupied a central place in social science of course. Relatively recent writing, however, has managed to move beyond the sterile debates that positioned agency in opposition to structure as primary explanations of human behavior for much of the history of social science. Instead, scholars have proposed an understanding of agency that is more fluid, situational, heterogeneous, and relational (Battilana, 2006; Emirbayer, 1997; Emirbayer and Mische, 1998; Fine, 1992; Giddens, 1984). Such a conception of agency is core to our understanding of social-symbolic work, as it suggests the possibility of actors engaging in purposeful, reflexive efforts to shape social reality while at the same time the social reality in which they are embedded is providing them with the motivations, resources, and constraints that shape those efforts.

Layered on top of this understanding of agency sits a swathe of scholarship exploring the work that goes into shaping specific kinds of social-symbolic objects—the growing body of research that prompted us to write this book in the first place. Although we situate this book primarily in relation to management and organizational research, interest in the work done to shape social-symbolic objects has emerged across the social sciences, including in sociology, psychology, economics, political science, and anthropology. The recognition of a wide and disparate range of social-symbolic objects has triggered writing on such forms of social-symbolic work as identity work, emotion work, values work, body work, strategy work, technology work, institutional work, and gender work. We will address the conceptual commonalties that bind these streams of writing together in Chapter 2, but for now it is sufficient to note that they all share an interest in what happens at the intersection of social construction and agency. They all ask a parallel set of questions—how, why, and in what contexts do people work to construct a social-symbolic object?

Returning to our example of "endangered species," the second important part of this example involves the ways in which the emergence of the concept "endangered species" and its application to denote particular sets of animals as "endangered" was the result of extensive efforts by a wide array of actors. In the language of this book, actors performed social-symbolic work to bring a social-symbolic object into being. While the appearance of the idea of an "endangered species" (with all of its complexity) was obviously not the result of the efforts of a single actor, the efforts of actors played an important role in bringing it into being. A whole range of environmentalists, academics, politicians, and many others played important roles in bringing this concept into being. At the same time, other actors worked to undermine the concept and argue for other conceptualizations of the natural world. To be clear, we are not claiming that the intentional efforts of actors represent the entire explanation for this concept's appearance, but we do believe that such efforts play an important, and for us fascinating, part of the processes of social construction that lead to the appearance of social-symbolic objects.

Map of the Book

Part I includes this Introduction and Chapter 2, and it is here where we develop the core ideas that animate this book. Chapter 2 begins by introducing the historical shifts that establish the book's context: the transitions to modernity and postmodernity that transformed social reality in ways that led to people's purposeful, reflexive efforts to shape parts of social reality that were previously accepted as immutable—given by nature or God. We then develop the concept of social-symbolic work, defining the concept, reviewing its theoretical underpinnings, and providing an integrated framework we will use throughout the book. We end the chapter by introducing the three forms of social-symbolic work—self work, organization work, and institutional work—that are examined in detail in the next part of the book.

Part II comprises six chapters. In Chapter 3 and 4, social-symbolic work becomes personal: "self work" describes the purposeful, reflexive efforts of individuals, collective actors, and networks of actors to construct and shapes specific selves, both their own and other's. In Chapter 5 and 6, we introduce "organization work," which we define as purposeful, reflexive efforts of individuals, collective actors, and networks of actors to construct and shapes organizations. This form of social-symbolic work has received less attention as a general category of social-symbolic work than self work, but is related to long-standing discussions of organizational culture, symbolism, and social networks. In Chapter 7 and 8, we consider "institutional work"—purposeful, reflexive efforts of individuals, collective actors, and networks of actors to construct and shapes institutions—which in many ways is the most visible form of social-symbolic work and the form that has the most developed overarching theoretical schema. While we believe these forms of social-symbolic work are the most useful from the point of view of management and organizational research, there are, of course, many other forms of social-symbolic work that may be of interest to other social scientists.

Chapters 3, 5, and 7 focus on conceptualizing the three different forms of social-symbolic work. Each begins with an archaeology of the social-symbolic object (the self, the organization, institutions) focusing on how it became the target of people's efforts to shape it. These sections mirror our discussion of the transitions to modernity and postmodernity that began in Chapter 2 and show how each of those transitions was associated with a reconstruction of the self, organizations, and institutions in ways that motivated and allowed greater flexibility in how those social-symbolic objects were constructed.

The chapters then go on to introduce the form of social-symbolic work associated with the social-symbolic object that it has discussed—self work, organization work, and institutional work. We orient these conceptualizations around three key dimensions of social-symbolic work: discursive, relational, and material. Rather than try to catalogue subcategories of each form of social-symbolic work, we argue that these three dimensions are present in every instance of social-symbolic work, although perhaps more or less obvious and important to its effects.

In Chapters 4, 6, and 8, we examine existing streams of management and organizational research that focus on types social-symbolic work. In Chapter 4, we examine emotion work, identity work, and career work as types of self work. In Chapter 6, we examine strategy work, boundary work, and technology work as types of organization work. In Chapter 8, we examine practice work and category work as types of institutional work. For each of these literatures, we review their emergence in management and organizational research and then explore the implications of understanding them as types of social-symbolic work.

Part III includes three chapters, in which we pan out and consider the relations among different forms of social-symbolic work, discuss how researchers might study social-symbolic work, and examine the implications of the social-symbolic work perspective for scholarship, action, and understanding the broader world around us.

In Chapter 9, we explore the opportunities a social-symbolic work perspective provides for research. We begin by examining how simultaneously considering multiple types of social-symbolic work or multiple social-symbolic objects might provide new conceptual opportunities.

In Chapter 10, we turn to the question of how social-symbolic work might be examined empirically. To do so, we provide an extensive guide to studying social-symbolic work, including suggestions for developing research questions, doing fieldwork, analyzing data, and writing up the results.

Finally, Chapter 11 concludes the book by revisiting our original motivation for writing it and discussing why social-symbolic work is interesting both academically and practically. We begin by exploring what's interesting about social-symbolic work from a scholarly perspective. We then discuss more practical issues, including implications of a social-symbolic work for social innovation, managing workforce diversity, and entrepreneurship. We conclude Chapter 11 by discussing how a social-symbolic work perspective can be helpful in understanding our day-to-day social, technological, and natural worlds.

A Postscript: Should You Read This Book?

We wrote this book to be thought-provoking and useful to people interested in how actors purposefully participate in the social construction of organizations. We are assuming that you are probably an academic or a student, but you may also be someone who is involved in changing organizations as a job or a passion. In any case, in this postscript we will try to provide some thoughts on why you might find this book worth reading.

This book will be useful if you are a graduate student studying management and organizations, either in business schools or in related areas, such as health administration, education, sociology, organizational psychology, and social work. Studying in these domains you will be aware of the tremendous interest that has emerged across the social sciences in the role of actors and agency in shaping organizations, communities, and societies. This book will allow you to participate in this growing research community by providing you with an integrative theoretical framework that can provide the foundation for empirical studies; concise reviews of eight distinct streams of related literature that include forms of work targeting the self, organizations, and institutions; archaeologies of the self, the organization, and institutions that clarify how each became the object of social-symbolic work; and suggestions of further resources if you wish to pursue particular topics in depth.

This book will also be useful if you are already engaged in research on a particular kind of social-symbolic work, such as identity work, strategy work, or institutional work. Although tremendous progress has been made in understanding many of these distinct kinds of social-symbolic work, the impact and insights associated with these streams of research have been constrained by the narrow focus adopted by most scholars who tend to explore individual forms of work, largely ignoring the overlaps and intersections with other forms. Recent research has begun to explore some points of connection between forms of social-symbolic work, but without an overarching framework these efforts have remained isolated and ad hoc. If you are studying one of these kinds of work, this book will provide a way of embedding your research in a broader set of problems and issues, a basis for connecting your findings to those in allied research domains, and a systematic approach to articulating the links between different forms of work.

You might also find this book useful if you are working in or inspired by social constructionist traditions, including interpretive methods, discourse analysis, practice and process theory, historical methods, narrative analysis, studies of organizational culture and symbolism, and the social studies of science and technology. Although these different traditions largely exhibit a mutual sympathy, their scholarly projects tend toward segregation rather than integration because they are typically motivated by or framed in terms of idiosyncratic issues rather than by some common set of problems. Thus, you might find valuable the theoretical framework we develop, which can accommodate a wide range of social constructionist methods and lenses, and provides a common point of departure for social constructionist studies of organizational life.

We also think you will find this book valuable if you are a management and organizational scholar who focuses on the role of agency in organizational processes and practices such as leadership, strategy, organizational change and development, creativity and innovation, and entrepreneurship. Although this book is not about these topics directly, we believe it has much to offer scholarship in these domains. Each of these organizational processes depends significantly on the ability of members to engage successfully in specific forms of social-symbolic work, as might be clearly illustrated by the importance of identity work, strategy work, and boundary work in launching an entrepreneurial venture. More broadly, the concept of social-symbolic work and the framework we provide could be of significant value in developing holistic analyses of complex organizational processes, such as the corporate transformations currently being triggered by digital technologies.

Finally, if you are someone who is not an academic but rather has a professional or personal interest in changing organizations, then we think that you, too, will find this book interesting. It contains a range of ideas and examples that will provide you with new ways to think about what organizations are and how they can be changed by actors working purposefully. Our discussions also include ideas about the self and society that we hope are helpful in conceptualizing and understanding what can be changed, how it can be changed, and who might be able to change it.

2

The Social-Symbolic Work Perspective

In this chapter we:

1. Discuss the cultural shifts that have made social-symbolic work increasingly common and important.
2. Define and explain the concept of social-symbolic work.
3. Present a process model of social-symbolic work useful in analyzing instances of work.
4. Summarize the forms of social-symbolic work on which the book will focus.

Introduction

In March 2010, the United States Congress passed the Patient Protection and Affordable Care Act (ACA), a far-reaching and controversial overhaul of its national healthcare system. Obamacare, as it came to be known, was intended to address the profound problems in American healthcare at the time: individuals paid higher out-of-pocket healthcare costs than in any other country in the world, while 18 percent of the non-elderly population had no health insurance, and another 22 percent were underinsured, despite the fact that the US spent more than 17 percent of the country's GDP on healthcare (while no other country spent more than 12 percent).

To make Obamacare a reality, the Obama administration had to create complex change on multiple levels and in the face of intense opposition. Just drafting and passing the ACA itself was a monumental task. Its 900 pages reflect the complexity of the issues, as well as the host of compromises and accommodations that accompany any major piece of legislation. Passing the ACA, however, marked only the beginning of the efforts to create change. Reducing the number of uninsured involved passing new laws requiring all

Americans to obtain insurance on their own or through their employers, which meant a dramatic expansion of the private insurance market in the US. This expansion demanded a huge legislative effort, as well as negotiations with state governments and industry groups to agree on changes to long-established practices in the health care system, including the creation of state-level "health insurance exchanges" intended to ensure understandable, comprehensive coverage at reasonable prices (Davidson, 2013).

The changes associated with Obamacare extended well beyond new laws and negotiating new agreements. There was also a great deal of work at the organizational level, including changes to hospitals, government agencies, and other health care organizations. It involved the creation of completely new organizational forms, including the "accountable care organization," an innovative new form of medical practice where doctors are rewarded financially when patients avoid hospital stays and other medical interventions, the opposite of traditional systems (Keller, 2013). Another new organizational form was the "patient-centered medical home" in which patients are cared for as a whole person through collaboration and teamwork, again a radical departure from traditional medical organizations (Sommers and Bindman, 2012). Developing these new kinds of organizations not only required new strategies for controlling health care costs through prevention and early intervention, but also investments in information technologies to more rapidly identify at-risk patients, and the formation of new relationships among doctors, nurses, care coordinators, and nurse practitioners.

Transforming a country's healthcare system turned out to also require important work at the individual level, as pharmacists, doctors, and nurses had to respond to legislative and organizational changes that brought new demands in terms of their practices and relationships. Pharmacists, for example, had to begin carrying out routine procedures such as blood pressure checks. Doctors faced significant challenges to their professional identities, as they were encouraged, and even required, to interact with other professionals in more collaborative, less hierarchical relationships, and focus on maintaining health rather than curing illness. Nursing was similarly transformed, with nurses taking on dramatically expanded roles, as seen in the expansion of nurse-managed health centers. These changes (and other parallel changes in other related professions) created real and ongoing challenges to the identities, relationships, and skill sets of healthcare professionals that required significant work on their part to make sense of and implement.

The efforts that went into making Obamacare a reality represent an extraordinary example of the phenomenon that motivates this book. Obama and the other elected politicians, civil servants, managers in hospitals and other healthcare organizations, doctors, nurses, and pharmacists all engaged in purposeful, reflexive efforts to change social arrangements—what we refer to as social-symbolic work. They did so to remedy what they saw as the worst ills of American healthcare by reshaping regulations, norms, beliefs, values, social boundaries, and identities—the social-symbolic objects that populate the American healthcare system. Understanding how this was accomplished is a daunting task. The scale, complexity, and practical importance of Obamacare make it a social change effort that deserves careful study, but it is not clear that our current toolkits for analyzing social phenomena provide an adequate foundation for understanding this broad, multi-level change.

As we discussed in Chapter 1, this book is devoted to exploring a new way of understanding and analyzing the social world. Our focus is on the efforts of interested actors working to affect the social and symbolic world around them. Rather than examining social structures and processes, as has come to dominate much of social science, we believe in the value of a perspective that highlights the actors and actions that shape those structures and processes, transforming them as well as holding them in place. We will argue that by focusing on the intentional efforts of people and groups to shape the social world, we can come to a richer understanding of the social world, how it came to be the way that it is, how it is held in place, how it changes, and perhaps most importantly, who makes all these things happen in the first place.

When we began writing this book, the story of Obamacare did not yet include the efforts of the Trump administration to undo the changes accomplished by Obama and the previous administration. These more recent efforts, though, reveal an important aspect of this story of social-symbolic work. The social-symbolic objects that were the focus of Obamacare are, like many social-symbolic objects, highly contested. Thus, the successful outcomes of the Obama administration's efforts provoked a counter-response by President Trump and his supporters. Not only was Trump motivated by belief in the superiority of an alternative healthcare system, but also, and perhaps especially, by a desire to undo these changes because they were the work of Obama and his supporters. Thus, the Trump administration's counter-efforts highlight the political nature of social-symbolic objects and social-symbolic work. They are important as they constitute social reality and limit and structure action.

The second important element added by Trump's efforts concerns the status of social-symbolic objects. Despite the extensive work done and the complex cultural, legal, and economic arrangements that constituted Obamacare, these arrangements, like all social-symbolic objects, are ultimately fragile—dependent not just on being left alone but on being actively supported and maintained. Thus, our interest in social-symbolic work includes efforts to change social reality, but just as importantly to maintain it.

In this chapter, we further develop the ideas that we outlined in Chapter 1 and that form the foundation for the rest of the book. We do so in four parts. First, we explore the historical changes that have made possible the vast amount of social-symbolic work we now observe. Then, we develop the concept of social-symbolic work in more detail, explaining its roots in studies of social structure and agency, and building up the conceptualization of it that animates our approach to understanding organizational life. In the third section, we present a process model of social-symbolic work. In the chapter's last major section, we describe three forms of social-symbolic work, each of which provides the basis for subsequent chapters. We end the chapter (as we do the subsequent chapters) with a list of resources for those who wish to further explore the ideas we have discussed.

The Possibility of Social-Symbolic Work

A key idea that underpins this book is that social-symbolic work depends on an understanding of social-symbolic objects as being subject to the influence of actors' intentional efforts to shape them. While the fact that social-symbolic objects can be purposefully shaped by actors may seem obvious from a modern, Western perspective, such an understanding was not always the case. The possibility of social-symbolic work is embedded in a set of historical shifts that transformed how people understood the social world that began in the seventeenth century and then dramatically accelerated in the latter half of the twentieth century.[1] At the core of these shifts was the idea that a social world that was once understood as fixed—rooted in nature or ordained by God—is not immutable, but can be improved (or at least changed) by agents acting purposefully. As this shift proceeded, it came to encompass much of the social world, including social categories like class and gender, as well as aspects of "human nature" such as emotions. One result of this shift has been the emergence of various technologies of change: social movements demanding change at the societal level, a huge range of ideas and approaches to organizational change and development, and a multitude of practices aimed at the reinvention and improvement of the self. In this section we review these shifts, focusing on the historical transitions to modernity and postmodernity, and the changes in social-symbolic objects that accompanied those transitions.

---

[1] The history on which we focus here is primarily of Western Europe and North America. Although similar transitions to modernity and postmodernity occurred in other places, the dates and specific dynamics of those transitions differ in important ways, with profound implications for the nature of social-symbolic objects and social-symbolic work.

Modernity and the Possibility of Social-Symbolic Work

The possibility of social-symbolic work as we understand it today is tied to a number of profound changes that began in Europe in the 1600s and evolved over the next three centuries. These changes are a part of the long arc from premodernity to modernity, and then to postmodernity. According to Giddens, modernity is: "a shorthand term for modern society," and is associated with "(1) a certain set of attitudes towards the world, the idea of the world as open to transformation, by human intervention; (2) a complex of economic institutions, especially industrial production and a market economy; (3) a certain range of political institutions, including the nation-state and mass democracy" (Tucker, 1998: 94).

Together, these characteristics create a form of society that is distinct from any previous form in that we live oriented toward the future rather than the past. This statement requires some unpacking. Whereas premodernity was characterized by a focus on the past and on tradition—things were as they should be—with modernity came an understanding of the world as manageable, and even perfectible, with the application of rational means and technologies. Looking back from the twenty-first century, it is easy to underestimate the degree of change involved in the transition from premodernity to modernity.

In Western Europe, where the move to modernity was first observed and was perhaps the most abrupt, there had been a 600-year period of relative cultural and social stability leading up to the seismic shifts entailed by the arrival of modernity. During this long period, there were, of course, important social changes, including the emergence of the first universities and the development of various technologies, but the everyday lives of most people changed little from generation to generation. People were born peasants, vassals, or lords, and lived out their lives as members of the same social category according to the dictates of religion and tradition. For many generations, the lives of grandchildren were indistinguishable from the lives of their grandparents. Stability was the defining characteristic of the patterned social arrangements that defined the lives of Europeans during this period.

Then modernity swept across the continent. With it came rational science, new technologies, new political systems, and a general belief in progress. Society began, as Giddens describes it, to live in the future, rather than the past. And with this new belief in the future, people began to improve and reinvent every aspect of society using the tools of rationality and innovation. The great migration to cities began in earnest. People began to believe that they could better themselves through education and hard work. In art, architecture, and music, innovation became the watchword, leading to new forms of artistic expression such as the novel and the modern play. The lives of everyday people were flooded with new technologies invented by the scientists and engineers who had appeared on the scene, and produced in the factories that had recently been invented. For the first time in 600 years, grandchildren's lives were fundamentally different than their grandparents as modernity roared into the future.

Our concern for the general change in social conditions associated with modernity is tied to our interest in the more specific changes in the status and understanding of social-symbolic objects that allowed people to engage in work to shape those objects in ways not previously understood as possible. In the transition to modernity, an array of social-symbolic objects were transformed in ways that allowed them to become targets of efforts to shape them. This included the institutions of the state, the organizations of the military, church, and industry, and individuals' senses of self and family.

If we look back at the story of Obamacare, for instance, we can see it depended on a host of social-symbolic objects which emerged in this period. Social-symbolic work focused on reshaping government health policy and regulation depended fundamentally on the idea of the nation state, a social-symbolic object that emerged with modernity. While this may seem like ancient history in relation to modern debates around governmental regulation of healthcare, those debates are inextricably tied to the social-symbolic work of early modernity that established the basic formulation of a nation state as an object, the ability of states to intervene in citizens' lives, and the legitimacy of citizens' participation in determining state policies. Similarly, the social-symbolic work in relation to organizational forms and professional identities associated with Obamacare depended on the emergence of formal organizations as social-symbolic objects with qualities such as hierarchy, rationality, and bureaucracy, as well as the emergence of professions as social-symbolic objects imbued with expertise and autonomy.

Of equal importance to our discussions here, the changes in society associated with modernity were accompanied by similarly profound changes in social science. With modernity came modernism. Driven by ideas about rationality, and inventions such as the printing press and the experimental method, modern science appeared on the scene. At the heart of this new endeavor were the natural sciences, but a range of applied sciences also appeared, including modern engineering, scientific medicine, and agricultural science. While these new sciences differed in focus and method, they shared an assumption that the application of rationality and rigorous methods could provide insight into the natural world, and that this insight would drive progress and move the world forward. The results were spectacular, producing a historically unprecedented accumulation of knowledge: from Darwinism and the structure of DNA, to understandings of the causes of illness and the invention of the computer, society was rapidly transformed by scientific progress.

But this new belief in rationality and perfectibility also brought with it an understanding of society as separate from the natural world. Combined with a general decline in the importance of religion, this led to the belief that human behavior and relationships required their own fields of study. This recognition led to the development of a science of society (sociology) and a science of the individual (psychology) that focused the tools of rationality on the social world. The social sciences were born, and their explicit purpose was to develop grand narratives that explained how society worked, what individuals were, and how both could be perfected. Modernism was the wellspring of the social sciences as the idea took hold that we could both understand and manage the social world if only we had the correct grand theories.

Postmodernity and the Fragmentation of the Modern Project

But the story does not end there. Beginning just before World War I, and then accelerating and broadening after World War II, another major historical shift swept across Western society. This societal shift had significant implications for the development of social-symbolic work as the belief in the possibility of change in social-symbolic objects began to lose the accompanying belief in their perfectibility. In this next era—postmodernity—people began to seriously question the idea that progress could be tied to the fulfillment of some "natural" order; instead, what progress might mean became a matter of politics or aesthetics. Social-symbolic objects in postmodernity thus remained the targets of efforts to shape them, but without the assumptions of manageability and perfectibility through rational means that had characterized modernity. Instead, social-symbolic objects became understood as somewhat arbitrary constructions created and held in place by social conventions and political power, rather than their closeness to some ideal. In the identity and social movements of the 1960s and 1970s, for instance, the meaning and status of gender, racial, and sexual preference were deeply contested, with similar dynamics in play in student movements that challenged the legitimacy of academic traditions and canons, and especially the privilege that accompanied them.

Although the contours of postmodernity may be less clear than those associated with modernity (perhaps because of the former's relative proximity to contemporary life), there are many instances of social-symbolic objects transformed in ways that clearly illustrate postmodernity's divergence from the perfectibility and rationality associated with modernity. The pop art movement, for example, disrupted taken-for-granted distinctions between pop culture and high culture. Roy Lichtenstein, a key proponent of pop art, produced paintings that used old-fashioned comic strips as inspiration, taking elements of comic strips and producing close copies in much larger sizes, emphasizing the Ben-Day dots and thick lines associated with the printing process of pulp comics from the 1950s and 1960s. In creating pop art—an art that spanned the previously impermeable boundary between pop culture and high art—Roy Lichtenstein, Andy Warhol, Richard Hamilton, and many others contributed to and drew on the broad current of postmodernity that was sweeping through Western culture.

In the music world, a powerful echo of the social movements marching in the streets was heard in the sounds of the Sex Pistols, whose single "Anarchy in the UK" distilled the sentiments of activists into an angry snarl and launched punk as a musical force. Although the life of the Sex Pistols as a performing band was short, the impact of their music, and especially its translation into the sounds of countless other bands, was enduring. In *Lipstick traces*, Marcus (1990) describes its essence:

> What remains irreducible about this music is its desire to change the world.... The desire begins with the demand to live not as an object but as a subject of history— to live as if something actually depended on one's actions ... Damning God and the state, work and leisure, home and family, sex and play, the audience and itself, the music briefly made it possible to experience all those things as if they were not natural facts but ideological constructs: things that had been made and therefore could be altered, or done away with altogether. It became possible to see those things as bad jokes, and for the music to come forth as a better joke.
>
> (Marcus, 1990: 5)

Crucial to this description is the last sentence. The music does not provide the truth, in opposition to the falsity of what it criticizes, but instead provides another, and perhaps better (amusing, insightful, energizing), story that itself is immediately understood as equally made up. As Marcus (1990: 22) goes on to argue, "Real mysteries cannot be solved, but they can be turned into better mysteries," so jokes are answered by better jokes, and mysteries by better mysteries.

The transformations associated with pop art and punk music may represent the extreme end of a move away from perfectibility through rational means, but they also symbolize a much broader shift in the conception of social-symbolic objects and the work done to create and manage them. Across a wide swathe of society, there emerged a new understanding of how social-symbolic objects could be produced and shaped, not just among elites and large organizations, but by everyone and involving the objects of everyday experience of life as well as broader social structures. The belief that such objects could be perfected through rational means began to disappear, or at least fracture, as the focus shifted to change for its own sake.

Just as had occurred with the shift to modernity, the changes associated with postmodernity dramatically affected academe. The humanities were the first to feel this effect, where ideas in philosophy and art about truth and beauty became highly contested in the early decades of the twentieth century. In the social sciences, modernism largely held fast until the 1960s, when the social upheaval on university campuses in Western Europe and North America spilled into the theoretical work of social scientists. Their confidence in the possibility of understanding and improving the social world on a large scale began to fracture as did their single-minded focus on quantitative empirical methods. Social science began to look less like a science in the grand sense imagined by its founders and more like a set of competing narratives with no privileged position from which to adjudicate among them (Lyotard, 1984). The breakdown of grand narratives led social scientists to seek local solutions to local challenges and especially local politics (around issues of gender, race, policing, community decision making, etc.) and solutions intended to transform the meaning of those issues through forms of what we call social-symbolic work.

An example of this dynamic can be seen in urban planning (see Harvey, 1989 for an extended discussion) in which the city as a social-symbolic object underwent a significant transformation. Modernist architects and planners had, since the early twentieth century, worked on a grand scale, designing whole neighborhoods and even whole cities to be perfect places for living. But the building of cities based on those grand plans resulted in rather imperfect "machines for living," filled with deprivation, crime, and failed neighborhoods where people refused to live. In the 1970s, as these neighborhoods began to be torn down, the failed grand narrative of urban planning and modernist architecture was replaced with approaches that conceived of more modest, more tractable urban communities as the focal objects (Jacobs, 1961). The construction of these objects came to shift from one rooted in planning and development that aimed for perfection, to an eclecticism of style that worked to integrate idiosyncratic urban histories and geographies.

Parallel trajectories occurred in many disciplines in the social sciences in which the social-symbolic objects on which they focused were reconstructed in pluralistic terms. In psychology, a postmodern alternative emerged that abandoned the search for a singular, comprehensive understanding of the mind to explore a plurality of stories through which people collectively constitute a network of selves (Gergen, 1977, 2009b). In organization theory, the search for the "ideal" organization—the perfect bureaucracy—was abandoned, first as it became clear that what worked best was contingent on the situation, and then even more profoundly with the recognition that both the situation and the organization were socially constructed (Hatch, 1997). In geography, there was an experiential turn that moved away from the search for idealized understandings of "space" toward a more localized and particularized approach that emphasized particular "places" (Tuan, 1975, 1977).

Thus, the search for complete understandings of essential social objects based on rational methods was replaced by an appreciation of the plurality of objects and a diversity of ways to explore and explain the social world.

This is perhaps easiest to see in the theories that were developed (or not as the case may be) to explain the new postmodern society. Scholars struggled to develop narratives to explain the direction society and social science had gone without being "totalizing" or claiming some sort of independent access to a universal truth. One of the proponents of postmodern social theory explained it this way:

> It is hard to discuss "postmodernism theory" in any general way without having recourse to the matter of historical deafness, an exasperating condition (providing you are aware of it) that determines a series of spasmodic and intermittent, but desperate attempts at recuperation. Postmodernism theory is one of those attempts: the effort to take the temperature of the age without instruments and in a situation which we are not even sure there is so coherent a thing as the "age," or zeitgeist or "system" or "current situation" any longer. (Jameson, 1991: xi)

The story we have told about societies and the social sciences is, of course, an idealized one. While the transformations we have described—from premodernity through modernity to postmodernity—have occurred and have had profound effects, that transformation and those effects are not evenly distributed or uniformly welcomed, and they are told from the rather particular perspective of Western Europe and North America. The world we live in, including our selves, our organizations, our societal rules and beliefs, and the social sciences that explore them, comprise a mix of the premodern, modern, and postmodern, and the story is a quite different one in other parts of the world.

While many people in many societies believe strongly in a world with, for instance, a plurality of sexual identities, many others believe in premodern notions of God-given sexes and sexual attractions, while still others subscribe to more modern conceptions of a moral (or other) hierarchy within the diversity of gender identities. The organizations through which we accomplish so much reflect a great deal of modern thinking, as well as both premodern and postmodern thinking: large corporations, government agencies, and non-profit organizations are structured significantly as traditional bureaucracies, with modern, rationalist thinking at the core of their layers of authority and spans of control.

At the same time, the social sciences mirror the confused situation in the social world. While postmodernism has been an important and powerful force in social science, and there has been a breakdown of grand narratives across many of the social sciences, these changes have not been uniform or uncontested. A great many, and perhaps even the majority, of social scientists believe in the potential for social science to achieve progress on a grand scale. For some, and we include ourselves in this group, the concepts associated with postmodernism represent a source of insight and a potential basis for new freedoms. But for others, and we include many colleagues and friends in this latter group, these concepts undermine the nobility and even the possibility of" with "purpose, and even perhaps the possibility, and even the possibility of social science. Grand narratives in areas as diverse as economics and positive psychology continue to be developed and promulgated by social scientists whose belief in rationality and progress remains undimmed. Perhaps ironically, postmodernism in social science is as fractured as the world the concept was coined to describe.

Thus, our aim in this section has not been to recount a comprehensive history, but rather to highlight the profound changes that occurred in societal understandings of social-symbolic objects during the transitions to modernity and to postmodernity as the first step in understanding the possibility of social-symbolic work. Social-symbolic work as a concept grows out of the complex interplay of the modern and postmodern that characterizes contemporary society. We turn now to developing an integrated understanding of the many forms of social-symbolic work that have emerged in the transitions to modernity and postmodernity.

The Concept of Social-Symbolic Work

In this section, we develop the concept of social-symbolic work. We begin by defining social-symbolic objects—the targets of social-symbolic work. We then develop a conceptualization of social-symbolic work rooted in writing on heterogeneous forms of agency, extended programs of human action, and repertoires of practice. Finally, we introduce three dimensions of social-symbolic work that we find helpful in understanding the wide variety of forms of social-symbolic work that have been identified in the literature.

Social-Symbolic Objects

We define the concept of a social-symbolic object as a combination of discursive, relational, and material elements that constitute a meaningful pattern in a social system. Unpacking this definition begins with the notion of a pattern, by which we mean a socially constructed, interpretable entity that describes some perceived consistency across space and/or time. Such patterns can be primarily ideational, such as sets of concepts and subject positions. Using the case of institutions as social-symbolic objects, we previously argued (Phillips et al., 2004: 635) that although there has been a "tendency among institutional theorists . . . to define the concept of institution in terms of patterns of action . . . institutions are constituted through discourse and that it is not action per se that provides the basis for institutionalization but, rather, the texts that describe and communicate those actions."

This argument, we suggest, applies not only to institutions but to other social-symbolic objects as well. If we think of organizational strategies and values, for instance, strategy has been defined as "a pattern in a stream of decisions" (Mintzberg and Waters, 1985: 257). Many social-symbolic objects also have significant material dimensions, including everyday physical objects such as furniture and tools, "natural" objects such as flowers and food, and social-symbolic objects tied to the human body. What makes these things social-symbolic objects is that they are meaningfully situated in social systems—they are social and symbolic objects, with meaning and (sometimes) functionality that are core to how we relate to them. Conceiving of emotions as social-symbolic objects, for example, focuses on their existence as culturally legitimate patterns of feeling and expression that include important bodily elements (Hochschild, 1979; Turner and Stets, 2006).

Two qualities of social-symbolic objects are key to understanding their role in generating social-symbolic work. The first involves the relationship between social-symbolic objects and day-to-day living. Social-symbolic objects are largely pragmatic and taken for granted. As Giddens argues, the "vast bulk of the 'stocks of knowledge' . . . is not directly accessible to the consciousness of actors," but rather is "inherent in the capability to 'go on' within the routines of social life" (Giddens, 1984: 4). The embeddedness of social-symbolic objects in everyday life means that efforts to shape them may require a degree of reflexivity that is often lacking. In order to have a hope of shaping the social-symbolic objects that populate social systems, people need first to have some conscious understanding of the workings of the social systems in which they live and the arbitrary nature of social-symbolic objects.

The second important quality of social-symbolic objects potentially motivates social-symbolic work: social-symbolic objects significantly affect the distribution of opportunities, benefits, and advantages within social systems. Social-symbolic objects, even if largely pragmatic, are not usually equally beneficial to all participants. They support unequal distributions of rewards and life chances, celebrating and compensating some positions while demonizing and penalizing others. Thus, to the extent that actors are aware of the impact of social-symbolic objects on their own situations and the dependency of social-symbolic objects on human action, these objects provide both the motivation and means for their potential transformation. When actors come to understand that their life chances and those of others are fundamentally shaped by social-symbolic objects, they may seek to change or maintain them depending on the benefits they are accruing. These two qualities—the embeddedness and taken-for-grantedness of social-symbolic objects and their impacts on the distribution of resources and opportunities in social systems—lead to an understanding of social-symbolic work as something that demands effort, reflexivity, and skill, and will sometimes involve significant contestation.

Consider as an example of a social-symbolic object the idea of a "refugee." Although now taken for granted, this social-symbolic object came into being in the modern, legal sense in 1951 when the United Nations passed the UN Convention Relating to the Status of Refugees. As a social-symbolic object, the idea of a refugee represents a meaningful pattern. It establishes as comparable the experiences of a vast number of people fleeing persecution or deprivation, as well as the experiences of those dealing with their needs, and the local and national responses to the demands that refugees place on communities. The idea of a refugee organizes these experiences, without which they would remain disparate.

The idea of a refugee is consistent with our description of social-symbolic objects as largely practical phenomena: the UN convention identified who qualified as a refugee and who did not (such as war criminals), and defined their rights. Ratified by more than 145 countries, the convention provides a set of practical resources for identifying and dealing with refugees, and specifying the responsibilities of host nations. And, perhaps more than many social-symbolic objects, the idea of a refugee and the UN convention in which it is embedded has been profoundly influential and highly contested. It has directly affected many hundreds of millions of people who have been determined to be refugees and are therefore legally entitled to protection and assistance from the nations that have signed the convention. The effects go well beyond those deemed to be refugees, of course, with the international politics of refugee settlement sparking tremendous conflict in many countries at the time of this writing, as "local" citizens embrace or reject the significantly increased numbers of people seeking refugee status.

Social-symbolic objects, such as an individual determined to be a refugee or the UN definition of a refugee, are the conceptual anchor for the perspective we are developing. Seeing social reality as composed significantly of meaningful patterns that act as practical resources and political triggers leads us directly to questions regarding how they are created, shaped, disrupted, maintained, and transformed. It is to these questions—questions of social-symbolic work—to which we turn in the next section.

Social-Symbolic Work

The concept of social-symbolic work connects social-symbolic objects to the potential for people to engage in purposeful, reflexive efforts to shape those objects. We develop our conceptualization of social-symbolic work by rooting it in broader social science concepts. More specifically, we suggest that the concept of social-symbolic work rests on three ideas: heterogeneous forms of agency, extended programs of human action, and repertoires of practice.

HETEROGENEOUS FORMS OF AGENCY

We begin with agency as it represents the foundational idea upon which any discussion of work needs to build. The relationship between agency and structure has posed a core dilemma in social science since its earliest beginnings, generating intense conflict among scholars for decades. The two most extreme positions are often referred to as structural determinism and voluntarism. Structural determinists argue that the actions, beliefs, and experiences of individuals are determined by the environments in which they find themselves. This view of the world leads to research that focuses on "the structural properties of the context within which action unfolds, and on structural constraints that shape individual or organizational behavior and provide organizational life with overall stability and control" (Battilana and D'Aunno, 2009: 33). In contrast, voluntarists emphasize the free will and autonomy of actors, such that individuals and collective actors represent "the basic unit of analysis and source of change in social life" (Battilana and D'Aunno, 2009: 33). The struggle between determinists and voluntarists was a central defining struggle in social science[2] for almost a hundred years, beginning with the early work of Weber and Durkheim at the end of the nineteenth century.

Happily, social science (or at least much of social science) has moved beyond these extreme positions to focus on understanding the simultaneous effects of structure and agency, and to develop conceptions of both that resonate with, rather than exclude, the possibility of the other. This shift has been facilitated by a reconceptualization of agency from one that was individualistic and unitary to relational and heterogeneous. The extreme positions of determinism and voluntarism asked the relatively simple question of whether individuals in a particular situation exhibited agency—did they engage in behaviors or hold beliefs that were matters of choice rather than conditioning? Such a conception of agency was bound to lead to polarized debates. In contrast, a relational, heterogeneous conception of agency looks at situations differently and asks different questions, focusing more on how agency is enacted in relationships, and what forms it might take at different times under different conditions and with what effect. The question is not whether people do or do not have agency, but what forms of agency manifest through what kinds of social relationships in what situations.

---

[2] This struggle is often referred to as the agency/structure debate (see Lawrence et al., 2009 for a more complete discussion).

In what has become a canonical treatment of agency as relational agency, Emirbayer and Mische (1998) argue for an understanding of agency that is heterogeneous and responsive to the situations in which people find themselves. They focus in particular on "temporal-relational contexts of action," the variations of which correspond to different forms of agency that they describe in explicitly temporal terms. Building on Giddens and Bourdieu, who emphasized the connection between human action and the past through habits and routines, Emirbayer and Mische (1998: 963) extend their conception of agency to include temporally diverse forms, including agency that is "informed by the past (in its habitual aspect), but also oriented toward the future (as a capacity to imagine alternative possibilities) and toward the present (as a capacity to contextualize past habits and future projects within the contingencies of the moment)." This "chordal triad of agency" is more succinctly composed of "habit, imagination, and judgment" (Emirbayer and Mische, 1998: 970).

This chordal triad of agency provides an inspiring starting point for social-symbolic work because it provides room for the sort of activity that Lawrence et al. (2011: 53) describe in relation to institutions as the "efforts of individuals and collective actors to cope with, keep up with, shore up, tear down, tinker with, transform, or create anew the institutional structures within which they live, work, and play, and which give them their roles, relationships, resources, and routines."

PROGRAMS OF ACTION

An important issue that we feel is underexamined in the sociological literature on agency is the ability of people to move between temporal forms of action, and especially from habitual action rooted in the past to present-focused practical action (i.e., action focused on solving a current problem) or future-oriented projective action (i.e., action undertaken to accomplish a future goal). Understanding such shifts is central to the psychology of judgment and decision making, both as developed in the Nobel Prize-winning work of Kahneman and Tversky (see the summary in Kahneman, 2011) and in the more recent work described as the new synthesis in moral psychology (Haidt, 2001, 2007, 2012).

Cognitive psychologists have for decades proposed a "dual-process" account of human action. Stanovich and West (2000: 658) describe the dual processes as "System 1" and "System 2," where System 1 thinking is "automatic, largely unconscious, and relatively undemanding of computational capacity," in contrast to System 2 thinking which "encompasses the processes of analytic intelligence." System 1 thinking includes both innate skills, such as recognizing objects and orienting attention, and others that become automatic through practice, including reading, interpreting social situations, and for some people advanced skills including diagnosing illness and making advanced chess moves. In contrast, System 2 thinking requires attention and is disrupted when attention is drawn away (Kahneman, 2011). Key to this distinction is the effort involved in System 2 thinking: it's not so much that System 1 thinking is necessarily faster than System 2, but rather that the latter requires effort and concentration, making appropriate the idea of "paying attention," as we only possess a "limited budget of attention" and so exceeding this budget leads to failure (Kahneman, 2011).

The psychological study of morality extends the basic dual-process idea in ways useful to our interest in purposeful, reflexive social action. Whereas traditional approaches to morality emphasized careful deliberation, contemporary research has connected morality to more basic emotional and cognitive processes (Haidt, 2007). Key to this new understanding of morality is the notion of "moral intuition," which involves "the sudden appearance in consciousness of a moral judgment, including an affective valence (good–bad, like–dislike), without any conscious awareness of having gone through steps of searching, weighing evidence, or inferring a conclusion" (Haidt, 2001: 818). This understanding of moral judgment is important for us because so much of what we think of as social-symbolic work involves a moral dimension—efforts to shape identities, emotions, social boundaries, practices, and categories are often motivated by moral concerns, while the outcomes of those efforts may be similarly affected by the moral judgments of others.

The dual-process account of human cognition, and the new moral psychology, complement the idea that agency exists in heterogeneous temporal forms (Emirbayer and Mische, 1998). Together, they move us toward a more realistic image of how people act and think, which is crucial, especially as prior attempts to infuse agency into sociological images of organizational life, such as institutional entrepreneurship (Hardy and Maguire, 2008), have been accused of creating profoundly unrealistic images of ultra-rational, hyper-muscular agents.

We draw on the relational notion of agency to support the possibility of social-symbolic work existing as purposeful, reflexive effort, but recognize, in line with the dual-process model of human action, the impossibility of continuously sustaining such action. At the same time, our image of social-symbolic work is not dependent on actors capable of continuously suspending habits and intuitions; rather, it depends on actors who are capable of moving back and forth between these modes of action and thinking, and most importantly connecting individual decisions, judgments, behaviors, and utterances so that over longer periods of time (days, weeks, and months), they can create programs of action that constitute social-symbolic work. Those actors are not only able to engage in moments of projective action, but are able to envision such actions in the future and reach back to previous such actions as resources and guides.

29

REPERTOIRES OF PRACTICE

Our conception of social-symbolic work also relies heavily on the concept of practice. People's purposeful, reflexive efforts to shape social-symbolic objects seldom occur as random or idiosyncratic actions, but are generally instances of practices that are legitimate within specific communities (Whittington, 2006). If we conceive of social-symbolic work as occurring in programs of action over extended periods of time, these programs of action are built up out of practices that actors learn, reproduce, and extend. Thus we draw on the sociology of practice (Bourdieu, 1977; de Certeau, 2011; Giddens, 1984; Schatzki et al., 2001) to inform our understanding of the repertoires and resources out of which social-symbolic work is composed.

In this tradition, practices represent "embodied, materially mediated arrays of human activity centrally organized around shared practical understanding" (Schatzki, 2001: 2). The sociology of practice is particularly interested in situated action that is in response to the demands of everyday life (de Certeau, 2011) and builds on an interest in social processes by examining the "internal life of process" (Brown and Duguid, 2000: 95). Practice-theoretic approaches to social life bring with them a specific ontology within which "phenomena of various complexities are not made of transcendental elements such as forces, logics, or mental models: instead, 'it is practicing all the way down'" (Nicolini and Monteiro, 2017: 111). Practices represent "the substructure beneath the busy surface of events" (Vaara and Whittington, 2012: 288). They define shared routines that guide behavior according to a situation (Goffman, 1959a; Pentland and Rueter, 1994) and belong to the social collective rather than to individuals (Barnes, 2001). A simple way of understanding practices and how they are distinct from simple behavior is that one can do practices "wrong," or at least wrong given a particular time, place, and social situation.

In the context of social-symbolic work, practices represent repertoires of available, legitimate routines from which actors draw strategies for shaping and maintaining social-symbolic objects. The key concepts when exploring social-symbolic practices are community, roles, resources, and learning: practices are specific to particular communities (Jarzabkowski, 2005), available to members dependent on their roles within those communities (Zietsma and Lawrence, 2010), dependent on access to specific material and social resources (Nicolini and Monteiro, 2017), and must be learned by the individuals and groups using those resources and taking on those roles (Brown and Duguid, 1991). The concept of social-symbolic work employs the concept of practice as a bridge between people's purposeful, reflexive efforts and the social-symbolic objects at which those efforts are aimed: concrete instances of social-symbolic work represent the combination of practices organized around social-symbolic objects and the intentions of people to shape those objects.

A DEFINITION OF SOCIAL-SYMBOLIC WORK

We have defined social-symbolic work as the purposeful, reflexive efforts of individuals, collective actors, and networks of actors to shape social-symbolic objects. Drawing on the literatures on agency, action, and practice allows us to elaborate this definition in specific ways. Social-symbolic work involves heterogeneous forms of agency that can be oriented toward the past, present, and future. It is bundled into programs of action that, while not continuous, are coherent in their aims and the actors involved. Finally, social-symbolic work involves the enactment of repertoires of practices available within a social system, and thus depends on the awareness, ability, and resources demanded of those practices.

Three Dimensions of Social-Symbolic Work

While our conceptualization of social-symbolic work in terms of heterogeneous forms of agency, programs of action, and repertoires of practice provides a foundational understanding of its core properties, reflecting on the empirical literature that inspired this book shows the variety in forms that such work takes on. Thus, to help unpack this variety, we extend our conceptualization by examining three key dimensions of social-symbolic work: discursive, relational, and material. Each of these three dimensions is present in all instances of social-symbolic work, though their importance may vary depending on the kind of work and the social-symbolic objects in question.

THE DISCURSIVE DIMENSION OF SOCIAL-SYMBOLIC WORK

In general terms, the discursive dimension of social-symbolic work describes those aspects of efforts to shape social-symbolic objects that rely on text and talk. While this is a reasonable place to start, we draw on a more specific understanding of "discursive" linked to writing on discourse analysis in the social sciences that conceives of discourse as constitutive of the social world, rather than simply reflective of it (Parker, 2014; Phillips and Hardy, 2002). By constitutive, we mean that in speaking and writing about the social world, we produce that world, and thus, "[w]ithout discourse, there is no social reality, and without understanding discourse, we cannot understand our reality, our experiences, or ourselves" (Phillips and Hardy, 2002: 2).

Central to our understanding of the discursive dimension of social-symbolic work are the relationships among texts, discourses, and social-symbolic objects. For our purposes, a good working definition of a discourse is "a system of statements which constructs an object" (Parker, 2014: 5). Unpacking this definition, systems of statements are "structured collections of meaningful texts" (Phillips et al., 2004: 636) where texts from this perspective include not only written documents, but "any kind of symbolic expression requiring a

31

physical medium" (Taylor and Every, 1993: 109) including audio recordings, photographs, and other visual material, as well as less obviously textual material such as clothing, flags, decorations, and home furnishings. Any of these can be associated with symbolic expression that is made enduring by the physical medium to which it is attached.

Discourses are more than collections of texts, however. They include the relationships among texts (that are often entrenched in other texts), along with the systems of production and consumption through which those texts come into being and are circulated. As illustrated by our example of endangered species in Chapter 1, these structured collections of texts and systems of production and consumption constitute a discourse when they bring an object or objects into being. Thus, the concept of an endangered species emerged out of the broader discourse of environmental conservation.

This conception of texts and discourses suggests that the discursive dimension of social-symbolic work shapes social-symbolic objects through a range of potential routes. Most simply, the discursive dimension of social-symbolic work involves creating texts intended to combine with other texts to construct or shape the social-symbolic objects associated with a discourse. The discursive dimension of social-symbolic work also focuses on shaping systems of production and consumption associated with a discourse in ways that affect the standing of a social-symbolic object, perhaps diffusing it more broadly through expanded systems of production and consumption, or limiting its availability by interrupting those systems. Moreover, the discursive dimension of social-symbolic work involves efforts to shape the interpretation of particular texts within specific communities.

THE RELATIONAL DIMENSION OF SOCIAL-SYMBOLIC WORK

As with its discursive dimension, the relational dimension of social-symbolic work is anchored in the intuitive idea that since all social-symbolic objects exist as parts of social systems, working on these objects will necessarily involve relying on and negotiating social relationships. As a simple example, imagine a person trying to change how a rule is interpreted in the organization in which they work: this will necessarily involve leveraging existing relationships with other organizational actors or establishing new ones. All social-symbolic objects are suspended in social networks and thus working on them will always involve engaging with those networks in some way.

At a conceptual level, understanding the relational dimension of social-symbolic work is aided by the idea of "relational work" from economic sociology (Zelizer, 2000, 2012). This concept describes "the creative effort people make establishing, maintaining, negotiating, transforming, and terminating interpersonal relations" (Zelizer, 2012: 149). Writing on relational work emerged as a way of conceptualizing economic activity that went beyond the idea that economic transactions were "embedded" in social structures, since the embeddedness argument left economic activity nested within the social, and thus itself fundamentally asocial. In contrast to this approach, Zelizer argues for an understanding of economic activity as occurring in what she refers to as "relational packages" that combine interpersonal ties, economic transactions (which might include purchases but also gifts or bribes), media through which those transactions are enacted (such as money, but also IOUs, food stamps, or casino chips), and the shared meaning of these combinations. A key point made by Zelizer is that relational work is in no way restricted to economic activity. So, if we generalize these combinations, we can substitute any value-creating process (such as love, cooperation, or competition) for economic transactions, and imagine appropriate combinations of interpersonal ties, media, and meanings that would accompany those processes.

These ideas—relational work and relational packages—provide a useful foundation for exploring the relational dimension of social-symbolic work, especially highlighting three issues. First, the concept of relational work suggests that the relational dimension of social-symbolic work will involve efforts to shape relationships among people, including establishing, maintaining, negotiating, transforming, and terminating those relationships. Second, it suggests that this kind of work will be found in all spheres of social life, even domains in which the study of interpersonal relationships have traditionally been marginalized, such as the market, and what might be intensely private domains, such as death. Third, the notion of relational packages points out important facets of relationships, the shaping of which might be the focus of actors' efforts, including the definition of the relationship, the value produced by it for those involved as well as those otherwise affected, the media through which the relationship is negotiated, and the meaning of the relationship in terms of the individuals directly involved and the broader social system.

To these ideas, our conceptualization of the relational dimension of social-symbolic work adds some important nuance. Most fundamentally, it shifts our understanding away from efforts to shape relationships as standalone forms of work to seeing such work as integrated with the discursive and material dimensions (discussed below) of social-symbolic work, and thus focused on multidimensional social-symbolic objects rather than relationships *qua* relationships.

This has three important implications. First, we see the relational dimension as an important dimension of all social-symbolic work, targeting all kinds of social-symbolic objects. Although the relational dimension of social-symbolic work describes work done through the shaping of relationships, it does not necessarily mean that those relationships are the target of the social-symbolic work—they may only be a means of shaping some more distal social-symbolic object, just as creating a text may not in and of itself represent the aim associated with the discursive dimension of social-symbolic work.

Second, relationships themselves can be the targets of social-symbolic work that includes discursive and material dimensions, as well as the relational dimension. This does not mean we think relationships are unimportant, but that they are important as one kind of social-symbolic object, with discursive, relational, and material dimensions, and thus the target of social-symbolic work that includes all of those dimensions.

Third, in conceptualizing the relational dimension of social-symbolic work we move away from an exclusive focus on people working on their own relationships: social-symbolic work is defined by the object rather than by the actors engaged in that work, and so the relational dimension of social-symbolic work may involve actors working on their own relationships, but is just as likely to involve actors, including collective actors such as organizations and communities, working to shape the relationships of others.

THE MATERIAL DIMENSION OF SOCIAL-SYMBOLIC WORK

Finally, we introduce the material dimension of social-symbolic work. As with the discursive and relational dimensions, we think of this dimension as a part of all instances of social-symbolic work, rather than occurring separately or occasionally. There are aspects of the discursive and relational dimensions of social-symbolic work that imply a material dimension: discourse depends on the materiality of texts and the systems through which they are produced and consumed; relationships depend on media through which they are negotiated and enacted, whether face to face or in some kind of virtual environment. More than that, though, management and organizational research has shown how the efforts of individual and collective actors to shape social-symbolic objects draw ubiquitously on aspects of the material world, including the natural environment (Bansal and Knox-Hayes, 2013; Kisfalvi and Maguire, 2011), manufactured tools and other objects (Gunn and Williams, 2007; Spee and Jarzabkowski, 2009), the built environment (Lawrence and Dover, 2015), and the human body (Dyer et al., 2008; Frank, 1997).

An important issue when considering the material dimension of social-symbolic work is the relationship between materiality and determinism/voluntarism as views of human action. As we discussed previously, determinism suggests that human behavior results from external forces beyond our control, whereas voluntarism suggests the opposite, that people have free will and thus shape their environments. An emphasis on materiality is often linked to a determinist position, but this is not a necessary connection, and indeed our interest in the material dimension of social-symbolic work depends on an understanding of humanity that allows for voluntary action.

Leonardi and Barley (2008: 161) provide the useful example of ergonomics as a discipline, which rests on the idea that technologies shape human behavior, but since "technologies are designed and because designs can be altered, humans can both intend and change the social effects of a technology by redesigning it or, failing that, by refusing to use it." These responses to technology—redesigning or refusing it—illustrate for us the material dimension of social-symbolic work. If we think, for instance, of organizations as incorporating technology-dependent routines, then redesigning those technologies exemplifies the material dimension of social-symbolic work—altering the material properties of some artifact or how those material properties are employed in practice in order to shape an organizational routine (a meaningful pattern in an organization and thus a social-symbolic object).

Along with the emergence of a general interest in materiality in management and organizational research, streams of research have emerged focusing on particular forms of materiality and social-symbolic work. In fact, attention to space in management and organizational research generally, and in relation to forms of social-symbolic work, has flourished since the early 2000s. There have been multiple theoretical reviews of the relationship between space and organizations (Clegg and Kornberger, 2006; Hernes, 2004; Taylor and Spicer, 2007) and also a growing number of empirical studies (Marrewijk and Yanow, 2010; Yanow, 1998) that have explored issues of gender performativity (Tyler and Cohen, 2010), creativity (Haner, 2005), and power (Dale and Burrell, 2008; Fleming and Spicer, 2004). Particularly important from our perspective have been the examinations of the roles that different kinds of spaces play in relation to individual and collective agency, such as Kellogg's (2009) important work on the role of "relational spaces" in facilitating institutional change.

Similarly, writing on organizations has begun to incorporate the body as a site of social-symbolic work, showing the range of ways that the body can be involved in social-symbolic work. Bodies can be sites of subjectivity, when actors "use" their own bodies to accomplish social-symbolic work (Dyer et al., 2008). Bodies can be the objects on which actors work, shaping their form and meaning (Gimlin, 2002). Bodies can also be integral to social interactions that are crucial to establishing the meaning and boundaries around social-symbolic objects, such as the boundary maintained by elder-care workers between "violence" and the acceptable "aggression" of patients toward staff that might include slaps and punches (Åkerström, 2002).

Incorporating materiality as a dimension of all social-symbolic work is consistent with the move in the broader social sciences toward sociomateriality as an anchoring concept in understanding the relationship between the physical and the social. This concept suggests that the social and material cannot be separated because they are mutually constitutive of each other. This duality of social and material provides a useful extension to the duality of agency and social structure that is at the heart of the social-symbolic work perspective. It forces us to consider the material whenever we are trying to understand agency and structure, and hence whenever we are discussing social-symbolic work.

Summary

Our aim in this section has been to develop a conceptualization of social-symbolic work that can provide a foundation for the rest of the book. We began by defining social-symbolic objects as meaningful patterns in social systems, and described them as largely pragmatic but often associated with political contests over their meaning and evaluation. We then defined social-symbolic work as the purposeful, reflexive efforts of individuals, collective actors, and networks of actors to shape social-symbolic objects. These efforts, we argued, occur through heterogeneous forms of agency bundled into programs of action that constitute the enactment of practices. Finally, we argued that all instances of social-symbolic work have discursive, relational, and material dimensions, the salience of which will depend on the intentions of actors, the practices in which they engage, and the social-symbolic objects in question.

A Process Model of Social-Symbolic Work

We have discussed the historical shifts that have made possible the kinds of social-symbolic work that actors perform today, and developed the concept of social-symbolic work in terms of its core elements and dimensions. We now turn to developing a model of social-symbolic work as a process. This model represents an important foundation for the rest of the book as it provides a more nuanced understanding of how the conceptual elements discussed above relate to each other in concrete instances of social-symbolic work and a means of exploring how different streams of management and organizational research have approached specific forms of social-symbolic work (e.g., identity work and emotion work, discussed in Chapter 3).

Our model connects the motivations, practices, and effects (including unintended effects) of social-symbolic work, and locates those in the context of sets of resources drawn on by actors to enact those practices, and the situations that affect each of the elements and how they are linked (see Figure 2.1). We propose this idealized process model as a platform for research and debate, rather than a representation of how we think social-symbolic work proceeds in the real world. Thus, what is important is that it highlights important facets of social-symbolic work, integrates our conception of social-symbolic work in an

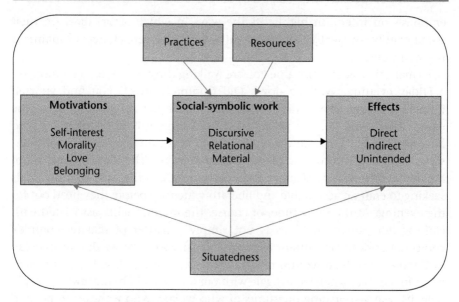

Figure 2.1. Integrated model of social-symbolic work

interpretable process, and points to potential connections that might motivate empirical research.

Motivations

The study of social-symbolic work depends on an important and potentially contentious assumption that when we study the social world, we need to pay attention to actors' intentions, and that intentions and the motivations that underpin them are available for examination and interpretation. This assumption is tied to our conception of social-symbolic work as involving heterogeneous forms of agency (Emirbayer and Mische, 1998) that draw on practices (Nicolini and Monteiro, 2017) enacted in programs of action (Kahneman, 2011). Social-symbolic work rarely occurs as a single isolated action, the intentions behind which might be difficult to assess both for the actors involved and for a scholar observing that action.

Instead, social-symbolic work tends to involve complex programs of action over time, which are far more likely to be associated with markers of intentionality that make the motivations of social-symbolic work potentially available for study. Paying attention to intention is important because the concept of work depends on purposefulness—work is the purposeful expenditure of effort toward a goal. Although actions that produce, reproduce, and transform social-symbolic objects can happen thoughtlessly or accidentally, these are not the actions that fit into the category of social-symbolic work. Our emphasis on intention highlights the ways in which actors draw on their social context in creative and innovative ways to create change or maintain the status quo.

To make this clearer, imagine you are walking through Soho, in London, on a Friday evening. Walking down Old Compton Street, you find yourself immersed in one of the most open and liberal gay neighborhoods in the world. All around you are young men (and some not so young men) who have worked hard to craft a gay identity drawing on carefully chosen hairstyles, items of clothing, and many hours in the gym. This identity work is not accidental or driven by abstract social structures. It is the work of individuals seeking to craft an acceptable and liberating identity before they head out for the evening. At the same time, of course, the intentionality associated with crafting our public identities is not simply a matter of making complex choices. A critically important feature of identity work (as we discuss in detail in Chapter 3) is the discontinuous patterns of intentionality. We go through times in our lives when we struggle with our identities in highly aware, deeply reflexive ways—pursuing questions of who we are, who we want to be, and who we ought to be—while at other times, we experience our identies as natural, inevitable, and taken for granted.

When we are exploring the motivations and intentions associated with social-symbolic work, it is important to keep in mind the potential importance of chains of intentionality. While some intentions might be understood as "direct" most intentionality exists in relation to multiple other intentions, such that some essential intentionality may be difficult to unpack. For example, a chain of intentionality occurs when intentions result from paid employment, so that social-symbolic work becomes a form of labor. In fact, the ubiquity of paid social-symbolic work is an interesting aspect of modern society that deserves special attention. We live in a time where there are many workers and organizations who are skilled at social-symbolic work and who are paid to carry it out. Lobbyists and trade associations, for example, represent rapidly growing categories of social-symbolic workers that, for better or worse, play an increasingly important role in modern democracies.

Practices

Once an actor is motivated to perform social-symbolic work, they draw on available practices to actually engage in social-symbolic work. This might include organizing a demonstration, setting up a website or Facebook page, or any of the range of practices that are available in a social setting. Some practices are highly standardized and routinized, others are more creative and improvisational. Although we might imagine a great deal of creativity associated with how people shape their social-symbolic contexts—including, for instance, their identities and emotions, as well as social categories and organizational boundaries—many forms of social-symbolic work involve practices that are well understood, and may even be taught in formalized educational programs. Think, for instance, of the myriad courses available on managing one's emotions, and especially "negative" emotions such as anger, or the growing number of university courses on social innovation and social enterprise.

But routinized and formalized practices only get actors so far. Much of the activity associated with social-symbolic work is necessarily improvised and creative. The importance of creativity is perhaps especially obvious when considering social-symbolic work focused on the construction and management of complex, individual identities. Essers and Benschop (2009), for instance, explore how women entrepreneurs of Moroccan and Turkish origin in the Netherlands construct their ethnic, gender, and entrepreneurial identities in relation to their Muslim identity. They argue (2009: 402) that these entrepreneurs engage in highly creative boundary work, such that "Islam is employed as a boundary...to make space for individualism, honour and entrepreneurship," while at the same time religious identities "are crafted to stretch the boundaries of what is allowed for female entrepreneurs in order to resist traditional, dogmatic interpretations of Islam." Thus, the very nature of social-symbolic work can make creativity and innovation central to success.

The rapid changes occurring in the social world also means that the roles of improvisational and routine forms of social-symbolic work are themselves often changing, with the most significant impacts potentially occurring when improvisational approaches to social-symbolic work become routinized and widely adopted by others. The example of microfinance, where an initial innovation in routines for lending money and supporting development in one social context became widely adopted and created widespread change, is a good illustration of the power of the combination of creativity and routinization. This process can often be most clearly seen when new forms of social-symbolic work, such as those associated with social innovation and social enterprise, are integrated into established educational enterprises and curricula.

Effects

Although social-symbolic work is defined by its intentions, rather than its outcomes, it is still important to integrate the effects of social-symbolic work into this process model. We imagine at least three important categories of effects for scholars examining social-symbolic work. The first category involves the social-symbolic objects that are the targets of the social-symbolic work under consideration. If an actor is sufficiently skilled, has access to the required resources, and engages in appropriate practices in a conducive situation, they might succeed in shaping the social-symbolic object that is the focus of their efforts. This might involve, for instance, maintaining the status quo in the face of pressures for change (e.g., protestors working to stop same sex marriage), adapting a social-symbolic object to fit with changing circumstances (e.g., the extension of "maternity leave" to create "paternity leave"), or completely disassembling one (e.g., campaigning to repeal sodomy laws).

The concept of a refugee discussed earlier illustrates this process. The concept of a refugee came into being due to a concerted effort by many working through the League of Nations and then the newly founded United Nations. Their motivations were largely driven by moral outrage over the Holocaust and the lack of a coordinated response to the plight of the Jewish people in Europe, along with a general feeling that a more integrated and fairer system was needed to determine who is a refugee and what should be done for them. The United Nations provided both a forum for taking the issue forward and legitimate sets of practices that could be drawn on to make decisions about refugees, to enshrine them in conventions, and then to gain the agreement of member states. The result is a convention on refugees, a UN agency tasked with managing refugee issues, and a global agreement establishing "refugee" as a legitimate identity and the principle that refugees should be given support and protection. While there are still significant and ongoing disagreements about who is a refugee and what rights they should have, the UN Convention on Refugees continues to have significant moral, legal, and practical effects in the world.

There are at least two other kinds of effects of social-symbolic work. First, there are the more distal effects that follow on from its first-order effects on targeted social-symbolic objects. We argued that one of the reasons that studying social-symbolic work is important stems from the effect of social-symbolic objects on the creation and distribution of resources in society: social-symbolic objects, including identities, rules, careers, social boundaries, and technologies, have profound effects on people's relationships, experiences, and opportunities. Thus, examining these second-order effects represents an important part of studying social-symbolic work.

Finally, although social-symbolic work is defined by its intentions—shaping social-symbolic objects—its status as social-symbolic work does not depend on achieving these aims. The complex combination of intentions, situations, tools and skills, and creativity and routines, creates a great deal of uncertainty in the causal paths through which actors work to shape social-symbolic objects. Indeed, social-symbolic work often fails. And, even when it does not fail completely, it often results in unintended effects. For example, Khan et al. (2007) describe how an initiative to stop child labor in the soccer ball industry in Pakistan had exactly the opposite result of the intentions of the actors who worked to stop it. Their intervention and the resulting changes to laws and practices resulted in more deprivation and a worse situation for the very children they were trying to help. Social-symbolic work is difficult and the social world it is intended to change is often more complex than the actors involved realize. Thus, failure and unintended effects are a common outcome.

These unintended effects are an important part of the process model we propose. The uncertain relationship between social-symbolic work and its effects suggests that focusing only on successful instances or on the parts of the work that are successful would be a serious error of omission. Instead of bracketing those unintended effects, we believe that their frequency and significance makes investigating them a critical part of studying social-symbolic work. Doing so will lead to a better understanding of the relationships between forms of social-symbolic work, the situations in which that work happens, and the outcomes to which it leads.

Resources

Although intentionality and practices are essential to social-symbolic work, they are not enough. All forms of work, including social-symbolic work, depend on resources, including skills, abilities, and tools (Jarzabkowski, 2004; Kaplan, 2010; Schatzki, 2001). The criticality of tools and resources for social-symbolic work in organizational life has been most clearly recognized in studies of organizational technologies (Bijker et al., 2012; Garud and Karnøe, 2003) and in the strategy-as-practice literature (Jarzabkowski, 2004; Kaplan, 1997). These literatures both highlight the degree to which material technologies, organizational practices, and the forms of work in which they are used are all intertwined, with the meaning of technologies, the viability of practices, and the intentions that underpin forms of work often difficult to unpack.

As an example, consider the importance of resources in the "Arab Spring." When, in 2011, citizens in Tunisia, Egypt, and Libya rose up in defiance of their rulers, demanding "personal dignity and responsive government" (Anderson, 2011: 2), the use of social media as an enabling technology was distinctively important. Critically, it provided a quick and interactive way to mobilize that was lacking in traditional ways of organizing such as leaflets, posters, and faxes (Eltantawy and Wiest, 2011). In Egypt, for instance, "activists created Facebook groups, personal blogs, and Twitter accounts to engage supporters and followers," including a Facebook group called "We are all Khalid Said," which was created following the outcry over the death of a young man at the hands of Egyptian police (Eltantawy and Wiest, 2011: 1213). These tools allowed the organization of large demonstrations by individuals and groups who had little access to official channels of communication. The availability of social media facilitated the social-symbolic work that these actors were conducting and allowed them to have an impact in ways that would not have been possible before.

Situatedness

The final component of our model could easily have been its first. All social-symbolic work is situated, with all that the concept implies. Perhaps most importantly, the concept of situatedness highlights that although social-symbolic work depends on intentionality, we are not arguing for uncondi-tioned free will. While we argue that social-symbolic work is fundamentally intentional, those intentions are also clearly shaped by the social world in which they are embedded. The connections among intentions, action, and social structure involve a complex array of recursive relationships, and we believe that the social-symbolic work perspective may be useful in unpacking this dynamic.

A great deal of virtual ink has been spilled exploring the "paradox of embedded agency" (Battilana and D'Aunno, 2009). Embedded agency is, of course, a critically important concept for understanding how people engage in forms of social-symbolic work that are aimed at shaping social-symbolic objects at the same time as those objects shape understandings of what is right, proper, or even possible, and provide the resources necessary for any kind of social action and interaction.

That agency exists and that it is embedded does not, however, seem to us to present a paradox, or even a problem. Agency is not complete, in the sense of being unbounded, unconstrained, and inevitable. But neither is it absent. And the situatedness of agency in social contexts challenges neither of these statements. Agency is heterogeneous in degree and form, and relational rather than individual. To foreshadow an example that we examine in depth in Chapter 3, the ability of people to control their identities differs significantly across contemporary cultures, and has changed even more significantly over history. Identities can be crafted, but the extent to which they can be crafted and in what ways is shaped by the social context in which the crafting occurs.

Social-Symbolic Work in Management and Organizational Research

While the concept of social-symbolic work is novel, research on this kind of activity in management and organizational research is not. In fact, the origins of this book lie in our observation that research on different kinds of "work" in management and organizational research was rapidly increasing, yet frag-mented. To gain a better understanding of this trend as we began to work out what became the social-symbolic work perspective, we sought to identify as many streams of management and organizational research on this form of work as we could. We began by reviewing the literature looking for forms of work, and then posted a request on the Academy of Management Organization and Management Theory Division listserv for anyone who was researching a new form of work to contact us.[3] We received more than thirty responses which, when combined with our review of the literature, allowed us to identify twenty distinct forms of social-symbolic work being examined in management and organizational research. We summarize the results in Table 2.1.[4]

In reviewing these disparate forms of work, three observations emerged. First, all of the forms of work involved actors engaged in a purposeful effort—a "conscious, intended try" as Hochschild (1979) put it—to manipulate some aspect of their social context. The aspect of the social context on which the actors focus is the "X" in "X work." What is notable about these "Xs" is that they are all social-symbolic in nature. Identity, emotion, institutions, ideas, aesthetics, values—they are all social in that they constitute and are constituted by sets of social relations, and symbolic in that they are constituted through language and other forms of symbolic expression. Moreover, common across these areas of research was a conception of agency as embedded, and particularly embedded in the very sets of social-symbolic structures they were aiming to affect (Battilana and D'Aunno, 2009). Watson's (2008: 129) discussion of identity work, for instance, describes it as a set of "mutually constitutive processes" that involve people both "striv[ing] to shape a relatively coherent . . . personal self-identity" and "com[ing] to terms with . . . the various social-identities which pertain to them."

Second, studies of these forms of work generally adopt a social constructionist epistemology that highlights the role of actors in socially constructing elements of organizations or their context previously understood as either "natural" or beyond the control of individual actors. Emotion, for instance, is traditionally understood in psychology (where research on emotion is most prevalent) as either emanating from cognitive interpretations of situations or directly from events themselves (Elfenbein, 2007), but not being the object of work done by interested actors. At most, such emotions might be understood as "expressed" and distinct from "felt" emotions, whereas a powerful aspect of Hochschild's writing on emotion is that it is people's "real," felt emotions that they were working on. Similarly, a part of the interest in institutional work

---

[3] We would like to sincerely thank the members of the Academy of Management OMT Listserv for their willingness to share their ideas on these new forms of work.

[4] We have not included all submissions from the OMT list or all of the times in the OMT literature reference was made to a kind of work. In particular, we restricted our list to forms of work aimed at affecting the social-symbolic context, rather than, for instance, characteristics of work (e.g., "dirty work") or more traditional types of work (e.g., "professional work").

Table 2.1. "New" forms of work in management and organizational research

	Type of work	Definition	Exemplary citations
1	Aesthetic work	"the employment of workers with certain embodied capacities and attributes that favourably appeal to customers and which are then organizationally mobilized, developed and commodified" (Warhurst and Nickson, 2009: 104)	Warhurst and Nickson, 2009
2	Age work	"the institutional work of organizational actors to pursue their particular interests and to (de) legitimize age inequalities" (Collien et al., 2016)	Collien et al., 2016
3	Authenticity work	"work involved in claiming authenticity" (Peterson, 2005: 1083)	Peterson, 2005; Svejenova, 2005
4	Boundary work	"'strategic practical action' for the purpose of establishing . . . boundaries . . . [through] expulsion, expansion, and protection of autonomy" (Lamont and Molnár, 2002: 179)	Kreiner et al., 2009
5	Contextualization work	The institutional work that sustains responsible investment "glocalization," including filtering, repurposing, and coupling	Gond and Boxenbaum, 2013
6	Cultural work	Action by actors to align themselves with prevailing societal preferences or attempts to shape cultural tastes and preferences	Glynn, 2000; Lounsbury and Glynn, 2001
7	Discursive work	Discursive activity carried out to influence processes of social construction (Hardy and Phillips, 1999)	Lawrence et al., 1999
8	Emotion work	"making a conscious, intended try at altering feeling" (Hochschild, 1979: 560)	Hochschild, 1979; Rafaeli and Sutton, 1987
9	Idea work	"activities concerned with generating, selecting, realizing, nurturing, sharing, materializing, pitching and communicating ideas in organizations" (Carlsen et al., 2012: 1)	Carlsen et al., 2012
10	Identity work	"forming, repairing, maintaining, strengthening or revising the constructions that are productive of a sense of coherence and distinctiveness" (Sveningsson and Alvesson, 2003: 1165)	Watson, 2008
11	Institutional work	"purposive action . . . aimed at creating, maintaining and disrupting institutions" (Lawrence and Suddaby, 2006: 215)	Lawrence and Suddaby, 2006
12	Interaction work	"the construction of recognizable social scenes or events" (Idrissou et al., 2016: 1989)	Idrissou et al., 2016
13	Intersectional identity work	"constructing an understanding of a mutually constituted self that is coherent, distinct and positively valued" (Atewologun et al., 2016: 4)	Atewologun et al., 2016
14	Meaning work	"struggle over the production of mobilizing and countermobilizing ideas and meanings" (Benford and Snow, 2000: 613)	Benford and Snow, 2000
15	Narrative identity work	"social efforts to craft self-narratives that meet a person's identity aims" (Ibarra and Barbulescu, 2010: 137)	Ibarra and Barbulescu, 2010
16	Practice work	"efforts to affect the recognition and acceptance of sets of routines" (Zietsma and Lawrence, 2010: 190)	Zietsma and Lawrence, 2010
17	Race work	Efforts to reconstruct the meaning, power, and privileges associated with race	Whitaker, 2005
18	Strategy work	Purposeful activities carried out in the production of strategies	Whittington et al., 2006

| 19 | Temporal work | "negotiating and resolving tensions among different understandings of what has happened in the past, what is at stake in the present, and what might emerge in the future" (Kaplan and Orlikowski, 2013: 965) | Granqvist and Gustafsson, 2016; McGivern et al., 2018 |
| 20 | Values work | "the work that is going on at any moment as values practices emerge and are performed" (Gehman et al., 2013: 2012) | Gehman et al., 2013 |

is that it captures the intuition of a set of scholars that actors engage in a wide range of efforts to affect the institutions around them; such an approach contrasts with more structural approaches to institutions that emphasize stability based on automatic social controls (Jepperson, 1991) and change based on exogenous shocks (Kondra and Hinings, 1998).

The third observation concerned the differences among these forms of work as much as their commonalties. Although each form of work specifies a particular social-symbolic object as the target, it is clear that they also connect to each other around broader classes of social-symbolic objects, in particular around the self, organization, and institutions. Building on this observation, we will now introduce three forms of social-symbolic work—self work, organization work, and institutional work—which we explore in depth in Chapters 3 through 8.

Self Work

Self work describes the efforts of individuals, collective actors, and networks of actors to shape the social-symbolic dimensions of a self, both their own selves and those of others. In Chapters 3 and 4, we explore self work, both as it exists in contemporary society and how it has emerged historically. Drawing on a diverse set of writings, we argue that self work describes the efforts of actors to construct a self, and examine the discursive, relational, and material dimensions of those efforts. In management and organizational research, self work has been the subject of sociologically and psychologically informed research since the 1970s. We review three literatures from management and organizational research that represent different degrees of development in the study of self work: emotion work, which is perhaps the longest standing area of research on self work; identity work, the study of which emerged more recently; and career work, which scholars are only beginning to examine as a form of self work.

Scholarly interest in emotion work traces primarily to Hochschild's (1979, 1983) explorations of how people engage in efforts to shape not only the expression of emotion in social settings, but their feelings. Hochschild documented the ways in which organizational members engage in emotion work, which she describes as "the act of trying to change in degree or quality an emotion or feeling." Importantly for our discussion, Hochschild (1979: 561) also notes that "'emotion work' refers to the effort—the act of trying—and not to the outcome, which may or may not be successful," and argues that "[f]ailed acts of management still indicate what ideal formulations guide the effort, and on that account are no less interesting than emotion management that works."

A second closely connected research stream focuses on identity work. The concept of identity describes the "various meanings attached to an individual by the self and by others" (Ibarra and Barbulescu, 2010: 137), and thus identity work refers to the purposeful ways through which individuals craft those meanings, through such strategies as humor, dress, personal style, and office decor (Elsbach, 2003; Ibarra, 1999; Kreiner et al., 2006; Pratt and Rafaeli, 1997; Pratt et al., 2006).

The third literature we examine in relation to the concept of self work focuses on careers as social-symbolic objects. The study of careers exemplifies research that has not traditionally been linked to other forms of social-symbolic work, but which could significantly benefit from more explicitly examining the social-symbolic work involved in constructing and shaping careers. This potential stems in part from the profound changes that have been occurring in the employment relationship, where we moved from organizational to boundaryless careers (Arthur and Rousseau, 2001) and now the gig economy in which careers involve sequences of tasks rather than jobs (Barley et al., 2017; Davis, 2016; Demetry, 2017).

Organization Work

We move to a discussion of organization work—efforts to construct and shape an organization—in Chapters 5 and 6. More precisely, it involves the work of individuals, collective actors, and networks of actors to construct the social-symbolic dimensions of an organization. Management and organizational research has long been concerned with the role of social-symbolic objects in organizational life, highlighting the importance of organizational culture (Barney, 1986), organizational symbolism (Pondy et al., 1983), and, somewhat more recently, stories, narratives, and other forms of discourse (Barry and Elmes, 1997; Boje, 1995). The emphasis in earlier work, however, was primarily on the impacts of these important social-symbolic objects on organizational life, rather than on the efforts of organizational actors to shape these objects.

More recently, three significant streams of research have emerged that emphasize the ways in which organizations as social-symbolic objects are constructed by actors. First, the strategy-as-practice literature reconceptualizes the notion of strategy from something an organization "has" to something its members "do" (Jarzabkowski, 2005; Maitlis and Lawrence, 2003; Vaara and

Whittington, 2012; Whittington, 2006). The idea of "strategy work"—the efforts of organizational actors to shape the strategies of their organizations (Vaara and Whittington, 2012)—is core to this perspective and is, from our perspective, a type of organization work. Whereas traditional views of strategy describe it as either "a pattern in a stream of decisions" (Mintzberg and Waters, 1985: 257) or an intended course of action (Schendel and Hofer, 1979), the notion of strategy work emphasizes strategy as a social-symbolic object.

Second, studies of boundary work have become an important stream in management and organizational research. The question of boundaries in and around organizations has long been a concern for organizational scholars, but had until recently been dominated by realist conceptions and functionalist explanations (Santos and Eisenhardt, 2005), rooted in traditions such as transaction cost analysis (Williamson, 1985). In contrast, recent writing on boundaries in management and organizational research treats boundaries as social and symbolic phenomena (Lamont and Molnár, 2002) and incorporates an explicit concern for the work of diverse actors to shape boundaries (Gieryn, 1983). Organizational scholars have also explored boundary work that involves the construction of boundary objects which facilitate cooperation across internal divisions (Carlile, 2002), the role of boundary spanners who negotiate meaning and relationships between organizational insiders and outsiders (Bartel, 2001), and the political contests over organizational and interorganizational decision-making boundaries (Zietsma and Lawrence, 2010).

A third kind of organization work focuses on the social-symbolic properties of technology. While a great deal of research has focused on the physical and functional properties of technology, an important stream of research concentrating on the social construction of technological systems in organizations has also emerged (Dodgson et al., 2008; Garud and Karnøe, 2003; Orlikowski, 1992). This literature has been significantly influenced by research on the "social construction of technology" (Latour, 1990; Pinch, 2008), which investigates how and with what effects technologies are socially constructed, often drawing on colorful examples to illustrate the social nature of even seemingly "hard" physical objects and facts, as in the study of the social construction of "missile accuracy" (MacKenzie, 2012). Research on technology work was initially focused on electronic communications systems (Fulk, 1993; Orlikowski, 1992, 2000), and more recently has broadened to consider the social and symbolic dimensions of the built environment more generally (Dover and Lawrence, 2010a; Leonardi and Barley, 2010; Orlikowski and Scott, 2008).

Institutional Work

We examine institutional work, defined as "the purposive action of individuals and organizations aimed at creating, maintaining and disrupting institutions" (Lawrence and Suddaby, 2006: 215) in Chapters 7 and 8. Within the tradition of research on institutional work, institutions are understood as, "rules and shared meanings...that define social relationships, help define who occupies what position in those relationships and guide interaction" (Fligstein, 2001: 108). An important dimension of institutions is the set of social control mechanisms that underpin them and hence ensure their stability and people's compliance (Jepperson, 1991; Phillips et al., 2000). Scott (2013) famously distinguishes between cognitive, regulative, and normative mechanisms, referring to them as the "three pillars of institutions." Thus, institutional work can be aimed at affecting rules and shared meanings, the social control mechanisms that support them, or both.

A wide variety of institutional work strategies have been catalogued across a range of contexts, but the literature has been dominated by studies of practice work, which represents the efforts of "actors [to] affect the practices that are legitimate within a domain" (Zietsma and Lawrence, 2010: 194–5). Studies have documented how practices are created and institutionalized through processes of institutional entrepreneurship (Battilana et al., 2009; Maguire et al., 2004) and institutional innovation (Gawer and Phillips, 2013; Hargrave and Van de Ven, 2006). The disruption of practices has also been explored, particularly in the context of social movements (Maguire and Hardy, 2009; Rao et al., 2000). More recently, researchers have begun to focus attention on maintaining the legitimacy of practices, and this form of work has been explored in relationship to centuries old traditions (Dacin et al., 2010), as well as newer sets of practices (Trank and Washington, 2009).

A recent addition to the study of institutional work has been research focused on creating, disrupting, and maintaining categories (Durand and Paolella, 2013; Navis and Glynn, 2010; Vergne and Wry, 2014). This form of institutional work is closely related to boundary work, but focuses exclusively on symbolic boundaries with particular attention to the boundaries between organizational categories and between product categories (Vergne and Wry, 2014). Although much of the organizational research on categories has emphasized their impact on organizations, Vergne and Wry (2014: 78) note the emergence of "a nascent research stream...[that] shows that producer organizations can act strategically to theorize new categories around 'codes' and 'attributes' which may be discounted within extant categories."

Conclusion

In this chapter, we have built on the introductory chapter to further explore the nature of social-symbolic objects and the social-symbolic work through which actors seek to shape them. Our intention has been to establish a perspective that will be useful in thinking about and researching how organizations, their contexts, and the selves that inhabit them are purposefully constructed, how this happens, and the contribution of this activity to the ongoing construction of the social world. While social construction is not, of course, completely driven by intentional action, we argue that the role of intentional action has been underemphasized and there is much to gain from a more comprehensive account of social-symbolic work in constructing organizational life.

Our review of self work, organization work, and institutional work suggests some important common threads among these streams of research that have thus far remained separate. Most fundamentally, research on all three categories of social-symbolic work has established the ability of individuals, collective actors, and networks of actors to purposefully and reflexively engage with facets of organizational life that were previously treated as influential but often outside the reach of intentional action. Earlier writing on social-symbolic objects, such as institutions, values, emotions, and identities, treated them as having powerful impacts on organizational members, but overlooked or understated the degree to which the causal arrow might be reversed.

Key Resources

The Turn to Work in Society

Social-symbolic work becomes important both theoretically and practically as members of a society begin to believe that they can change the social world through the application of directed effort. The development of this belief, and the resulting rapid change in society that resulted, has been discussed by social scientists and by keen observers of society. Foucault provides a fascinating example of how agents conduct self work, organizational work, and institutional work over time in *The birth of the clinic*. His book chronicles how doctors worked to change medicine from something done by hacks and barbers to a high-status scientific endeavor. In *Lipstick traces*, Marcus provides a fascinating and accessible discussion of a related set of social movements, philosophical trends, and musical genres that were influential in changing the social world. The website of the Young Foundation provides a great window onto the activities of a social innovator at work today and the way they think and conduct their activities as they seek to create social change. Finally, *And the band played on* provides a gripping retelling of the dramatic events that led to the constitution of AIDS as a disease.

Foucault, M. 1973. *The birth of the clinic*. (A. M. Sheridan, trans.). London: Tavistock.
Marcus, G. 1990. *Lipstick traces: A secret history of the twentieth century*. Cambridge, MA: Harvard University Press.
Shilts, R. 2011. *And the band played on: Politics, people and the AIDS epidemic*. Souvenir Press.
Spottiswoode, R. 1993. *And the band played on*. <https://www.youtube.com/watch?v=ua5RrxvfVJU>.
The Young Foundation. <http://youngfoundation.org/>.

49

Epistemology in the Social Sciences

This book is underpinned by the idea that the social world is not pre-existing and external to human activity, but rather is constituted in social interaction. *The social construction of reality*, by Berger and Luckmann, really started this revolution in thinking about the social world within the social sciences (although this discussion had been going on in philosophy and the humanities for some time prior to its publication) and is worth reading to understand how social construction works. In *Philosophy and the mirror of nature*, Rorty develops and extends these ideas, using them to challenge the conception of language as a "mirror of nature," and the associated idea that our goal should be to develop language that is exact and a reflection of the natural and social world. We suggest another book by Foucault here, *The history of sexuality*, because it builds on this strong form of social constructionism and fundamentally challenges thinking about sexuality and gender as essential categories. Finally, in *An invitation to social construction*, Gergen provides an accessible and interesting introduction to social construction and its ramifications for social science and our understanding of social life at a practical level.

Berger, P. L., and Luckmann, T. 1966. *The social construction of reality: A treatise in the sociology of knowledge*. New York: Anchor.
Foucault, M. 2012. *The history of sexuality: An introduction*. New York: Random House.
Gergen, K. J. 2009. *An invitation to social construction* (2nd ed.). London: Sage.
Rorty, R. 2009. *Philosophy and the mirror of nature* (30th anniversary edition). Princeton, NJ: Princeton University Press.

Social Structure and Agency

Social-symbolic work, by definition, requires agents to act purposefully and in their self-interest in a world characterized by social structure. But what, exactly, is agency and how and when is it constrained by social structure? A good place to start in understanding this question is Gidden's book *The constitution of society* where he explains the complex interaction of agency and structure; more specifically, how agency is conditioned by structure at a moment in time, but over time how the activity of agents changes structure. Sewell delves deeper into this question of agency and structure, in his article "A theory of structure," with a focus on how the relationship between the two leads to change in social structures. Finally, in a comprehensive treatment of agency, Emirbayer and Mische's now foundational piece, "What is agency?," dives deeply into the discussions of agency in social science and the humanities to provide a highly useful framework for understanding different types of agency.

Emirbayer, M., and Mische, A. 1998. What is agency? *American Journal of Sociology*, 103(4): 962–1023.
Giddens, A. 1984. *The constitution of society: Outline of the theory of structuration*. Cambridge: Polity Press.
Sewell, W. H. 1992. A theory of structure: Duality, agency, and transformation. *American Journal of Sociology*, 98(1): 1–29.

Modernism and Postmodernism

The importance of social-symbolic work follows the changes in society that have led people to see their selves, the organizations they inhabit, and the broader societal context as things they can work to influence. This change is, as we have already argued, part of the broader shift from premodernity to modernity and then postmodernity. Cooper and Burrell provide an accessible and concise introduction to this topic that we highly recommend to anyone with little familiarity with these ideas. For a more theoretically challenging discussion of modernism and postmodernism, Harvey's *The condition of postmodernity* provides an interesting perspective that highlights the link between postmodernism and cultural change. In two more focused works, Lyotard's classic *The postmodern condition* focuses on the doubt about meta-narratives that comes with the move to the postmodern, while Weedon's *Feminist practice and poststructuralist theory* focuses on what the advent of postmodernism means for feminism.

Cooper, R., and Burrell, G. 1988. Modernism, postmodernism and organizational analysis: An introduction, *Organization Studies*, 9(1) 91–112.

Harvey, D. 1989. *The condition of postmodernity: An enquiry into the origins of cultural change*. Oxford: Blackwell.

Lyotard, J.-F. 1984. *The postmodern condition: A report on knowledge*. University of Minnesota Press.

Weedon, C. 1987. *Feminist practice and poststructuralist theory*. Oxford: Blackwell.

Part II

3

Self Work

In this chapter we:

1. Review the history of the self as a social-symbolic object.
2. Conceptualize self work as a form of social-symbolic work.
3. identify the key dimensions of self work.
4. Explore the variety of actors engaged in self work.

In 1998, Maria Patiño, Spain's top woman hurdler, found herself at the center of an unexpected and unwelcome whirlwind of gender "assignment" (Fausto-Sterling, 2008). Having arrived for the 1985 World University Games without a certificate verifying her sex (something required of all competitors), Patiño was subjected to routine chromosomal testing. It was a complete surprise to Patiño when the tests revealed that the cells scraped from her cheek contained a Y chromosome. Moreover, tests showed that her labia hid testes she didn't know existed, and that she had neither ovaries nor a uterus. Patiño's life was turned upside down. She was immediately barred from international competition, and when the story went public, she was stripped of previous titles by Spanish track officials, barred from further competition, deserted by her boyfriend, and excoriated in the press. As she describes it, "I felt ashamed and embarrassed. I lost friends, my fiancé, hope, and energy" (Martínez-Patiño, 2005: S38).

For her part, Patiño fought back: "I could hardly pretend to be a man; I have breasts and a vagina. I never cheated. I fought my disqualification" (Martínez-Patiño, 2005: S38). She spent thousands of dollars consulting with doctors to find out that she had a rare condition called androgen insensitivity that meant her cells could not utilize the testosterone her testes produced, and thus her body never developed male characteristics, while the estrogen that her body (and all humans) produce caused her breasts to grow, her waist to narrow and her hips to widen: "[d]espite a Y chromosome and testes, she had grown up as a female and developed a female form" (Fausto-Sterling, 2008: 2). Patiño insisted on her womanhood: "I knew I was a woman...in the eyes of medicine, God and most of all, in my own eyes" (Carlson, 1991: 27). With the help of Alison Carlson, a biologist opposed to sex testing as well as a former Stanford University tennis player, Patiño began to build a case that she was a woman. She was examined by doctors who "checked out her pelvic structures and shoulders to decide if she was feminine enough to compete" (Vines, 1992: 41).

In the end, she made history. After a two-and-a-half-year battle, the International Amateur Athletic Federation (IAAF) reinstated her, and she rejoined the Spanish Olympic squad. Patiño was the first woman to successfully challenge sex testing for female athletes. Having spent all that time fighting instead of training, however, she missed qualifying for the 1992 Olympics by 1/10 of a second.

The story of Maria Patiño shows that sex is not a simple matter of assignment to a category based on obvious and unchanging physical markers. Not only is the question of whether a person is a "man or a woman" not straightforward, but the assignment of sex can become the matter of significant work by interested parties. The self work done in relation to sex and, even more so, gender[1] has meant that the fluidity of these constructs has evolved significantly since 1985, when Patiño ran into her problems. A simple illustration of these changes involves signing up for a social media account: when filling out a Facebook profile in 2018, the choices for gender include not only Male and Female, but "Custom," which provides a box to fill in using one's own terms, along with the choice of Male, Female, and Neutral "preferred pronouns."

Maria Patiño's story vividly illustrates the focus of this chapter—the purposeful, reflexive efforts of individuals, collective actors, and networks of actors to shape an individual's self. It highlights the intensely personal—as well as political, economic, social, and material—nature of this self work. The story also shows the multidimensional nature of self work, including a discursive dimension that in this case involved letters, reports, legal documents, and public speeches; a relational dimension that involved forming, maintaining, ending, and leveraging interpersonal and interorganizational relationships; and a material dimension that relied on a range of physical objects, including scientific testing equipment and, crucially, the human body. Patiño's story also highlights the range of actors who can become involved in defining a self,

---

[1] Although the traditional distinction between sex and gender (with sex being attached to biological characteristics and gender to social identity) is made problematic from a social-symbolic work perspective, where both sex and gender are social accomplishments, they remain distinct as social-symbolic objects, since the resources drawn on to socially construct a person's sex revolve around the meaning of biological characteristics, whereas this is less the case with gender.

including the person whose self is the object of those efforts as well as any number of other individuals and organizations. In Patiño's case, determining what is often considered to be one of the most basic dimensions of the self—sex—involved a host of interested actors, including organizations such as the IOC and the IAAF, the Spanish government, Spanish sports bodies, and the media, as well as many individual medical and sports professionals, reporters, and even Patiño's friends and family.

Our exploration of self work in this chapter is broken into two main parts. First, we examine the history of the self as a social-symbolic object and how that history has shaped how self work is performed. We then conceptualize self work as a form of social-symbolic work, including its dimensions and the kinds of actors who might engage in self work. We end the chapter, as with the others, with a set of additional resources for investigating this form of social-symbolic work.

The History of the Self as a Social-Symbolic Object

The concept of self work begins with the concept of the self. At one level, the self is simply you and me. We look in the mirror and we see our "selves." We fall off our bikes and we hurt our "selves." From this perspective, our selves are simply another way of describing our bodily limits. And indeed, this is an important feature of the self as we consider it in this chapter. The body and its limits form an important facet of the self that shapes how we understand both ourselves and our selves.

At the same time, the self is more than a body and provides a paradox in its familiarity:

> Nothing could be more intimate to us than [the] self. It is not just close to us, it is all we are.... But perhaps it's not so simple. For if we try to grasp our self, it is always just out of reach. We see, hear, and touch particular things, but can't see who is seeing, hear who is hearing, touch who is touching.... Our self, which to our immediate perception is the surest of all things, is at the same time the hardest to pin down. (Heehs, 2013: 1)

The availability and meaning of a self as a social-symbolic object has, moreover, changed dramatically over time. In this section, we explore the history of the self, focusing on its transformation in modernity, and then its reformulation in postmodernity. The history of the self as a social-symbolic object is crucial to the purpose of this book; the status of the self in social life is what makes it an object upon which social-symbolic work can be performed, and its constitution in different periods and places establishes the ways in which people can work to shape it.

The Modern Self

A history of the self might seem a strange and confusing possibility because a core element of popular culture, informed significantly by religious traditions, is that there exists and has always existed "something eternal and immutable in us that is our essential self" (Heehs, 2013: 2). In Judeo-Christian terms this is often cast as the "soul"; in Hinduism, there exists the "atman"; in Jainism, the "jiva." In secular terms, the presumption of a universal, ahistorical self is echoed in our ideas of "authenticity" and "sincerity" which suggest a constant self from which deviation is problematic. But, regardless of whether the soul, atman, or jiva are eternal, the terms "soul," "atman," and "jiva" are not: these terms came into being at a certain point in the development of these religions and have undergone significant changes in use and meaning over the centuries (Heehs, 2013). As we shall discuss later in this chapter, the possibility of an authentic self has similarly emerged only over the last few centuries. Thus, in tracing the history of the self, our concern is not with its metaphysical status, but its emergence as a social-symbolic object on which people could reflect and work to improve or at least to change.

The first historical transition we are concerned with occurred during the transition from premodernity to modernity. As we discussed in Chapter 2, this transition was remarkable for its turn away from traditional habits and customs, to social forms and practices that sought change and progress. Over time, the social world, along with the natural world, became something that could be managed and, if done so using rational means and technologies, potentially perfected. This was not only in terms of large-scale institutions and structures, but in ways that "radically alter[ed] the nature of day-to-day social life and affect[ed] the most personal aspects of our experience" (Giddens, 1991: 1).

Most important to us here is the fact that the self became an object of work in the transition to modernity as its relationship to society became more complex and less deterministic. In medieval times, the relation of one's self to society was simplified by two sets of beliefs: the equivalence between a person and his or her role in society, and faith that fulfilling one's role would give life meaning and fulfillment because that role was designed and assigned by God (Baumeister, 1987). While the "role equals self" equation was direct and linear in premodern times, the advent of modernity required people to construct selves in relation to multiple, often competing discourses. In modernity, the self became a "reflexive project." Where life transitions prior to modernity were ritualized as rites of passage with clearly identified changes in identity, as in the transition to adulthood, life transitions in modern societies demanded that "the altered self . . . be explored and constructed as part of a reflexive process of connecting personal and social change" (Giddens, 1991: 34).

An important part of the emergence of the modern self was its interiorization. Whereas the self had previously corresponded to our behaviors and commitments, in this period it became the invisible force behind those behaviors and commitments. This shift made the previously knowable self uncertain and mysterious. Through the Renaissance and the revolutions in knowledge associated with the Enlightenment, and the tremendous changes that occurred during the industrial revolution, people gained certainties with respect to nature, but faced new uncertainties with respect to the self (Baumeister, 1987). In response, literary and scholarly innovations emerged—in particular the portrait, diary, and biography—that represented efforts to render visible what had become abstract, hidden, and mysterious (Porter, 1997). These visual and literary cultural forms both reflected and constructed the new and distinctly modern problem of knowing oneself.

The individualization and interiorization of the self brought with them the potential for self-improvement in a way not possible when the self was the sum of a social position and the behaviors that enacted that position. Ideas such as "self-control" and "self-discipline" emerged as important features of life. Not only did the self become an object of social-symbolic work, the work itself became explicitly examined as a set of rational means to preferred ends. Representative of this quest for self-improvement were the "conduct books" that emerged in Western Europe in the sixteenth century. Conduct books focused on the "refinement of manners and greater delicacy in public with regard to eating, excreting, cleanliness and the body generally" with the aim of creating Christian gentlewomen and gentlemen (Smith, 1997: 56).

Another important literary innovation that gained significance in this period for similar reasons was the diary. Whereas we might today conceive of diaries as private spaces in which to confess our secrets and explore our thoughts and desires, early diaries were understood as a means of reflection and self-control, to the extent that "[s]erious Puritans recommended the diary as a discipline for the soul's steady contemplation of its proper ends" (Smith, 1997: 56). Protestant diaries of the sixteenth and seventeenth centuries were volumes racked with anxiety. The Reformation had left Protestants with a fear of damnation that could not be resolved through confession; only those "elected" by God would ascend. The anxiety led to a search for signs of what Calvin called "proofs of the indwelling of the spirit and signs of divine election." As Weber (2001: 69) argued: "[h]owever useless good works might be as a means of attaining salvation," they are indispensable for "getting rid of the fear of damnation." This anxiety was often expressed in diaries of the time in terms of self-loathing, as in the case of a Rhode Island woman who wrote "that her heart was 'a sink of sin, more loathsome than the most offensive carrion that swarms with hateful vermin!'" (Heehs, 2013: 57).

The self that emerged with the transition to modernity was, in summary, the site of reflexive consideration and anxious cultivation. The philosophical articulation of this new self, separate from our behaviors and thus from our bodies, gained its most pithy rendering in Descartes's famous pronouncement, "I think, therefore I am." Descartes's notion established as foundational the separation of mind and body which governed, and continues to heavily influence, modern conceptions of the self. The writing—both professional and personal—of the time, along with the visual renderings of individual people, give us a strong sense of the anxieties that people experienced in relation to questions about who they were and the lives they were meant to lead. This changed idea of self is reflected in modern preoccupations with "personal feelings, personal wealth, personal fulfilment, personal health, personal privacy and much else 'personal' besides" (Giddens, 1991: 13).

The Postmodern Self

As with the transition to modernity, the transition to postmodernity did not occur all at once or uniformly across geographies or domains of social life. Where modernity was associated with a self that could be improved, and ideally perfected, through rational means anchored in scientific, religious, or other moral traditions, postmodernity brought a deep skepticism with respect to the modern ideals that underpinned that possibility. Change remained highly valued, but became unanchored from perfection or even improvement in some objective sense. Instead, the selves of postmodernity could be the targets of change efforts, but the motivations for those efforts would be more likely aesthetic or political than rational, and the means radically plural rather than singularly rational.

To understand the self in postmodernity, it is helpful to consider Gergen's (1991) discussion of a "saturated self." By saturated, Gergen means a self that has been fractured by the radical multiplicity of social relationships resulting in a plurality of more or less conflicting selves: "Social saturation furnishes us with a multiplicity of incoherent and unrelated languages of the self. For everything we 'know to be true' about ourselves, other voices within respond with doubt and even derision" (Gergen, 1991: 6–7).

The foundation of Gergen's argument is that modern technologies have transformed social life. The printing press, trains, automobiles, a postal service, radio, and telephones, and more recently air travel, television, and instant electronic communications, mean we engage in relationships and daily contact with vastly more people, and consequently greater varieties of information and expression. Along with these technologies has come a globalization of experience, in part through mass media that expose us to the cultures of distant populations, and in part through the mass migrations of the afflicted and the global travel of the affluent, that marked the twentieth century.

In 2017, Gergen's 1990s description of social saturation seems almost quaint; in today's social media-infused landscape, people number their "friends" in the hundreds, flick through photos and videos of friends, family, and acquaintances, as well as celebrities and random strangers over breakfast, and are overwhelmed with the scores of emails received each day (unless they are young enough or hip enough to have forsaken email altogether). And the movement of cultural values and practices has only accelerated: mass migrations are a constant (if highly contested) feature of the twenty-first century; and visual exposure to distant people and events has increased exponentially through the uploads of individuals on YouTube, Facebook, and Instagram.

Gergen's point, though, remains valid and useful. These technologies and their impacts on our lives have had a profound effect on our selves: a *"populating of the self,* the acquisition of multiple and disparate potentials for being...that undermine the traditional commitments to both romanticist and modernist forms of being" (Gergen, 1991: 69). One dimension along which this populating occurs is in terms of the values that people hold. As people participate in more and more relationships, and are familiar with greater numbers of cultures, they work to "hold an increasing number of values with an increasing level of importance" (Ovadia, 2003: 241). This populating of the self with experiences, relationships, values, and information leads to a situation in which people no longer constitute themselves as a consistent "I" and variable "Me"s, as suggested by the symbolic interactionists, but rather a plurality of "I"s—a plurality of "images (not of essences) which are part of relationships (not of the individual)" (Tseëlon, 1992: 120). The modern and postmodern selves differ in their ontology, with the modern self existing as a Cartesian duality that contrasts the private and the public, while the postmodern self exists as a pragmatist plurality in which the self is constituted in and through situated, discursive, and material practices (Gergen, 1991; Goffman, 1959a; Tseëlon, 1992).

While the abstract descriptions are mysteriously inviting, the question that remains is what the postmodern self is in practical terms. As an answer, we suggest two key images: a self anchored in local routines and practices, and an agential self with nearly (but not quite) limitless potential for transformation.

The first image is rooted in the day-to-day adjudication of the self that occurs in a vast array of institutionalized routines and practices, including schools, hospitals, offices, prisons, counseling rooms, self-improvement courses, welfare agencies, and day-cares. These disparate organizations constitute "sites of interpretative practice" in which "the self remains a central category for attaching subjective meaning to experience" (Gubrium and Holstein, 1994: 690). The self is thus not simply free-floating, but nor is it rooted in global discourses of God and Truth; instead, the self is produced, fixed, and adjudicated in local, practical terms by interested parties who negotiate its meaning in relation to specific projects and needs.

The second image of a postmodern self stands in apparent contrast to the first: it describes the transformational agent who takes control of their self in ways that previously seemed impossible. Two categories of transformation illustrate this image: class and gender. At this point in history, the possibility of people transcending and reconstructing their social class, at least in most developed Western economies, is taken for granted. It's not that this is easy, or that most people are successful in moving across class lines, but we no longer see class as a fixed category into which one is born and can never escape. Indeed, the potential for redefining oneself in terms of one's class (through education and "hard work") is a core myth for many Western democracies, and its possibility is reinforced by the life stories of many actual people.

The possibility of transforming one's gender is a more recent innovation, but one that has, in many societies, become not only taken for granted at a cultural level, but enshrined in law and supported by a range of institutionalized practices around education, healthcare, and workplace protections. In the United States, Caitlyn Jenner's[2] story is now a part of the everyday worlds of even the most conservative parts of the population.

So, does this mean anything goes for the postmodern self? No—and this is the meeting point for the first and second images of the postmodern self. The ability of people to transform their selves depends on the sets of negotiations and practices that are institutionalized within specific times and places. Take, for instance, the matter of race and its potential as an object of purposeful shaping or reshaping, and the case of Rachel Dolezal,[3] who gained notoriety when her parents stated publicly that she was a white woman passing as black. At that time, Dolezal had been the president of the National Association for the Advancement of Colored People (NAACP) in Spokane, Washington since 2014, as well as an instructor in Africana studies at Eastern Washington University. In the aftermath, Dolezal resigned from the NAACP and lost her position at Eastern Washington University. Since then, her claims of "blackness" and her arguments for the possibility of someone being "transracial" have been the focus of intense debate, with comparisons to transgender identities being decried by members of both the transgender community and the black community.

---

[2] Caitlyn Marie Jenner is an American television personality and retired Olympic gold medal-winning decathlete. She was born William Bruce Jenner on October 28, 1949 and publicly transitioned to a woman in April 2015. She is one of the most famous openly transgender women in the world.

[3] <https://en.wikipedia.org/wiki/Rachel_Dolezal>.

Core to these criticisms are two arguments. The first is that "passing" as black is a choice, unlike transitioning gender to one's "true" gender. An editorial by a transgender person in the *Guardian*, for instance, argued that "The fundamental difference between Dolezal's actions and trans people's is that her decision to identify as black was an active choice.... Dolezal identified as black, but I *am* a woman, and other trans people *are* the gender they feel themselves to be" (Talusan, 2015, emphasis original).

The second argument is that "passing" as black is a choice with hostile political effects on black people, whereas transitioning genders has no effects on anyone but the person in question. As one commentator on her claims argued, "By performing 'blackness', she made a joke of our oppression.... Instead of using her privilege to help move the cause forward, she used it to de-center black people within our own movements" (Gibson, 2015). In a much-publicized interview with Dolezal, Ijeoma Oluo, a black woman, summarized it this way, "I couldn't escape Rachel Dolezal because I can't escape white supremacy. And it is white supremacy that told an unhappy and outcast white woman that black identity was hers for the taking" (Oluo, 2017).

In these responses to Rachael Dolezal and her claims about the possibility of a "transracial" self, we see the intersection of the transformative, postmodern agent and the locally situated and adjudicated actor. While the self has become increasingly detached from broad, globalizing discourses, it remains deeply attached to the local discourses and communities of interpretative practice through which the standing of the self is evaluated. The postmodern self is, thus, layered on top of the modern self. In the debates over Rachel Dolezal and her "blackness," we see the contours provided both by the local and historical politics of race and gender, and by references to the "latest science" which might suggest that transgender people's brains are more like the brains of the genders to which they have transitioned.

The Contemporary Self

At this point in history, the self as a social-symbolic object is a complex layering of its premodern, modern, and postmodern versions, and it is this complexity that makes self work complex and challenging, and fascinating to study. We are, of course, still born in locations with social, cultural, and economic traditions, and into families with ethnic, religious, and occupational legacies. These legacies, however, represent starting points, not final destinations. The idea of absolute agency, where everyone can simply reshape their self in the way they wish, is a myth, but so is any strong form of structural determinism. People, especially in liberal Western democracies, weave their lives, as well as the lives of those with whom they are in relationships, from the threads of multiple discourses that together provide significant opportunity for self-definition. At the same time, this process is dependent on those societal discourses, which still vary tremendously in terms of their benevolence, accessibility, and malleability.

Conceptualizing Self Work

Central to our discussion of the self as a social-symbolic object is the contrast between the self as the simple awareness of the distinction between ourselves and the world (something that we share with many animals), and the self as a product of thought, reflection, and action—the result of our ability to take one's self as the object of attention (Leary and Tangney, 2003). The latter is a uniquely human attribute and a product, at least in part, of human effort. This leads directly to the concept of self work, which we defined at the beginning of this chapter as purposeful, reflexive efforts of individuals, collective actors, and networks of actors to shape a self.

Although self work is far from the whole answer to the question of how selves are produced, it is a crucially important part of the answer and the one that arises directly out of our more general concept of social-symbolic work. If the self is a social-symbolic object, then what sorts of social-symbolic work can be performed to shape it and who can do this sort of work? To answer this question, our conceptualization of self work as a type of social-symbolic work requires unpacking and we also need to understand the boundaries of self work (that is, what is and what is not self work).

Before we explore the concept of self work, it is useful to more closely examine the idea of purposeful, reflexive effort. By this, we mean that self work occurs when the efforts of some actor or actors are focused on a self (and not necessarily their own self), and that that focus is intentional and reflexive. Self work, in the way we talk about it, is not done by accident or thoughtlessly. Moreover, it is effortful in the sense that it requires an investment of time, attention, and social and material resources. And it is important to emphasize that by self work we do not mean the efforts of actors to shape the *concept* of the self—the psychologists, philosophers, poets, and novelists who have, over the ages, portrayed and debated the self as an idea, including its location, limits, and potential. We are interested in this work, but as a kind of institutional work, rather than a kind of self work, and we will return to this form of work in Chapters 7 and 8.

It is also important to note that, as with all kinds of social-symbolic work, there is no direct or linear relationship between self work and the self. The link between self work and the self is complicated by at least two dynamics. First, selves are the product of a host of social, cultural, technological, and biological processes beyond self work. Genderedness as a dimension of the self, for instance, is more malleable now, not only because of the efforts of individual people working to shape their own genders, but because of technological and biological advances that have led to medical and pharmaceutical options to shape the self that were previously unavailable (and perhaps unthinkable).

Second, selves are sites of contestation. The construction of a self involves self work well beyond the individual whose self is in question. There are a host of individual and collective actors interested in the shaping of selves, beginning with parents and families, continuing on to schools, religious organizations, and other child-focused agencies, and eventually involving workplaces and the wide array of businesses and organizations devoted specifically to the shaping of the self, such as gyms, fashion firms, psychologists and other counselors, and recovery organizations. The complications associated with understanding the connection between self work and the self do not diminish the importance of self work. The transitions to modernity and postmodernity are associated with, and to some extent defined by, the emergence of self work as a preoccupation. We spend more time, effort, and money than ever on our efforts to define and redefine our selves. In this section, we examine self work from two angles: its dimensions, and who does it.

Dimensions of Self Work

In order to adequately conceptualize self work, we need to account both for its heterogeneity—the wide array of activities through which people work to shape selves—and the commonalties among these activities. Rather than trying to categorize kinds of work, as has been commonly done in other writing on social-symbolic work (e.g., Lawrence and Suddaby, 2006), we focus on describing key underlying dimensions that cut across forms of work. Thus, our aim is not to catalogue kinds of self work, but rather to develop a language that can be used to describe and compare instances of self work.

This is not, of course, an original problem. Other writers have identified dimensions of particular forms of social-symbolic work, and thus we draw on discussions of identity work and institutional work (Hampel et al., 2017; Snow and Anderson, 1987) that have identified three key dimensions: discursive, relational, and material. These dimensions are not types of social-symbolic work; rather, they represent three dimensions that underpin all instances of social-symbolic work. Different instances of social-symbolic work may be more or less clearly associated with one dimension rather than the others— for example, some instances of self work are largely discursive—but all instances of self work involve all three dimensions at least to some degree.

THE DISCURSIVE DIMENSION OF SELF WORK

We begin by exploring the discursive dimension of self work, which describes the efforts of actors to shape or construct a self through the production of verbal or written language. In the context of self work, some forms of discourse play especially important roles in the construction of selves. A wide range of writing on the self has highlighted the central role of narrative, suggesting that "human beings think, perceive, imagine, and make moral choices according to narrative structures" (Sarbin, 1986: 8). From this perspective, narrative is more than just a way in which humans make sense of their world; it is the key organizing principle for such activity. Furthermore, unlike many other organizing principles common in psychology, such as heuristics (Kahneman and Tversky, 1984), narrative is an accomplishment: it is an "achievement that brings together mundane facts and fantastic creations," and "allows for the inclusion of actors' reasons for their acts" (Sarbin, 1986: 9). A narrative can also be rewritten, with important implications for the self it plays a role in constituting.

By suggesting a narrative dimension to self work, we mean that much of the effort that people put into constructing selves involves telling stories either about that self, or in which the self features prominently, such that they tell us something important about the self. This work is illustrated by the diaries and biographies we discussed in relation to the emergence of the modern self, but it also includes more mundane, day-to-day storytelling, as when we recount the story of "our day" to a loved one, or a story about a funny or interesting thing that happened to a friend or work colleague.

These narratives are not separate from our selves, or even reflective of our selves, but rather productive of our selves in the sense that they constitute our selves as objects on which we are able to reflect, and which inform our understandings of the world and our place in it. Our ability to construct narratives in which we constitute our selves does not naturally or inevitably occur; people need to learn how to construct such stories. Narratives have structures that make them more or less convincing and compelling, and they draw on broader cultural ideas and themes that allow others to locate those stories in relationship to their own selves and communities. People learn to do this kind of narrative work in many ways, much of which occurs in childhood through pretend play (Kyratzis, 1999) and listening to adult conversations (Miller et al., 1990).

A compelling context to explore the discursive dimension of self work involves the narratives of individuals who have faced serious illness and construct themselves and their situations through stories. Frank (1997) refers to these people as "wounded storytellers"—people "for whom illness is not just a topic of a story, but the very condition of having a story to tell" (Williams, 2008: 714).

An important facet of illness narratives is their historical evolution, from premodern stories as illustrated by a North African woman who describes how, "In the old days...folk didn't know what illness was. They went to bed and they died" (Bourdieu, 1977: 166, quoted in Frank, 1997), to the contemporary version of such a story, which involves a great deal more "knowledge," including symptoms, causes, and treatments, all articulated in the scientific language of medicine (and much of it in recent times thanks to Google). Writing on narratives of illness points to postmodern possibilities of such stories, where people experiencing illness might resist dominant discourses of illness, injury, old age, and infertility, thus producing more hopeful narratives (Ezzy, 2000; Maitlis, 2009). Particularly inspiring is the idea of a "polyphonic" narrative characterized by "interwoven and often contradictory stories and values," told in a way that welcomes rather than suppresses contradictions and tensions (Ezzy, 2000: 613). Such a narrative contrasts with the emphasis on certainty and linearity typical of scientific, medical narratives, and thus allows people with serious illnesses to reject standard, universal illness plots in favor of particular and uncertain life paths (Ezzy, 2000: 616).

The discursive dimension of self work involves efforts to shape a self through discourse, but it also points to a more profoundly discursive understanding of self work in which the self is understood as a discursive object, rather than simply an object influenced by discourse. Research on narrative and the self has shown the value of making this shift from narrative effects on the self to a narrative self. The idea of a narrative self emphasizes the human need and ability to assemble sequences of "experienced events and proposed actions into unified episodes," integrating them into a plot so that they "take on significance and meaning" (Polkinghorne, 1991: 142). The narrative self goes beyond packaging sets of events into story units, though, extending to our whole lives:

> Like each episode singly, my life as a whole—that is, my self—is something temporal that unfolds in time...As such, the self calls for the same sort of structuring and similar principles of unity and coherence as other storied orderings of temporal events. It is the narratively structured unity of my life as whole that provides me with a personal identity and displays the answer to "Who am I?"
>
> (Polkinghorne, 1991: 143)

Conceiving of a narrative self implies a kind of self work that involves creating and shaping a discursive object, not as a means of influencing some distal target, but as an end in itself. The image of self work this suggests involves an infinitely recursive process in which people engage in the reflexive construction of stories about themselves, constituting themselves as discursive objects, knowing that that is what they are doing, and thus including in some fashion the construction of their selves as part of their self-narratives. We are not suggesting a paradox, but perhaps a kind of tension, or at least the need to develop a set of skills and resources that allow one to narrate one's own self.

THE RELATIONAL DIMENSION OF SELF WORK

The discursive dimension of self work begins to break down the boundaries around the self, suggesting a more social than individual object. Narrative is social in many ways. Stories represent, of course, an important medium through which social life transpires, and telling a story requires a listener and a protagonist. We tell and retell stories—about ourselves, about others with whom we are connected, and about people, things, and events about which only we are aware. Stories are also social in a deeper way. The structure and content of stories, along with legitimate and effective ways of relating stories, are socially negotiated and socially learned—how to tell a story is not an art we are born with but one that is learned with and through others. Narrative and other discursive forms always exist in relationships. Without social relations, there would be no need, opportunity, or ability to narrate the self. Thus, the discursive dimension of self work means that self work also has a relational dimension.

The relational dimension of self work begins with the idea that the efforts of actors to construct selves, their own and those of others, occur in the context of relationships that motivate, facilitate, and restrict those efforts. The relational dimension of self work, and social-symbolic work more generally, involves work on relationships—establishing, maintaining, and transforming relationships—as a means of shaping a self, as well as self work that leverages relationships as they already exist.

Self work necessarily involves a relational dimension because selves are fundamentally social constructs—they describe people not as isolates but as situated members of families, groups, organizations, communities, and societies. As with the narrative dimension of self work, there are two key facets to its relational dimension—the ways in which relationships are involved in actors' efforts to construct selves, and the ways in which the self is constructed as a relational object.

The importance of relationships in self work is highlighted by research on close relationships and on relatively distant relationships. Writing on close relationships among adults suggests that our selves are "constantly under construction and reconstruction, with the architects and remodelling contractors largely being those with whom we have close interactions" (Aron and Nardone, 2011: 521). The metaphor is apt. It is not that close relationships have some kind of direct effect on our selves; instead, they provide opportunities and resources for self work, both on one's own self and the selves of those with whom we have those close relationships. Such opportunities arise as people in close relationships enhance or diminish the other's self-esteem, support or fail to support important goals, and confirm or disconfirm expectations through their actions (Aron and Nardone, 2011). The critical role of close relationships in self work is highlighted by their centrality in a range of psychotherapeutic traditions that focus on families of origin and intimate partners as keys to understanding and responding to problematic self narrations (Magnavita, 2000; Strupp et al., 1988).

Although close relationships are undoubtedly powerful contributors to self work, sociological research has for decades also shown the importance of weak ties in shaping how we construct and reconstruct our selves, particularly by providing novel opportunities and information. While our intimate relationships show us who we are, our more distant relationships often show us what we might become and give us access to different social worlds. The first important study to show these effects was Granovetter's (1973) examination of how people get jobs. Unsurprisingly, Granovetter found that most people got jobs through personal connections, but surprisingly he found that those connections tended to be somewhat distant acquaintances who connected them with job opportunities embedded in social networks outside their immediate spheres. Since this landmark study, a large body of research has confirmed the "strength of weak ties," as Granovetter put it, not only in terms of the opportunities they provide but the wide array of kinds of information they allow individuals to access, which people use to imagine and enact new selves (Dobrow and Higgins, 2005; Ibarra and Deshpande, 2007).

Like the narrative dimension, the relational dimension of self work goes beyond suggesting that relationships contribute to people's efforts to shape the self to suggest an ontological shift in our understanding of the self as a social-symbolic object, in this case to the idea of a relational self. The concept of a relational self inverts the traditional idea that individuals exist and then form relationships (Gergen, 2009a; Mason, 2004). It proposes instead that a self is the product of the relationships in which it is engaged. The ontological flip required by the idea of a relational self is propelled by a broader relational ontology that posits a relational foundation for the existence of all things. A relational ontology suggests that to the extent anything has meaning, it is as part of a social relationship. So, things exist, but they only come to have meaning—to be "some thing"—in and through social relationships where the meaning of those things is determined: things exist but come to be "mountains," "trees," and "the sun" through the social relationships in which they gain those meanings (Gergen, 2009b: 37).

Extending this ontology into the social world, we see that human actions, in and of themselves (or at least by themselves), have no meaning: "There are no acts of love, altruism, prejudice, or aggression as such. In order to *be anything at all*, they require a supplement, an action by at least one other person that ratifies their existence *as something*" (Gergen, 2009b: 33, emphasis added). Applying this logic to the self suggests that our selves do not exist outside of relationships. It is in relation to other selves that the self as a social-symbolic object comes into existence *as something*—as friends, as colleagues, as Tom, as Nelson. To be clear, this is not a metaphysical argument. The idea of a relational self does not imply that things (including people) do not exist outside relations, but that they only exist *as something* in relations. It is in co-action that we are produced both as individuals and as participants in relationships.

The concept of a relational self is both a reaction to individualistic notions of self that dominate contemporary psychology and an extension of traditions that focus on the person in relationship to others, particularly from feminist work in psychology and education (Gilligan, 1982; Noddings, 2003). Feminist writing has led the social sciences in appreciating and understanding the relational self and self work. A landmark in this tradition was Gilligan's (1982) study of women's moral development that located "care" for others at the center of a mature ethics. Gilligan argues that for women, the world of relationships is the central "focus of attention and concern" (1982: 168). This focus on relationships even inverts what were seen as traditional conceptions of power, so that power is equated with giving and care: "while men represent powerful activity as assertion and aggression, women in contrast portray acts of nurturance as acts of strength" (Gilligan, 1982: 168).

Bringing together the discursive and relational dimensions of self work, we see self work as the efforts of individuals, collective actors, and networks of actors to construct selves that only exist in relation to others and that originate in sets of partial, fragmented stories. They do this by drawing on the intimate and distant relationships in which they are involved, and their ability to assemble experience, memory, and anticipation into reasonably coherent narrative structures. This process is often characterized by conflict and tension as different actors work to shape selves in ways that are incompatible and the self that is constituted is characterized in important ways by these unresolved differences.

Self work is thus not the province of individuals, and especially not individuals *qua* individuals. Rather, self work is a form of coordinated activity that we do with and in relation to others. How we describe our past, present, and future, and how we develop narratives that connect them, are not activities done in isolation by individuals constructing their own self. They are done in relation with others who sometimes participate as a passive audience, but often as co-producers of those narratives, asking questions, prompting explanations, filling in blanks, providing possible templates, or even leading the process, as parents, teachers, professors, counselors, lawyers, and doctors, as well as friends, lovers, and siblings (and even collective actors like churches,

---

Box 3.1. THE SELF WORK INDUSTRY

The fact that selves are not simply constructed by individuals for themselves opens up the possibility of self work as a commercial arena, in which actors work to benefit economically from their roles in the construction of the selves of others. At the time of writing this, Amazon.com listed 361,960 books in its "Self-Help" section, covering a vast range of topics from "abuse" and "anger management," through "death and grief," to "sex" and "time management." In the US alone, consumers spend more than $11 billion a year on books, seminars, CDs, coaching, and stress management programs (Lindner, 2009). At the same time, the US market for psychologists, social workers, and marriage counselors is estimated at $15.4 billion.

The size of this industry reflects both the importance we place on our selves and our belief in our ability to improve those selves physically, psychologically, emotionally, sexually, practically, professionally, or otherwise. It also reflects a strong desire across a wide variety of people to simplify the path to improvement into a series of "steps," including "5 Steps to Master Any Skill in 20 Hours," "7 Simple Steps to Becoming More Grateful in 7 Days," and "5 Simple Steps You Need to Know to Achieve Mindfulness and Live in the Moment," and even the ironic "How to Become a Grown-up in 468 Easy(ish) Steps." Perhaps the most profoundly important steps, however, are the "12 Steps," a phrase so well understood that most readers could enumerate some of those steps, at least in part—"believe that a Power greater than ourselves could restore us to sanity," make a "list of all persons we had harmed, and...make amends." The 12 Steps originally published in the 1939 book, *Alcoholics Anonymous: The story of how more than one hundred men have recovered from alcoholism,* has become one of the most compelling and influential templates for self-help.

The self-help industry points to two important aspects of self work as social-symbolic work. First, that its outcome may often be less important than the work itself. This is evident in much of the language associated with the self work industry, where notions like "doing the work" and "practice" have become institutionalized. Second, social-symbolic work, while perhaps the most social of activities, often becomes commercialized and is performed by trained professionals of various sorts who perform social-symbolic work as a job. We will come back to this point as we discuss various kinds of social-symbolic work.

---

schools, governments, and companies, see Box 3.1). Even enemies and rivals work to construct selves, although their activities are not always appreciated and often resisted.

THE MATERIAL DIMENSION OF SELF WORK

Self work involves more than "just" talking or thinking about our selves—it is both embodied and material and can involve a wide range of artifacts and forms of effort. While selves are constructed through narrative work and in relation to others, there are always important material aspects that help or hinder the narrative and that must be managed to maintain a self or to change it. Put another way, the self is not just narratively constituted, but also depends on material artifacts and practices that support and instantiate the self.

The importance of the material dimension of self work is clear in this account of a gay man working in the UK civil service who felt he could not come out at work without creating a new self:

> I thought the only way I can [be openly gay] is to move, change jobs, move to a new office and a new town and a new city. Move home and change my name and completely come up with a brand new life. . . . I severed all connections with my previous life. (Ward and Winstanley, 2005: 460)

This person's self work went well beyond thinking or talking about being "out" as a gay man—it involved years of concrete, effortful material change. We need to incorporate these physical, material, and geographic facets so that our images of self work are not restricted to those more easily captured in texts and images, and thus more likely to enter discourse (Phillips et al., 2004). The material dimension of self work, as illustrated by this story, involves, at a minimum, technologies of consumption and production, space, and the body.

In the context of modern capitalism, material technologies of production and consumption are key to self work. Beginning with technologies of production, the objects we use in our day-to-day working lives are tools, but their functionality goes beyond their practical usefulness; these objects are also important tools for self work through which we fashion aspects of our selves as social-symbolic objects. The computers we use to create and communicate; the desks, chairs, and shelves that populate our workspaces; the instruments and devices we use to maintain our bodies: all of these objects expand our abilities in ways that alter our selves and help define us in terms of occupations.

Today, perhaps nothing exemplifies this better than the smartphone, which has become a permanent attachment for most people (and with an estimated 6.1 billion smartphone users by 2020, we will be well past "most"). The ubiquity and impact of smartphones led Leslie Perlow to engage in research with the Boston Consulting Group to see if they could rescue their consultants from the constant pressure for responsiveness that these technologies engendered (Perlow, 2012). The experiment was successful, but establishing "predictable time off" from using smartphones required coordinated action by teams of consultants with the support of the organization as a whole. So integral was the smartphone to the selves of consultants, that no consultant or executive on their own could even temporarily extract smartphones from their role.

A similar dynamic involves objects of consumption. Through consumption we construct "extended selves" in which we come to "regard our possessions as parts of ourselves" (Belk, 1988: 139). The role of possessions in defining the self is certainly not new: clothing and other objects have played important roles in constructing our selves for all of human history. But the role of consumption has taken on special significance in an age of global capitalism where companies spend billions making products meaningful and symbolically attaching them to certain identities. This activity means that people, at least in wealthy developed countries, have access to a tremendous variety of highly symbolic consumer products through which they can define who they are and how they relate to the world. The mass consumption that marks global capitalism has been associated with a movement of values from being embodied in persons to being embodied in objects. A perhaps unexpected effect of that shift has been the fostering of diversity in identity and expression, as people are able through purchase and display to construct complex selves more quickly and easily than through other means, such as production, profession, or developing relationships (Miller, 1988).

An interesting example of consumption as a form of self work is found in the home, where people work to acknowledge and reconcile multiple, sometimes conflicting, selves. Decorating one's home, or someone else's home as a profession or favor, represents an important form of self work that offers the potential to incorporate different facets of the self—familial, cultural, ethnic, sexual, religious, etc. Material homemaking practices connect, through physical proximity and arrangement, different parts of fragmented selves, potentially constructing a unified self within a single setting. This possibility may be especially important for marginalized people whose sense of self is "not affirmed or easily performed in the public sphere" (Gorman-Murray, 2008: 284).

In a study of the homemaking practices of gay men and lesbians, for example, the author describes the home not as "not a fixed space, but remade over and over again through everyday homemaking practices...through which identities are ongoingly re-embedded in the home" (Gorman-Murray, 2008: 287). For Maria, a study participant, home was:

> a space of your own, filled with the things that you love and the people within it and that there is a sense of permanency. Photos of your loved ones and books you have read and loved. Things you have bought in your travels to remind you of the places you have been.

The self work in which Maria was engaged was relatively simple—maintaining, arranging, and displaying cherished possessions—but through that work she connected the different facets of her life, such that, as she put it, "The things within [my home] reflect who I am as a whole" (Gorman-Murray, 2008: 291–2). Although we are emphasizing the material dimension of choosing and arranging household objects as a means of constructing a self, it is easy to imagine the discursive and relational dimensions of this work, as people describe their homes and the arrangement of household objects to friends and family.

A second important site for the material dimension of self work is the body. We began this chapter with the story of Maria Patiño, whose body, or more precisely other people's adjudication of her body, triggered a long process of self work by many individuals and collective actors. More generally, we suggested that the body is inextricably linked to the self, our bodily limits often defining our selves. In our history of the self, we remembered the separation of body and self (formulated as mind) emerging in modernity, as captured by Descartes. Patiño's experience, however, highlights how problematic it can be to divide the body and the self. In the transition to postmodernity, the body has become a project "increasingly open to human intervention and . . . made subject to constant revision" (Giddens, 1991: 218).

As a project, though, the self and the body are even more inextricably bound up, such that imagining a self working on the body is misleading. Instead, it is more useful to think of the body as both as a site of self work and a resource in that process. The self work around the body involves not only efforts to shape our physicality in certain ways—losing weight, gaining weight, changing hair color and style, tattoos, piercings, etc.—but also the social negotiation of the meaning of both the outcomes of those efforts and the efforts themselves.

An illustration of these complex dynamics comes from the experience of young women dealing with pressures to make their bodies conform to idealized images. In one study, the responses of young women took on a somewhat unexpected turn, such that it included normalizing a pathological relationship with their own bodies: "having a problem with the way one looks was interpreted as quite a 'normal' relationship [with their bodies], so, rather than feeling as though one's body was abnormal and in need of transformation, it was that very feeling which was normalized" (Budgeon, 2003: 44). This inversion—where having a problem with one's body becomes being normal—points to the importance of including the body in our understanding of self work, but not as a separate, physical resource to be used or altered. Instead, the body, including its physicality, meaning, and social location, is understood as a dimension of the self, inextricable from its other dimensions, subject to a reflexive gaze, but not separable as a distinct object. This understanding of the body in self work moves us away from reductionist approaches to the body, "away from questions about what . . . bodies mean to questions about what . . . bodies can do" (Budgeon, 2003: 52).

Thinking about the body as a part of self work brings us to the point we also reached with respect to the discursive and relational dimensions of self work, that materiality might usefully be understood not as a separate realm we draw on to shape the self, but rather as a facet of the self—a material self. The concept of a material self leads us to imagine a self imbued with material properties, and to incorporate questions and answers that might not usually connect to the self. Questions of affordances, material decay or enhancement, and physical interconnections.

Latour (1999) provides one version of this line of thinking in suggesting a relationship between materiality and the self in which we see material objects and people as comprising integrated units. A widely cited example of this argument is in relation to the debate over gun control, and what to make of the National Rifle Association's claim that "guns don't kill people; people kill people." Latour (1999: 179) responds to this claim by proposing that we think of this debate in terms of a new hybrid agent, the "person-gun," which has different properties than either of its components alone: "You are different with a gun in your hand; the gun is different with you holding it. You are another subject because you hold the gun; the gun is another object because it has entered into a relationship with you." The self in this case is not the person holding a gun but a version of Belk's "extended self," with new abilities and a different social location that results from the risks and potential benefits to others associated with this person-gun hybrid.

Less dramatically, the same reasoning can be applied to any significant technology—computers, cell phones, automobiles—where the person and material object together combine to make a material-social unit with distinct abilities and relationships to others. This hybrid material-human self is important for understanding self work because it is so often the focus of what we are trying to achieve. Contemporary self work is often focused on establishing our selves as hybrid material objects with distinct, and usually more powerful, abilities and social influence. This may be especially true in organizational life, where material-human hybrids are often at the center of organizational productivity.

ADDING UP THE DIMENSIONS OF SELF WORK

We have argued in this section that self work can be usefully understood as made up of three dimensions—discursive, relational, and material. It is important to restate that we are not arguing for instances of self work being categorizable in terms of these dimensions; there are not instances of discursive self work and other instances of relational or material self work. Instead, episodes of self work involve all three dimensions as actors work to shape selves through the construction of narratives that draw on and are motivated by relationships and employ a variety of material resources to make them "real." More profoundly, discourse, relationships, and materiality not only act as resources for self work, but are also dimensions of the self, such that self work becomes concerned with the construction of narrative selves, relational selves, and material selves. Such a conception allows us to move beyond strictly cognitive conceptions of the self to see more complex selves with diverse abilities and constraints.

Who Does Self Work? The Political Economy of Self Work

Although the literatures in management and organizational research that address self work (reviewed in the next section) tend to focus on the efforts of individuals to manage their own selves, the examples we have discussed describe self work engaged in by a wide variety of actors well beyond the focal individual. They have also shown how the construction of a self is often a highly contested arena, in which individual and collective actors in relation vie for dominance over definitions of selves.

The story of Maria Patiño, for instance, points to the social, political, and economic stakes that motivated self work by a wide variety of actors. Whether Patiño was a woman and was therefore allowed to race had significant material and symbolic benefits not only for Patiño, but for her country, her sponsors, her teammates, and her competitors—implications that led to a wide range of actors engaging in self work focused on the construction of Patiño's sex as female. In contrast, the IAAF engaged in high-stakes self work focused on constructing Patiño as a man, work that was motivated by its belief in the need to preserve sex-based segregation of sports as a core element of its operations. Still other actors engaged in self work focused on Patiño's sex that was rooted in a moral position regarding the politics of gender and sport. The result of all of this was a complex arena of different actors conducting self work as they tried to shape Patiño's sex in ways that corresponded to their interests and moral positions.

Despite the variety of actors who might engage in self work, little research has been conducted to better understand this aspect of these complex processes. Thus, one of the contributions of exploring self work is to make this dynamic more visible and available for research. In this section, we explore the work of individuals, collective actors, and networks of actors to construct selves.

INDIVIDUALS AS AGENTS OF SELF WORK

The most obvious actors involved in self work are the individuals themselves. As individuals, we spend considerable time and effort constructing our selves and, in many cases, resisting the self work performed by others as they attempt to shape our selves in ways with which we do not agree. Self work done by individuals involves the three dimensions of self work we have discussed as people work to shape the narratives through which they define their selves, the relationships they are embedded in, and the material manifestations of their selves. It is this aspect of self work that has received the most attention in the literature and, even if not framed directly as self work, about which we have the most developed theoretical understanding.

Considering self work in organizational life highlights the potential efforts of at least two more sets of individuals to shape the selves of others. Central to self work in organizations is the role of leaders. Leadership in organizations is essentially concerned with influencing others, and a key mechanism through which that influence occurs is shaping how others understand themselves and their relationship to the organization. Aspects of the self including social identity, for instance, may be directly affected by behaviors associated with charismatic leadership, and in turn lead to greater cooperation and the pursuit of common goals (van Knippenberg et al., 2004). A second set of individuals who are important agents of self work in organizations are mentors, who help protégés by providing information and interpretation regarding the informal functioning of the organization and access to a broader network than might otherwise be available (Rigg et al., 2012). Mentoring in organizations can involve people in intense relationships that may go on for extended periods (Scandura, 1992), which provides opportunities for more experienced organizational members to significantly influence junior members in more direct and personal ways than might be available to formal authority figures.

COLLECTIVE ACTORS AS AGENTS OF SELF WORK

Along with individuals, collective actors such as organizations often act as agents of self work. A common example of this occurs in the context of onboarding and initial socialization of new members, processes that focus on inculcating individuals with the "beliefs, values, orientations, behaviors, skills, and so forth necessary to fulfill their new roles and function effectively within an organization's milieu" (Ashforth and Saks, 1996: 149).

Self work by organizations is especially important where organizational success depends on organizational culture, and thus control is effected through informal, clan-like mechanisms. In such situations, organizations work to gain control over their members not only by establishing and enforcing formal rules but by shaping the experience and relationships of members in ways that will align members' identities with organizational strategy and cement the organizational commitment of members. This kind of self work is, however, "a precarious and often contested process involving active identity work, as is evident in efforts to introduce new discursive practices of 'teamwork', 'partnership', etc." (Alvesson and Willmott, 2002: 621). Organizational members are not passive, blank slates on to which organizational values can be inscribed. The histories and social networks of members connect them to a plurality of values and ideas from which they construct their selves.

A powerful and resonant example of socialization in an organization dependent on its culture for social control is found in Anteby's (2013) ethnography of Harvard Business School (HBS) from the perspective of a new faculty member. Anteby shows how HBS works to construct the selves of faculty members through a wide range of discursive, relational, and material practices. Anteby (2013: 3) argues that although all organizations develop a "distinct perspective" among their members, some organizations "purposely aim to produce a particular perspective, often with moral undertones" through the exertion of "normative control." In the case of HBS, the core of the organization's work was to produce routines that required "significant decision making on the part of those involved, with little direct guidance from higher authorities," but which are "embedded in [organizational contexts] rich in normative signs" (Anteby, 2013: 8). These routines establish situations in which self work is shared between the organization and the individual who's self is being shaped: a great deal of self work is done establishing these routines that subtly steer the individual toward particular moral perspectives, but the routines also require significant self work on the part of the individual who must struggle to divine the appropriate sets of actions and the morality of those actions.

NETWORKS OF ACTORS AS AGENTS OF SELF WORK

Along with individuals and organizations, self work can be carried out collectively by networks of actors in a social system. While we could reduce these efforts to the work of the individuals and organizations who occupy the social system, we believe there is value in separately recognizing the self work of these networks of actors because of its distinct dynamics and effects on the self in question as well as the social system as a whole.

An interesting example of self work carried out by a social system comes from the world of self-taught art (Fine, 2003). This world is interesting because the biographies of self-taught artists are so important to an artist's success, heavily influencing the legitimacy and price of artworks. However, unlike the world of elite art, where artistic biographies are often associated with elite credentialing, the key biographical quality in the world of self-taught art is authenticity rooted in struggle and outsider status. In the case of Kentucky sculptor Edgar Tolson, for example, "his many children, violence, primitive religion, alcoholism, lung problems, poverty, and rural isolation all added to the value of his work" (Fine, 2003: 172). As one collector argued, "In many cases with this work, the story is far more important than the art is, and people are buying the story as opposed to the piece of art for art's sake" (Fine, 2003: 172).

The distributed self work of networks illustrated by that done in the self-taught art world also highlights the role of selves as commodities, with economic value available to actors beyond the focal individual whose self is being shaped. Distributed self work also occurs in a range of social systems in which commodification and economic exploitation is not the main motivation. Business schools, for instance, are explicitly designed and organized around shaping selves, in part by imparting knowledge and skills, but also through the inculcation of values, beliefs, morals, attitudes, and affecting the self-esteem and efficacy of participants. The very significant budgets of careers offices in business schools and the various forms of self work they carry out (e.g., teaching students how to dress for an interview, how to narrate their selves to potential employers, and how to network) is evidence of the degree to which the selves of the students are important in their future employment. In work contexts, professional communities often share these broad self work agendas, shaping the ethics and normative commitments of members (Abbott, 1983).

Summary: A Conceptualization of Self Work

In this section, we have developed a conceptualization of self work that is consistent with our more general understanding of social-symbolic work, embedded in contemporary scholarly discussions of self, and resonant with the conversations about self that are occurring in society. To integrate these changes into our discussion of self work, we have drawn on discursive, relational, and material understandings of the self. Together, these ideas provide an image of self work that involves ongoing, effortful, skillful, creative efforts on the part of individuals, collective actors, and networks of actors to construct not only evidently malleable elements of self, such as friendships, career choices, and economic and social success, but less obviously malleable dimensions of self, such as sex, gender, and race.

Conclusion

In this chapter, we have explored how people work to construct selves—their own and others. Our initial focus was on understanding the self as a social-symbolic object and how understandings of the self have changed dramatically along with the transitions to modernity and postmodernity. We have argued that the self has gone from being something that was natural and fixed to a social-symbolic object that is often contested and the focus of a reflexive project involving an array of individual and collective actors. As Maria Patiño's story shows, the dimensions along which selves are constructed now extends to many aspects of self previously understood as being fixed at birth, although some dimensions of the self remain largely outside the remit of this important form of work (race, for example). Building on an understanding of selves as socially constructed, we proposed a conception of self work that highlights its discursive, relational, and material dimensions, and is carried out by people working to shape their own selves and those to whom they are connected, as well as by organizations and broader social networks. Clearly, self work represents a complex assembly of practices, skills, and resources with potentially powerful consequences—intended and otherwise—carried out by a complex network of individuals and collective actors who all have an interest in working to construct particular versions of the self.

Key Resources

The Self

At the center of any discussion of self work is, of course, the self, and how it has evolved since the emergence of modernity. An accessible entry point to understanding these changes is Curtis' documentary film, *The century of the self*, which explores the rise of mass consumerism in relationship to the self, and especially its relationship to the ideas and influence of Sigmund Freud. *Writing the self* extends this discussion by examining the intertwined histories of the self and self-expression, exploring first-person writing, such as diaries and memoirs, as they have changed from the Romantic period to the late twentieth century. In *The self after postmodernity*, Schrag adopts a more theoretical approach to the changing self. In this adaptation of a series of lectures, he provides a portrait of the human self-understanding as discursive, action-oriented, communal, and transcending. Finally, in *Selfie: How we became so self-obsessed and what it's doing to us*, Storr explores the history of the self, from ancient Greece to modern times, to understand contemporary depictions of the beautiful, successful, slim, socially conscious, and extroverted individual that our culture has decided is the perfect self, and its consequences for how we live.

Curtis, A. 2002. *The century of the self*. London: BBC Two. <https://freedocumentaries. org/documentary/bbc-the-century-of-the-self-happiness-machines-season-1-epi sode-1>.

Heehs, P. 2013. *Writing the self: Diaries, memoirs, and the history of the self*. New York: Bloomsbury Academic.

Schrag, C. O. 1999. *The self after postmodernity*. New Haven, CT: Yale University Press.

Storr, W. 2018. *Selfie: How the west became self-obsessed and what it's doing to us*. London: Picador.

Examples of Self Work

Finally, we would like to provide some resources that simply provide compelling examples of people doing self work, outside of traditional academic studies. In her memoir, *Crossing*, McCloskey (previously Donald now Deirdre) tells the poignant story of how—at age fifty-two, established as a renowned economist and historian, and a husband and father—she began the process of transitioning to become a woman. Benigni's beloved film, *Life is beautiful*, is set during the Holocaust, and tells the fictional story of a Jewish librarian who, amid the horrors of a concentration camp, uses humor and imagination to protect his son. In an equally powerful documentary film, Livingston explores the subculture of "voguing" and the ways that young gay men constructed complex identities through their participation in New York City's "ball culture." Finally, Tizon's essay, "My family's slave," recounts the story of Lola, who lived in servitude in America for most of her life. The story is remarkable on its own terms, and for us it provides a powerful depiction of the challenges (and possibility) of self work under extraordinarily difficult circumstances.

Benigni, R. 1999. *Life is beautiful.*
Livingston, J. 1990. *Paris is burning.*
McCloskey, D. N. 2000. *Crossing: A memoir.* Chicago, IL: University of Chicago Press.
Tizon, A. 2017. My family's slave. *The Atlantic.* June. <https://www.theatlantic.com/magazine/archive/2017/06/lolas-story/524490/>.

4

Self Work in Management and Organizational Research

In this chapter we:

1. Review the study of emotion work in management and organizational research and explore how conceptualizing emotion work as a type of self work can extend this well-developed literature.

2. Review the study of identity work in management and organizational research and explore how conceptualizing emotion work as a type of self work can contribute to the continued development of this rapidly growing literature.

3. Review the study of career work in management and organizational research and discuss how conceptualizing career work as a type of self work can aid the development of this newly emerging stream of research.

Introduction

Although the self has been a core concept in the social sciences for at least a century, the systematic study of how actors intentionally shape selves only began to emerge in the 1960s and 1970s. Led by scholars such as Goffman (1959a), the idea that we shape our own and others' selves as a normal part of everyday life was a groundbreaking idea that now informs a range of scholarly communities across a broad swathe of social science including fields as diverse as social psychology, nursing, and education.

In management and organizational research, interest in the social construction of selves sits primarily within more "micro" traditions and we focus in this chapter on three streams of research that represent well-established and emerging topics within this literature. First, we examine emotion work as one of the more long-standing, well-developed areas of self work research in management and organizational research. Second, we discuss the large and growing body of research on identity work that has developed somewhat more recently. The study of both emotion work and identity work began outside of management and organizational research, but have been associated with productive streams of research exploring these types of self work in and around organizations. In contrast, we examine career work as a nascent topic in management and organizational research; the idea that careers might be understood as social-symbolic objects, and thus the focus of career work, is only beginning to emerge and represents an area with tremendous potential as a site of self work research. For each literature, we review their evolution as research domains, and then explore how understanding them as forms of self work might influence future scholarship.

Emotion Work

Arlie Hochschild (1979: 561) coined the term "emotion work" to describe "the act of trying to change in degree or quality an emotion or feeling." Emotion work is an active, reflexive set of activities, as illustrated by Hochschild's respondents' descriptions: "I *psyched myself up* . . . I *squashed* my anger down . . . I *tried hard* not to feel disappointed . . . I *made* myself have a good time . . . I *tried* to feel grateful . . . I *killed* the hope I had burning" (1979: 561, emphasis and ellipses in original).

The concept of emotion work is consistent with our the idea of self work in that it "refers to the effort—the act of trying—and not to the outcome, which may or may not be successful" (Hochschild, 1979: 561). Moreover, the concept of emotion work highlights the degree to which people can manage their emotions and do so in response to social norms and pressures, thus standing in contrast to long-held conceptions of emotion that suggest it is "unbidden and uncontrollable, . . . not governed by social rules" (1979: 551).

Three qualities of emotion work are important to highlight in relation to self work. The first is its temporality: as we argued in relation to self work, emotion work often occurs as programs of action, over extended periods of time as people engage in ongoing attempts to manage their emotions. As one of Hochschild's (1979: 561) respondents described her efforts in the context of a romantic relationship: "Anyway, I started to try and make myself like him. I made myself focus on the way he talked, certain things he'd done in the past. . . . When I was with him I did like him, but I would go home and write in my journal how much I couldn't stand him."

The second is the sets of practices through which it is accomplished, which include cognitive strategies intended to shift beliefs or thoughts and in so doing affect associated emotions; bodily strategies, such as slowing one's breathing, in order to manage the physical symptoms of an emotion; and expressive strategies engaged in to affect an inner feeling. All of these strategies, like other forms of self work, can be "done by the self upon the self, by the self upon others, and by others upon oneself" (Hochschild, 1979: 562).

Third are the contexts in which it occurs: emotion work is motivated, shaped, and constrained by the social contexts in which it occurs and the social-symbolic resources available to those involved. Hochschild focuses on two features of the social context: social structure, particularly as it is constituted in the form of economic exchange, class, and child rearing; and feeling rules, which describe socially prescribed expectations for emotional display and experience in particular circumstances.

An important development in the study of emotion work was the recognition of its potential commoditization, captured in the concept of "emotional labor." The concept of emotional labor is differentiated from the more general concept of emotion work by its association with paid employment. Interest in commodified emotion work is rooted in Hochschild's (1983) study of Delta flight attendants—individuals working in a context where feeling rules intersect with the supply of and demand for emotional expression, and with the authority structures and practices of a large corporation. The world of Delta flight attendants provided a striking example of commodified emotion work, and particularly its relationship to how individuals relate to their own emotions. Hochschild (1983: 89) argues that, "[w]hen rules about how to feel and how to express feeling are set by management, [and] ... workers have weaker rights to courtesy than customers do," there is the potential created for an uncomfortable tension between employees' feelings and their expressions of feeling. But, since corporate demands for emotional expression are unlikely to yield to that discomfort, individuals will instead work to bring their own feelings in line with the obligatory emotional display. This process is what makes the commercialization of feeling possible, and its difficulty is what makes it so potentially valuable: "Even when people are paid to be nice, it is hard for them to be nice at all times, and when their efforts succeed, it is a remarkable accomplishment" (Hochschild, 1983: 118).

Emotion Work in Management and Organizational Research

The earliest research on emotion work in management and organizational research focused on emotional displays associated with specific organizational roles, such as front-line service personnel (Ashforth and Humphrey, 1993; Grandey et al., 2010; Rafaeli and Sutton, 1990). This work examined the impact of emotional display rules on the behavior of employees (Rafaeli and Sutton, 1990; Sutton and Rafaeli, 1988), organizational performance (Sutton and Rafaeli, 1988; Van Kleef et al., 2010), and employee well-being (Brotheridge and Grandey, 2002; Grandey, 2003).

In an early example of this research Sutton and Rafaeli (1988) explored the impact of positive emotional displays on sales performance in convenience stores. The motivation for this study was the assumption, widely held at the time, that positive displays of emotion would be associated with more satisfied customers and better organizational performance. The surprising finding was that this was not the case. Instead, there was a negative association between positive emotional displays and store sales. This surprising association was explained by the specific display rules of this chain of stores, in which speed and convenience were the dominant customer service values: as described by store clerks, "our customers just want to get in and out quickly [and] . . . don't care if the clerk is perky" (Sutton and Rafaeli, 1988: 474).

Although early studies of emotion work tended to portray it as emanating from individuals responding to organizational display rules, research has moved toward a more relational understanding of the phenomenon in which emotional display can be understood as a coordinated, collective accomplishment (Boje, 1995). In a study of criminal investigators and bill collectors, for instance, Rafaeli and Sutton (1991) found that emotion work involved collective effort on the part of two individuals, each of whom played a definite and sustained role for the duration of an interaction with the target. Study participants described these strategies as central to their role effectiveness, and included sequential and simultaneous good cop/bad cop variations, as well as one person playing both roles. As one investigator described,

> I just finished an interrogation that I did with a younger guy who would yell and scream at people 20 years older than him. Of course, they would ignore him. I'd always let this guy go before me because he really annoyed the suspects and when I walked into the room and spoke like a civilized person, they were ready to talk.
>
> (Rafaeli and Sutton, 1991: 761)

All of these strategies rely on the ways in which the salience and meaning of emotional displays change in relation to other such displays, and the ability of investigators and bill collectors to effect convincing positive or negative emotional displays.

Although most research on emotion work in paid employment has focused on emotional display, some research has investigated how people manage both felt and expressed emotion. In a study of "emotional boundary work," for example, Allan and Barber (2005) describe how changes to the role of fertility treatment nurses led to emotion work that was less about appropriate emotional display than about establishing sustainable, effective relationships between nurses and patients. The rule changes heightened the physical intimacy of nurses and patients, as nurses were directed to take on medical care previously administered by doctors, such as ovarian ultrasound scanning, egg collection, and embryo transfer. The vulnerability and uncertainty associated with these procedures led patients to bond with nurses, who had to respond with emotion work that aimed to "maintain a position between emotional closeness and distance as a defense against the anxiety of [patient] emotions." Nurses engaged in what is described in the nursing literature as the "therapeutic use of self," in which a nurse "employ[s] her/his entire person . . . as a tool for promoting health and limiting disease" (Uys, 1980: 175).

Emotion Work as Self Work

We were initially motivated to write this book by our recognition that many kinds of social-symbolic work were being examined in management and organizational research without any seeming awareness that they belonged to a broader theoretical family. Thus, for each of the streams of management and organizational research we review in this book, we explore how they might be influenced by recognizing their relationship to other forms of social-symbolic work. To guide this exploration, we draw on the process model introduced in Chapter 2 (reproduced here in a simplified version as Figure 4.1), and explore its implications for each type of self work. So, for emotion work, we review the treatment of each element of the process model (e.g., motivations, practices) in the emotion work literature, and explore the implications of reframing emotion work explicitly as a type of self work.

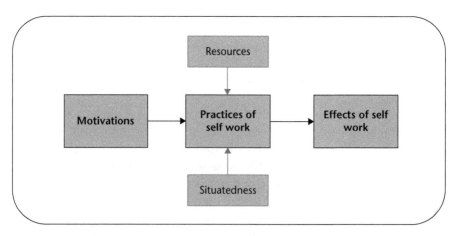

Figure 4.1. A process model of self work

MOTIVATIONS FOR EMOTION WORK

Starting from the left side of Figure 4.1, the process model begins with the motivations that drive social-symbolic work: put simply, why are people engaging in this work? The concept of social-symbolic work is premised on the idea that people are able to (at least at times) intentionally and reflexively engage in efforts to shape social-symbolic objects, and thus understanding the roots of those intentions is a core problem for the perspective we are developing.

The literature on emotion work in organizations highlights three main motivations. First, emotion work is performed in response to organizational demands concerning the sorts of emotions that are appropriate or required in specific workplace situations. Consider, for example, the Delta flight attendants originally studied by Hochschild (1983): these individuals worked in the context of socialization and control processes meant to ensure that their emotional responses remained polite and positive even on long flights with difficult passengers.

A second motivation for emotion work is rooted in the desire to produce better organizational outcomes, such as more effective service encounters. For example, Van Kleef et al. (2010) showed that leaders who worked to be "happier" generally had higher-performing teams. In other words, leaders who do the necessary emotion work to appear happy (despite whatever they are actually feeling) have a positive effect on the performance of their team.

A third motivation for emotion work found in management and organizational research is rooted in people's efforts to navigate difficult organizational situations where unmanaged emotional responses might result in ineffective or unpleasant dynamics. This motivation is illustrated by studies of nurses who engage in careful emotion work to avoid unpleasant, difficult to control situations with patients who are sick and frustrated (Hunter, 2005). By working to manage their emotional reactions, nurses working in this environment can avoid escalating unpleasant situations.

Together, these three motivations provide an important foundation for understanding the "why" of emotion work in organizations, particularly highlighting the embeddedness of motivations for emotion work in specific jobs and organizational roles. At the same time, when we shift to an understanding of emotion work as a type of self work, we begin to see a broader set of triggers and motivations than have been explored in the emotion work literature. It is not just instrumental organizational requirements that lead to the performance of emotion work. Instead, there are many other reasons for doing emotion work that deserve discussion and investigation.

One such motivation would involve the everyday efforts of people to maintain appropriate levels of distance and intimacy with organizational colleagues through both the expression and suppression of emotion. While much of the emotion work literature has been focused on practical outcomes such as happy customers or motivated staff, there are areas of interaction between colleagues that underpin friendships and other complex relationships between organizational members (Crary, 1987). Understanding and managing appropriate organizational relationships is a challenging area of self work that deserves much more attention as a research area.

Another motivation is associated with the work of organizational members to establish and maintain their images as "healthy" individuals, free from depression, anxiety, or other mental health issues. While this may seem an esoteric motivation for emotion work, the prevalence of depression and anxiety in organizations, and the stigma associated with such conditions (Ahmedani, 2011), makes this kind of emotion work a widespread, important, and underexamined form of self work.

Finally, conceptualizing emotion work as self work highlights the important and underemphasized fact that it is not just individuals doing emotion work for themselves. Reflecting on our discussion of the range of actors engaged in self work, we begin to see that extensive emotion work is done by actors trying to manage others' expression and experience of emotions. One context in which such dynamics are commonplace is in organizations where managers provide guidelines for the emotional displays of employees. Consider this example from the employee handbook of a gourmet deli (Steinberg and Figart, 1999: 9):

> Under no circumstances should a customer ever wonder if you are having a bad day. Your troubles should be masked with a smile. Tension can be seen and received negatively resulting in an un-happy dining experience, or what is called *frustrated food*...Once an un-happy or dissatisfied customer walks out the door, they are gone forever!

In addition, managers and other employees commonly work to shape the responses of individuals to stress, frustration, or disappointment by suggesting narratives that contextualize the problematic experience, by providing techniques for dealing with stress, or by providing examples where a particular kind of situation was responded to in a more effective emotional way. Despite their importance and intuitive ubiquity, relatively little research has focused on the emotion work of actors in relation to the emotions of others.

PRACTICES OF EMOTION WORK

If we move to the middle of our process model, we come to the practices—shared routines that conform to a group's social expectations—through which people engage in self work. In the case of research on emotion work, the most central practices, first identified by Hochschild (1983), have been "deep acting" and "surface acting." In surface acting, an actor works to modify the external display of emotion, whereas in deep acting, the actor works not only to shape the display of emotions, but also the feelings that are experienced. These practices draw on a dramaturgical understanding of social life and the role of emotion in it; deep acting, rooted in the idea of "method acting," has become a central, though contested, focus for the study of emotion work.

Although the importance of deep and surface acting in organizations has been amply demonstrated, their dominance in the literature has stifled recognition of other emotion work practices. The reaction of some nursing scholars to these practices is informative in this regard. Although notions of deep and surface acting have become important features of nursing research (Mann and Cowburn, 2005; McQueen, 2004), some nursing scholars have railed against the image of nurses as engaged in any form of acting. They argue that although nurses engaging in emotion work may at times be responding to employers' demands, focusing strictly on acting as a metaphor provides:

> too limited an account . . . for it fails to allow for the sense of moral concern and justice that may drive such efforts. Nurses are not serving customers as flight attendants do, they are responding to the needs of vulnerable, often frightened and suffering people who are partially, or totally, dependent on their help.
>
> (de Raeve, 2002: 469)

This argument is not rejecting emotion work as a possibility, but the implication that such work will always be inauthentic in some way.

Even if we don't think of deep and surface acting as necessarily inauthentic, they do rely on an understanding of emotions and the self, and consequently emotion work and self work, as separate (or at least separable) from each other. Any kind of acting as a basis for emotional experience and expression seems to suggest that emotions might be managed against the backdrop of a stable self that either manipulates emotional expression or forms the foundation for it. If instead, we think of emotions as a part of the self, then acting may be an unhelpful metaphor.

Inspiration for alternative metaphors for emotion work practices can be found in the discursive and relational dimensions that we highlighted in our conceptualization of self work. Emotion work might, for instance, be understood in terms of the weaving of emotions into the narratives through which we constitute selves. It might also be more explicitly conceived of as relational, with emotion work practices including empathy, attending, reflecting, and the negotiation of emotional roles and routines through which relationships (and thus selves) are constituted.

EFFECTS OF EMOTION WORK

Moving on to the effects of emotion work, research has tended to focus primarily on two sets of effects: on the person engaged in the emotion work, and on the interactions with customers and colleagues. The effects of emotion work on the person engaged in emotion work have been of significant interest throughout the history of the concept, with particular interest in the unintended, and often negative, consequences of emotion work for people's psychological well-being (Brotheridge and Grandey, 2002; Giardini and Frese, 2006; Zapf, 2002). Emotion work in service industries has been linked to stress and burnout, though with inconsistent results, with some studies finding no relationship, perhaps because of the positive effects of emotion work on relationships between the focal individuals and their clients (Grandey, 2003). The link between emotion work and negative psychological consequences has also been tied to the strain stemming from the "mismatch" between required emotional displays and the emotions that the participants wished they could display (Zapf et al., 1999). Although most studies of the effects of emotion work have highlighted its negative effects on the individuals involved, recent research has also shown its potential positive contributions (Zapf and Holz, 2006): Grant (2013), for instance, shows that engaging in emotion work leads people to speak up constructively in organizations, and in turn to better performance evaluations.

Along with the personal effects of emotion work, management and organizational research has focused on its impacts on immediate organizational relationships such as with clients and colleagues. In an extensive review, Van Kleef and colleagues (2012) show that emotional expression in the workplace affects customer service, group decision making, negotiations, and leadership through a combination of triggering affective reactions and shaping inferences among the people who observe the emotional display. These effects are nicely illustrated by the work of Rafaeli and Sutton (1990, 1991, 1987), who explored the impacts of emotional expression by convenience store clerks, criminal interrogators, and bill collectors.

Reframing emotion work as a form of self work again broadens the focus, this time to sets of effects that go beyond the immediate psychological and organizational impacts of emotion work. Understanding emotions as part of the self, and thus emotion work as partly constitutive of the self, suggests that the ways in which we actively shape our emotions will also shape our selves. As with our discussion of emotion work practices, conceptualizing the self and emotions as integrated rather than as separate parts of an individual problematizes the relationship between emotion work and experiences such as stress and psychological strain, or at least leads to a somewhat different conceptualization of these experiences. We have argued for an understanding of the self as discursive and relational, and thus for a radically plural self with multiple "I"s as well as multiple "Me"s.

This argument has important implications for understanding the effects of emotion work, as it leads to the possibility of stress and strain as potentially emanating from the challenges associated with managing multiple selves that are somehow in conflict with each other. There may also be a more general impact of sustained emotion work. In shaping the self on an ongoing basis, emotion work might make salient social or organizational demands for a different self, and thus breed dissatisfaction with the self one has shaped. This could be because one has succumbed to those pressures and constituted a different self for others, or because one has failed to do so and hence has failed in their organizational role. In either case, constructing the self in a particular way, or not doing so, might result in feelings of stress and strain due to the complexity and incompatibility of the demands to be a certain "kind of person."

SITUATEDNESS OF EMOTION WORK

Finally, we consider the context in which emotion work takes place—its situatedness. This situatedness was critically important to Hochschild and has remained so for the scholars who have followed her in investigating empirical instances of emotion work in a variety of contexts. To make the situatedness of emotion work explicit, Hochschild explored the role of social structure and introduced the notion of feeling rules. In addition, research on emotion work has highlighted gender as a central aspect of its situatedness, as in the many studies of flight attendants and nurses where the connection between gender and particular kinds and styles of emotion work has been highlighted. The effect on emotion work of particular occupations, including service work, care professions, and high-conflict work such as bill collection, have also been explored. Recent research has extended this work to explore emotion work in the context of specific organizational cultures, as in Barsade and O'Neill's (2014) exploration of affection, caring, compassion, and tenderness in cultures of companionate love. Collectively, this research has profoundly shifted our understanding of emotion from something universal, rooted solely in individual psychology, to a phenomenon that is profoundly social, with every aspect of our emotional lives, including emotion work, shaped by the social context in which it occurs.

As with the other aspects of emotion work, how we understand its situatedness is affected by conceptualizing emotion work as a type of self work. At least three issues arise from this move. First, it complicates the relationships among feeling rules, emotion work, and the self. Hochschild's conception of feeling rules, and the ways in which they have been explored empirically since then, suggest a stable self set against a changing social backdrop: the women who worked as flight attendants for Delta were understood as coping with the job's requirements by learning to engage in particular forms of emotion work. While such a conception of emotion work and feeling rules powerfully highlights the impact of organizations and organizational roles, it significantly overlooks the potential fluidity of the self, the creative agency that people bring to those situations in how they construct their selves, and how those selves can leverage those situations and act as sites of resistance.

A second important consideration is the changing context of much emotion work as more and more of our lives are lived online, and how this context can dramatically affect the relationship between emotion work and the self. Most immediately, the question becomes what emotion looks like when social interaction is digitally mediated. How much of the research on deep and surface acting as methods of emotion work is relevant when emotional expression occurs through the production of text, or even emoticons and "likes"?

Finally, and perhaps most fundamentally, there is the question of how we think about the self online. As the classic *New Yorker* cartoon observes, "On the Internet, nobody knows you're a dog." The unknowability and hence radical instability of identities in virtual contexts makes the question of feeling rules dramatically more complicated. Even if feeling rules exist in virtual spaces, such rules are traditionally applied with an understanding of to whom they are being applied: a person's gender, age, ethnicity, physical ability, and attractiveness can all play important roles in the interpretation and enforcement of feelings rules (Warhurst and Nickson, 2009). When those cues are unavailable or unreliable, the ability of participants to enforce feeling rules diminishes, just as it increases the ability of people to creatively shape their selves and the range of legitimate emotional expression.

SUMMING UP

Looking across the different elements, we see that conceptualizing emotion work as a form of self work expands the possibilities for theorizing by embedding efforts to manage emotions in the broader project of constructing a self. As suggested in our review of the history of the self, this project has become increasingly important and widespread, especially over the past century. To date, emotion work has primarily been explored in isolation of other forms of self work, with the focus on emotional labor in particular highlighting its immediate connection to work and organizations. The link between emotion work and self work has largely been ignored from both sides of this relationship. Research and writing on emotion work have tended to situate emotions as separate from the self, unwittingly reinforcing an essentialist view of the self as separate from the emotions that this literature has shown are constructed reflexively and with purpose. A different sin of omission has been committed by writers focusing on self work who either ignore emotions altogether or position them as simply an extension of the self being constructed, rather than an important and distinctive facet of the self.

Identity Work

The relation between self and identity, and hence between self work and identity work, is a complex one, with the terms sometimes used interchangeably in the literature. For our purposes, we distinguish the two in a relatively simple way. The concept of self is the more general one, describing the self-knowledge that results from "the human capacity for reflexive thinking—the ability to take oneself as the object of one's attention and thought" (Leary and Tangney, 2003: 6).

We anchor our use of the concept of identity in social identity theory, in which it depends on one's relatively stable relationships to others and is based on group identification: "people tend to classify themselves and others into various social categories, such as organizational membership, religious affiliation, gender, and age cohort" (Ashforth and Mael, 1989: 20). Although a range of theoretical approaches to individual identity exist (cf., Roberts and Creary, 2013), we focus on social identity theory because of its dominance in management and organizational research (Ashforth and Mael, 1989).

From a social identity theory perspective, identities describe "the internalized meanings and expectations associated with the positions one holds in social networks and the roles one plays" (Oyserman et al., 2012: 74). It is about who we are in relation to others and is organized around roles like mother, accountant, or customer. This conception of identity emphasizes the social basis of identity, separate from what is sometimes called "personal identities" that reflect "characteristics that may feel separate from one's social and role identities" (Oyserman et al., 2012: 74) and the broader aspects of the self that we discussed earlier.

Identity work, therefore, refers to the efforts of individuals, collective actors, and networks of actors to shape how individuals are understood in relation to group memberships and related roles. Snow and Anderson (1987) established identity work as a core sociological concept with their study of how individuals who are identified as homeless constructed and communicated their identities. The study examined how people "at the bottom of status systems" establish identities that "provide them with a measure of self-worth and dignity," and identified a complex set of strategies used by homeless people to "create, present and sustain personal identities" (Snow and Anderson, 1987: 1336).

The identity work strategies identified by Snow and Anderson were multimodal, involving talking about one's identity, establishing and maintaining associations with other people, and managing physical settings and props, including one's personal appearance. Although establishing the relationships among role, identity, and self-concept would become the paper's most significant theoretical contribution, the focus on homeless people set a lasting direction for the study of identity work, inspiring a range of scholars to examine situations that challenged people's legitimacy, status, and value (e.g., Ashforth and Kreiner, 1999; Brewis and Linstead, 2000).

Identity Work in Management and Organizational Research

Research investigating identity work in management and organizational research can be roughly divided into two approaches. The first approach has focused on the identity work that people do in relation to their own identity. This stream of research established the concept of identity work in management and organizational research, documented it in a range of organizational and social contexts, and examined different kinds of identity work. The second approach has focused on how identity work can be done by other individual and collective actors. This research provided important insights into the relationship between institutional work and other concepts, especially power and control. We explore the two approaches in the following subsections.

IDENTITY WORK AND INDIVIDUAL SOCIAL IDENTITY

Early management and organizational research on individual identity work focused on showing that identity work exists across different organizational contexts. Alvesson (1994: 544), for example, explored how advertising executives constructed themselves as professionals, with "special instincts" for how to effectively communicate ideas. A key strategy involved advertising executives disparaging their "rather careless" clients: "They lack stamina, jump from one campaign to another, and their campaigns differ greatly from one another. This means that they can never realize their plans or achieve their goals" (Alvesson, 1994: 548). Through this identity work, advertising professionals positioned themselves as professionals by distancing themselves from their clients, who they associated with an "amateur" understanding of advertising.

Following a related line of research, Fine (1996: 90) examined "occupational rhetorics" in restaurant kitchens, where he focused on the identity work of restaurant cooks who employ "rhetorics of profession, art, business and labor to shape how they think of themselves as workers." Fine's study showed that although we tend to use occupational labels implying homogeneity within a category—lawyer, professor, doctor—we know that such categories are internally differentiated in ways that can be important, both symbolically and instrumentally, to members.

As well as documenting its existence, early research work focused on categorizing and labeling different kinds of identity work. Ashforth and Kreiner's (1999: 413) discussion of "dirty work," for instance, explored "tasks and occupations that are likely to be perceived as disgusting or degrading." Like the homeless in Snow and Anderson's original study of identity work, the challenge for those engaged in dirty work is to "construct an esteem-enhancing social identity," which members accomplish through processes of reframing and selective social comparison. Research on dirty work highlights the flexible, nuanced nature of identity work, showing how it draws on specific social categories for comparison and contrast, and discursive strategies that require detailed occupational and social knowledge. One dirty work strategy, for example, is to "condemn the condemners," which is "to impugn the motives, character, or authority . . . of critical outsiders as moral arbiters," such that members of a dirty work occupation can "dismiss the condemners' perceptions" (Ashforth and Kreiner, 1999: 424).

Along with the discursive identity work that has been prevalent in the literature, research in this stream has attended to its material dimension, which involves the employment of physical artifacts such as dress (Buckingham and Willett, 2013; Pratt and Rafaeli, 1997; Rafaeli and Pratt, 2013). In their study of a rehabilitation unit of a large hospital, Pratt and Rafaeli (1997: 874) found that disagreements about appropriate dress among nurses reflected a deeper issue: "nurses attempted to answer the abstract and complex question, Who are we as nurses of this unit?, through discussing the question, What should we wear?" In this way, dress was integral to identity work: choices of clothing were nested in a complex web of social identities structured around divisions between rehabilitation and acute care identities, and between manager and floor nurses (with a rehabilitation identity and a manager nurse identity tied to wearing street clothes, rather than scrubs).

IDENTITY WORK AND SOCIAL CONTROL

The second stream of research on identity work we examined focuses on the identity work of others, and its relationship to social structures and processes, including power and control. Studies of the relationship between identity work and power/control have emerged out of a much longer tradition of labor process studies, which were concerned with understanding, criticizing, and influencing the relationship between labor, management, and capital in contemporary work organizations (Burawoy, 1979; Jermier et al., 1994). The introduction of identity and identity work to this area of scholarship was connected to the transformations that were occurring in the world of paid employment, where traditional labor–capital divisions and dynamics were breaking down, but the questions of power and control were enduringly important.

Central to discussions connecting identity work to power has been Knights and Willmott's (1989: 535) attempt to theorize "the connectedness of power and subjectivity in the organisation of social life," which extended the labor process tradition by integrating an account of power rooted in the work of Foucault (1979). They argue that "the very exercise of power relies upon the constitution of subjects who are tied by their sense of identity to the reproduction of power relations" (Knights and Willmott, 1989: 536–7). The relationship between institutional work and power is tied to the insecurities associated with identity in contemporary capitalism. With the foundations of the self having changed over time, from assigned and hierarchical to those increasingly involving "choice" of some kind, identity work has become more necessary and tied more tightly to circuits of power. For Knights and Willmott (1989: 549), there are both "positive" and "negative" implications of these changes:

> Positively, the modern subject is constituted as "independent" and "responsible", partly as a result of the institutionalisation of "natural" rights and obligations of democratic self-autonomy. Negatively, individuals have been "split" off from one another, and this is experienced as a vulnerability to the judgements of "significant others".

Thus, their argument is not that identity is only a matter of control and subjugation, but that the relationship between power and identity work is more subtle: although the exercise of power may provoke resistance when it threatens valued identities, it will at least as often enroll its targets by virtue of its enabling, productive qualities (Knights and Willmott, 1989).

A more explicitly critical approach to identity and power is taken by Alvesson and Willmott (2002: 620), who highlight the potentially unobtrusive political effects of identity work, forging chains of control in organizations that are both less visible and more effective than external mechanisms of control. Alvesson and Willmott articulate a wide range of forms of identity work that target different elements of organizational life: identity work that focuses on the employee by defining him or her in reference to some other; identity work that focuses on forms of action, defining how people should be relating to particular fields of activity; and identity work that targets the relationships of organizational members, defining spheres of belongingness and differentiation, and defining identities in terms of how they fit into broader social, organizational, and economic landscapes (Alvesson and Willmott, 2002).

The world of commercial airline pilots provides an example that illustrates the contentious and distributed politics of identity work. As a profession, US commercial pilots are among the worst in terms of gender and racial diversity: 95 percent of pilots are men and 98 percent are white (Ashcraft, 2005). Although being male has been constructed as central to the professional identity of pilots, this has not always been the case. Corn (1979) documents the period in the 1920s and 1930s when women played an important role as pilots in US commercial aviation: a role that was ironic in that it was rooted in sexist beliefs regarding the inability of women to engage in heroic or technical tasks, and so their ability to pilot aircraft was intended to demonstrate to the public that flying must indeed be a safe, relatively mundane activity. This need underpinned the hiring of approximately 500 women as commercial pilots in this period. These women not only piloted planes, but raced them, sold them, and worked as "test pilots, flight instructors, aerial photographers and flying chauffeurs" (Corn, 1979: 556–7). Once the public had been convinced of the safety of air travel, however, the role of women as pilots largely disappeared, and women were moved to the back of the plane where, as stewardesses, they could put their nurturing "feminine qualities" to a new use for aviation. In contrast, the pilot's seat became associated with an "elite, civilized, rational, technical, omniscient, and thoroughly heterosexual and paternal figure" that was the powerful male counterpart to the sexy stewardess (Ashcraft, 2005: 76).

Looking across the research connecting identity work and power, this relationship seems inevitable for at least two reasons. First, identities, and especially organizational and occupational identities, are negotiated in the context of relationships in which power and control are of immediate concern. Employees and managers, but also customers, suppliers, and other stakeholders, are involved in these political games of identity construction. Second, identities themselves are inherently political as they are rooted in social categories and roles that carry with them different levels of legitimacy, status, and privilege. In the case of the commercial airline pilot, for instance, its relationship to a privileged gender category—masculinity—changed over time, first solidifying as flying became accepted as a relatively safe endeavor, and then recently being challenged as new technologies and changes in practices have undermined the paternal role of the pilot in relation to the crew.

Identity Work as Self Work

As we have just done with emotion work, we now discuss the implications of understanding identity work as a type of self work. We again draw on the process model established in Chapter 2 that connects motivations, practices, effects, resources, and situatedness (see Figure 4.1). For each part of the model, we discuss its relevance to identity work and how understanding emotion work as self work might shape theory and empirical research.

MOTIVATIONS OF IDENTITY WORK

Beginning with the motivations that lead actors to perform identity work, it is useful to distinguish between identity work undertaken by actors in relation to their own identities, and work done to shape the identities of others.

Management and organizational research has identified several motivations that drive actors to perform work to shape their own identities. One such motivation is to manage the relationships among group identities, both connecting groups and differentiating between them. This motivation was evident both in Fine's (1996) study of restaurant kitchens, where cooks engaged in work to connect their work to other professions, and in Alvesson's (1994) study of advertising agency employees who worked to distinguish their identities from those of clients. A second motivation prominent in management and organizational research is to defend threatened identities (Ashforth and Kreiner, 1999; Brewis and Linstead, 2000; Maitlis, 2009). Actors are understandably motivated to carry out identity work when they feel their identities are threatened in some way or when they face unwanted pressure to change their identities (Snow and Anderson, 1987).

Research on actors working to shape the identities of others has largely focused on identity work as a form of social control in the workplace (e.g., Alvesson and Willmott, 2002), and a way of managing associations between the identities of organizational actors and other facets of the organization (e.g., Ashcraft, 2005). In the first case, identity work is performed primarily by managers to craft identities for others that, if they are accepted, function to shape behavior in ways positively valued by the organization. In the second case, the identity work is carried out by managers or organizational members to make sense of their identities in relation to their organization or workgroup. Tracey and Phillips (2016), for example, discuss how changes to the organizational identity of a social enterprise in response to organizational stigmatization resulted in challenges to the identity of many individual employees who were then motivated to perform identity work to make sense of their identities relative to the new organizational identity.

From a social-symbolic work perspective, our understanding of the motivations driving identity work changes if we think of identity work as a type of self work. In particular, such a move suggests exploring deeper and more distal motivations for identity work. At present, management and organizational research exploring identity work has tended to focus on triggers and motivations that are relatively easily identified in people's immediate social and organizational contexts. If, instead, we worked from the three basic motivations established by current research—group association and differentiation, defending threatened identities, and social control—but expanded our search for the triggers of such identity work beyond people's proximal environments, we may well see identity work as part of a wider set of processes through which people work to construct and maintain selves. A need to differentiate, feelings of threat, and the desire for social control might, for instance, be anchored in people's relationships that are relatively distant from the exercise of those motivations. This is where a relational understanding of the self becomes important. If we see the self as a nexus of relationships, then how we work to construct identities—our own and others'—will be significantly influenced by the interplay of those relationships. We are not suggesting a return to an "I" and multiple "me"s, but rather the interplay of "I"s negotiating situational prominence and reaching temporary settlements.

PRACTICES OF IDENTITY WORK

Moving to the practices associated with identity work, researchers have paid the most attention to linguistic practices, with somewhat less attention to managing physical appearances, manipulating artifacts, and associating with particular groups or individuals. Following the broader interest in linguistic methods that emerged in the 1990s (Phillips and Oswick, 2012), management and organizational scholars have been concerned with how language is used by actors to construct identities. Linguistic methods include a range of approaches, including discourse analysis, narrative analysis, and the study of rhetoric. The tendency in studying linguistic methods has been to examine specific discursive strategies such as contrasting, whereby people use text and talk to juxtapose their own identities with those of others, usually establishing in some way their own superiority (e.g., Alvesson, 1994). There is also an extensive literature on the narrative construction of identity, looking at the stories that actors craft to make sense of their identities and to communicate them to others (e.g., Ibarra and Barbulescu, 2010).

Smaller streams of organizational research have attended to the ways in which identity work depends on managing appearance or relationships. People in organizations engage in cosmetic forms of identity work that involve managing one's appearance in order to shape identity, through different forms of dress (Pratt and Rafaeli, 1997) or body markings such as tattoos or piercings (Phelan and Hunt, 1998). This form of identity work can signal group membership or be an attempt to construct a unique identity. People also work to construct identities through association with physical artifacts or particular groups. The cliché of a middle-aged man buying a sports car, for example, represents identity work performed as part of an effort to construct a new identity during a "mid-life crisis." Alternatively, membership in an exclusive members club or an activist organization like Greenpeace may be used to signal aspects of identity such as wealth or social awareness.

Shifting to an understanding of identity work as a form of self work expands our attention to a more diverse set of identity work practices. Our conceptualization of self work emphasizes the roles of its relational and material dimensions, providing a useful corrective to the overly discursive focus that has characterized research on identity work research. Injecting the relational dimension more fully into research on identity work asks how people construct their identities in and through others. More fundamentally, it draws on the notion of a relational self to suggest that all identity work is relational because our identities are relational, even when we think of them as "personal" rather than "social." Concretely, we would stop seeing identity work as being accomplished "by an actor," and instead see it as being accomplished by networks of actors, negotiating the meanings of a self and its connections to others.

A similar effect will occur as we began to emphasize the materiality of identity work as self work. At a minimum this would mean ensuring attention to the body—its place in identity work and its inextricable tie to identity. Inspiration comes from writing on "body work" that has brought together what might seem like disparate activities, including the management of physical appearance, the caring for others' bodies (both abled and less abled), embodied emotional experience and display, and the body-modifying effects of labor (which are often debilitating) (Gimlin, 2007). All of these activities should be explored as both identity work and self work. Going back to our discussion of the material dimension of self work, it is important we also pay attention to the "cyborg" nature of identity (Haraway, 1985) as we increasingly attach our bodies to technologies at work and create material-social hybrids (Latour, 1999).

EFFECTS OF IDENTITY WORK

Research on the effects of identity work has tended to focus on its impacts on the person directly associated with the identity in question or on the other actors conducting identity work. Scholars have explored how, for instance, the identity work of homeless people allows them greater autonomy and dignity, and how the identity work of professionals shapes their organizational cultures. Other important effects that have been observed include the effects on organizations (usually employers) that benefit from the control and motivation resulting from individuals taking on particular identities. Identity work also provides access to resources associated with particular social networks or roles. Consequently, identity work that supports the construction of multiple social identities provides both the focal individual and others, including their managers, with access to broader arrays of resources (Creary et al., 2015).

Beginning to think of identity work as a type of self work extends our attention to some less well-understood effects, including the broader spillovers on others of work performed to shape one's own identity, or the effects of work performed by others on third parties related to the person occupying that identity. The third parties might include work colleagues, friends, or family, who may be positive or negatively affected both by the identity work and the identities in play. If we think, for instance, of the identity work of professionals, and especially new professionals, in consulting, law, or medicine, where a key facet of identity is associated with working long hours and being always available to the organization (Seron and Ferris, 1995; Zerubavel, 1981), we can begin to understand the costs to families and friends of such an identity being borne by the individual who gains the occupational prestige. A self work perspective focuses attention on this broader set of identity effects and in doing so opens up new areas for study.

RESOURCES FOR IDENTITY WORK

Turning to the question of resources in the study of identity work, we see that the emphasis on discursive forms of identity work has led to a preoccupation in the literature with related resources such as "discourses" (Watson, 2009), "rhetorics" (Fine, 1996), and "ethics" (Kornberger and Brown, 2007). The assumption underpinning scholarly concern for such resources is that people largely "talk" their way into identities, establishing who they are in relation to others through arguments, conversation, declarations, and questions. Some studies have also highlighted the cognitive resources that underpin discursive identity work: for example, in a study of people who simultaneously hold and identify with multiple jobs over extended periods of time, Caza et al. (2018: 726) show the value of cognitive resources, such as "identity authorship," which they define as "efficacy in grappling with, developing, and authenticating multiple identities."

There has also been some attention paid to the sorts of resources used by organizations as they work to shape the identities of employees and associates. These resources include financial resources as well as organizational routines and processes. Early labor process studies that connected identity to social control (Burawoy, 1979), for instance, identified such resources as "targets and bonus schemes, wage differentials and career systems," which were argued to have deleterious effects "on both workers and management in separating individuals off from one another and turning them back on themselves" (Knights and Willmott, 1989: 547–8).

As we argued in relation to the practices of identity work, moving to a conception of identity work as a form of self work directs attention to more heterogeneous resources, including relational and material resources. We believe that the heterogeneity of resources used in identity work has been neglected because identity work projects have been understood in an unnecessarily narrow way. When we conceive of instances of identity work as embedded in lifelong projects of self work, involving ever-changing casts of individuals and collective actors in addition to the persons themselves, and involving relational and material dimensions in addition to discursive resources, that we begin to see how important heterogeneous sets of resources are to such work.

If we go back to the example of Maria Patiño, the work done by individuals and collective actors drew on a broad range of discursive, relational, and material resources ranging from medical tests and financial resources to Patiño's body. Simply looking at the discursive resources would have missed much of the broad range of resources that were drawn on by the various actors who performed the broad range of work done in the reconstruction of Patiño's self.

Embedding identity work in the concept of self work raises a second important issue regarding resources. Although resources are critical to self work, there exists a starkly unequal distribution of resources useful in identity work in modern societies and across different societies. To engage in identity work requires access to skills, social networks, and material and symbolic assets, as well as time, energy, and security. Thus, although the ability of people to shape their own identities is often taken for granted, conceiving of it as self work highlights the challenges associated with such work in the face of an unequal distribution of resources. Although the mass production, mass consumption, and legally enshrined personal rights that characterize contemporary, developed Western societies create the generalized possibility of thinking of oneself as an individual, this possibility can be frustrated by a lack of critical resources. Self work requires "a surplus of personal resources that [people] can invest in reflecting on themselves and in building an autonomous identity"; inequality is not only a matter of material gains and losses, but "of unequal access to the new resources of individuation" (Melucci, 1996: 500).

The profound impact of a lack of resources on identity work can be seen more clearly if we consider it in relation to the discursive, relational, and material dimensions of identity work. We will start with the material dimension, as it may be the most obvious. To the degree to which identity work requires material objects, especially those associated with consumption or production, then poverty and unemployment may dramatically undermine one's ability to engage in identity work. Economic inequality is also associated with an inequality in the time and space available to people to engage in the discursive and relational dimensions of identity work. To put it simply, the ability of a wealthy, married professional to engage in identity work far outstrips that ability in a single-parent worker on minimum wage whose time, energy, and wealth are consumed by meeting her family's basic needs.

But the reality of the unequal distribution does not stop with the material dimension. Identity work demands discursive and relational resources, the availability of which depends on the context and the kind of identity work in question. The symbols and narratives, for example, of what it means to be a lesbian and how to live as a lesbian are more readily available and well developed in San Francisco than in Jeddah. Similarly, the willingness of others to participate and support this effort—the relational dimension—is also more developed and readily available in some societies and some parts of societies. To continue the example, for someone to be able to easily and publicly connect with others who are constructing their identities in similar ways, and receive their support and help, makes the work of constructing a lesbian identity much more likely to succeed.

SITUATEDNESS OF IDENTITY WORK

The question of situatedness is clearly important in research on identity work, where organizational, occupational, and technological dimensions of people's situations feature prominently. Perhaps the most common contextual dimension on which discussions of identity work focus is people's organizational and occupational affiliations. Studies of identity work have, for instance, emphasized the distinctiveness of identity work in occupations such as Amway representatives (Pratt, 2000), the priesthood (Creed et al., 2010), eBay business sellers (Curchod et al., 2014), and sex workers (Brewis and Linstead, 2000).

Less considered, despite its significance, is the historical context of identity work. A classic example that illustrates the importance of history on identity work comes from the early days of the Ford Motor Company (Meyer, 1981). Ford's use of identity work as a means of social control stemmed from problems it was facing with employees, including an annual turnover rate of 416 percent and daily absenteeism between 10 and 20 percent. In response, Ford established a profit-sharing plan for employees, but made it available only to those it deemed to be living a moral life, including men who lead "a clean, sober and industrious life," and women "who are deserving and who have some relatives solely dependent upon them for support." To support these rules, Ford established a Sociological Department that investigated workers' home lives and actively intervened with training and advice intended to lift standards of morality and living conditions.

SUMMING UP

Our discussion of the different elements of identity work suggests that conceptualizing identity work as self work provides an opportunity to extend current concerns with situatedness by incorporating a broader conception of context. Our discussion of motivations suggests that the situation in which identity work occurs may involve broader social networks than have been typically considered. Similarly, our suggestion that identity work research pay closer attention to the unintended effects of such work brings in less obviously affected actors, such as families, friends, and communities. The points we made in relation to practices and resources also highlight the need to enrich our analysis of context to include people's access to social, economic, and material resources that facilitate or constrain their ability to engage in identity work. Although we have not focused on it here, recent writing has begun to move research in ways consistent with this expanded view of identity work. Brown (2017) notes the emergence of discursive, dramaturgical, symbolic, and psychodynamic views of identity work that extend and challenge dominant conceptions associated with social identity and social categorization perspectives. Embracing this broader set of approaches to the study of identity work would help integrate more diverse sets of motivations, practices, resources, and effects, and provide creative links to other types of self work.

The directions we have suggested point to a richer, more deeply embedded examination of identity work. But they also point in the opposite direction— to the need for more comparative studies that cut across contexts and are thus able to systematically establish the causal roles of different situational elements. Identity work research has been dominated by qualitative methods that have provided detailed accounts of what identity work looks like in specific situations, by specific sets of actors, and with specific sets of effects. Less progress has been made, however, in integrating across these situations to provide a theory of variation in identity work, its motivations, and its consequences (Brown, 2015). Thus, conceptualizing identity work as a form of self work may provide a significant opportunity for the development of a more comprehensive theory.

Career Work

Our examination of the careers literature from a self work perspective will be relatively exploratory in contrast to our discussions of emotion work and identity work, both of which have more developed streams of research that are more immediately consistent with the approach we are developing here. At the same time, we believe the study of careers represents a tremendously exciting opportunity for the study of self work in part because of this gap, and because the traditional concept of a career is being challenged by a profoundly dynamic, challenging work environment, where we have moved from organizational to boundaryless careers (Arthur and Rousseau, 2001) and more recently to a workforce increasingly dependent on the gig economy in which careers are composed of sequences of tasks rather than long periods in conventional jobs (Davis, 2016; Kwok, 2017).

Career Work in Management and Organizational Research

Where the study of emotion work and identity work provide well-developed bodies of research to support our review of those areas, we anchor our discussion of career work more broadly in the study of careers, and highlight the threads in that literature we believe can contribute to a move to studying career work. The study of careers has a "long and chequered history" (Evetts, 1992: 1), which we draw on, first reviewing traditional approaches to the study of careers as objective sequences of employment and as subjective experiences. We then turn to research on careers that has emphasized their social construction, including the symbolic-interactionist tradition of the Chicago School, and writing that has drawn on institutional and structuration lenses. Finally, we turn to writing on careers that is focused on the recent changes in labor markets that have led to "boundaryless" careers and the gig economy.

CAREERS AS OBJECTIVE SEQUENCES AND SUBJECTIVE EXPERIENCES

Two approaches dominate traditional career research, the first of which defined a career as "sequences of work experiences over time" based on the simple idea that "Work gets done. Time passes. Careers . . . unfold" (Arthur and Rousseau, 2001: 3). This definition is explicitly general, intended to apply to all people who work. In the sociology of occupations and professions, early research on careers focused on organizational career structures, so that careers were understood as organizational phenomena, existing independently of the people who traversed those structures. Within this tradition, one approach was organization-focused, conceptualizing careers as organizational "frame-works which link together posts and positions with different functions and at different levels," and which included dimensions such as salary progression and professional development. A second approach focused on employees as the units of analysis, defining a career as "the succession of posts and positions through which employees have moved during their working lives," within an organization or a profession (Evetts, 1992: 4).

For researchers, it was attractive to conceptualize careers as a sequence of stepping stones within an organization or profession toward ever greater responsibility and compensation, especially when it seemed that such an image corresponded to most working people's experiences, or at least with the idealized versions of those experiences. But that image no longer holds, and in fact was always problematic. As Evetts (1992: 7) argues, a significant consequence of the objective approach to careers was that it produced an "assumption regarding what is the 'normal' career and hence what are 'abnormal' career patterns" that marginalized many women's careers, as well as the careers of the many men who for reasons of choice or circumstance moved across organizations and occupations in "abnormal" ways, or entered and exited the workforce in a rhythm inconsistent with the idealized continuous progression over many years.

The second long-standing tradition in the study of careers has focused on people's subjective experiences, exploring the "perspectives and understandings of career builders themselves" (Evetts, 1992: 9). From this perspective, a career is defined as an "individually perceived sequence of attitudes and behaviors associated with work-related experiences and activities over the span of the person's life" (Hall, 2001: 12).

A key idea in this tradition is that of a "vocation," which suggests an image of careers as long-term commitments that require training, and are sometimes driven by external or internal "callings" (Inkson et al., 2014). The psychological approach to understanding careers initially conceived of both people and jobs as relatively static, and thus emphasized the importance of "fit," which led to the rise of an industry devoted to assessing fit based on identifying job requirements and psychometric testing of individuals. Only relatively recently have psychological approaches to career research and counseling incorporated more fluid conceptions of careers and people, with insights from social-learning and information-processing theories pointing to the possibility of people shaping their relationships to employment and careers (Mitchell et al., 1979; Peterson et al., 1991).

THE SOCIAL CONSTRUCTION OF CAREERS

In contrast to the objective or subjective phenomena described above, the symbolic-interactionist approach conceptualized careers as a distinctly social phenomenon, and one imbued with agency. This approach applied the concept of a career not only to paid work, but to any context in which "one's life touches the social order" (Hughes, 1958: 64). This approach to studying careers was established by the Chicago School of Sociology between the 1930s and the 1960s (Barley, 1989), and applied to a wide range of lived experiences beyond formal employment, including sex workers (Weitzer, 2009), female crack dealers (Dunlap, Johnson, and Manwar, 1994), hit men (Levi, 1981), and graffiti writers (Lachmann, 1988). In this tradition, the notion of a career describes "the progress of an individual through a linked set of role learning experiences" (Evetts, 1992: 10) and is rooted in Goffman's (1959b) concept of a "moral career."

In the interactionist approach to careers, the concept of a "career strategy" evolved as a central explanatory tool. A career strategy describes the moves that an individual makes to "maintain, protect, develop and enhance their own positions and interests in particular situations" (Evetts, 1992: 11). The concept of a career strategy shifts the idea of a career from something emanating directly from organizational or occupational structure to a set of perceptions, choices, and behaviors on the part of individuals. This represents an important distinction, which highlights the roles of individual agency and meaning in the construction of careers: it highlights the "meaning-building, self-actualizing, and liberating potential" of career work (Tams and Arthur, 2010: 634; see Hall, 2001). Managing and shaping one's career can involve, for instance, asserting idiosyncratic definitions of what it means to achieve success, which can provide both freedom and energy. Thus, the symbolic-interactionist approach opens the door to a social-symbolic work perspective by focusing on the meaning and agency of individuals, but stops short by adopting an objective understanding of social structure and an apolitical understanding of human agency.

A related stream of writing on career work as a product of social construction evolved as organizational scholars adopted institutional and structuration lenses to explore the careers associated with a range of occupations and occupational categories, including scientific and technical occupations (Barley and Kunda, 2011; Duberley, Cohen, and Mallon, 2006a), and traditional professions like law and medicine (Duberley et al., 2006b; Hotho, 2008).

Key to this approach has been an integration of the social context into an understanding of careers, moving away both from careers as objective features of organizational structures, and from careers as the subjective experiences of individuals. In contrast, this stream of work, drawing on structuration theory, describes careers in terms of the ongoing interplay of structure and agency. Barley (1989), for instance, highlights the ways in which people draw on institutional resources to enact career scripts, which in turn can shape those same institutions.

This stream of work provides the strongest foundation for a social-symbolic work perspective on careers, as it has the potential to conceptualize careers and the notion of a career itself as socially constructed through the efforts of interested actors. Thus, as with emotions and identities, the study of careers has evolved in ways that allow an understanding of careers as social-symbolic objects that can potentially be reflexively examined, shaped, and leveraged by interested actors. Tams and Arthur (2010: 630) describe efforts to shape careers as "career agency," which they define as "a process of work-related social engagement, informed by past experiences and future possibilities, through which an individual invests in his or her career."

BOUNDARYLESS CAREERS AND THE GIG ECONOMY

A major shift occurred in the study of careers with the introduction of the notion of a boundaryless career (Arthur and Rousseau, 2001; Tams and Arthur, 2010). The boundaryless career emerged in contrast to the notion of an organizationally bounded career that "saw people in orderly employment arrangements achieved through vertical coordination in mainly large, stable firms" (Arthur and Rousseau, 2001: 1). Arthur and Rousseau (2001) suggest that there exists a wide range of boundaryless careers, including those that move "across the boundaries of separate employers," are validated by a market "outside the present employer," or are "sustained by external networks or information." Common across all of them, however, is "independence from, rather than dependence on, traditional organizational career arrangements" (Arthur and Rousseau, 2001: 3).

More recently, scholars and popular commentators have argued that even this boundaryless notion of a career has become a quaint relic of a bygone economic era, as changes in the labor markets of developed countries have led to careers that involve contingent and precarious forms of work, including work in the gig economy, in industries subject to automation and offshoring, and in project-based organizations (Barley et al., 2017). In this context, careers are composed of sequences of tasks rather than jobs (Davis, 2016).

One manifestation of these changing conditions that has gained considerable popular attention is the "side hustle," where people are engaged in a primary form of work, often in paid employment, and at the same time are engaged in an entrepreneurial venture that stems from an interest or passion. This is a common story in the world of pop-up and underground restaurants where amateur and moonlighting professional cooks create temporary restaurants, often as a strategy aimed at eventually opening a more traditional restaurant (Demetry, 2017).

The possibility of multiple parallel careers challenges traditional notions of careers, and highlights the value of conceptualizing careers as social-symbolic objects, rather than as some kind of sequence of work activities or even the subjective experience of those activities. These dynamics are evidenced even in more traditional kinds of work, where increasingly mobile careers lead people to craft "portable selves" that are "endowed with definitions, motives, and abilities that can be deployed across roles and organizations over time" (Petriglieri et al., In press). These portable selves rely on trans-organizational institutions as career anchors, which provide a basis for both "agentic direction and enduring connection" in the face of uncertain, highly mobile employment trajectories (Petriglieri et al., In press).

Career Work as Self Work

Careers from a social-symbolic work perspective relate to sequences of work over time but are not objective descriptions of those sequences, either as lived or as formalized by human resources departments, and neither are they purely subjective phenomena; instead, careers as social-symbolic objects represent relationally situated, materially enacted, narrative accomplishments. These narratives focus on sequences of work and their significance for individuals, their personal and professional networks, the firms that employ those individuals, and the communities in which those individuals and firms are situated. From this perspective, career work involves the social construction of people's "careers." By mapping research on career work to the process model of social-symbolic work we introduced in Chapter 2 (see Figure 4.1 for a simplified version), we can identify areas of connection between existing careers research and a social-symbolic work perspective, as well as opportunities for new research and theory.

MOTIVATIONS FOR CAREER WORK

As with emotion work and identity work, we begin by considering what we know about the motivations that animate career work. And, as with those other forms of work, this turns out to be a surprisingly complex question. We start with the familiar case of a person engaging in career work in relation to their own career, which has been explored primarily in terms of the psychological mechanisms that might trigger and drive such behavior. Despite this seeming a rather obvious activity in relation to careers, and a long-established topic in management writing (Whyte, 1956), systematic consideration of the motivations for "career self-management" has only recently emerged as a significant consideration in the study of careers. King (2004) constructs career self-management as a form of control-seeking behavior that emerges in response to a perception of impediments to desired career outcomes, which are rooted in "career anchors" (Schein, 1996). The desire to gain control of an important part of one's life conditions one's self-efficacy in regards to the career domain, such that people "are likely to use career self-managing behavior to a greater extent where they feel competent to do so" (King, 2004: 123). This image of the motivations for career self-management provides a useful starting point for understanding why people engage in career work, but is limited by its conception of careers as a subjective experience, rather than a socially negotiated social-symbolic object.

If we think of careers as a facet of the self, then the motivations that might drive career work become more complex. Rather than people only engaging in career work to gain career outcomes through future work experiences, career work would also involve the social construction of one's career as a discursive object that makes interpretable both previous and future work experiences. So, people would be motivated to engage in career work not only when they want to shape future work experiences, but when they want to re-narrate previous work experiences. One could, from this perspective, easily imagine the career work of retired people, or the career work of people looking for jobs and thus wanting to re-narrate the meaning of their previous work experiences.

Moreover, as part of the self, there are a range of people who might be motivated to engage in work that shapes the meaning and evolution of a career, including the focal person but also including people in relationships with that person. Spouses, children, and parents, as well as our bosses, subordinates, and colleagues, may all be motivated to shape a person's career.

In organizations, managers will often be motivated to construct careers from employees' already experienced and possible work experiences, so that the paths through organizational life are more meaningful and rewarding, and employees are in turn more likely to stay and work hard. More generally, careers, like identities, represent bridges between people and social structure that make people's lives meaningful and at the same time provide stability to social structures.

PRACTICES OF CAREER WORK

Moving to the question of practices, an important contribution of conceiving of career work as self work could be that it encourages the integration of what have previously been understood as separate sets of practices associated with careers. The careers literature has tended to divide "doing the work" and "talking about the work" as separate and sometimes loosely coupled parts of a career. Where the earliest writing on careers emphasized the pattern of doing the work that evolved over a person's life, equating that pattern with the person's career, more recent writing has focused on an interpretive view of careers as narratives told by multiple people about an individual's working life. Those two conceptions have, however, remained quite separate, despite the move in other parts of the social sciences to undermine what might be understood as an arbitrary and unrealistic divide.

The divide is arbitrary and unrealistic in two ways. First, it suggests that doing the work has no significant narrative component: "doing" work seems to involve an unreflexive actor engaging in routine or creative tasks without considering or shaping those tasks as part of a larger story of their work and self. This separation is denied by the growing literature on how people "craft" their jobs, which highlights the integration of discursive and practical dimensions of working lives (Wrzesniewski and Dutton, 2001; Wrzesniewski et al., 2003). Second, it suggests that telling stories about one's career is divorced from doing the work—that doing the work may at best serve as a narrative resource. In contrast, the concept of self work suggests that these two elements—doing and talking about work—are deeply integrated, with each not only informing the other but partly constituting the other. Such an understanding of career work is rooted in our conceptualization of the self and self work as simultaneously discursive, relational, and material.

EFFECTS OF CAREER WORK

Examining the effects of career work as self work points to a complex and heterogeneous set that includes both "objective career outcomes," such as mobility, income, and status, as well as deeper facets of the self, including a sense of "personal agency" that might be tied to "the daily practice of doing one's craft ... or from making subjectively meaningful and empowering career choices" (Tams and Arthur, 2010: 638). Indeed, a strength of careers research has been a sensitivity to the consequences of people's careers for their broader lives. Conceiving of career work as self work pushes this sensitivity further and in new directions by highlighting the ways in which efforts to shape a career can have consequences that extend not only beyond the person's relationship to employment, but beyond the person to include their networks and the network of actors connected to the employment situation, such as colleagues and customers.

RESOURCES FOR CAREER WORK

Although the issue of resources has not traditionally been central to research on careers, it has become a pivotal issue in research on the careers of women and visible minorities. Beginning with Kanter's (2008) groundbreaking study of the careers of men and women in a large corporation, the impact of identity on people's careers and their access to the resources necessary to forge a successful career have been studied across a variety of contexts and with attention to a range of resources (Sullivan and Baruch, 2009).

One important resource that has been investigated with respect to gender and race has been the availability and impact of organizational mentors. In an early study of these dynamics, it was shown that MBA program graduates who were able to establish mentoring relationships with white men gained nearly a US$17,000 salary advantage over those graduates with mentors who were not white men. Not surprisingly, this valuable resource was more available to white, male MBA students than to African American, Hispanic, or female students. The impact of race and gender also influences the dynamics within mentoring relationships, such that the degree to which mentor–protégé pairs perceive themselves as similar increases their mutual liking, satisfaction with the relationship, and frequency of contact (Ensher and Murphy, 1997). These studies illustrate not only the importance of specific resources for successful career work, but also the unequal distribution of those resources in ways often beyond the control of those trying to shape careers.

Embedding the study of career work in the broader concept of self work would, we believe, further energize research that attends to the role and distribution of career work resources. Conceiving of a career as part of a self highlights the importance the resources connected to the three dimensions of self work—discursive, relational, and material. Unlike some types of self work, the discursive dimension of career work, and thus the role of discursive resources, has been significantly under-researched. For instance, because careers have primarily been understood as either objective employment sequences or the subjective experience of those sequences, the resources needed to narrate a career have been left relatively unexamined. This is a shame because the ability of people to tell the story of their own or another's career can have significant consequences for their work situations and more broadly. Moreover, the discursive dimension of career work depends not only on rhetorical and narrative skills, but an actor's discursive legitimacy and the opportunities they are given to tell a story.

THE SITUATEDNESS OF CAREER WORK

Unlike the study of either emotion work or identity work, careers research has been explicitly organized around changes in the economy and society that have affected how and whether people can engage in career work. The evolution of the study of careers has closely followed the changes that have occurred in the economic landscape, beginning with the focus on careers as organizational ladders to be climbed, through the emergence of boundaryless careers, to studies of the gig economy in which careers are composed of sequences of tasks rather than jobs. These changes have radically changed the meaning of a career and the resources available to people to construct their careers.

Conceiving of career work as self work pushes us to explore these changes not only in terms of people's economic activity, but their broader conceptions of self including their relationships, material living conditions, and the narratives they construct in order to make sense of their lives for themselves and others. We can imagine that for the growing proportion of the population engaged in the gig economy, the boundary between self and career will be increasingly less meaningful—separating who I am, how I live, and what I do is highly problematic for a person who works on a task-by-task contract at home or from their car. These shifts highlight the distinctive nature of career work as a form of self work: perhaps more than any other kind of self work, career work exists at the intersection of the self, society, and the economy.

SUMMING UP

Conceiving of career work as a type of self work provides the opportunity for exciting and important new directions in exploring the agency people bring to their careers and those of others. It pushes us to examine how careers are shaped to fit with, enhance, and compensate for other parts of people's lives. It also highlights the importance of seeing a career as a social-symbolic object that affects and is affected by a whole network of actors, including but also well beyond a person's work relationships. Career work, from this perspective, is an artful endeavor that depends on skills and resources that allow people to narrate notions of success and achievement, embed it in supportive relationships, and support it with material resources. And, as highlighted by writing on boundaryless careers and the gig economy, career work is a matter of significant public importance, as we move to economic and technological conditions that challenge how we have traditionally constructed careers, and the economic rewards and social accolades that have accompanied those constructions.

Conclusion

In this chapter, we have focused on research on how people work to construct selves—their own and others. Research on management and organizations has examined a number of forms of self work, including emotion work, identity work, and career work. Unfortunately, little attention has been paid to their relationships to each other or their potential standing as members of a broader theoretical family. Studies of these forms of self work have provided important insights into organizational life and revealed previously overlooked opportunities for agency on the part of marginalized members. But left isolated, they each paint a monochromatic image of agency in relation to the self that could be made far more vivid and realistic if expanded and integrated. In the chapters to come, we consider social-symbolic work aimed at organizations and institutions, and the streams of management and organizational research that have examined each of them, before circling back to explore how all those forms of social-symbolic work might be integrated theoretically and studied empirically.

Key Resources

Emotion Work

The study of emotion work revolves around two compelling texts by Hochschild, "Emotion work, feeling rules, and social structure" and *The managed heart*, in which she lays out the core arguments regarding the possibility of people managing their emotions, both displayed and expressed, drawing on the dramaturgical notions of deep and shallow acting. In Bryman's book, *The Disneyization of society*, he explores the broader connections between emotion work and what he describes as performative labor in the context of Disney theme parks and a range of other societal contexts he describes as being subject to the process of Disneyization.

Bryman, A. 2004. *The Disneyization of society*. London: SAGE.
Hochschild, A. R. 1979. Emotion work, feeling rules, and social structure. *American Journal of Sociology*, 85(3): 551–75.
Hochschild, A. R. 1983. *The managed heart: Commercialization of human feeling*. Berkeley, CA: University of California Press.

Identity Work

As with emotion work, the study of identity work is tied closely to a single individual: Goffman's *The presentation of self in everyday life* and *Stigma* provide a foundation for all modern scholarship on identity work. In the first of these texts, Goffman adopts a dramaturgical perspective (like Hochschild) to consider the everyday performances of people in ordinary work situations, as they work to present themselves to others and manage the impressions they create. In the later book, Goffman extends his analysis of identity and identity work to focus on negative identities, and the work both of the stigmatized individual and those around her to shape and manage that tainted identity. The study of identity work was reinvigorated by Snow and Anderson's examination of "Identity work among the homeless" in Austin, Texas, which provided a broader understanding of identity work that included material and relational, as well as discursive/performative dimensions.

Goffman, E. 1959. *The presentation of self in everyday life.* Garden City, NY: Anchor Doubleday.

Goffman, E. 1963. *Stigma: Notes on the management of spoiled identity.* Englewood Cliffs, NJ: Prentice Hall.

Snow, D. A., and Anderson, L. 1987. Identity work among the homeless: The verbal construction and avowal of personal identities. *American Journal of Sociology,* 92(6): 1336–71.

Career Work

Coming to an understanding of career work involves reconceptualizing everyday understandings of what we mean by a career. It involves a shift from representational descriptions of a person's progress through jobs, responsibility, and pay, to careers as social constructions. This shift is central to a new wave of writing on careers that reflects changes that have occurred over the past couple of decades, beginning with Arthur and Rousseau's edited book on *The boundaryless career*, which provides an array of resources for understanding careers outside of traditional corporate ladders. Although not referred to as "career work," managing careers as social-symbolic objects is also a key facet of current writing aimed at individuals wanting to better understand and manage their own careers. In *Working identity*, Ibarra presents a model for career reinvention that suggests knowing how to do something is the result of doing and experimenting. Career transition is not a straight path toward some predetermined identity, but a crooked journey along which we try on a host of "possible selves" we might become.

Arthur, M. B. and Rousseau, D. M. (Eds.) 2001. *The boundaryless career: A new employment principle for a new organizational era.* Oxford: Oxford University Press.

Ibarra, H. 2004. *Working identity: Unconventional strategies for reinventing your career.* Cambridge, MA: Harvard Business Press.

5

Organization Work

In this chapter we:

1. Argue for the usefulness of understanding organizations as social-symbolic objects.

2. Explain the historical evolution of organizations as social-symbolic objects.

3. Define organization work and discuss its discursive, relational, and material dimensions.

4. Explore some of the individual and collective actors who engage in organization work.

Introduction

"News matters" declared the *Denver Post* front-page editorial on April 6, 2018. It had been eight years since the newspaper was bought by Digital First Media, one of the largest newspaper chains in the United States, which was in turn owned by the New York City hedge fund Alden Global Capital. During that time, the 125-year-old *Post* had suffered through round after round of layoffs, repeated reorganizations, and the relocation of its newsroom from downtown Denver to offices in its suburban printing plant.

As a result of the layoffs, newsroom ranks had been reduced from nearly 300 in 2010 to a hundred at the time of the protest, which was itself sparked by a directive from the owners to let go of thirty more news staff. The April 6 editorial was part of a public rebuke of the newspaper's owners by its staff that included nine pieces by *Post* writers calling for someone to "step up and save the Denver Post," asking "Who will 'be there' when journalists are gone?" and calling its owners "vulture capitalists." These followed an earlier march outside the *Post*'s building by fifty newsroom staff wearing T-shirts proclaiming "#newsmatters."

The protests of newsroom staff were more than the grumblings of belea-guered layoff survivors. They were, in fact, challenges to the hedge fund owners over the form and purpose of the organization. Buoyed by the experi-ences at newspapers such as the *Los Angeles Times* and the *Berkshire Eagle,* where local business people and philanthropists took back control of their local flagship papers from hedge fund owners, the *Post* staff were trying to convince local citizens and politicians to wrest back local control of their newspaper.

In a guest editorial, a beloved former editor argued that, "Government, business, media, community and civic leadership should brainstorm solutions and come up with a strategy to preserve The Post" (Moore, 2018). Other staff members put it even more bluntly. On Twitter, a *Post* reporter declared, "The @denverpost is being murdered by its owners. It's the most heartbreaking, panic-inducing thing I've seen in 20-plus years of writing for daily news-papers. We need a new owner, or we are going to get shut down (and soon)" (Wenzel, 2018).

The actions of the new owners of the *Post*, and the desperate responses of the *Post* newsroom staff, represent interesting examples of "organization work"—purposeful, reflexive efforts to shape an organization as a social-symbolic object. As with self work, the actors involved in organization work can be heterogeneously connected to the social-symbolic object in question; the nature of organizations makes this potential relationship between actor and object even more complex.

In the case of the *Denver Post*, the most obvious actors were the newspaper's employees and owners, but work was also done by other media organizations and by local politicians arguing for changes in the management of the news-paper. The work itself is also highly varied: in this case its discursive dimension is most obvious, but it also involved an important relational dimension that revolved around the connections among newsroom staff, and between staff and owners, and a material dimension involving the digital and physical technologies used by staff to realize their protest, as well as the location and nature of the offices and equipment used in the production of the newspaper.

The efforts of the newsroom staff and other actors in this case highlight some of the potential targets of organization work and provide insight into important features of organizations as social-symbolic objects. The actions of the new owners, and the resulting calls for changes in the ownership and priorities of the newspaper from the staff, point to issues of organizational strategy, structure, boundaries, identity, and membership. Unlike many organizational conflicts which occur well outside of public view, the compet-ing forms of organization work aimed at shaping the *Post* were more than simply visible, they depended, at least for *Post* staffers, on enrolling actors outside of the organization in support of their project. Newsroom staff constructed the *Post* as an organization with significant local importance, as well as a part of an important national institution that was under threat.

In this chapter, we explore how individuals, collective actors, and networks of actors engage in organization work. We first discuss the historical evolution of organizations as social-symbolic objects, focusing particularly on the transitions to modernity and postmodernity. Those transitions affected the dimensions and characteristics of organizations as social-symbolic objects, and thus the possible forms of organization work in which people might engage. We then conceptualize organization work, focusing on its dimensions—discursive, relational, and material—and what kinds of actors are involved. Third, we explore three areas of management and organizational research that represent kinds of organization work—strategy work, boundary work, and technology work—tracing the development of each and exploring the implications of conceptualizing them as organization work. We close the chapter, as always, with some personal reflections on the significance and potential of organization work, and a set of additional resources for further study.

The History of Organizations as Social-Symbolic Objects

Understanding organization work begins with an understanding of organizations as social-symbolic objects. An organization is commonly understood to be two or more people who interact on an ongoing basis around a shared goal. While this definition is useful for many purposes, such an image of organizations fails to capture much of what we mean when we talk about organizations as social-symbolic objects. Rather than a group of people, we argue that organizations exist as meaningful patterns arising from the interactions of such a group. As social-symbolic objects, much of what is important about organizations lies in the shared understandings held by members and interested external actors, and in the heterogeneous relationships among and between this network of actors. Just as the self is not synonymous with the person, organizations are not synonymous with the assemblies of people that animate them. Rather, organizations as social-symbolic objects represent patterns that lie in the social-symbolic realm—the realm of relations and meaning rather than the realm of physical bodies (even though, of course, those bodies are essential to the organization).

Organization work, then, describes the purposeful, reflexive efforts of individuals, collective actors, and networks of actors intended to shape organizations as social-symbolic objects. It is the work of creating, changing, maintaining, and destroying organizations (see Box 5.1). At the same time, although we will argue that organization work goes on all the time in

117

Box 5.1. TERRORISM AS ORGANIZATION WORK

A recent and vivid example of organization work intended to both construct and destroy organizations is the rise of the terrorist organization ISIL (or Islamic State as they refer to themselves) as an organization and a political project. While a horrifying example of destruction and carnage, it is also an impressive example of organization work in two ways: first, in the sense that the founders of the movement have been frighteningly effective in creating a new and original form of organization in a relatively short period of time; and second, in the sense that the terrorist acts carried out by ISIL are in many cases forms of organization work aimed at organizations that ISIL seeks to destroy.

It is useful to begin with the organization work that Abu Bakr al-Baghdadi and the rest of the ISIL leadership conducted to bring ISIL into being. Interestingly, what we see is a constellation of work that looks remarkably like the sorts of organization work carried out by a traditional entrepreneur founding a new business venture. They needed to develop a strategy, an identity, obtain resources, and construct an organizational boundary. The beheadings, suicide bombings, ethnic cleansing, and destruction of ancient artifacts can be seen to be as much about creating an identity for the organization and reinforcing the organizational boundary as they are about any actual practical implications of these horrific acts. Understanding their actions from this perspective makes many seemingly random acts of extreme and pointless violence more understandable and even rational. It also makes it more understandable how these acts are successful for ISIL even when they obviously don't threaten Western civilization.

Second, ISIL has been conducting a campaign of organization work to bring down foes such as the Syrian and Iraqi governments. In addition to the military campaign they have been conducting, they are also working hard to undermine the basic structures of these organizations. Through campaigns of suicide bombings, they struck at the heart of the narrative of public security that underpins both governments. Unsurprisingly, the Syrian and Iraqi armies struggled with morale and a sense of purpose in the face of the resolve and commitment of ISIL suicide squads. As a result, the overwhelming technology of the Iraqi army in particular seemed to have little effect in this situation; the Iraqi army as an organization evaporated on the battlefield, leading to undisciplined mass retreats and the abandonment of large amounts of equipment. Well-conducted organization work by ISIL overwhelmed superior military technology and training again and again. Even allied airstrikes often made little difference in the face of ISIL's deft organization work.

Furthermore, if we step back a bit, the organization work perspective also provides a useful approach to understanding not just what the leadership of ISIL has done to construct the organization and what the goals of the organization are, but also a way to think about how to undermine terrorist organizations like ISIL. While military action to destroy these organizations is often demanded, what we know about organizations and organization work would suggest that this might be counterproductive on at least some occasions. What a social-symbolic work perspective suggests is a much more nuanced strategy, which looks at the forms of work that could be directed at ISIL (and other similar organizations) to undermine the organization. For example, organizational identity work can be conducted to undermine the core narrative that supports the organization, or the organizational boundary could be undermined and weakened in many more subtle ways. Alternatively, the organization's digital presence could be degraded in ways that would produce deep and lasting impacts on the organization, without the counterproductive impacts of military action that often do more to help the leaders of the organization than it does to undermine their efforts.

organizations, not all of the purposeful effort that occurs in organizations is part of what we refer to as organization work. It is therefore important to distinguish organization work from two other kinds of work tightly tied to organizations.

The first is the work done in organizations to produce goods and provide services, but which takes the organization for granted. As a simple example, the work done by employees to assemble a car using established technologies and taken-for-granted organizational routines is not organization work. In contrast, the work done at a car assembly plant to make the production line more efficient, to reorganize workers, to introduce new values, and to increase its influence and standing in the broader company, are all instances of organization work. Organization work is not about *work done in* organizations, but about *working on* organizations.

The second related form of work that is not organization work as we define it involves the efforts of actors to shape the idea of an organization; for example, the work done by actors in the United States to establish the "B corporation" as a type of organization. For us, organization work involves efforts to shape specific organizations (e.g., Nike, the UN, the US Treasury Department, Bob's Barbershop), whereas work focused on changing the way we understand "organization" as a concept, how we understand a kind of organization (what, for example, constitutes a bank), or to introduce a new form of organization (a "B corporation"), is institutional work (which we discuss in Chapters 7 and 8).

The possibility of organization work depends on actors' recognition of organizations as social-symbolic objects. But these objects, like the self, have undergone significant transformations as part of the broader social changes in the transition from premodernity to modernity and postmodernity. This evolution began in earnest with an increasing belief in the perfectibility of organizations through the application of rationality that accompanied modernism. It continued, and was enhanced by, the evolution of organizations in postmodernity to more and more complex social objects with increasing numbers of dimensions available for actors to work on. In this section, we explore how the evolution of the organization as a social-symbolic object has engendered and shaped organization work.

Premodern Organizations

Before we discuss premodern organizations as social-symbolic objects, it is useful to begin with a brief discussion of the human capacity for organizing upon which organizations depend. Humans working together to achieve a goal is not, of course, a modern development. Since the appearance of *Homo sapiens*, humans have shown a remarkable ability to flexibly organize into informal groups to solve problems of all kinds. The ability of humans to organize to support one another in hunting, war, child rearing, and other activities is a large part of the explanation of how an otherwise unremarkable species became the dominant species globally and is arguably the reason we evolved large brains and linguistic abilities (Gamble et al., 2014).

In premodern societies, the ability to organize allowed relatively small, semi-permanent groups of humans—tribes—to succeed as hunter-gatherers. By living in a tribe and forming temporary organizations of subsets of members around particular tasks (e.g., hunting, foraging, canoe building), premodern groups thrived in difficult environments. Tribes generally remained small,[1] however, and their forms of organizing were characterized by flexibility, temporariness, and lack of formal hierarchy. They were organizations, but only of the most ephemeral sort.

Where tribes became more successful at solving basic problems like security and access to sufficient food supplies (by, for example, discovering how to grow a dependable food supply), the size of the group would begin to increase and more permanent organizations emerge. At this point, we begin to see something that would fit our definition of a social-symbolic object. These organizations were generally small, but they were enduring and had some limited hierarchy, formalization, and specialization. These new organizations were very different from the flexible, problem-based groups formed by members of tribes to deal with particular challenges: they are what we would consider premodern organizations that fit our definition of social-symbolic objects.

These premodern organizations tended to be one of two forms (Weber, 1958). First, with the availability of surplus, charismatic leaders who were able to raise an army and conquer territory began to build governance structures to administer the newly conquered territories and an increasingly complex military. A concrete example of this can be found in the exploits of Genghis Khan. Starting from nothing, he built the largest contiguous empire in history. But he also had to build a system to run his vast empire. To do so, he created the *Yassa*, an administrative and military code, as well as governance structures to administer the code and collect taxes. Interestingly, he also recognized that as nomads, his Mongol followers were not well suited to administering cities, so he appointed ethnic Chinese or other non-nomadic ethnicities to these positions. The result was a sizable system of administration made up of a variety of organizations in different parts of the empire all structured along similar lines and administering the same administrative and legal code.

---

[1] In fact, researchers have argued that the size of these groups is limited by Dunbar's number. In monkeys, this number is about fifty while in humans about 150. In humans, this is the limit of the size of a group without formal organization.

Second, while many of the governmental and military systems that grew up around successful charismatic leaders disappeared with the death of the leader, some did not. Some of the charismatic leaders were able to create the conditions for the organizations they created to survive their deaths. Returning to Genghis Khan, his empire and the administrative structures that he built outlived him and became the standard way to organize across the Mongol empire long after his death. The organization successfully survived his death and changed from a charismatic organization built around him as a leader, to a traditional organization based on principles of organizing that were seen as legitimate because of their links to the past. The organizations he created to administer his empire therefore remained resolutely premodern; there was little trace of the focus on rationality and progress associated with modern organizations.

Modern Organizations

Organizations as a recognized social-symbolic object emerged with modernity and reflected modern concerns for rationality and perfectibility. In fact, it wasn't until the late 1700s that the word "organization" even entered the English language as a way to describe "[a]n organized body of people with a particular purpose, as a business, government department, charity, etc."[2] (OED, 2004). So, when we refer to premodern social groups as "organizations," it is worth keeping in mind that we are using a modern concept to make sense of entities that were rather differently understood at the time.

To understand the nature of modern organizations, and especially their association with rationality and perfectibility, consider the Prussian Army of the eighteenth and nineteenth centuries—the first "modern" army. Following defeat by France in the battles of Auerstedt and Jena in 1806, Prussian military and political leaders set out to reform their army. The standard solution at the time would have been to further professionalize the army by hiring a larger number of mercenaries. This model had proven successful for the British in the Peninsular War (1807–15) and represented the dominant European conception of a great army. Instead, the Prussian leadership constructed a novel, even revolutionary, approach to establishing an army: it would be a rationally managed army of citizens. The conceptual underpinnings of such an army were rooted in the ideas of the Enlightenment, and particularly "the development of the social contract and the prestige of the natural sciences" (Avant, 2000: 44).

With the invention of the modern state, a new social contract emerged between citizens and nations that made possible the idea that citizens would

---

[2] Earlier uses of the word "organization" beginning in the 1400s were in reference to biological organisms.

121

enthusiastically defend their nation. From the rise of the natural sciences and natural philosophy, came the belief in rationality that diffused into the social realm, and implied that the army should be organized in a strictly rational way.

Together, these ideas allowed the establishment of an army that worked to a highly systematic, structured plan in which a small standing army was supplemented with a large reserve force (Gray, 1992). New citizen soldiers were integrated into the existing army through a system in which local regiments were responsible for conscripting and training soldiers. Young men were drafted at age twenty, served for three years on active duty, and then were allowed to shift to a reserve pool for a further four years during which they would report to their regiment for regular further training periods. This new system meant that the standing army functioned as a school for training soldiers who would make up a large reserve force available for duty in the event of war. The new citizen soldiers would be motivated by patriotism, while the small standing army would keep costs manageable for the state.

This new form of citizen army proved to be highly successful. After the Prussians defeated Napoleon in the great Franco-Prussian war, their model was adopted by nearly every major power around the world (Gray, 1992). The march of modernism led to a complete transformation from mercenary armies fighting for money on behalf of the king to patriotic citizen armies fighting for their countries. Similar transformations occurred across many areas of activity leading to the emergence of modern organizations as a dominant feature of the social landscape. These organizations shared three key features that we argue underpin the possibility, and shape the nature, of social-symbolic work in relation to modern organizations: rationality, independence, and character.

The first feature of modern organizations that creates the possibility of organization work is the taken-for-granted application of rationality within organizations to achieve modern concerns for efficiency and effectiveness. In the transition to modernity, rationality emerged as a dominant idea, describing the capacity of humans to "overcome the restrictive limitations of authority and tradition" through the application of reason (Rutgers, 1999: 21). The belief in rationality brought with it an "attitude of optimism" with respect to people's ability to understand and affect their worlds, and an appreciation of novelty and innovation that defied premodern concerns for stability (Miller, 2009: 158).

In this environment, modern organizations were conceived of as machines, with the rationality of their structure and processes determining their legitimacy. It was no longer enough to say we do things this way because we have always done them this way or because the king said we should; instead, organizations should be rational. The continuous application of rational principles to improve organizations led to the diffusion of rational tools like modern accounting, time and motion studies, and myriad other management methods developed in the drive for efficiency and effectiveness. From the ashes of the medieval court emerged Henry Ford's assembly line and the immense bureaucracies that govern modern nation states.

The second key feature of modern organizations was their status as independent actors: separate in identity, aims, and accountability from their members. With the transition to modernity, organizations developed distinctly different relationships both to their members and to other organizations, including the state. As a part of the emergence of the modern self, people gained new autonomy from the collective bodies with which they were associated. Rather than being fully incorporated into collective bodies as was the case in the Middle Ages, when one's membership in guild or village was more or less complete, such associations became partial and contingent in modernity. People's relationships to collective bodies became matters of negotiation with only specific duties being owed to the collective.

In a reciprocal manner, organizations gained the ability to "pursue interests that were not simply aggregates of the interests of their members" (Scott, 2003: 151). This newly developed independence of people and organizations came with the vesting of rights in both sets of actors. As people gained "rights to make contracts on their own," thus becoming "persons before the law with a certain set of rights," so too did the new corporate organization, with "a variety of rights to free and expansive action" (Coleman, 1974: 28). The idea of modern organizations as "legal persons" was more than metaphorical—it allowed organizations to participate in contracts, to launch and be subject to lawsuits, and even to enjoy some "human" rights, such as the right to free speech. This transformation meant that the interests of organizations might diverge from the interests of members: whereas the interests of premodern organizations were either identical to those of the group in the case of a tribe, or of a leader in the case of charismatic leaders, the organization now had its own interests and rights to be respected. We see these interests and rights reflected in the entire apparatus of corporate governance that has emerged to ensure that members, including leaders, respect the interests of their organizations.

Finally, if organizations exist separately from their members, can act independently, and have interests and rights, then it is only a small step to see organizations as social actors, each with an idiosyncratic organizational "character." This possibility was noted most prominently by Selznick (2011), who argued that an organization could become more than a functional means to desired goals, that it could become infused with value above and beyond its stated purpose. The possibility of organizational character inspired scholarship and practice, especially in the second half of the twentieth century, focused on understanding and managing organizational culture and values (Kanter, 1983; Van Maanen and Barley, 1984).

More broadly, it has been suggested that the cultural and institutional processes in organizations lead to a situation in which organizations develop "a personality that becomes stamped with values around which future leaders deliberate and make important strategic decisions" (King, 2015: 151). The idea that organizations might have character (or personality) is important for our conception of them as social-symbolic objects. But the idea needs to be considered carefully. When King suggests that organizations have become social actors, equivalent in many ways to human actors, we agree—sort of. It is the case, we would argue, that organizations have become more equivalent to human actors, but that change has happened at the same time that our understanding of human actors has also been changing (as described in the Chapter 3).

In sum, as Western societies have moved from the premodern to the modern era, our understanding of organizations has evolved from a functional mechanism extending the power of individuals or the traditions of a community, to a social-symbolic object imbued with rationality, agency, and character. These changes were shaped by the efforts of interested actors and have in turn shaped the possibility of further organization work. Much of the social-symbolic work focused on modern organizations involved the application and elaboration of science-based rationality aimed at increasing the efficiency of organizations: the development and employment of new technologies, beginning with the assembly line and ultimately involving a vast array of physical and digital technologies; the socialization of employees as a mechanism for encouraging specific behaviors and attitudes; and reducing the variance in people's experiences of organizational life.

Organization work in the modern era has also been tightly tied to the status that organizations have gained as independent actors, with agency separate from the agency attributed to their members. Much of the organization work connected to this feature of modern organizations has involved managing the tension between facilitating organizational agency and the agency of members, often protecting organizational agency and intentionality by establishing constraints on the choices and resources of individual members including both front-line workers (e.g., physical and electronic workplace surveillance) and senior executives and board members (e.g., contractual limitations to disclosure and monitoring of conflicts of interest).

Finally, a wide range of organizational practices has emerged, and a whole set of industries tied to organization work around constructing, maintaining, and narrating the idiosyncratic character of organizations. Inside organizations, the work of a range of departments including marketing, corporate relations, strategy, and organization development is often focused on ensuring that the organization has and can project a "special" set of qualities that separates it from its competitors. Externally, public relations and other kinds of consulting firms emerged in the modern era to offer specialty services intended to help organizations achieve that distinctiveness. As we will see in the next section on postmodern organizations, the transition to postmodernity has both further enabled and transformed these efforts.

Postmodern Organizations

As with the transition to modernity, the transition to postmodernity has had important ramifications for the evolution of the organization as a social-symbolic object. At its most basic, postmodernity has been associated with a radical reflexivity that has made previously taken-for-granted aspects of organizations open to creativity and experimentation. The modernist goal of constructing the one best—i.e., most rational and effective—way of organizing has been replaced with a more flexible, and sometimes playful, approach to organization design. As a result, the idea that there are universal design principles, or even best practices, that should drive the construction of organizations has increasingly weakened.

To explore the transformation of organizations in postmodernity, we first look at some of the organizational forms that have emerged in this period, and then suggest a way of conceptualizing the shifts that have allowed the emergence of these disparate kinds of postmodern organization. We begin with polyarchy, and then discuss platform organizations, and finally network organizations, before we return to the broader question of what is a postmodern organization.

FROM RATIONALITY TO RATIONALITIES: THE POLYARCHY

The core idea around which modern organizations are structured is the bureaucracy, with its hierarchical form of control, formalization of routines, and specialization of roles. Modern organizations are structured into a pyramid of levels with more levels added as organizations grow so that managers can effectively maintain control. Alongside hierarchy, organizational growth is associated with shared practices established as formal routines, inscribed in organizational rules and procedures, and the delineation of separate, specialized tasks to increase efficiency. These are central organizing principles associated with modern organizations, enshrined in both normative and descriptive organizational writing.

The first kind of postmodern organization we examine takes as its starting point the abandonment of the central principles of bureaucracy, and in particular the abandonment of hierarchy. The concept of a polyarchy comes from political science, where it describes a form of democracy characterized by a high degree of permissible public contestation and relatively complete inclusiveness in decision making (Dahl, 1973). Modern democracies have varied significantly along these dimensions, with twentieth-century Switzerland providing an extraordinary level of public contestation but not allowing women to vote in federal elections until after the referendum in 1971. In contrast, there exist a large number of ostensible democracies with high degrees of inclusiveness (formal rights of participation), but extremely limited allowable public contestation of political ideas and decisions (China or Russia, for example).

Employing the concept of polyarchy in the context of organizations brings with it a commitment to participation and contestation, but in the service of organizational goals rather than democratic ideals. It describes "a form of radical decentralization—not a mere flattening of organization structure, but bestowing full autonomy of judgment, decision, and execution to decentralized individuals and subunits" (Felin and Powell, 2016: 83).

A well-known example of polyarchy in contemporary business organizations comes from Valve, a developer and distributor of video games. Valve's commercial success is based on its games, and especially Steam, its distribution platform. But its notoriety as a polyarchy stems from the widespread dissemination of its *Handbook for new employees* after it was leaked onto the internet. The handbook is described as "an abbreviated encapsulation of our guiding principles" and makes clear the commitment in Valve to polyarchy—a commitment illustrated by headings in the handbook such as "Welcome to Flatland," "Why do I need to pick my own projects?," and "Choose your own adventure." The commitment to polyarchy extends throughout the organization: "Valve is flat. It's our shorthand way of saying that we don't have any management, and nobody 'reports to' anybody else. We do have a founder/president, but even he isn't your manager . . . You have the power to greenlight projects. You have the power to ship products" (Valve Software, 2012: 4).

Although Valve represents a famous example of polyarchy, it is not unique in the corporate world: other prominent polyarchies include the online shoe retailer Zappos, groupware developer Basecamp, and tech consultant Menlo Innovations. What connects these organizations, and what makes polyarchy a postmodern form of organization, is a commitment to a conception of rationality that diverges from the unitary understanding of rationality associated with modernity, a move away from a belief in one best way and the ability of experts to divine that best way. Polyarchy is premised on a plurality of rationalities, and a belief that effective collective action will emerge from the unbridled participation and influence of a wide range of actors all pursuing their own passions, making decisions based on their idiosyncratic knowledge and experience, and collaboratively connecting those passions and decisions in fluid, emergent ways.

FROM CONTROL TO CONNECTION: THE NETWORK ORGANIZATION

The Ford Motor Company was founded by Henry Ford on June 16, 1903 in Detroit, Michigan. For its first few years, the company produced only a few cars each day using parts purchased from various suppliers assembled by men working in teams to build entire cars from the ground up. Within a few years, though, Ford had become the largest producer of cars in America and transformed the car from a luxury product for the rich into a standardized affordable product for the middle classes. While the assembly line was at the center of this highly rationalized organization, Ford's production system also involved a vertically integrated supply chain that ran back to rubber plantations in Brazil and iron smelters in America. And above this complex system of production was a large bureaucracy of managers and planners who handled the complex flows of materials, the many tens of thousands of workers, and the production systems that produced the millions of Model Ts that revolutionized transportation in America. The Ford Motor Company was, by the middle of the twentieth century, the archetype of the modern organization.

Fast forward to 2017 and the production of automobiles looks very different. While cars are still produced on assembly lines, the whole system of production that was internalized in Fordist production is now outsourced. While automobile companies still produce millions of cars, they now focus narrowly on assembly, design, and quality control while outsourcing the production of components to a network of suppliers who themselves often outsource elements of production to a second tier of suppliers. Rather than mass production based on the rational integration of all activities within a single organizational boundary, the automobile companies produce cars by coordinating hundreds of subcontractors in a flexible network.

Network forms of organizing, like the modern automobile manufacturers, are collections of individuals and organizations embedded in webs of relationships that facilitate joint activity in the production of goods or the provision of services. Where modern organizations worked to bring activities within the organizational boundary to enhance control and predictability, network organizations move activity outside of their boundaries to enhance flexibility and allow for increased specialization of network members. Network organizations as postmodern organizations reflect a willingness to move away from the basic principles of control and hierarchy. Rather than vertical integration, network organizations are about specialization within the organization and diversity among the organizations across the network. This creates uncertainty as activities are no longer inside of a single organization and controlled by a single hierarchy. But it also creates flexibility, agility, and highly specialized organizations focused on a narrow range of activities whose capabilities can be developed and honed based on their specialization.

FROM PRODUCTION TO FACILITATION: THE PLATFORM
ORGANIZATION

Mechanical Turk is an online platform developed by Amazon that began operating in November 2005.[3] According to Amazon, the service provides "Artificial Artificial Intelligence"—allowing humans to support machines by doing small tasks where human intelligence is superior to machine intelligence. The name harks back to "The Turk," a chess-playing automaton that toured Europe in the eighteenth century, beating both Napoleon and Benjamin Franklin. It was eventually revealed, however, that The Turk wasn't an automaton at all, but a dummy manipulated by a chess master cleverly concealed inside.[4]

Mechanical Turk, as its name suggests, similarly provides the "human inside the machine." It operates by bringing together "requesters" with tasks to be completed and "providers" who complete those tasks, which include a range of activities that machines find challenging, such as interpreting photos (e.g., searching for missing boats on satellite images) or judging the aesthetics of signage. Mechanical Turk acts as a facilitated marketplace that allows requesters and providers to connect and a financial conduit for payment. So, although Mechanical Turk represents a significant piece of business for Amazon, the company itself does not complete or control the core tasks that requesters are paying for.

Mechanical Turk is a platform organization—a postmodern form of organization that provides value to customers by bringing together buyers and sellers without becoming directly involved in the transactions between them. Platform organizations might accomplish this through a website like Mechanical Turk or through a physical technology like the PC bus architecture provided by Intel that connects PC makers and component manufacturers. Whatever the medium, platform organizations provide an "interface" that standardizes and facilitates the interactions of interested parties.

In providing a platform for interaction, platform organizations also move away from modernist organizing principles. In organizing in a way that the actual transactions are carried out between suppliers and customers without the direct involvement of the organization, it gives up the sort of control that was the focus of the vertical integration and internal specialization of modern organizations like the Ford Motor Company. Instead, the platform designers inject uncertainty by simply providing an infrastructure through which other organizations can connect and then facilitating that connection. This means much of what happens on the platform is not controlled by the platform organization. It is shaped and facilitated of course, but it is neither directly

[3] <https://www.mturk.com/mturk/welcome>.
[4] <https://en.wikipedia.org/wiki/Amazon_Mechanical_Turk>.

arranged nor controlled by the platform. In injecting this uncertainty into the transactions that flow through the platform the organization is moving some distance from the predictability and controllability of the assembly line or the bureaucracy.

POSTMODERN ORGANIZATIONS AS OBJECTS OF SOCIAL-SYMBOLIC WORK

Looking across these emerging forms of organization, we see some important changes in organizations as social-symbolic objects in postmodernity. The emergence of polyarchies pushes back against the idea of a unitary rationality around which organizations should be structured and managed. It embraces the idea that there are a multitude of legitimate voices and opinions in organizations, which need to be accommodated and integrated if organizations are to make the most of their resources. Platform and network organizations similarly shift away from the idea of organizations as independent agents seeking control through vertical integration or other means. Instead, they see organizations as existing in complex ecologies, with the participants and relationships that define those ecologies making it possible to achieve much more than could ever be accomplished alone.

So, postmodern organizations reject independence and a singular rationality, but they celebrate an idiosyncratic character and personality as key features of organizations. This need not be understood as inconsistent, however, since a move toward greater attention to organizational character and a move away from control and independence may both reflect a greater reflexivity on the part of organizational actors with respect to their organizations as social-symbolic objects. Fundamentally, it means that previously taken-for-granted aspects of organizations are open to experimentation and innovation. Design principles have become a toolkit that can be applied or not depending on the inspiration of the individuals crafting the organization. Constructing organizations is no longer engineering, but art, and the actors working to construct the organization need to be as much inspired artists as rational engineers.

As we discussed earlier, the transition to modernity brought with it the idea of organizations as machines that could (and should) be optimized through the application of rationality. The move to postmodernity relaxed this notion and led to a move away from hierarchy, formalization, and unitary rationality. This is still a work in progress: the results are often radical and still emerging, but the process is still incomplete. But what is clear is that postmodern organizations do not conform to a single form. Instead, postmodernity has seen a variety of different forms of organization emerge, which together defy the modernist assumption of "one best way of organizing."

The emergence of postmodern organizations has been shaped by and shapes the organization work of a variety of actors. Relaxing hierarchy and bureaucracy in organizations, for instance, does not mean doing "less" organization work, but rather organization work of different kinds and sometimes by different people. Whereas the design and implementation of bureaucracies was a largely planned, top-down affair, the construction of polyarchies, as illustrated by Valve, is a continuous process of organization work involving members at all levels of the organization. The deep understanding of organization work embedded in a polyarchy is illustrated by the diagram in Valve's employee handbook showing the "Method to move your desk," and instructions for employees to: "Think of [your desk's] wheels as a symbolic reminder that you should always be considering where you could move yourself to be more valuable.... You'll notice people moving frequently; often whole teams will move their desks to be closer to each other" (Valve Software, 2012: 6). Organization work in Valve thus depends on purposeful, reflexive efforts by employees across the organization making choices that continuously reconstruct the organization.

Similar dynamics are associated with network organizations, in which organization work is demanded of a wide range of participants in a responsive, continuous manner, triggered by the need to adjust the network in response to changing environmental and market conditions, as well as by the intersecting, and occasionally conflicting, aims and strategies of network members (Agranoff and McGuire, 2005; Dyer and Nobeoka, 2000). Platform organizations also require and allow distinctive kinds of organization work, where the focus of the work is not on controlling members, so much as on creating efficient, effective markets for buyers and sellers to come together (Alstyne et al., 2016).

Organizations Today

If contemporary societies are societies of organizations (Perrow, 1986), then the landscape we see is one of organizations that vary dramatically in their postmodern, modern, and premodern characteristics. The organizations that tend to receive the most attention, because of their novelty, recent emergence, and economic importance tend to have noteworthy postmodern qualities: Amazon, Google, Uber, and other technology-driven firms gain much of their power from their status as successful platforms. At the same time, these high-tech postmodern juggernauts are also constituted significantly as rational, modern organizations, with large swathes of their operations devoted to efficiency-driven rationality. Looking more broadly, we also see the continuing importance of religious and other premodern organizations devoted to the maintenance of traditions (including many parts of one of our universities), as well as a wide variety of organizations driven by charismatic leaders who, while dressed differently, have much in common with Genghis

Khan. Thus, while there has been a progression toward the postmodern, organizations today are a complex mélange of premodern, modern, and postmodern elements, and the sorts of organization work that happens in organizations is conditioned and enabled by this complex mix of elements.

Conceptualizing Organization Work

Building on our conception of organizations as social-symbolic objects, we can begin to explore the key activities underpinning organization work. From our perspective, organization work describes the purposeful, reflexive efforts of actors to establish, shape, and disrupt organizations. This form of social-symbolic work includes discursive, relational, and material dimensions that interact in complex ways in concrete instances of organization work such as signing a document, designing a logo, or voting on a vacation policy. In this section, we explore the discursive, relational, and material dimensions of organization work, and then discuss the kinds of actors involved.

Dimensions of Organization Work

THE DISCURSIVE DIMENSION
The production, dissemination, and consumption of texts intended to shape the social-symbolic objects that populate and constitute an organization are integral parts of organization work. The development of a business plan for a new venture; the construction of a new strategy in an existing organization; or the disruption of an established understanding of a product category in an industry are all activities that contribute to constructing organizations and are carried out primarily through the production, dissemination, and consumption of texts. Thus, almost all of what we think of as organization work has a significant discursive dimension.

To explain the discursive dimension of organization work, we first need to recognize that organizations exist as discursive objects, constructed and maintained in texts of various kinds. This is not to suggest that organizations exist only in language: as Mumby and Claire (1997: 181) argue, a discursive perspective on organizations does not "claim that organizations are 'nothing but' discourse, but rather that discourse is the principle means by which organization members create a coherent social reality that frames their sense of who they are." Organizational discourse analysis has evolved as an extension of the broader discursive perspective to encompass "a range of approaches that share an interest in the role of discourse in the constitution of organizational life" (Phillips and Oswick, 2012: 2). Research in this area focuses on how organizational reality is constituted in discourse and, from a work perspective, is of

131

direct interest as much of the organization work that occurs in organizations is discursive.

The discursive dimension of organization work involves the construction and shaping of organizations through the production and dissemination of texts, as well as the establishment of systems through which this process occurs. If we consider, for example, work performed to construct a socially responsible corporation, this might involve work such as creating and disseminating documents describing how new policies and procedures should function as part of the establishment of corporate social responsibility programs, the production and dissemination of documents announcing the creation of senior organizational positions responsible for social responsibility, such as a Vice President of Corporate Social Responsibility and the naming of that individual who will occupy the new position, as well as the communications to stakeholders demonstrating how the organization is achieving its social responsibility targets. Without this discursive dimension, the other forms of work that might be linked to social responsibility would likely fail to construct the socially responsible organization as a social-symbolic object in the lives of its members and stakeholders.

Discourse studies have investigated the construction of a wide range of social-symbolic objects and kinds of discursive activity, and how this organization work effects the organization, its members, and the broader interorganizational context in which it occurs. Mantere and Vaara (2008), for example, explore how the discursive dimension of organization work can shape participation in strategy processes: they show that strategy discourse that includes themes of "self-actualization," "dialogization," and "concretization" lead to strategic processes that engender greater participation by organizational members.

Narrative studies have highlighted the role of stories and storytelling in the discursive dimension of organization work (Fenton and Langley, 2011). This stream of research has shown "how people perform stories to make sense of events, introduce change, and gain political advantage during their conversations" (Boje, 1991: 106). Dalpiaz et al. (2014), for example, explore the role of narratives in making sense of succession processes in family firms, focusing on the case of Italian design firm Alessi as the leadership of the firm passed from uncle to nephew. They (2014: 1376) argue that despite being largely overlooked by entrepreneurship scholars, narratives play a crucial role in stabilizing the process of family business succession, as "the meaning of family, the eligibility of the prospective head, and the appropriateness of appointing from within all come under scrutiny."

In a very different organizational context, Allen (2001) describes how nurses told "atrocity stories" that reinforced the boundaries inside a hospital between nurses and other hospital professionals, especially doctors. Atrocity stories relayed "dramatic or shocking events that may take on a legendary or apocryphal status in the oral culture of an occupational group" (Allen, 2001: 76). These stories played a dual role in the organization work of nurses: the content of the stories focused on doctors' incompetence or negligence, and thus maintained the boundary between them and the nurses; moreover, by telling the stories among themselves, nurses reinforced their membership inside the boundary. This latter dynamic was often strengthened by nurses engaging in collective storytelling, where a story was initiated by an individual but then added to and elaborated on by others in the group.

Along with narrative studies, a variety of discursive approaches to research on organization work have emerged, including studies of rhetoric (Brown et al., 2012; Zbaracki, 1998), semiotics (Barley, 1983; Fiol, 1989; Wilf, 2012), and hermeneutics (Nyström et al., 2003; Phillips and Brown, 1993; Robinson and Kerr, 2009). Looking across these studies highlights different aspects of the ways in which actors draw on discourse to construct organizations. They also, however, highlight the important differences among forms of discourse as organization work. Studies of rhetoric, for instance, focus on the structure of the arguments that actors construct in their attempts to influence others' beliefs and attitudes, tying rhetoric closely to the discursive dimension of social-symbolic work. In contrast, research adopting a semiotic and hermeneutic approach examine the ways in which meaning is constructed in organizations and how that meaning shapes behavior and beliefs.

THE RELATIONAL DIMENSION

Although we argued that the traditional definition of organizations as comprising groups of people interacting around shared goals was insufficient for our purposes, its focus on the relationships among people is helpful in that it highlights the importance of the relational dimension of organizations and of organization work. Just as an organization exists in part as a discursive object, so too does it exist as a fabric of relationships that includes connections between individuals, among members of teams, and between units within an organization, as well as externally between an organization and its partner organizations. These relationships emerge out of a complex set of processes, many of which are emergent and unintended, but many of which are also the product of intentional efforts on the part of actors to create and shape relationships.

Perhaps the most concrete manifestation of the relational dimension of organization work is the organization's formal structure that defines lines of authority and the boundaries of specialized groups. Formal organizational structure represents both a long-time concern of management and organizational research and one that has traditionally been understood as the focus of organization work. Indeed, the early roots of management and organizational research in studies of administrative and workplace efficiency strongly emphasized organization structure as the outcome of purposeful, analytical effort directed at identifying and establishing the most efficient means of achieving organizational goals (Barnard, 1968; Taylor, 1914). Interest in organizational structure as a focus of purposeful work re-emerged in the late twentieth century as new, post-bureaucratic forms of organizing became associated with organizational goals like innovation, quality, and employee well-being (Drucker, 2011; Handy, 2012).

The relational dimension of organization work also involves managing the less visible network of informal relationships that cut across more formal lines of reporting and responsibility. As Krackhardt and Hanson (1993: 104) argue, "informal networks can cut through formal reporting procedures to jump start stalled initiatives and meet extraordinary deadlines"; but they can just as easily sabotage the "best laid plans by blocking communication and fomenting opposition to change." A number of different aspects of informal relationships in organizations shape the relational dimension of organization work, including the strength of those ties and their quality.

Classic research in the sociology of work and organizations has shown the distinctive contributions provided by both strong and weak relationships, where strong relationships—characterized by multiple forms of connection and frequent interaction—can provide the trust and continuity required to be productive over extended periods of time, whereas weak relationships are more likely to offer novel information and opportunities that stem from their role in connecting people across networks. Establishing and leveraging strong and weak relationships also require, however, organization work with distinctive relational properties. Managing strong relationships demands significant investments of time and energy, as well as care in maintaining trust and goodwill. In contrast, managing and exploiting weak ties is more likely to require shorter episodes of engagement facilitated by broader networks of reciprocity and reputation.

Recent writing that focuses on the "quality" of relationships in organizations points to the significant, positive impacts that such relational dimensions of organization work can provide (Spreitzer et al., 2005). "High quality connections" are described as "life giving," operating like a "healthy blood vessel that connects parts of our body, a high-quality connection between two people allows the transfer of vital nutrients" (Dutton and Heaphy, 2003: 263). Such connections, it is argued, are associated with higher emotional carrying capacities, an ability to bend and withstand strain, and a high degree of generativity (Dutton and Heaphy, 2003: 266). Creating such connections can depend on the organization work of the people involved, who can foster them through "respectful engagement" and "task enabling," as well as by leaders who can facilitate high-quality connections by shaping organizational values, reward systems, routines, and physical spaces (Dutton, 2006).

A third facet of the relational dimension of organization work focuses on the emergent properties of the networks in which actors are involved. Social networks have important emergent properties associated with structural patterns that affect the quality and effects of individual relationships. These structural patterns include the number of ties linking an actor to others (Putnam, 2001), the number and extensiveness of structural holes in the network (Burt, 2009), and the number of broad, cross-cutting interconnections (Coleman, 2000). Network patterns such as these have been shown to affect the performance of individual members, groups, and the organization as a whole, as well as their behaviors, beliefs, and attitudes (Dobrow and Higgins, 2005; Dyer and Nobeoka, 2000; Krackhardt and Hanson, 1993; Snow et al., 1992). As a consequence, actors engage in organization work to both shape and respond to network patterns, as illustrated by the large scholarly and practical literature exploring the costs and benefits of different "networking" strategies and tactics. Inside many large organizations, professional development efforts are commonly made to increase members' skills and understanding with respect to how to shape and utilize their informal networks.

Finally, the relational dimension of organization work also extends across the organization's boundaries. In addition to the intra-organizational relationships discussed above, important interorganizational relationships exist between individuals inside and outside the organization (as with an organization's sales reps and their clients), between organizational members and external organizations (membership in a professional organization, for example), and between the organization and other organizations (such as between a bank and its regulator). The qualities of these interorganizational networks echo those described in relation to organizations' informal internal networks and have stimulated a parallel set of theoretical and practically oriented inquiries.

An important form of organization work that revolves around these interorganizational networks are brokerage strategies through which organizational actors manage and leverage their interorganizational networks. Brokers in organizational networks exploit structural holes—gaps between actors who are only connected by the broker (Burt, 2009). Although the immediate impact of network brokerage is on the flows of information and other resources between organizations, it is also an important way in which actors construct specific organizations. Effecting a brokerage strategy shapes not only the organizations to which the broker is connected, but also the boundaries, strategies, and identity of the broker.

THE MATERIAL DIMENSION

While our conceptualization of organization work has a distinctly social constructionist flavor, our intention is not to deny the inherent materiality associated with organizations as social-symbolic objects. Organizations typically occupy some sort of physical space (an office, factory, store, or service center); they are full of tools, machines, and files (even though many of those are digital in today's organizations); and the people who work in them are material both in the sense of taking up physical space and in terms of requiring rest, light, warmth, and food. All of this means that while discussions of organizations may sometimes focus on the ideal and social, there is an important material aspect to organizations and therefore an important material dimension to organization work.

Early research that recognized the importance of materiality as constitutive of organizations focused on the impact of particular technologies on how manufacturing and other processes were organized and managed (Woodward, 1958). Although this early work recognized the important role of materiality in shaping organizations, technology and organizing were conceived of as separate from each other, with technologies determining the most appropriate forms of organizing (Perrow, 1967). This assumption of separateness limited the ability of organizational scholars to appreciate the ways in which material and social dimensions of organizations are interwoven. While scholars have made considerable progress in developing insights into many aspects of organizing, "these insights are limited in large part because the field has traditionally overlooked the ways in which organizing is bound up with the material forms and spaces through which humans act and interact" (Orlikowski, 2007: 1435). In contrast, more recent writing has moved toward a conception of the material and social dimensions of organizations as inextricably tied to each other, and even mutually constitutive (Carlile et al., 2013; Leonardi et al., 2012).

Our approach to organization work follows this more recent explicit focus on the material context and consequences of constructing organizations. While a great deal of research on organization work has tended to focus on its discursive and relational dimensions, there is also an unavoidable material dimension to the work done to construct and shape organizations as social-symbolic objects. At the very least, individual actors engaged in organization work employ a wide range of tools that range from the pens and pencils (or tablets and keyboards) of office workers fashioning organizational strategies and workflows, to the screwdrivers and wrenches (or signal tracers and logic analyzers) of plant floor technologists constructing more efficient production processes. Organization work also involves materiality on much larger scales, of course. Office buildings, manufacturing plants, server farms, and a host of other large material structures are integral to contemporary organizations.

These large material forms are important in structuring activity and their physical arrangements place limits on activity, produce patterns in the movements of people, and shape their communication and interaction. They are also generative, of course, providing spaces within which things can happen and where processes of social construction and practical activity can take place.

When exploring the material dimension of organization work, an important issue concerns the plasticity of material objects. Early contingency theories of the impact of technologies emphasized their rigidity—showing how the material features of technologies directly affected organizations and organizing (Woodward, 1958). In contrast, recent writing on the social construction of science and technology has tended toward an extreme understanding of the plasticity of material objects: "At its extreme, the social constructivist position holds that technologies themselves hardly matter at all...What matters, instead, are the ways in which those technologies are used in the context of work or other social settings" (Kallinikos et al., 2012: 4). For understanding the material dimension of organization work, an intermediate position is more useful, one that recognizes the flexible ways in which material objects are used to shape organizations, but at the same time acknowledges the limits of that flexibility driven by the affordances of those material objects (Leonardi and Barley, 2008).

If we consider the role of physical spaces in organization work, for example, we begin to see the interaction between the social construction of physical spaces as organizational places, and the material limits of those spaces especially in relation to human bodies and other forms of material technology that might be installed within them (Gieryn, 2002; Marrewijk and Yanow, 2010). This interaction leads to the idea that organizational places are "doubly constructed" in the sense they are "built or in some way physically carved out" and "interpreted, narrated, perceived, felt, understood, and imagined" (Gieryn, 2000: 465).

This process of double construction plays out in complex and unexpected ways. In a study of a "wet weather mat program" for homeless people established in a network of suburban churches, for instance, Lawrence and Dover (2015) show how the geographical location, size, and layout of the churches interacted with the identities and strategies of the organizers, as well as the material and social resources of the homeless, to provoke both significant resistance and later significant commitment to the program by local community members.

A simple example of this interaction involved the movement of homeless people to the churches in the evenings, and from the churches in the mornings as the churches returned to their more typical daily uses. Because the churches used for the mat program were located in residential neighborhoods of a middle-class suburb, a considerable distance from the river valley in which most homeless people were camping, buses were used to transport clients. This was done in part to make the program more accessible, and significantly to avoid local community members encountering homeless people walking through their neighborhood.

The story of the mat program points to the importance of a specific form of materiality in organization work—the human body. The use of buses, churches, and even the need for indoor mats in wet weather, were all a function of the needs and abilities of the human body. More broadly, we see that the design of buildings, manual tools, physical and digital technologies, modes of transportation, etc. all revolve around what the human body requires, what it is able to accomplish, and what potentialities we imagine for it. Even more than other forms of materiality, the role of the human body in organization work has been relatively neglected, except in specialized fields of research, such as ergonomics, workplace safety, and the design of health-care organizations.

Even in the latter, we have seen a surprising neglect of the body in designing and building safe health facilities (Kohn et al., 2000). In the past couple of decades, the body has entered research on the efforts of actors to shape organizations through the provision of seemingly basic requirements, such as food and clothing. As Altman and Baruch (2010: 128) describe, "[m]eals drive an aspect of organizational life that embodies organizations and which is inherently relational." What people eat, when, and with whom not only tells us a lot about organizations, it also shapes those organizations in important ways, establishing foundations for trust and understanding among members, and providing occasions for communication, and celebration.

Who Does Organization Work?

There is no simple, predictable relationship between the object that is the focus of organization work and the actor who engages in that work. Although organizational leaders are important agents of organization work, so too are rank-and-file organizational members, as well as a wide range of extra-organizational actors who work to construct the organization indirectly by exerting pressures, constructing narratives, establishing regulations, and providing or withholding resources. Inside organizations, a range of roles exist that are specifically devoted to organization work, from marketers responsible for managing the organization's brand identity, to computing specialists engaged in designing and implementing the organization's information architecture, to human resource managers analyzing the organization's future workforce needs.

The prominence of specialized organization work is nicely (and somewhat surprisingly to us) illustrated by the US Bureau of Labor Statistics' 2012 prediction that industrial-organizational psychologists would be the fastest growing job category between 2012 and 2022.[5] As described on the profession's website, the role of industrial-organizational psychologists is to "understand and measure human behavior to improve employees' satisfaction in their work, employers' ability to select and promote the best people, and to generally make the workplace better for the men and women who work there" (SIOP, 2018). In other words, the fastest growing job category is one that is completely focused on organization work! In the remainder of this section, we explore who does organization work, including specialists like industrial-organizational psychologists, organizational members, extra-organizational actors, and organizational leaders.

ORGANIZATIONAL LEADERS
In 2011, Nokia was in trouble. Sales were falling, Apple was pulling ever further ahead, and Android smartphone sales had just overtaken Nokia smartphone sales. Stephen Elop, the CEO, needed to do something dramatic to create a sense of urgency around the changes he was trying to implement at Nokia. His famous "Burning platform memo" was his attempt to capture the attention and imagination of Nokia employees:

> There is a pertinent story about a man who was working on an oil platform in the North Sea. He woke up one night from a loud explosion, which suddenly set his entire oil platform on fire. In mere moments, he was surrounded by flames. Through the smoke and heat, he barely made his way out of the chaos to the platform's edge. When he looked down over the edge, all he could see were the dark, cold, foreboding Atlantic waters. As the fire approached him, the man had mere seconds to react. He could stand on the platform, and inevitably be consumed by the burning flames. Or, he could plunge 30 meters in to the freezing waters. The man was standing upon a "burning platform," and he needed to make a choice. . . . We too, are standing on a "burning platform," and we must decide how we are going to change our behaviour.
>
> (See Ziegler, 2011 for the entire memo)

Elop's memo illustrates some important characteristics of how leaders engage in organization work. First, his aim was to shape the organization's overall direction and to do so he relied on the discursive dimension of organization work by telling a story he hoped would provide a common understanding of the gravity of Nokia's situation. The discursive dimension is key to organization work by leaders, whose role and ability to shape the organization often

---

[5] <http://www.bls.gov/ooh/fastest-growing.htm>.

depends on their ability to articulate the future they seek to achieve through stories, speeches, and conversations (Fairhurst, 2008; Fleming, 2001).

A second important feature of Elop's memo was its intended audience. Elop used his position as CEO to address all of Nokia's employees simultaneously, a capacity few other actors enjoy. Moreover, his leadership position provided him with distinctive legitimacy in declaring an organizational emergency. As CEO, his relationship to organizational members and to external stakeholders was clear and direct. Thus, there is also an important relational dimension to a leader's organization work illustrated by Elop's memo. The relational dimension of organization work by leaders extends beyond this broadcast mode of engagement: in many organizations, authority is diffused in ways that demand collective efforts on the part of organizational leaders to engage in organization work (Denis et al., 2001).

The importance of the discursive and relational dimensions of leaders' organization work is not exclusive to Elop or even CEOs. Leaders at all levels are distinctive in their need to work through others to shape organizations— they "do" by getting others to "do"—and thus are reliant on the discursive dimension of organization work to communicate, motivate, and persuade others to effect the changes they seek (Bartunek, 1984). Similarly, this need to engage in organization work indirectly through others elevates the importance of the relational dimension of organization work. Organizational leaders rely on colleagues and direct reports, as well as networks of formal and informal relationships, to understand the organization and its environment, and shape its responses to threats and opportunities.

ORGANIZATIONAL MEMBERS

It is not, of course, just leaders that engage in organization work. Rank-and-file organizational members represent important agents of organization work both in terms of the formal tasks associated with their positions and as a result of their more idiosyncratic responses to problems they confront in their everyday organizational lives. And, while leaders often do discursive organization work with the potential for broad impacts, it is work combining all three dimensions—discursive, relational, and material—done by members of the organization far down the hierarchy that determines much of the actual fabric of organizations.

Some of this work is done by organizational members as a formal aspect of their jobs, as illustrated by Lounsbury's (2001) study of the introduction of recycling programs into universities. The universities in his study established formal, mandated recycling in two different ways: through the creation of a new, dedicated positions responsible for implementing the recycling programs; or through the addition of this responsibility to the activities of an existing person or persons. The difference mattered, as organizational members in new dedicated positions did much more organization work, including making alliances with student organizations within their own university, as well as people in similar positions at other universities, and creating programs to educate people on the importance of recycling.

In contrast, those for whom recycling was simply added to their existing roles, "conceptualized recycling much more narrowly as the collection of potential recyclables and rarely worked with student groups or spent time on educating people to 'reduce, reuse and recycle'" (Lounsbury, 2001: 34). While the formal job descriptions and goals of the two different forms of recycling manager were similar, the forms of work in which they engaged differed due to the motivations and interests of the two different groups of managers. The differences observed in this study highlight the ways that organization work interacts with self work: the construction of organizational roles significantly shaped how the occupants of those roles understood their own motivations and careers.

The same domain—organizational recycling—provides an interesting illustration of an organizational member doing organization work that was much more informal, yet had a profound impact on an organization, and eventually an industry. In 1989, Jacki Graham, an American Airlines flight attendant in San Jose, California, was frustrated by the lack of recycling by her employer and began an informal program to collect aluminum soft drink cans on her flights (Laabs, 1992). Her efforts were quickly noticed by other flight attendants who began to do the same thing on other routes. Soon, this local activity gained the attention and support of the airline's senior management, which led to adoption of the new practice across the company and the development of new systems, processes, and policies around recycling. By 1992, the airline had recycled over 200,000 pounds of aluminum and their activities had gained the attention of the media and environmental groups, putting pressure on other airlines to do something similar.

The informal organization work done by Jacki Graham to create a system to collect aluminum cans on her flights led to organization work by other flight attendants, the management of her airline, and eventually to other airlines, leading to a change in practices across an industry. This example highlights not only the importance of organization work by rank-and-file members, its relationship to the organization work of leaders, and the resources and contexts associated with each. The initial organization work done by Jacki Graham was triggered by her immediate connection to the problem and enabled by her influence over material conditions and relationships local to the planes on which she was flying. The American Airlines executives who rolled out the company-wide recycling program were able to leverage the initial organization work, which created on-board recycling as a meaningful practice, and use their access to broader, but more distal, resources to engage in organization work on a bigger scale.

EXTERNAL ACTORS

Despite the long-standing interest in the activities and impact of external actors on organizations in management and organizational research, the roles that external actors play in organization work has been largely overlooked. External actors are the focus of numerous streams within management and organizational research, including competitive strategy, stakeholder theory, contingency theory, resource dependence theory, and population ecology. All of these approaches to understanding organizations emphasize the important effects of external actors on the structure and behavior of organizations.

If we take stakeholder theory as an example, a prominent argument suggests that the "salience" of external actors determines the degree to which they are likely to influence organizations. Salience is understood as "the degree to which managers give priority to competing stakeholder claims" and is based on three attributes of the organization–stakeholder relationship: urgency, legitimacy, and power (Mitchell et al., 1997: 854). Organizational managers, it is argued, are most responsive to stakeholders whose claims are interpreted as most urgent, have the greatest legitimacy, and control critical resources that give them the most power. It is to these stakeholder demands that organizational actors will respond. Thus, from this perspective, external actors shape organizations, but they do so indirectly through their ability to influence the actions of organizational managers. This approach is echoed in a range of management and organizational research in which external actors are conceptualized as "forces" or "factors."

From a social-symbolic work perspective, external actors are capable of taking much more direct action in relation to the construction of organizations as social-symbolic objects. Staying with stakeholder theory, adopting a social-symbolic work perspective to the issues it raises would shift the focus from understanding salience as a factor that influences organizational managers, to one in which salience becomes a potential measure of the degree to which the social-symbolic work of a stakeholder is likely to successfully affect the organization. Thus, from a social-symbolic work perspective, salience acts as a resource that can support the organization work of external actors who are trying to shape an organization with which they have some kind of relationship. Moreover, salience from a social-symbolic work perspective becomes itself a potential focus of social-symbolic work: the salience of a relationship is socially constructed, valuable, and contested, and thus the target of external actors who might work to increase the salience of their relationship to an organization, as well as work to diminish the salience of other external actors.

Adopting a social-symbolic work perspective on the relationship of organizations to external actors thus shifts the focus and reveals new potential insights associated with exploring the role of these actors in organization work. While the social construction of organizations has become widely accepted, the role of external stakeholders is generally framed as "influencing" and the work they are doing and the role they are playing in the construction of organizations is not explored. This seems, to us, to be an important and interesting potential area of research as we seek to understand organization work and organizations as social-symbolic objects.

If we start to look at the specific sets of external actors involved in organization work, perhaps the most visible are activist interest groups and social movements. For large, highly visible organizations, these groups can be important actors as they seek to shape policy and practices in a particular organization (for example, to stop large oil companies drilling for oil in the Arctic). The organization work done by these external stakeholders is often highly discursive but can also involve important relational (e.g., lobbying) or material (e.g., boycotts) dimensions.

But in addition to the more diffuse external stakeholders who seek to influence the firm, there is a set of external actors with a more direct role. A critically important set of actors for some firms are shareholders who perform distinctive forms of work through corporate governance mechanisms. Consultants are also often key external actors who perform highly influential forms of organization work. The National Health Service (NHS) in the UK spent almost US$1billion on external consultants and advisors in 2014, whose sole purpose was to carry out organization work. Finally, industry associations and professional associations are also important actors whose role has often been overlooked in the organization theory literature (see Box 5.2).

Governments are also key actors. Through a number of mechanisms, they play a central role in shaping organizations of all types. Their ability to pass legislation, create regulators, and provide and withdraw resources, makes them one of the central actors for all modern organizations. In fact, the necessity of a legal existence for modern organizations makes government a uniquely important external actor with the authority to bring organizations into existence as well as make them disappear.

SUMMARY: A CONCEPTUALIZATION OF ORGANIZATION WORK
In this section, we developed the concept of organization work as a form of social-symbolic work. Like other forms of social-symbolic work, organization work comprises discursive, relational, and material dimensions. Each of these dimensions highlights distinctive qualities of organizations as social-symbolic objects, as well as specific sets of resources and skills employed by actors engaged in organization work. Key to our argument is that these dimensions are present in all instances of organization work, even if not always equally apparent or important (for an illustration of research that shows the integration of discursive, material, and relational dimensions, see Smith and

---

Box 5.2. INDUSTRY ASSOCIATIONS

The Obama administration's $900 billion healthcare reform bill was forged against a backdrop of intense political and societal debate and acrimonious ideological differences. During this process, the input of industry associations such as the Pharmaceutical Research and Manufacturers of America (PhRMA) was discreet but highly influential. Aware of the legislation's long-term implications for the industry, PhRMA played a crucial role on behalf of its member companies by engaging with the government on the bill's design and implementation and ensuring the interests of its members were represented during the proceedings.

But the role of PhRMA went far beyond simply informing public policy. In fact, PhRMA worked strategically to ensure maximum impact on the legislative process. Memos released in 2012 by the US House of Representatives Energy and Commerce Committee revealed that the Obama administration coordinated a $150 million advertising campaign, funded by PhRMA and its members, in support of the 2010 Affordable Care Act. An investigation launched by a Subcommittee on Oversight and Investigations confirmed that PhRMA was so influential that the Obama White House felt compelled to "cut a deal" with PhRMA to promote and ultimately pass the controversial healthcare bill.

Trade associations like PhRMA play an increasingly important role in the policy-making process in many countries. They range in size and nature from the niche Fine Chocolate Industry Association with annual corporate membership fees of $350, to the US Aerospace Industries Association with 158 full and 219 associate members paying annual membership dues ranging from $3,000 to $400,000 depending on total sales. Despite their differences, they are united in their efforts to influence regulation and government policy, and sometimes public opinion, on behalf of the collective needs and objectives of their members.

In addition to this visible external role, they also serve as agents for disseminating and exchanging information within a given industry and often act as informal regulators of industry activity where they set voluntary standards of behavior for industry members. As such, they are influential organizations within their industries and in society more broadly who are deeply involved in many forms of consequential organization work, and they therefore deserve sustained attention from anyone interested in the inner workings of industries and in the influence of companies on government.

Besharov's (2017) study of the organization work involved in maintaining structured flexibility in a hybrid organization). We also explored three key categories of actors engaged in organization work—organizational leaders, organizational members, and external actors—all of whom bring distinctive resources to organization work, and are thus able to shape the organization as a social-symbolic object in different ways.

Conclusion

Our aims in this chapter have been to introduce the idea of organization work, provide a historical understanding of its possibility and how that possibility has changed with the advent of modernity and postmodernity, and develop a conceptualization of organization work as involving discursive, material, and relational dimensions.

The concept of organization work is based on a conceptualization of organizations—as social-symbolic objects—that is, distinctive from dominant understandings that emphasize their status as social aggregates, rather than as multidimensional objects. We have argued that organizations are modern phenomena, not only because of the need to organize industrial work processes and large-scale state enterprises that emerged in the seventeenth and eighteenth centuries, but also because of the broad changes in Western beliefs about rationality, change, and perfectibility that brought with them the possibility of bureaucracy as an ideal organizational form. Similarly, postmodern organizations emerged from both the revolutionary changes stemming from digital technologies, and the cultural shifts following World War II that led to widespread questioning of grand narratives and uniform rationality. Thus, our understanding of organizations as social-symbolic objects includes their functional existence as goal-driven social aggregates, which emphasizes their relational dimension, but incorporates a broader conception of organizations that includes discursive and material dimensions.

Our conceptualization of organization work similarly incorporates discursive, relational, and material dimensions. As with other forms of social-symbolic work, we argue that all instances of organization work involve all three dimensions, though not necessarily with equal obviousness or importance. The discursive dimension of organization work is tied to the role of discourse in constituting organizations and in the experience of everyday organizational life. Stories, lists, rules, speeches, conversations, instructions, jokes, arguments, announcements—these are the stuff of organizational life for many people. This has become even more the case as the predominant forms of employment have shifted from manufacturing to services, where discourse may be the only obvious form of connection among employees or between employees and other stakeholders. At the same time, organizations and thus organization work is inherently relational. Organizations do not exist only as ideas that can be conveyed through talk and text; they also exist as sets of people in relationship with one another, individually and collectively, and so to work on organizations is to work on relationships. Finally, organizations are inextricably material and so is organization work. At a minimum, the materiality of organizations is tied to the human bodies involved and to the material forms necessarily taken by text and talk. But, for nearly all organizations, materiality goes well beyond these rudimentary forms to include built environments, physical tools, and concrete outputs in some form.

Key Resources

Organizations as Social-Symbolic Objects

All social-symbolic work revolves around particular social-symbolic objects, in this case organizations, which emerged as widely recognized social-symbolic objects in modernity and then transformed again in postmodernity. Thus, to guide further inquiry into organization work, we start with a set of resources that tap into these fundamental shifts and the organizations that emerged alongside them.

Modern Organizations

Stewart Clegg provides a useful guide to modern organizations, particularly in Chapter 2 of his book, appropriately titled, *Modern organizations*. In this chapter, he lays out a concise introduction to the standard argument regarding the relationship between modernity and organizations. This summary is useful for its insights both into this relationship and the limits of this relationship, which are explored in the remainder of Clegg's book. To understand the archetypal modern organization, we suggest Meyer's *The Five Dollar Day*, which explores the technological and social structuring of the early years of the Ford Motor Company. This study presents a fascinating account of the integration of material, discursive, and relational dimensions of the company, done in explicit and visible ways. Finally, as a visual complement to these texts, we suggest Charlie Chaplin's film *Modern Times*, a humorous but poignant account of life as an employee in the modern organization.

Chaplin, C. 1936. *Modern Times*. <http://www.imdb.com/title/tt0027977/>.

Clegg, S. R. 1990. *Modern organizations: Organization studies in the postmodern world.* Ch. 2. London: SAGE.

Meyer, S. 1981. *The Five Dollar Day: Labor management and social control in the Ford Motor Company, 1908–1921*. Albany, NY: State University of New York Press.

Postmodern Organizations

Postmodern organizations are by their nature diverse, and so our aim in this section is not to cover all of the territory they occupy. Instead, we provide some interesting and informative examples that might spark further investigation. The employee handbook from Valve (*Valve: Handbook for new employees*) opens the door to one of the organizations that has come to exemplify postmodernity. Chen's study of *The organization behind the Burning Man event* offers an intriguing account of an organization that tightly couples premodern, modern, and postmodern elements to achieve the extraordinary annual event in the Nevada desert. Finally, Scott's sci-fi masterpiece *Blade Runner* continues to provide a compelling and disturbing image of a postmodern society where capitalism has destroyed the environment, the privileged are moving off-planet, and what it means to be human has become increasingly unclear as androids become indistinguishable from humans. and Chen, K. K. 2009. *Enabling creative chaos: The organization behind the Burning Man event*. Chicago, IL: University of Chicago Press.

Scott, R. 1982. *Blade Runner.* <http://www.imdb.com/title/tt0083658/>.

Valve Software. 2012. *Valve: Handbook for new employees.* Bellevue, WA: Valve Corporation. <https://assets.sbnation.com/assets/1074301/Valve_Handbook_LowRes.pdf>.

Organization Work

In order to guide further explorations of organization work, we suggest a set of academic articles and books that revolve around its discursive, relational, and material dimensions. Although we suggest that all instances of organization work involve all three dimensions, writing to date has tended to concentrate on a single dimension. For a look into the discursive dimension of organization work, Boje's "The storytelling organization" describes how people tell stories in a large office-supply firm, and shows how those stories are implicated in sensemaking, change-making, and politicking. Moreover, the stories don't live up to what had been a traditional image of stories as the complete narratives of individuals, but instead were fluid, partial, and co-constructed. To access the relational dimension of organization work, we suggest Kreiner and colleagues' study of "Balancing borders and bridges." In this study, they explore how people construct the boundary between their home life and their work organizations, drawing significantly on relational strategies to do so. Finally, we recommend a book and an article as ways to continue exploring the material dimension of organization work. Leonardi et al. provide a sophisticated and engaging examination of *Materiality and organizing* that will take the reader a long way in understanding this complex relationship. For an easier way into this dimension, Altman and Baruch explore "The organizational lunch."

Altman, Y., and Baruch, Y. 2010. The organizational lunch. *Culture and Organization*, 16(2): 127–43.

Boje, D. M. 1991. The storytelling organization: A study of story performance in an office- supply firm. *Administrative Science Quarterly*, 36(1): 106–26.

Kreiner, G. E., Hollensbe, E. C., and Sheep, M. L. 2009. Balancing borders and bridges: Negotiating the work–home interface via boundary work tactics. *Academy of Management Journal*, 52(4): 704–30.

Leonardi, P. M., Nardi, B. A., and Kallinikos, J. 2012. *Materiality and organizing: Social interaction in a technological world.* Oxford: Oxford University Press.

6

Organization Work in Management and Organizational Research

In this chapter we:

1. Review the study of strategy work in management and organizational research and explore how conceptualizing strategy work as a type of organization work can assist researchers in further developing this established literature.

2. Review the study of boundary work across areas of social science and explore how conceptualizing boundary work as a type of organization work can help organize and extend this diverse literature.

3. Review the emerging stream of literature on technology work and explore how conceptualizing technology work as a type of organization work can help to shape and direct research in this area.

Introduction

The question of how the concept of organization work connects to the existing literature in management and organizational research is a complex one. While, at one level, the whole field is focused on understanding the work of creating and running organizations, research that focuses on organizations from a perspective compatible with the ideas we have developed here represents a narrower, more specific set of discussions. Several streams of research have, however, emerged in management and organizational research that are based on a view of organizations compatible with a social-symbolic work perspective and that focus on activity that fits with our definition of organization work. In this chapter, we discuss three types of organization work that have been the subject of significant scholarly investigation and that illustrate the potential value of an organization work perspective: strategy work, boundary work, and technology work.

Each of these three literatures represents an area that has significantly advanced our understanding of organizational life beyond what was possible prior to its development. Although the concept of strategy is used widely across a range of disciplines, from military studies and political science, to sociology and psychology, it is in management and organizational research that strategy work has become systematically examined as a focus of scholarly inquiry (Vaara and Whittington, 2012). In contrast, the study of boundary work represents an active focus of management and organizational research, but is also prominent in a range of social sciences including sociology, accounting, environmental studies, and education (Åkerström, 2002; Eden et al., 2006; Gieryn, 1983; Hoppe, 2010). In contrast to both, the study of technology has a long tradition in management and organizational research, but the study of technology work is relatively nascent within management and organizational research, whereas it has emerged as an independent sub-field of sociology, known as the social studies of science and technology (Bijker et al., 2012a; Hackett et al., 2008). Thus, the location of these research domains relative to management and organizational research presents different sets of opportunities for integration into the study of organization work.

Strategy Work

Strategy work focuses on a specific social-symbolic object, the existence and shape of which, like many of the social-symbolic objects we examine here, is tied to the transitions to modernity and postmodernity. Strategy emerged as a word in the English language in the seventeenth century, originally referring to a plan developed by an army or government, and then in the nineteenth century came to describe "the art or practice of planning the future direction or outcome of something" (OED, 2016). It has only been since the middle of the twentieth century, though, that strategy has been associated with business organizations (Bracker, 1980), first describing a series of actions embedded in an economic game (von Neumann and Morgenstern, 1944) and later as the analysis of and response to a firm's competitive situation (Drucker, 1954). These descriptions position strategy as a distinctly modern social-symbolic object, imbued with the same concerns for rationality and perfectibility that characterized the modern organization more generally. Strategy work, in turn, refers to the purposeful, reflexive efforts of actors to shape an organization's strategy, including such elements as defining an overarching direction for the organization, articulating key resources, mapping the competitive landscape, and creating a narrative that communicates the organization's strategy to members and external stakeholders.

Strategy Work in Management and Organizational Research

Although research on strategy emerged alongside the idea of organizational strategy in the mid-twentieth century, and flourished since the 1980s with the establishment of the *Strategic Management Journal* and the Strategic Management Society, it is only since the mid-1990s that strategy work has been become a focus of scholarly inquiry (Whittington, 1996). While early strategy research adopted either a structural lens, focusing on industry and organizational structures (Miles and Snow, 1978; Porter, 1980), or a process view (Pettigrew, 1992; Van de Ven, 1992), research on strategy work adopted a practice approach (as evident in its self-styled label, "strategy as practice") and focused on understanding the people and practices that make strategy happen in organizations (Jarzabkowski, 2005). The possibility of strategy work as an academic concern was prefigured by writing in the early 1990s that drew on poststructuralism to problematize the concept of strategy, particularly highlighting its historical ties to specifically US corporate history (Knights and Morgan, 1990, 1991). Research on strategy work maintained this social constructionist epistemology, but shifted its focus away from strategy as a societal discourse to strategy as a social-symbolic object in organizational life.

Research on strategy work fits neatly into our conception of social-symbolic work in its focus on organizational strategies as social-symbolic objects and the work of organizational actors to develop and put them into practice. This includes the actors involved, the practices in which they engage, the frameworks and ideas they draw on, the physical objects and technological systems they use, and discursive and material means through which strategy is shared among organizational members and stakeholders (Burgelman et al., 2018; Vaara and Whittington, 2012).

Strategy work involves a variety of activities and a diversity of actors: strategy work activities can involve "board meetings, management retreats, consulting interventions, team briefings, presentations, projects, and simple talk"; it includes "the routine and the nonroutine, the formal and the informal, activities at the corporate centre and activities at the organizational periphery" (Whittington, 2006: 619). The growing community of strategy-as-practice researchers explore "who does it, how do they do it, what they use, and what implications this has for shaping strategy" (Jarzabkowski and Spee, 2009: 69). Instead of considering strategy as a finished product or an objective description of an organization's competitive position, this perspective focuses on the complex, ongoing forms of work through which strategies are constructed that were previously overlooked in the strategy literature.

The literature on strategy work has evolved rapidly as the emphasis in this stream of work has shifted from broad overviews and conceptual discussions to detailed empirical research identifying and explaining the dynamics of how strategy work is accomplished (Vaara and Whittington, 2012). The first articles and book chapters on strategy work echo the early writing on other forms of social-symbolic work that focused on establishing theoretical roots, conceptual definitions, and empirical illustrations (Jarzabkowski, Balogun, and Seidl, 2007; Johnson, Melin, and Whittington, 2003). And like several of the streams of research that emerged around other forms of social-symbolic work, conceptualizations of strategy work rested heavily on the practice theory of such authors as Giddens (1984), Bourdieu (1977, 1980), and de Certeau (2011). An important conceptual move in this early literature was focusing attention on "the practical competence of the manager as strategist," including not only the ideational aspects of strategy—"the getting of ideas, the spotting of opportunities, the grasping of situations"—but also the "perspiration—the routines of budgeting and planning as they unwind over the year, the sitting in expenditure and strategy committees, the writing of formal documents, the making of presentations" (Whittington, 1996: 732).

As the study of strategy work has evolved, its focus has broadened from the activities and actors associated with strategy work to include the tools and artifacts used in it. Research on the materiality of strategy work recognizes that understanding such work is not just about what people do, but also about the tools they use in creating strategies. Strategy tools include a wide array of objects, from PowerPoint and social media (Kaplan, 2010; Whittington, 2015) to Lego blocks and furniture (Jarzabkowski et al., 2015; Roos et al., 2004) to conceptual tools such as SWOT and rational decision-making frameworks (Cabantous et al., 2010; Jarratt and Stiles, 2010). These "technologies of rationality" (March, 2006) offer "models of causal structures, provide spaces for collecting data, and establish decision rules for selecting among alternatives" (Jarzabkowski and Kaplan, 2014: 538).

The development of research on strategy work has also seen the emergence of research interests that echo those associated with research on self work, particularly with respect to its discursive dimensions. Following research on other forms of social-symbolic work (e.g., identity work and emotion work), studies of strategy work have conceived of strategy as tightly tied to what people say and think in organizations, and thus explored a variety of forms of discourse, including narrative and conversation (Fenton and Langley, 2011; Maitlis and Lawrence, 2003), as well as people's sensemaking and emotions (Liu and Maitlis, 2014; Rouleau, 2005). The importance of these kinds of strategy work stem from their connection to the broader understanding of organizations as social-symbolic objects constituted, to a large degree, in the talk and text of organizational members and stakeholders.

Studying Strategy Work as Organization Work

As we did with the forms of self work considered in Chapter 4, we will now explore how the study of strategy work might be advanced by embedding it in the broader framework of organization work. From our perspective, strategy work represents a particularly important type of organization work given its focus on an important social-symbolic object around which frequent organizational struggles occur. By defining what the organization does, what it doesn't do, and what it is good at and why, strategy work plays a key role in defining what the organization is and what makes it special, as well as who benefits from and who is excluded by those definitions. We again proceed from the process model of social-symbolic work introduced in Chapter 2 (reproduced in simplified form in Figure 6.1).

MOTIVATIONS FOR STRATEGY WORK

Our model of social-symbolic work begins with the motivations that drive actors to perform work. Within strategy work research, this question is primarily explored in terms of the roles and identities of strategy practitioners. Explicitly sociological, the strategy-as-practice perspective takes the position that, "practitioners are never simple individuals: they are social beings, whose socio-political and rhetorical skills and even national culture and gender, all make a difference to how they work" (Vaara and Whittington, 2012: 304).

From this perspective, motivations are a question of where actors are located in networks of relationships, activities, and discursive formations. The social-symbolic work perspective shares this interest in understanding motivations as socially situated phenomena, not products of isolated individual cognition and emotion. Moreover, motivations may be the idiosyncratic products of the

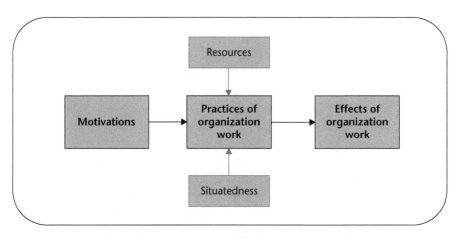

Figure 6.1. A process model of organization work

specific discursive, relational, and material locations occupied by individuals. While it is useful to think of "professionals," "middle managers," or "senior executives" as informative categories with respect to interests and motivations, it may be necessary to go beyond these kinds of descriptions in order to understand why people engage in strategy work.

Despite the potentially complex motivations suggested by strategy work scholars, research in this domain has tended to explore motivations in relatively simple terms, based primarily on the organizational and occupational locations of actors. Motivations are primarily interpreted in terms of interests and roles, rather than more complex configurations of discourses and subjectivities (e.g., Fauré and Rouleau, 2011; Jarzabkowski and Balogun, 2009; Kaplan, 2008). This research has continued the tendency in studies of strategy process of tying strategy work to formal responsibilities, though expanded beyond the traditional focus on "top management teams" (Nag et al., 2007).

Strategy work research has, for instance, paid significant attention to the role of middle managers in shaping strategy (Balogun and Johnson, 2004; Huy, 2011; Rouleau, 2005), as well as that of board members, strategy specialists within organizations, and strategy consultants (Hendry et al., 2010; Kornberger and Clegg, 2011; Maitlis, 2004), all of whom have been relatively neglected in traditional strategy research (Vaara and Whittington, 2012). Although strategy work research has expanded the range of actors considered, conceptions of their motivations for engaging in strategy work have remained somewhat narrow, confined primarily to structural and interest-driven political conceptions of why actors might expend effort to shape organizational strategies.

An interesting contribution that significantly broadens our understanding of why actors engage in strategy work comes from a study of "strategy consumption" which describes how managers use organizational strategy in creative ways (Suominen and Mantere, 2010). Drawing on an ethnography of strategy work in three organizations, Suominen and Mantere (2010) identify three sets of consumption tactics. The "instrumental" use of strategy, they argue, is rooted in managers' personal goals and purposes, to justify their decisions, establish the legitimacy of their actions, or solve a practical problem by labeling it "strategic." In contrast, the "playful" use of strategy takes it "more creatively and less seriously," ridiculing strategy through irony or jokes, often as a means of subverting or resisting strategy as a top-down control mechanism (Suominen and Mantere, 2010: 235). Finally, the "intimate" use of strategy involves managers using strategy to define their own identities, perhaps as "fearless and brave agents" as in one of the organizations, or as devoted company agents at another (Suominen and Mantere, 2010: 236). Together, these consumption tactics suggest a wide range of motivations for engaging in strategy work, from trying to "get things done," to simply amusing

153

oneself and others, to constructing one's identity. Just as importantly, they suggest the need to imagine a much wider set of potential motivations than has been explored in either the traditional strategy process literature or in strategy work research.

Finally, in the traditional strategy literature, the focus has been on the relationship between strategy and firm performance, a focus that rests on the assumption that companies need strategies and so managers produce them. The motivation is therefore a simple organizational one: senior managers are motivated to develop strategies to drive firm performance. While strategy work research has focused on how people in organizations actually make strategies, it has retained this implicit functional understanding of why actors do strategy work in the first place. But, this conception of the relationship between strategy work and its motivations ignores the vast amount of organizational behavior and social-psychological research that has systematically examined what motivates behavior in organizations. Thus, the centrality of actors in strategy work points to the potential for strategy work research to benefit from a stronger and more creative connection to existing theories of motivation and decision making in the organizational behavior literature and in social psychology. The actors doing strategy work are people, and their motivations are complex and deserve much more study from an organizational behavior point of view.

PRACTICES OF STRATEGY WORK

Practices are a core issue in understanding any form of social-symbolic work, and have been at the center of research on strategy work, as suggested by the term, "strategy as practice." From the outset, strategy work scholars have been focused on practices and adopting "practice theory" (e.g., de Certeau, 2011; Giddens, 1984) as their main orienting theoretical framework. As Vaara and Whittington (2012: 286) explain, a key insight of strategy-as-practice research "has been that strategy work ('strategizing') relies on organizational and other practices that significantly affect both the process and the outcome of resulting strategies."

Conceiving of strategy work as a form of organization work, however, suggests that the approach to practices typical of this tradition may have limited its ability to fully appreciate the embeddedness of strategy work in broader networks of practices, objects, and relationships, and thus to understand its role in constructing organizations and organizational life. Research on strategy work has, perhaps necessarily, established boundaries around its domain of interest; in order to create a meaningful, identifiable area of inquiry, strategy of practice scholars have restricted themselves to organizational events, processes, and practices that seem "strategic," either by virtue of their connection to organization-level strategic decisions and positions, or by virtue of their overarching importance to the firm, as in practice studies of strategic change. While this boundary has allowed the area to maintain a coherence to its scholarship and its community, it has also neglected the important interactions among different kinds of practices that are involved in organization work.

For strategy work research, this represents an important, missed opportunity, the contours of which emerge when we consider the expanded set of actors that have been identified as involved in strategy work. The importance of middle managers, for instance, has been made clear by the detailed strategy-as-practice research examining their strategic roles and activities. Missing in that discussion, however, has been the interplay of middle managers' strategy work and the myriad other forms of organization work in which they engage. An important but overlooked question, for instance, involves how their strategy work complements or competes with their work shaping the selves around them, including the emotions, identities, and careers of their direct reports. Similarly, the practices through which they manage all kinds of change may have critically important connections to their roles in strategic change. An organization work perspective thus connects the practices of strategy work to questions of day-to-day management and the many varieties of organizational work. By viewing strategy work as a kind of organization work, these connections become clear, and the ways in which strategy work contributes to, coexists with, and sits in tension to the other ways that actors shape organizations is highlighted.

EFFECTS OF STRATEGY WORK
Shifting now to the effects of strategy work, we come to an issue that has been more seriously considered in the traditional strategy literature than in more recent research on strategy work. This question of effects has been a defining interest of the traditional strategy literature, in which the focus has been on linking strategy to corporate success measured as sustainable profitability. According to Kenichi Ohmae (1982: 36), "the sole purpose of strategic planning is to enable the company to gain, as efficiently as possible, a sustainable edge over its competitors." In a similar vein, financial performance and the extraction of economic rents have been central to the scholarly strategic management conversation (Mahoney and Pandian, 1992). In stark contrast, when research on strategy work has not completely ignored its effects, it has tended to focus on either its broader social effects (Knights and Morgan, 1990, 1991) or its effects on organizational members.

Adopting a view of strategy work as organization work highlights the missing connection between the traditional strategy literature that focuses on financial performance and the strategy work literature, with its more focused studies of micro consequences and broader social ramifications.

These literatures remain strangely separate, despite the obvious connection between the practices of strategy making and the effectiveness of strategies once developed and implemented in companies.

Conceiving of strategy work as organization work may help explain why these two literatures are not more closely connected. An organization work perspective highlights the considerable distance between strategy work and its effects, and the importance of other forms of organization work in explaining how strategy work affects financial performance and other traditional measures of the impact of strategy. Put simply, it is difficult to observe the effect of an instance of strategy work on firm performance, especially when considered in isolation from other forms of organization work—technology work, boundary work, organizational identity work, etc. Instances of strategy work by themselves are unlikely to achieve much, but may be highly influential when put together with other types of organization work. It is these connections and their combined effects on organizational performance that become apparent when one shifts focus from strategy work to organization work.

RESOURCES OF STRATEGY WORK

The study of resources in relation to strategy work has extended theorizing in ways that echo our conception of organization work as involving discursive, relational, and material dimensions: attention to discursive resources began with early strategy work research that explored the important role of narrative and rhetoric in shaping organizational strategies (Barry and Elmes, 1997; Fenton and Langley, 2011; Hendry, 2000; Ruebottom, 2013; Samra-Fredericks, 2005); some limited but important research has begun to look at how relationships inside organizations shape strategy work (Hendry et al., 2010; Huy, 2011; Liu and Maitlis, 2014); and, recently, there has emerged a significant interest in how material resources are used in and shape strategy work, echoing the broader interest in materiality that has infused research on social-symbolic work and highlighting the roles of commonplace physical objects found in workplaces, as well as more specialized technologies and materials imported into strategy work, such as Lego blocks (Jarzabkowski et al., 2015; Roos et al., 2004).

While all of this attention to the resources used in strategy work is useful and important, it has tended to focus on resources as contributors to rather than constitutive of organizational strategy. In our exploration of the discursive, relational, and material dimensions of organization work, we found that taking these seriously as dimensions of organization work opened up the possibility that these dimensions, and the practices and resources tied to them, reveal a complex ontology of social-symbolic objects as discursive, relational, and material patterns. Pushing the study of resources in strategy work in this direction, we argue, may provide significant insight into how strategy work occurs in organizations, and especially how it plays a role in constituting organizations.

SITUATEDNESS OF STRATEGY WORK

The interest in the day-to-day activities that make up strategy work have made scholars in the area sensitive to the situations in which it occurs. As is common in studies of social-symbolic work, strategy work scholars are energized by locations, events, and circumstances that trigger and shape actors' efforts to build and shape strategy. Scholars have chronicled strategy work in such situations as "away days" (Bourque and Johnson, 2008), board meetings (Hendry et al., 2010), public events (Kornberger and Clegg, 2011), executive meetings (Liu and Maitlis, 2014), and strategy presentations (Kaplan, 2010), each of which has been shown to have its own dynamics and influence strategy work in specific ways.

This research explores the effects of the location and resources, but also who is present, the relationships and history of the participants, and the social status they have relative to each other. While perhaps trivial from the perspective of traditional strategy research, anyone who has been involved in a strategic planning exercise can attest to the critical importance of social and physical micro situatedness in the effects of strategy work. As in the case of resources, however, strategy work research has tended to treat these situations as relatively isolated from each other, rather than exploring how arrays of situations are linked together through forms of organization work that give them broader meaning and significance. Developing an integrated understanding of strategy work across situations thus represents an important opportunity, especially if it incorporates an inclusive conception of organization work and links those dynamics to performance effects.

SUMMING UP

Looking across the literature on strategy work, we believe there is significant value in embedding it more broadly in conversations about organization work and social-symbolic work. The identification of strategy work as a distinctive activity in organizations was an important conceptual move for early research in this domain; in proposing a new concept, scholars are obliged to demonstrate its meaning and its distinctiveness from existing concepts. Thus, the emphasis on showing that the concept of strategy work described a significant part of organizational life, and that it was different from other kinds of work, was understandable and echoed the intellectual history of other forms of social-symbolic work such as emotion work and identity work. At this point in its development, however, we believe it is time to reconnect strategy work with its older sibling—managerial work (Mintzberg, 1973)—and explore their relationship in detail. Moreover, looking at both as kinds of organization work has the potential to reveal unexpected connections and influences that are important for understanding strategy work.

Boundary Work

Unlike many of the social-symbolic objects we have discussed that emerged with modernity, social boundaries as social-symbolic objects have a long history, and long traditions of study in anthropology, sociology, and political science. In general terms, social boundaries describe "objectified forms of social differences manifested in unequal access to and unequal distribution of resources (material and nonmaterial) and social opportunities," which are "revealed in stable behavioral patterns of association" (Lamont and Molnár, 2002: 168). More simply, a social boundary represents the limits of a social group.[1]

Although social boundaries have been around as long as humanity, the kinds of boundaries and the bases for these boundaries changed with the advent of modernity and the transition to postmodernity. Premodern social boundaries rested on the same foundations as the rest of social life: kinship, religion, nature, and tradition provided the bases of the most important social groups until the Renaissance, when the rise of the nation state and the industrial revolution furnished new boundaries that were more clearly understood to be the outcomes of human activity. Postmodernity challenged modern social boundaries, throwing questions of essentialism and purity into question as ways of delineating who is in and who is out of any social group. Postmodern critiques of social boundaries have highlighted their arbitrary politics, not by throwing out the idea of a boundary altogether, but by allowing a far greater range of bases for constructing and shaping those boundaries.

Boundary work thus describes the purposeful, reflexive efforts of individuals, collective actors, and networks of actors to shape a social boundary. Given the array of boundaries that exist in the social world, and the importance to actors of where they are located, it is not surprising that there is a large and varied literature on boundary work spanning sociology, psychology, and political science. The concept of boundary work is also appearing with increasing regularity in more applied areas, such as education and environmental science, where the concept is used to develop insights into

---

[1] Although the term "boundary" is also used to describe "symbolic" boundaries, which describe "conceptual distinctions made by social actors to categorize objects, people, practices, and even time and space" (Lamont and Molnár, 2002: 168), we restrict our discussion here to social boundaries, leaving a discussion of symbolic boundaries to Chapter 4 where we explore them in the context of "category work," a form of institutional work.

important questions about the role of boundaries and boundary work in phenomena like efforts to apply science and technology to sustainability where researchers find that these efforts are more likely to be "effective when [actors] manage boundaries between knowledge and action" (Cash et al., 2003: 8086).

While there is an extensive literature on boundary work, our focus is on boundary work as a type of organization work—work performed by actors to change or maintain a boundary in or around an organization. The practical necessities of managing organizational boundaries demand the time and energy of both organizational members and external stakeholders like government regulators and suppliers. Security guards in large manufacturing firms, for example, spend much of their time ensuring the integrity of the organization's physical boundaries; alumni affairs officers work to ensure that students who have finished their studies remain emotionally a part of the university; and attorneys in technology companies define, patrol, and defend their firms' intellectual property boundaries. All in all, boundary work is an important form of organization work in both new and established organizations and has been the focus of a significant amount of research in management and organizational research.

Boundary Work in Management and Organizational Research

Boundary work has been an important focus of attention for management and organizational scholars since the beginnings of the field. In fact, the idea of an organization is inseparable from questions about where the boundary of the organization lies and how it is maintained. There are also important boundaries inside of organizations: the boundaries between departments, teams, and functions are central to modern organizations. In this section we review boundary work in management and organizational research, beginning with research on the external boundaries of organizations, and then discuss the work that is carried out on the boundaries inside organizations.

ORGANIZATIONAL BOUNDARIES

A central question when considering boundary work as a form of organization work is what organizational boundaries actually are. In general terms, an organizational boundary describes "the demarcation between an organization and its environment" (Santos and Eisenhardt, 2005: 491). Such a definition says little, however, about how people can see and know that demarcation or, even more, how they might work on it. In fact, the very ubiquity and obviousness of organizational boundaries hides a complex phenomenon that requires unpacking. Santos and Eisenhardt (2005) suggest a useful typology of organizational boundaries that points to distinctive kinds of boundary work.

The most basic organizational boundary in modern organizations is the legal boundary that defines what is and what is not owned by the organization, including physical equipment, intellectual property, and employment contracts with members. While relatively simple conceptually, the legal boundaries around organizations are often the subject of intense and sometimes dramatic contests. In the world of professional services, for instance, client relationships are an immensely valuable resource, but ownership of those relationships is sometimes only decidable in the courts when members leave to join or start a competing firm. Similarly, the legal ownership of intellectual property is often in dispute when employees leave the organization.

The boundary that defines the legal limits of an organization is tied to at least two important forms of boundary work. The first is specifically legal in nature—defining through legal procedures and processes what is "inside" the organization. This includes negotiating employment contracts that distinguish employees from outsiders, launching financial instruments that specify ownership, and establishing patents, trademarks, and copyrights that define the organization's intellectual property. The second is analytical, and often carried out in anticipation of the legal boundary work. It involves the efforts of actors to establish rational bases for legal boundaries, which may be rooted in the economics of production and the transaction costs associated with outsourcing different organizational activities (Santos and Eisenhardt, 2005; Williamson, 1985). It also includes strategic considerations, as the legal boundaries around organizations facilitate distinctive kinds of competitive positions that either increase or decrease monopoly power, with the organizational integration of supply or distribution chains, for instance, potentially creating significant barriers to new organizations entering an industry (Porter, 1980).

Although the legal boundaries of organizations may be the most obvious and intuitive, other boundaries exist around organizations that involve distinct kinds of boundary work. Santos and Eisenhardt (2005) suggest three additional organizational boundaries, based on a firm's (1) sphere of influence, (2) competencies, and (3) organizational identity. The organizational boundary defined by its sphere of influence includes within it those other actors over which the organization has power: a supplier may, for example, be legally separate from its customer, but if the customer purchases all of the supplier's production then a resource dependence relationship may bring the supplier inside of the customer's sphere of influence (Pfeffer and Salancik, 1978).

Boundary work in terms of an organization's sphere of influence includes an organization's efforts to increase its influence over external actors by creating resource dependencies, or to defend against the efforts of other actors to reduce the organization's influence. Walmart, for example, owes much of its global success to its extremely efficient system for managing supply chains in a way that produces highly dependent suppliers who have little choice but to provide the yearly price reductions Walmart demands.

Competency-based boundaries define the limits of the organizations in terms of its unique bundles of resources (Wernerfelt, 1984). The boundary work engendered by this kind of organizational boundary involves both assessing the distinctiveness and value of particular competencies and establishing control over those competences deemed strategically important. More specifically, this kind of boundary work involves activities like outsourcing processes which are deemed non-core, as well as strategic investments in new areas of competence (imagine, for example, a financial institution creating and staffing an Islamic banking subsidiary).

Finally, organizational identity boundaries are based on cognitive frames produced through collective sensemaking that provide an answer to the question of "who are we as an organization?" (Albert and Whetten, 1985). Boundary work connected to this boundary, therefore, revolves around the construction, diffusion, and maintenance of cognitive and discursive resources that answer that question for organizational members and stakeholders. For example, extensive identity work has been done by large oil companies who have worked to become "energy companies" in order to make their excursions into renewable and alternative energy sensible for organizational members.

MANAGING THE ORGANIZATIONAL BOUNDARY

From a social-symbolic work perspective, two existing areas of research on managing organizational boundaries are particularly interesting—the literature on boundary spanners, which identifies a specific organizational role associated with boundary work, and research on the boundary between work and home lives, which explores organizational boundary work often performed outside of any obvious organizational context. We will consider them in turn.

Scholarship on boundary spanners is one of the oldest streams of research focusing on organizational boundary work. Boundary spanners are individuals who link "organizational structure to environmental elements" (Aldrich and Herker, 1977: 218), and thus function "as exchange agents between the organization and its environment" (Leifer and Delbecq, 1978: 41). Boundary spanners are internal "communication stars" who have substantial connections beyond their unit (Tushman and Scanlan, 1981). Two main functions performed by boundary spanners are "information processing and external representation" (Aldrich and Herker, 1977; see also Friedman and Podolny, 1992): they face outward and are able to communicate important information across organizational boundaries. In line with this activity, boundary spanners are often specialists such as marketing and sales representatives, personnel recruiters, and purchasing agents. They engage in boundary work that is focused not on changing organizational boundaries, but on managing the complexities of working across a boundary.

In contrast to the special boundary work done by boundary spanners, research on boundary work in relation to home and work lives explores a nearly universal phenomenon (Kreiner et al., 2009). This work–life boundary work, as it is sometimes described, involves managing the organizational boundary so that one's work life doesn't spill over into one's home life or does so in a controlled fashion—as well as managing the self, including identity, emotions, and career (Nippert-Eng, 1996). From this perspective, the organizational boundary demarcates a domain of activity—work—that people move into and out of not only when they enter the physical worksite, but also, and especially problematically, at home as they engage in work-related activities including communication with colleagues.

Although managing this tension has traditionally been conceptualized in terms of role conflict, more recent research and writing has understood it as a kind of boundary work (Ashforth et al., 2000; Desrochers and Sargent, 2004; Fonner and Stache, 2012; Kreiner et al., 2009). This stream of research has conceptualized boundaries as "means of simplifying and ordering the environment" (Ashforth et al., 2000: 474), and boundary work as efforts to shape "temporal, spatial, and other boundaries"(Ashforth et al., 2000: 482) and thus create "more or less distinct 'territories of the self'" (Nippert-Eng, 1996: 569). In this emerging perspective, the boundary between work and home is "crafted as an ongoing, 'situated' accomplishment" (Kreiner et al., 2009: 705). This boundary work is important because the ability to actively manage the boundary between work and home increases people's feelings of well-being (Kossek et al., 2006). More broadly, shaping the work–home boundary has implications for other kinds of social-symbolic work, especially identity work: in a study of Australian men, for example, workplaces were shown to be central sites in the construction of their masculinity, while home represented a pivotal site of conflict in this regard (Smith and Winchester, 1998).

BOUNDARIES INSIDE ORGANIZATIONS

Along with the boundary around organizations, other important boundaries exist, and form a focus for boundary work, inside organizations—between groups, teams, departments, areas, and divisions. The differentiation of organizational members into groups based on such criteria as function, geography, and market served is a central characteristic of modern organizations. Even in postmodern organizations, such as holocracies that seem to have abandoned bureaucracy, members still assemble into units, the boundaries of which may be more permeable than in traditional hierarchies, but which are still evident and important. In Valve, for instance, configurations of self-moved desks demarcate who is in a particular team, no matter how informally it got to be that way. The boundaries inside organizations are crucial to understanding boundary work as organization work, with much of the contemporary literature on boundary work in management and organizational research focusing on these boundaries.

Boundary work inside organizations has been shown to be particularly consequential in domains such as healthcare and social work, where there are morally charged boundaries between "caring" and "administrative" groups and activities, and between occupational groups with distinct relationships to clients' well-being. These dynamics were clearly evident in the 1990s UK social service sector when attempts at imposing efficiency-driven reforms led to boundary work by front-line staff aimed at maintaining the separation of "caring" which was traditionally associated with social work, and "costing" which was associated with accounting and managerial positions (Llewellyn, 1998). An important boundary work strategy involved refusing to take costs into account when making care decisions for clients, reinforcing both internally and to clients the organizational division between these activities and concerns.

In another study of internal organizational boundary work, Young (1989) emphasized the complexity of the boundaries between occupational groups and how the same artifact—roses purchased by a group of female sewing machine operators on St. George's Day—could be used by actors to both enhance cohesion within one subgroup (the operators engaged in the production of "Work-Wear" who bought the roses) and to highlight the internal boundary between sewing machine operators who produced "Work-Wear" and those that produced "Bags." The purchase and public display of the roses on St. George's Day was, among other things, an organized form of boundary work by the "Work-Wear" sewing machine operators.

Another important focus of research on boundary work inside organizations has been the role of boundary objects. Originally examined in the social studies of science and technology, boundary objects represent mechanisms used to coordinate and communicate across boundaries. For boundary objects to play this role, they need to be "plastic enough to adapt to local needs and constraints of the several parties employing them, yet robust enough to maintain a common identity across sites" (Star and Griesemer, 1989: 393). The origins of the concept are in a study of the Museum of Vertebrate Zoology at the University of California, Berkeley, which identified a range of boundary objects, including "ideal types," which are abstractions that provide "good enough" guides (e.g., a species), and "standardized forms," which provide common means of communication across groups (e.g., forms given to amateur animal collectors). The paradox associated with boundary objects is that they "have different meanings in different social worlds but their structure is common enough to more than one world to make them recognizable means of translation" (Star and Griesemer, 1989: 393).

Although boundary objects do not necessarily affect organizational boundaries directly, they facilitate boundary work in which organizational members negotiate boundaries between their domains and the meaning of those boundaries. In Carlile's (2002) study of new product development, for instance, members of design engineering and manufacturing engineering made use of design drawings as a boundary object to reinforce the boundary between the groups and at the same time make it manageable. Boundary objects are often employed to accomplish tasks that require coordination across organizational boundaries and thus represent an important resource for maintaining those boundaries. It is important to note that objects can only serve as boundary objects in the context of boundary work: "particular objects may serve as a bridge between different groups, but the answer to what makes them 'do it' does not reside in the properties of this or that object but in the network within which they are nestled" (Lainer-Vos, 2013: 516). Thus, boundary objects function to bring diverse groups together and allow them to collaborate only when appropriate boundary work has been conducted. In this sense, boundary objects are inseparable from the boundary work that brings them to life.

Studying Boundary Work as Organization Work

The study of boundary work in management and organizational research consists of a disparate, relatively disconnected set of conversations. This fragmentation makes outlining the implications of studying boundary work as organization work a challenge. However, we will do our best, drawing again on our simplified model of organization work from Figure 6.1.

MOTIVATIONS OF BOUNDARY WORK

The many kinds of organizational boundaries, and wide range of actors who may be interested in shaping those boundaries, lead to a great variety of motivations to engage in boundary work. One set of motivations stems from the impact that organizational boundaries have on the capacities and performance of organizations and groups within organizations. The organizational boundaries identified by Santos and Eisenhardt (2005) bring with them distinctive sets of motivations for boundary work. Research on the legal boundaries of firms, for instance, emphasizes efficiency gains and losses as motivating the work done to establish and maintain legal boundaries. In contrast, boundary work done to affect an organization's sphere of influence is intended to "maximize strategic control over crucial external forces" (Santos and Eisenhardt, 2005: 495). We are not suggesting that these motivations describe the personal aims of everyone involved in organizational boundary work, as those are likely to be highly heterogeneous and idiosyncratic. Instead, these motivations describe collective motivations that exist as discursive and relational phenomena, rather than simply (or even) in the minds of individuals. Research on boundary objects highlights similarly functional motivations, with actors creating and using boundary objects to coordinate and collaborate across boundaries inside organizations.

But there are motivations beyond the practical desire to improve organizational and group performance. One important implication of studying boundary work as organization work is to highlight the motivations associated with relatively overlooked actors, occasions, and kinds of organizational boundaries. Hiring processes in both large and small organizations involve sets of actors who may be significantly motivated to shape the organization's boundaries: networks of family and friends commonly work together to open the boundary to those in their network and exclude others; at the same time, regulators and external stakeholders may become involved in efforts to reshape boundaries that are considered discriminatory or exclusionary; and external actors like universities carry out boundary work to ensure their graduates have access to hiring processes. Boundary work can also be triggered by specific occasions rather than occurring as day-to-day activity. If we examine outsourcing decisions, for example, these are often motivated by efficiency and cost considerations, but they also lead to boundary work that is motivated by politics and emotions, as people recognize the threat of losing their jobs, their positions, or their influence in the organization.

More broadly, although Santos and Eisenhardt have provided a useful typology of organizational boundaries, and pointed to important forms of and motivations for boundary work, there is a broader range of organizational boundaries and boundary work that are significant forms of organization work. The physical boundary of an organization, for example, is often the site of many forms of work that are motivated by the need for security and access control (security guards and the fences they patrol), as well as to communicate (think of the logos and signs that marketers erect), and the desire to facilitate the transfer of goods across the boundary (think of loading docks and piers). By focusing on boundary work as organization work, we are able to highlight a wide range of motivations that are often underemphasized in current research and that deserve more attention.

PRACTICES OF BOUNDARY WORK

Looking across the management and organizational research that has examined boundary work, we can identify two broad categories of practices: those that involve establishing or disrupting boundaries within and around organizations, and those that are focused on managing tasks and relationships across boundaries. Although boundaries in and around organizations have long been of immense interest in management and organizational research, much less attention has been paid to the concrete efforts of individual and collective actors to manage them. This lack of attention may stem from historically rooted biases in management and organizational research that approached the problem of boundaries as an analytical problem, with the key issues being how to best identify the most efficient and effective organizational boundaries, largely neglecting the work necessary to construct those boundaries once identified. Such an approach may have been appropriate in relation to modernist organizations with clear, unambiguous divisions between organizational members and non-members, or between departments and groups within organizations. In contemporary organizations, however, where boundaries are more fluid and contested, both inside and around organizations, then the analytical dimension of boundary work is only one small part.

The second main category of organizational boundary work practices are oriented toward managing tasks and relationships across boundaries, which sometimes involve shaping the boundaries directly, but more often focus on coping with or exploiting those boundaries. Although the concept of boundary work, particularly as developed in the sociology of science and of the professions, has emphasized the efforts of actors to establish or disrupt social boundaries, management and organizational research on boundary work has instead focused primarily on the work of organizational actors to cope with existing boundaries through the production of specialized objects (boundary objects) and the creation of specialized roles (boundary spanners). These literatures have flourished, perhaps reflecting the realities of organizational life in which members have far greater opportunities and abilities to manage around organizational boundaries than to alter them directly. As with boundary work that is focused on directly shaping organizational boundaries, the study of this kind of boundary work in management and organizational research would be facilitated by the development of an integrative approach that could bring together insights from the study of boundary spanners and boundary objects as two key ways in which organizational actors work to manage tasks and relationships across organizational boundaries.

Despite examining a wide range of practices, the boundary work literature has left largely unexplored the connections to other forms of organization work. Conceptualizing boundary work as a form of organization work shifts the focus somewhat, from trying to understand how and why actors work to shape organizational boundaries, to asking how and why that work is done as a part of constructing organizations as social-symbolic objects. Locating the study of boundary work in this way demands that we understand how boundary work practices interact with, complement, and compete with other forms of organization work. For instance, if we take seriously the idea that organizational boundaries can have significant competitive effects through their impacts on costs, competencies, and identities, then boundary work practices immediately become potentially intermingled with strategy work. The actors, motivations, skills, and resources associated with those boundary work and strategy work practices become difficult to understand in isolation. Similarly, while an important boundary around organizations is connected to its identity (Santos and Eisenhardt, 2005), little has been done to connect boundary work and identity work. This intersection promises a potentially valuable area of research, exploration of which could enrich understanding of identity work, boundary work, and organization work more generally.

Another overlooked opportunity involves connecting the study of boundary work to the broad stream of literature on organizational change (e.g., Poole and Van de Ven, 2004), as well as to related literatures on the organizational aspects of mergers and acquisitions (e.g., Stahl and Mendenhall, 2005), the management of international expansion (e.g., Zaheer, 1995), and the challenges of structuring strategic alliances (e.g., Parkhe, 1993). This is an area of intense interest from a practitioner point of view and has, unsurprisingly, led to the development of a large literature on how different aspects of organizations can be changed, the barriers to change that make change challenging, and the sort of boundary work practices that increase the likelihood of success. Although not all of this literature is relevant to thinking about boundary work, connecting boundary work research to these literatures could significantly expand the practical value of boundary work research and its appeal to a large community of scholars.

EFFECTS OF BOUNDARY WORK

Significant attention has been paid to the effects of boundary work, though largely on its intended, functional effects and the degree to which those were achieved by specific boundary work strategies. As with the motivations that fuel boundary work, its effects are largely conceived of in terms of the performance of the organization, or the ability of actors to manage across or cope with existing boundaries. Although these are important effects to consider, two issues arise from the existing focus in the literature: first, the disparate nature of research on boundary work in management and organizational research has led to a situation in which our understanding of its effects is fragmented and incomplete; and second, important effects of boundary work remain largely overlooked.

What we have in the study of boundary work in and around organizations is a rich set of ideas and findings with respect to how people interact with organizational boundaries; what we lack, however, is a systematic theory of when that interaction will be effective—under what conditions will the aims of boundary work will be realized, what boundary work strategies are most effective, and what social positions are most able to effectively engage in boundary work. The potential utility of such a framework is highlighted by the possible negative, unintended consequences of boundary work. Tracey et al. (2011), for example, describe how a decision made by the founders of a social enterprise to franchise (a change in the legal boundary) led to the demise of the firm: extensive boundary work intended to expand the activities of the social enterprise through franchising led to a financial crisis and bankruptcy.

An important but overlooked set of effects revolve around the experience of people engaging in such boundary work and its, likely unanticipated, effects on their resources, skills, and social positions. The research on the work–life boundary is instructive in this regard, as it is the only boundary work literature that deals explicitly with both its functional aims and outcomes, and its effects on the people engaged in the work in terms of their experience, emotions, relationships, and careers (Kreiner et al., 2009). Such effects are, however, not restricted to boundary work managing the separation of home and working life: the work of boundary spanners often demands that they negotiate liminal spaces in which their organizational membership is complex and potentially ambiguous; creating and managing boundary objects may require people to move, at least cognitively and emotionally, across organizational boundaries that otherwise provide them with identities, meaning, and security.

SITUATEDNESS AND RESOURCES

Situatedness and resources refer to the effects of the context within which the social-symbolic work is carried out and the bundles of resources that are available to the individual and collective actors performing the social-symbolic work. When considering the context of boundary work, there are obvious and important implications for why boundaries are easier or harder to construct in some contexts. So, for example, it is easier to found a company in some places than in others due to the characteristics of the context and the resources available. In fact, the World Bank publishes a yearly "Ease of Doing Business" report that includes a ranking of how easy it is to start a company in different countries.[2] This ranking refers, of course, primarily to the legal boundary of a firm, but it highlights how important context is for understanding the challenges of performing boundary work. Similarly, the context can also result in the failure of boundary work. Uber's attempts to locate their drivers outside the legal boundary of the organization, for example, have failed

---

[2] <http://www.doingbusiness.org/rankings>.

in some cities due to court rulings that establish drivers as Uber employees and thus firmly inside the organizational boundary.

The boundary work required to establish and manage boundaries around new ventures is a particularly interesting and helpful example. There are, of course, a wide range of tasks necessary to establish a new venture, but an important subset of those revolve around establishing its boundaries. If we take, for instance, the case of a university scientist wishing to convert their academic knowledge into commercial activity, significant boundary work will be required to distinguish the property, activity, and value of the new firm in relation to the university. Such boundary work may be contentious or straightforward, depending significantly on the experience of the university in such negotiations, and the regulatory frameworks in place that guide the entrepreneur and other stakeholders as they construct these new boundaries. At one extreme, the legal boundary around the firm might include only the entrepreneur and the intellectual property to be sold or licensed to other firms; alternatively, the boundary might incorporate labs, staff, equipment, patents, and production facilities intended to directly commercialize the scientific ideas. The creation of the latter new venture will require a much more complicated and extensive variety of boundary work, along with many other types of organization work.

SUMMING UP

In this section, we have used a social-symbolic work framework to organize and discuss the literature on the organization work through which boundaries are created and maintained, and the closely related work on different forms of organizational boundaries. While our discussion was necessarily broad ranging, we hope we have succeeded in highlighting the usefulness of a coherent and structured framework for thinking about this important form of organization work.

What is particularly striking to us about considering boundary work as organization work is that it brings together such a range of different conceptualizations of boundaries and boundary work that are based in different theoretical traditions and that therefore conceptualize boundaries in different ways. Furthermore, some of these conceptualizations have been in conflict for some time. While writers like Santos and Eisenhardt (2005) have done an excellent job of pulling together different streams of literature based on the simple observation that there are different literatures all focused on the same empirical object—organizational boundaries—we believe that a social-symbolic work perspective provides a more powerful way to connect these different perspectives and to include a concern with agency and actors as well as connect in an useful and interesting way to other forms of social-symbolic work.

Technology Work

The last type of organization work we examine—technology work—is concerned with shaping the technologies upon which organizational activity depends. Technologies as social-symbolic objects "have a dual nature in being constituted by both physical form and social function" (Faulkner and Runde, 2009: 443). Thus, technology work describes the purposeful, reflexive efforts of individuals, collective actors, and networks of actors to shape a technology's material form, as well as the understandings and practices associated with it. Although the term "technology work" has not been widely used in management and organizational research, an extensive literature has explored technologies as social-symbolic objects in organizations.

The Social Construction of Technology

The study of technology work is rooted primarily in the more general study of the social construction of technology (Bijker et al., 2012a). This perspective can be traced to a single edited volume published in 1984 that, for the first time, focused on "how technological artifacts were developed and changed" (Bijker et al., 2012b: xiv). Central to this perspective is a focus on the idea of a "seamless web" in which the boundaries between social and technical aspects of creating and producing technologies are post-hoc accomplishments rather than predetermined by essential differences (Hughes, 1986). A favorite example of the volume's editors was the web that Edison constructed "between his Menlo Park laboratory and Wall Street to invent technology and raise capital in a seamless way" (Bijker et al., 2012b: xvii).

What makes this perspective so important to our understanding of technology work is its shift from traditional views of technology that told the stories of "how heroic inventors and engineers stole great ideas about technology from the gods and gave them to mere mortals" (Bijker et al., 2012b: xvii), to a focus on describing and understanding how distributed networks of actors engaged in efforts to shape the evolution of objects that are inherently flexible in their meaning, use, and material constitution. This flexibility is critical both to the social construction of technology perspective and to our notion of technology work, since without it there would be no room for organizational actors to creatively shape the development and employment of technology in the social construction of organizational life.

The social studies of science and technology have established two characteristics of technology that are key to our discussion of technology work. First, technology is not something that develops according to some inner technical logic, but is itself a social product (Pinch and Bijker, 2012). As such, the nature and direction of technological change is not predetermined simply by the material reality of the technology (although it is undoubtedly affected by it). Instead, it is also shaped by the social world of which it is a part. More specifically, it is shaped by the efforts of networks of actors who have an interest in the ways that the technology might intersect with organizational life. As a result, the direction of a technology's development and the particularities of its implementation are the result of complex interactions between the social context and the material characteristics of the components of the technology.

The second important characteristic of technology stems from the first: the uncertainty associated with how a technology will develop means that the impact of technology on organizations is also uncertain, as it is also shaped by the social context. Both the nature of technologies and their impacts are mediated by the social environments in which they are shaped by individual and collective actors performing technology work. Thus, there is a recursive relationship between the social world and the technological objects that make it up: while the physical characteristics of material technologies open up and limit their potential uses, the implications of these limits are conditioned by the social context in which the technology is situated.

TECHNOLOGICAL FRAMES

The role of social processes in technology begins well before anyone starts to use it. Engineers, scientists, and designers are all embedded in what Bijker (2012) calls a "technological frame" that fundamentally shapes the technology in question. The technological frame includes understandings of what the technology is for, who will use it for what purposes, and the backgrounds and relationships of the technologists involved in producing the technology. Imagine the early days of bicycle technology (see Pinch and Bijker, 2012): the bicycle designs produced depended on what the designers imagined the purpose of the bicycle to be (racing versus transportation), who the users of the bicycle were (young men or ladies), and what materials were understood as appropriate for bicycles (wooden wheels or hard rubber tires).

The importance of technological frames makes them an unsurprising focus of technology work in organizations. When actors work to change the technological frame surrounding a technology, they are performing technology work, and this technology work can have important ramifications for the technology that is subsequently developed in the organization. But this also means that once a technology is designed and built, the meanings of that technology within the organizational context are still not set. For example, Kling (1991) explored how, as computers began to be used in organizations, they became enmeshed in webs of social relationships which shaped the meaning of the computers for users and observers. In a similar way, texting was originally envisaged by phone companies as a service for broadcasting to customers (such as sending someone their bank balance). Individual users, however, discovered the facility and began to use it to send personal messages to friends, and in so doing profoundly shifted the mode of use and the meaning of texting (Ansari and Phillips, 2011).

TECHNOLOGY WORK AND ORGANIZATION WORK

As with strategy work and boundary work, the kinds of technology work on which we focus here are those that are a part of organization work. Although a great deal of effort goes into shaping technologies that are not organizational, we restrict our analysis to technology work that involves technologies that make up organizations. Two simple examples illustrate this distinction. Both are from the world of "creative consumers" who "adapt, modify, or transform a proprietary offering" (Berthon et al., 2007: 39).

First, Jose Avila constructed furniture exclusively from Federal Express boxes and displayed them on his website, www.fedexfurniture.com (and then promptly faced a cease and desist order from FedEx) (Philipkoski, 2005). Avila's creativity with FedEx boxes and the company's response to that creativity illustrate the interpretative flexibility that surrounds even mundane objects and the potential significance of those interpretations for interested actors. Avila's efforts, however, do not constitute what we think of as technology work as a form of organization work (at least in part because of the reaction by FedEx), since they were never intended to shape FedEx as an organization, and nor did his activity last long enough to become a new entrepreneurial organization.

In contrast, the second example shows how some companies recognize and incorporate the efforts of users in their own technology work. The BBC did this in their backstage.bbc.co.uk project. "Backstage" was a five-year project in which BBC services and content were made available to outside developers and hackers to experiment with through a variety of application programming interface (APIs). The Backstage project led to the development of more than 160 prototypes made by over a hundred people, including some that became commercially successful and others that significantly influenced the BBC's internal development efforts (Forrester et al., 2011; Kiss, 2011). The BBC project illustrates both the potential of technology work as organization work, and the wide range of potential actors who can engage in that work.

Technology Work in Management and Organizational Research

The study of technology work in management and organizational research is not a single, distinct stream of research, but rather a set of related streams that have emerged over time. To understand how the study of technology work has evolved in management and organizational research, we focus on three important "moments" in the study of technology and organizations: the sociotechnical systems approach, the application of structuration theory to organizational technologies, and the development of sociomateriality. The study of technology and organizations has, of course, spanned a much broader set of themes, but each of these three represents a turn away from technological determinism and the conceptualization of technology as separate from the social dimension of organizational life, toward one in which the technical and social, and ultimately the material and social, are not only interrelated but inextricably intertwined.

SOCIOTECHNICAL SYSTEMS
The sociotechnical systems approach represents the first attempt by organizational scholars to wrestle with technologies as bound up with the social contexts in which they are employed. Emerging in the 1950s (Trist and Bamforth, 1951), the sociotechnical approach conceives of "any production system" as requiring "both a technology—machinery, plant layout, raw materials—and a work–relationship structure that relates the human operators both to the technology and to each other" (Cooper and Foster, 1971: 467).

One of the earliest studies of this type examined "coalgetting," an innovation in the organization of coal mining in South Yorkshire. Coalgetting refers to a form of work organization that emerged alongside the increasing mechanization of coal mining, but that revived practices common prior to mechanization. In contrast to the Tayloristic breakdown of coalmining into smaller and smaller discrete tasks, which was the dominant approach at the time, the miners at Haigh Moor had taken advantage of a technical breakthrough to organize themselves into autonomous work groups with responsibility for the whole cycle of coalgetting.

The importance of this research for us is twofold. First, it is important due to its conceptualization of the "longwall method" of coalmining, which they regard "as a technological system expressive of the prevailing outlook of mass-production engineering and as a social structure consisting of the occupational roles that have been institutionalized in its use" (Trist and Bamforth, 1951: 5). Second, it is important due to the insight that the analysis of social and technical dimensions of organizations needed to be integrated, and thus a sociotechnical approach was born. Not coincidentally, the integration of material and social originated in a team of authors, one of whom came "from a mining family and spent the first eighteen years of his working life at the coal-face" (Trist and Bamforth, 1951: 38).

While a review of the extensive literature on sociotechnical systems is beyond what we can offer here, it is useful to note the general path through which this stream of research developed. As recounted by Trist (1981), the study of sociotechnical systems originated in the study of "work systems."

173

This early work focused on a systematic approach to the design of jobs that included the technical and the social, and began with an understanding of the "transformations (changes of state) of the material or product that take place . . . whether carried out by men or machines" (Trist, 1981: 33).

This concern evolved over time to incorporate larger social aggregates, first moving to examine whole organizations as sociotechnical systems scholars became convinced that innovations in work organizations would likely not survive unless they were embedded in organizations that were changing in the same direction (Trist, 1981). Central to this move was a new image of organizations as jointly optimizing the technical and social, in contrast to the traditional view of organizations as following "the technological imperative which regards man simply as an extension of the machine and therefore as an expendable spare part" (Trist, 1981: 42).

Finally, sociotechnical systems research moved to the "macrosocial" level to include an explicit concern for interorganizational systems including industries, communities, problem domains, and networks. Central to our discussion of technology work was the focus on the interplay of technical and social dimensions of organizational life, and the potential to manage that interplay in an active, and potentially emancipatory fashion. Recent work in this stream of literature has extended these concerns to explore the idea of innovation systems at the industry and national levels as sociotechnical systems (Geels, 2004).

STRUCTURATION THEORY AND TECHNOLOGY WORK IN ORGANIZATIONS

Following the sociotechnical systems approach, studies of technology in organizations shifted back toward a technological determinism that stemmed in part from a new emphasis on information and communication technologies, as computerization became a dominant concern in organizations and in related work in management and organizational research. The fascination with the new information technologies seemed to decouple technology from its social context in organizational research. This focus on information and communication technologies has remained an important one, spawning large literatures examining the implementation of information technologies in organizations, and the management of information technology as a strategic resource (Mansell et al., 2007).

Information and communications technology research consistently reflected a positivist philosophy, echoing the natural sciences, until the early 1990s when interpretivist approaches began to appear (Fulk, 1993; Orlikowski and Baroudi, 1991; Walsham, 1995). In the context of information technology research, an interpretivist perspective highlights the ways in which these technologies revolve "around shared meanings, interpretations, and the production and reproduction of cultural and social realities by humans" (Orlikowski and Baroudi, 1991: 18). Thus, it is this interpretivist tradition in the study of information and communication technologies that ties the literature to our conception of technology work as a form of organization work, and brought with it the study of organizational technology employing Giddens' concept of structuration as a theoretical anchor.

In a review of this tradition, Jones and Karsten (2008) identify 331 articles on information systems published between 1983 and 2004 that draw explicitly on structuration theory. They attribute the popularity of structuration in information and communication technology research to Giddens' account of the structure–agency relationship and his conceptualization of social structure as being continuously produced and reproduced through situated practice. Together, these ideas make structuration particularly useful in research on the interplay of information technologies and social structures, and the processes of organizational change that this interplay brings about.

As we reviewed in Chapter 2, Giddens proposes an understanding of social structure and agency in which they constitute a duality, in the sense that structure and agency are not independent, contributing factors in social phenomena, but rather mutually constitutive of one another, and thus jointly constitutive of social life. The application of structuration theory to information and communication technology research has focused, perhaps not surprisingly, on topics in which the social factors are more obviously important, such as decision support and virtual teams, as well as on change processes, mirroring the employment of structuration theory more broadly in management and organizational research. This view has obvious ramifications in terms of the nature and importance of technology work.

Two key articles provide important examples of the insights that structuration theory has brought to the study of technology in organizations, and its potential to contribute to an understanding of technology work. In the first empirical study applying structuration theory to organizational technology, Barley (1986) explored the introduction of CT scanners in two hospital radiology departments. This study shows how technology "might occasion different organizational structures by altering institutionalized roles and patterns of interaction" (Barley, 1986: 78). In this case, identical technologies triggered similar processes but with distinctly different organizational outcomes, with one radiology department becoming far more decentralized than the other. It was not that the material properties of the technology had no impact, but rather that their effects depended on "the specific historical process in which they [were] embedded" (Barley, 1986: 107).

Orlikowski's (2000) essay extends a structurationist perspective on technology by distinguishing between technologies as artifacts and technologies in practice. A key theoretical move that Orlikowski makes is to turn away from the idea that "technology is developed through a social-political process which results in structures (rules and resources) being embedded within the technology" (Orlikowski, 2000: 405). This idea, she suggests, allows for social construction only in the development of technologies, after which their material form becomes deterministic. This divide breaks down "in the face of empirical research that shows people modifying technologies and their conceptions of technology long after design and development" (Orlikowski, 2000: 406).

Thus, a structurationist perspective on technology and organizations provides important contributions to our understanding of technology work. It highlights the recursive interplay of the physical and social dimensions of technologies, showing how, when people in organizations adopt, implement, or use a technology, they are doing technology work. They do this by combining its physical properties, the intentional designs as signaled through those properties and the texts that accompany the technology, and their own additions to its physical properties and place in the social order. This combination is described by Orlikowski as a "technology in practice," and represents an important type of technology work.

SOCIOMATERIALITY AND TECHNOLOGY WORK IN ORGANIZATIONS

The third theme we examine takes a step further toward an integration of the social and technical in exploring technology work in organizations. The concept of sociomateriality describes an approach to the study of technologies in organizations that involves a shift from "focusing on how technologies influence humans, to examining how materiality is intrinsic to everyday activities and relations" (Orlikowski and Scott, 2008: 455). Unlike research on sociotechnical systems and structuration theory, writing on sociomateriality in organizations is spread across a set of diverse traditions, including actor-network theory (Callon, 1986; Latour, 1986), the sociology of science (Pickering, 2010), and the sociology of algorithmic finance (Mackenzie, 2008).

What connects these different traditions is their focus on the ways in which "the social and the material are constitutively entangled in everyday life" (Orlikowski, 2007: 1437). This understanding of the social and material differ from previous approaches in two important ways (Orlikowski and Scott, 2008: 454). First, it suggests a continuousness to the relationship between the material and the social, distinct from the idea of technology providing an "occasion" for structuring (Barley, 1986), as has been emphasized in the literature examining the adoption, adaptation, and implementation of technology in organizations (Leonardi and Barley, 2010). Second, and more profoundly, it moves away from an image of the "technology-human (or organizational) relationship as involving distinct entities or processes that interrelate in some way" (Orlikowski and Scott, 2008: 454). Instead, a sociomaterial approach proposes a relational ontology that treats the boundaries between technologies and humans as accomplishments, rather than as fixed either by the actors involved or the researchers observing the situation (Latour, 1990; Pinch and Bijker, 1984).

A sociomaterial understanding of technology in organizations provides a powerful basis for the study of technology work, as it shifts the focus from understanding the relationships between entities to, in our terms, the constitution of objects through the purposeful efforts of organizational actors. Although the emphasis in writing on sociomateriality has been on the entangled nature of the social and material, and on "composite and shifting assemblages," it does not deny the presence of social-symbolic objects in the world. Consistent with our arguments, these objects exist due to the efforts of actors who are able to pull from these assemblages some "discrete" object to be identified and employed in their ongoing organizational activities.

From a sociomaterial perspective, these objects are simultaneously real and imaginary. They are not discovered by actors sifting through the sociomaterial morass, nor are they created in some heroic fashion; instead, they are assembled by disparate networks of competing and collaborating actors, as intended and unintended effects of their purposeful work. As has been documented in regard to a plethora of technology objects, from bicycles to Bakelite to medical imaging, the social construction of these objects is always a result of complex sociomaterial interactions driven by human interests and emotions, the availability and affordances of material objects, and the histories of both. In other words, by technology work.

Studying Technology Work as Organization Work

In this section, we will explore the ramifications of thinking about technology work as organization work. We again use Figure 6.1 to explore how understanding technology work as a kind of organization work highlights new ways of thinking about technology work, new connections among areas of research, and new areas that would benefit from further study. For each of the elements of Figure 6.1—motivations, practices, outcomes, and situatedness and resources—we first examine what insights might emerge from research on sociotechnical systems, structuration theory, and sociomateriality, and then reflect on how conceiving of technology work as organization work might build on and extend these traditions.

MOTIVATIONS OF TECHNOLOGY WORK

The literatures we have reviewed suggest a layering of motivations for engaging in technology work, beginning with more instrumental motivations identified by research on sociotechnical systems, to more creative motives suggested by structuration theory, and finally to more existential impulses pointed to by a focus on sociomateriality.

From a sociotechnical systems perspective, the motivation to engage in technology work flows from the impacts of the technical and social dimensions of production systems on organizations and organizational life. Core to this perspective is the idea that technologies are tools—that a fundamental aim in designing and using technologies in organizations is to make work more effective, efficient, and satisfying. An important focus of sociotechnical systems is on how work groups (rather than organizations) shape their use of technology. Thus, this perspective brings our attention to motivations attached to these more proximal sets of actors, especially with respect to their productivity and satisfaction with their work and working environments.

The structuration perspective brings in ideas of appropriation and enactment—shifting from the image of technologies as tools, to technologies as platforms for practice. Thus, the motivations that it attends to include those of individuals and groups using technology to overcome local problems that may or may not coincide with organizational goals. A key issue in understanding the motivations highlighted by structuration theory is its conception of actors as knowledgeable agents with respect to the possibilities afforded by technologies, and especially the possibilities that lay beyond the intentions of the designers. This might involve, for instance, the use of formal channels of communication for informal, even subversive, intensions, as when early corporate email systems were co-opted to enact non-hierarchical networks in organizations (Tyler et al., 2005).

Although a sociomaterial perspective on technology work does not deny either the instrumental motivations highlighted by sociotechnical systems or the emergent motivations pointed to by structuration theory, it adds a set of existential motivations that stem from the ongoing, negotiated nature of the boundary between technology and humanity in organizational life. Rather than seeing technologies as separate from humans in predetermined ways, this perspective sees those separations as negotiated in an ongoing way, such that they represent both opportunities for expanding human agency and threatening human "existence."

The existential motivation for technology work is highlighted by current debates around the ethical limitations of artificial intelligence (AI), but is in fact a long-standing issue, as illustrated by the reaction of scholars of the time to the emergence of the printing press. Although there were practical objections regarding the impermanence of typeset pages and the ugliness of mechanical fonts, the more fundamental objections focused on the relationship between mechanical printing and the humanity that the technology might displace. The fifteenth-century abbot Johannes Trithemius, for instance, argued that the copyist "is by the very act of writing introduced in a certain measure into the knowledge of the mysteries and greatly illuminated in his innermost soul" (Brann, 1981: 156). Moreover, the laboriousness of copying texts was not a problem to be overcome, but inherent to its virtues. Although not what we might typically think of as technology work, the writing of Trithemius was explicitly intended to shape conceptions of a new technology by establishing its limitations in relation to existing social practices.

Looking across the writing we have reviewed on technology work in organizations, we see a variety of motivations, including productivity, satisfaction, enablement, and existential threat. Largely missing in this discussion of motivations for technology work, however, are the motivations that might stem from a focus on technology work as organization work—as work done significantly to shape the organization in which it is embedded. This goes beyond engaging in technology work to meet organizational or local goals. It involves understanding technologies as partly constitutive of the organization as a social-symbolic object, giving the organization meaning and shaping its place in a network of individual and collective actors. Imagining the discussions among technicians in front of the CT scanners, we might imagine that those actors were motivated not only by a desire to shape their professional relationships, but also by a desire to shape the kind of organization in which they worked—how centralized it would become, how much control and independence different actors might enjoy, how much respect it shows for traditional professional relations.

This line of reasoning pushes us to problematize the distinction between technology and organization. The dividing line between organizations and the machines "inside" organizations is, from a social-symbolic work perspective, a social accomplishment, not predetermined by some essential characteristics of technology or organizations. Thus, a central motivating impetus for technology work is to construct that boundary. This dynamic is especially evident in contemporary technology-driven organizations, previously with the so-called dot.com companies, and more recently in the world of social media. Distinguishing between Twitter and Facebook as companies and as technologies is a non-trivial accomplishment, but one that has been repeatedly critical as they faced controversies around the privacy and veracity of their platforms. Connecting the motivations driving technology work to the social construction of organizations provides important opportunities to integrate the study of technology work into the literature on new organizational forms (Puranam et al., 2014).

PRACTICES OF TECHNOLOGY WORK

Technology work involves not only shaping the material properties of technologies but also shaping the social relationships and practices in which those material objects are embedded. Sociotechnical systems, structuration theory, and sociomateriality all see the relationship between technology and humanity as requiring work that engages with the material and social properties of both, and shapes them jointly and mutually.

Sociotechnical systems research highlights technology work practices that include the design, adoption, and implementation of technologies, and—critically—the design and modification of work processes in ways that leverage the material properties of those technologies. An important aspect of these practices is the idea that the design and modification of work processes in relation to technologies is best done by those organizational members most directly in contact with the technologies, rather than by designers working from a distance.

The key practice added by structuration theory is appropriation, which describes "the process by which people adopt and adapt technologies, fitting them into their working practices" (Dourish, 2003: 465). Although appropriation seems closely related to the more general notion of customization, it is associated with more ongoing, social, and transformative qualities (Desanctis and Poole, 1994; Dourish, 2003). Appropriation is fundamentally concerned with situating technologies in systems of meaning, both by ascribing meaning to the technologies (perhaps in terms of their utility or the experience of using them) and by conveying meaning through technologies (perhaps suggesting the meaning of other actors, such as customers in a customer relationship management system) (Dourish, 2003).

A sociomaterial perspective on technology work pushes our conception of technology work practices even further. Starting from the relational ontology that is at the heart of this perspective and that "dissolves analytical boundaries between technology and humans" (Orlikowski and Scott, 2008: 455), the question becomes what kinds of practices are entailed by this move. At a general level, it suggests that technology work involves ongoing efforts to socially construct the human and technological in relation to each other. Thus, technology work practices may overlap significantly with those we have associated with self work and with other forms of organization work. This perspective suggests that technology work includes the social construction of technologies and actors, whether individual or collective, in relation to those technologies.

From a sociomaterial perspective, we might think of "constituting" as an umbrella term for technology work practices. This is an exciting idea for the study of technology work, as it brings the exploration of how people interact with technologies much closer to our understanding of technology work as organization work. At the same time, it potentially overshoots with respect to the scope of how we define technology work: from a sociomaterial perspective, people are negotiating the boundaries between technology and the social world on an ongoing basis, both purposefully and not. While such a description makes sense for examining the social construction of organizational technologies in general, it moves beyond what we think of as technology work, which we associate strictly with purposeful, reflexive efforts.

The broader question we ask here is how thinking about these technology work practices might be affected by conceptualizing them as kinds of organization work. Perhaps the most immediate answer to this question comes from the sociomateriality perspective and its emphasis on the efforts people engage in to establish and maintain the boundary between technology and humanity. In doing so, technology work connects with the previous discussion of boundary work and we begin to ask questions about the boundaries between organizations and technologies, but also the boundaries between technologies and the social world within organizations. Technology work is therefore about the social construction of technologies within organizations and also about constructing the relationship between the organization as a social-symbolic object and the technologies upon which organizing depends.

EFFECTS OF TECHNOLOGY WORK
Shifting to a consideration of the effects of technology work on organizational life, we see that the sociotechnical systems, structuration, and sociomateriality approaches provide interesting insights into this question. While the different perspectives highlight different effects of technology work, what is clear from all three perspectives is that technology work plays a significant role in the ongoing construction of organizations.

Sociotechnical systems research was explicit with respect to the effects on which it focused: the efficiency of production systems and the satisfaction of individual workers in those systems (Cooper and Foster, 1971). The unintended effects highlighted by sociotechnical systems research are the obverse—inefficiency and dissatisfaction. From a sociotechnical systems perspective, technology work is about shaping the nature of the social and technological aspects of organizations to produce an effective sociotechnical system that is effective and efficient, and avoid sociotechnical systems that do not.

Structuration theory as a lens on technology in organizations broadens both the conception of technology work and our understanding of its effects. In particular, the wider array of practices pointed to by structuration theory are associated with a broader set of potential outcomes, such that technology work leads to organizational structures (Barley, 1986) and practices (Orlikowski, 2000). In Barley's study, for instance, we see that the technology work of radiologists and technicians creates interaction orders that maintain or transform status hierarchies. Thus, the effects of technology work from this perspective include the creation and transformation of roles and relationships, as the affordances of technologies intersect with the interests, values, aims, and abilities of organizational actors, both enabling and constraining actors depending on the shape of that intersection. Effects also include reimagined technologies: actors engaged in appropriation and enactment transform the possibilities associated with specific technological tools, and consequently the possibilities associated with the work roles in which those tools are employed.

The important addition that the sociomaterial perspective makes to our understanding of the effects of technology work involves the ways in which that work shapes not only the technologies in use, and the work practices and processes in which it is involved, but also the actors—the individuals and groups—who interact with those technologies. Negotiating the boundary between technology and humanity means that engaging in technology work may have significant, and even profound, consequences for the construction of selves and organizations.

In sum, a technology work perspective changes our understanding of the effects of the social construction of technology: it highlights the functional effects of technology work both leading up to and following the adoption of technologies in organizations, as well as the deeper effects of doing this work on the constitution of selves and organizations. Technology work is a fundamental form of organization work, as the effects of this activity socially construct the technologies and the relationships between technologies and the organizations in which they are constructed. As new digital technologies increasingly dominate the workplace and replace activities carried out in traditional ways, technology work becomes ever more important—the effects of technology work penetrate every facet of contemporary organizational life.

SITUATEDNESS AND RESOURCES OF TECHNOLOGY WORK

We have focused on three moments in the study of technology work in organizations—sociotechnical systems, structuration, and sociomateriality—each of which is marked by a distinct and increasing concern with the situatedness of technology work and the resources employed in that work.

Although it might now seem trivial, the attention that sociotechnical systems research paid to the situatedness of technologies in organizations was extraordinary at the time. In particular, sociotechnical systems elevated the importance of the local working conditions, including the relationships among workgroup members, their situated understanding of the technologies, and their local aims. Rather than working from an uncontextualized understanding of technology as had been common in previous scholarship, sociotechnical systems research conceived of technology work as focused on production systems that included both technologies and social relationships.

Structuration theory provides a different, yet equally important contribution to our understanding of the situatedness of technology work and the resources used in that work. In a theoretical move that still causes confusion at times, structuration theory describes reproduced social practices as social systems, and the generative rules and resources that actors draw on in enacting those practices as social structure. The situatedness of technology work from a structuration theory perspective is not, therefore, only the social system and the technology, but also people's memory traces and their evolution through time. This conception of situatedness highlights the capacity of actors to collect, store, and retrieve knowledge of the social world in ways that allow them to act purposefully and reflexively. Thus, technology work from this perspective always involves the interplay of sets of material properties and the knowledgeability of actors as they appropriate those properties for their own aims.

Sociomateriality does not so much add discrete dimensions to the situatedness of technology work as much as it complicates the dimensions already suggested. The key complication involves the boundaries between technical and social objects—technology and humanity—such that the situatedness of human action is itself an accomplishment of that action (Jones, 2014). This idea echoes Weick's notion of enacted environments, but pushes it toward an ontological argument in which not only are environments enacted, but the boundaries between people and their environments are also constituted through ongoing effortful action.

An important issue raised by attending to the situatedness and resources of technology work concerns the impacts of the myriad digital technologies shaping organizational life in the twenty-first century. While the importance of technology has long been recognized in management and organizational research, the question of how the shift to digital infrastructure is shaping the way people work and organize is only beginning to receive consistent attention.

From an organization work perspective, the growing ubiquity of digital technology in organizations raises three intriguing questions. First, as digital technologies become more central to the functioning of organizations, we need to ask how actors are using these technologies to perform other types of organization work. So, for example, how are new digital tools being used by organizational actors as they carry out strategy work and how is this changing the strategies that result? Second, what kinds of technology work are occasioned by digital technologies? For example, Salesforce is a digital client management system that significantly changes the sales and marketing departments in which it is adopted. Adoption triggers both customization of the technology and a reciprocal adaptation of the organization's internal routines and relationships. Finally, and perhaps most profoundly, is it possible for digital technologies to "do" organization work. For example, AI and machine learning are increasingly being used in recruiting new employees. Entelo,[3] one recent entry into the market, uses AI and predictive analytics to analyze data scraped from social media to identify candidates who are likely to leave their jobs. The ability of machines to carry out organization work may require a significant reconsideration of the nature of agency and our theories of organization work.

SUMMING UP

Technology work is fundamental to organizations. The development of modern and postmodern organizations has depended on a whole range of communication, management, and production technologies that allowed and supported, first the rational organization of people in large numbers, and then the turn toward more flexible rationalities. Modern and postmodern organizations are thus inseparable from technology. Thus, the study of organization work inescapably involves the study of the technologies, and how they are created and used by organizational members.

Although the pervasive presence of technology in organizations is undeniable, technology is still notable primarily by its absence in management and organizational research (Orlikowski and Scott, 2008). One reason for this is the lack of a theoretical bridge between studies of organization that focus more on the human aspects of organizations and studies of technology that tend to be concerned with "affordances." We believe that technology work, as a type of organization work, provides a potential bridge by connecting the efforts of organizational members to construct the organization—a key concern of organizational researchers—to technology in organizations. This bridge, we suggest, might lead to a number of fruitful areas that deserve further attention from management and organizational researchers.

Most generally, the term "technology work" has not been widely used in management and organizational research, which highlights the potential for a research area that embraces and extends the existing literature on technology and organizations. Research in the social construction of technology, as well as the management and organizational research literatures we have reviewed here, provide an important foundation for the study of technology work. They have had considerable success in theorizing and empirically investigating the ways in which technology is shaped and made meaningful, though as we have shown, they have paid significantly less attention to the motivations and outcomes of that work, especially with respect to the organizations in which it occurs. Conceptualizing this activity as "technology work" highlights the role

---

[3] <https://www.entelo.com/>.

of the actor performing the work, and makes who does the work, why do they do it, and what resources they draw upon, important areas for investigation.

Conclusion

Reviewing research on organization work represents an interesting challenge. Despite the long-standing interest in studying organizations and organizing, streams of research that conceive of organizations in ways consistent with a social-symbolic work perspective have only begun to emerge in the past decade or so. Moreover, the links between these streams of research are not well recognized, beyond a general affinity with practice theories. Thus, reviewing strategy work, boundary work, and technology work together—as types of organization work—provides a potentially generative foundation for developing research that embraces the broader context in which each of these specific types of work occur.

In looking across the reviews of the three types of organization work, we also see specific possibilities that are created by conceiving of them in this way. One possibility is the development of an integrated approach to studying how actors work to construct organizations and organizational life, beyond the specific concerns with individual facets, such as strategy, boundaries, and technology. An integrated research stream on organization work would marry contemporary interests in the social construction of organizational life to the traditional concerns that established organizations as the focal point for management research, a focus that many scholars have bemoaned the loss of. A second possibility is that conceiving of strategy work, boundary work, and technology work as types of organization work could generate interest in how actors work to construct a wide range of features of organizational life: strategy work as organization work, for instance, could inspire parallel investigations of operations, marketing, and finance, with correspondent shifts away from trying to explain only the outcomes of these activities, but also to understand them as forms of organization work, and thus linked to other forms of organization work, and at the same time analyzable in terms of motivations, practices, effects, and resources.

Key Resources

Strategy Work

The study of strategy work is a relatively young literature that has matured rapidly through the intensive work of a dedicated community of management and organizational scholars. Consequently, we recommend starting your exploration of this

185

literature with a relatively recent summary of the field. In "Strategy-as-practice: Taking social practices seriously," Vaara and Whittington provide a cogent summary of the field and point to some important directions for research in this area to take. Then, for a useful empirical example of strategy work, Jarzabkowski's "Shaping strategy as a structuration process" explores how top managers in three universities engage in strategy work shape their organization's strategies in the action and institutional realms.

Jarzabkowski, P. 2008. Shaping strategy as a structuration process. *Academy of Management Journal*, 51(4): 621–50.

Vaara, E., and Whittington, R. 2012. Strategy-as-practice: Taking social practices seriously. *Academy of Management Annals*, 6(1): 285–336.

Boundary Work

The study of boundary work was originally anchored outside of management and organizational research, and so we suggest beginning with Gieryn's classic examination of "Boundary-work and the demarcation of science from non-science," in which he explores how scientists engage in boundary work to demarcate their community and activity. For an article more clearly focused on organizational boundaries, we recommend Zietsma and Lawrence's study of "Institutional work in the transformation of an organizational field." Although they focus on institutional processes, the boundary work they examine involves a range of organizational boundaries, including within those defining individual organizations as well as collaborative groups across organizations.

Gieryn, T. F. 1983. Boundary-work and the demarcation of science from non-science: Strains and interests in professional ideologies of scientists. *American Sociological Review*, 48(6): 781–95.

Zietsma, C., and Lawrence, T. B. 2010. Institutional work in the transformation of an organizational field: The interplay of boundary work and practice work. *Administrative Science Quarterly*, 55(2): 189–221.

Technology Work

As with boundary work, we recommend starting with the classic literature outside of management and organizational research to better understand technology work. There is no better place to start in this domain than with Bijker et al.'s edited volume on *The social construction of technological systems*. As discussed earlier in this chapter, this edited volume marks the beginning of contemporary approaches to the social construction of technology (and it's full of fascinating stories). The entry point we suggest for management and organizational research on technology work is Orlikowski and Scott's review of "Sociomateriality," which in fact provides a review of reviews. They summarize three reviews of research focused on technology as discrete entities and three more on technology on mutually dependent ensembles, before discussing the emerging stream of research associated with the concept of sociomateriality. Lastly, we recommend Faulkner and Runde's article "On the identity of technological objects and user innovations in function," which develops a theory of how actors socially construct the technical identity of technological objects, and provides a fascinating account of the transformation of the turntable into a musical instrument in hip-hop.

Bijker, W. E., Hughes, T. P., and Pinch, T. J. 2012. *The social construction of technological systems: New directions in the sociology and history of technology* (Anniversary). Cambridge, MA: MIT Press.

Faulkner, P., and Runde, J. 2009. On the identity of technological objects and user innovations in function. *Academy of Management Review*, 34(3): 442–62.

Orlikowski, W. J., and Scott, S. V. 2008. Sociomateriality: Challenging the separation of technology, work and organization. *Academy of Management Annals*, 2(1): 433–74.

7

Institutional Work

In this chapter we:

1. Review the history of institutions as social-symbolic objects.
2. Conceptualize institutional work as a form of social-symbolic work.
3. Identify the key dimensions of institutional work.
4. Explore the variety of actors engaged in institutional work.

Introduction

In 2008, a programmer known as Satoshi Nakamoto published a proposal for a new currency entitled *Bitcoin: A peer-to-peer electronic cash system*. The online proposal described a form of "electronic cash" that "would allow online payments to be sent directly from one party to another without going through a financial institution" (Nakamoto, 2008). The next year, the bitcoin network went live, with Satoshi Nakamoto "mining"[1] the very first block of bitcoins. The first bitcoin transactions followed shortly thereafter, negotiated by individuals on the bitcointalk forum with one notable early transaction involving the use of bitcoin to purchase two pizzas from Papa John's.

Since its relatively obscure beginnings, bitcoin has emerged as a cultural and economic phenomenon. Spending bitcoins has been described as being "as easy as sending an email" and the number of firms that accept bitcoins has risen rapidly. While writing this chapter, we searched on spendbitcoins.com for hotel and travel companies in London and Oxford that accept bitcoin and found a wide range, including major firms such as Expedia, Airbnb,

---

[1] "Mining" refers to the process of solving complex mathematical problems whose solution is a key that allows the miner to edit the blockchain in order to clear transactions and be rewarded with bitcoins. These problems become increasingly difficult to solve as the number of bitcoins increases, providing an effective limit to the number of bitcoins in circulation.

VRBO, and Virgin Atlantic, as well as smaller companies such as 9flats.com, CheepAir, and Yassu Tour Uzbekistan Travel. More broadly, the popularity of bitcoin led to the emergence of a range of cybercurrencies, including Litecoin and Ethereum, and the rise of large digital currency trading venues, such as coinbase.com, as well as energizing the discourse around blockchain technologies more generally.

Bitcoin represents a fascinating example of individuals and collective actors working to effect change at a broad societal and cultural level. They were not only attempting to launch a currency, but one with remarkable properties: it has been described as "the world's first completely decentralized digital currency," which is "frictionless, anonymous, and cryptographically astonishingly secure" (Salmon, 2013). Central to the significance of bitcoin is that it relies on no state, bank, or central clearing house, but instead uses a decentralized system distributed across a network of independent computers.

These features of bitcoin are significant because of the context in which bitcoin was born, and that made it more than an obsession of the paranoid and technologically advanced. Nakamoto's bitcoin proposal was published in 2008, when the financial crisis of the time had significantly diminished public trust in governments to manage the money supply:

> The Federal Reserve was introducing "quantitative easing," essentially printing money in order to stimulate the economy. The price of gold was rising. Bitcoin required no faith in the politicians or financiers who had wrecked the economy— just in Nakamoto's elegant algorithms. (Wallace, 2011)

Bitcoins offered an alternative to the banks and governments in which individuals around the world were losing faith. People mining, holding, and spending bitcoins would not have to worry, as Nakamoto (2008) declares, about banks lending their money "out in waves of credit bubbles with barely a fraction in reserve."

The creation, distribution, and use of bitcoins clearly illustrates what we refer to as institutional work: purposeful, reflexive efforts of individuals, collective actors, and networks of actors intended to shape a society's ideas, beliefs, values, rules, and assumptions, in this case through the construction and implementation of a new financial technology. Bitcoins represent much more than a way to engage in financial transactions: they challenge the normative order with respect to who can create money, how money can be used, how it is tracked, what forms of trust underpin its value, and how it is connected to the "material" world. The answers to these questions ripple outwards through the relationships among individuals, banks, corporations, and the state, as well as changing our beliefs regarding the nature and purpose of money and thus the nature of the economy.

In this chapter, we explore institutional work and develop a framework for analyzing the purposeful, reflexive efforts of individuals, collective actors, and networks of actors to shape the institutional arrangements within which they live, and which influence their experiences, opportunities, and actions. Our starting point for this chapter is the concept of an institution: we begin by defining and illustrating this concept as a foundation for understanding institutional work. As with the self and the organization, we explore the history of institutions as social-symbolic objects, focusing on how they changed in the shifts to modernity and postmodernity; here, we explore language as a prototypical institution, tracing its evolution through the transitions to each of these historical periods. We then develop the concept of institutional work in more detail, first discussing its discursive, relational, and material dimensions, and then outlining a set of distinctive roles associated with it. We again end the chapter with a set of additional resources for investigating this form of social-symbolic work.

The History of Institutions as Social-Symbolic Objects

As scholars who have worked for many years in the field of institutional theory, the most common question we have faced is the deceptively simple query, "What exactly is an institution?" The confusion surrounding this term stems in no small part from its use, both in social science and in everyday life, to describe both an "established organization or foundation, especially one dedicated to education, public service or culture," and "a custom, practice, relationship, or behavioral pattern of importance in the life of a community or society" (The Free Dictionary, 2015).

What then, do we mean by an institution? For our purposes, institutions are better understood as something closer to the second definition. They are, put simply, "conventions that are self-policing" (Phillips et al., 2004: 637). To unpack this definition, let's begin with what we mean by a convention. A convention is some kind of pattern, or "typification" (Berger and Luckmann, 1967) that describes a practice, technology, or rule. What is critical to this definition is that the institution is not the practice, technology, or rule as such, but rather its shared, social understanding (Phillips and Malhotra, 2008). So, for instance, the practice of clear-cutting forests involves a combination of routines, skills, tools, and machines, while clear-cutting as an institution is the shared understanding of that combination, as well as its place in the field of professional forestry and its relationship to the broader social milieu in which it occurs (Zietsma and Lawrence, 2010). Importantly, clear-cutting as an institution can, from one time to another, be reconstructed from being a responsible forestry practice to being an environmental crime, as well as evolving in terms of techniques and practices (see Box 7.1 for a more developed example of an institution).

The second part of our definition of institutions describes them as self-policing. By this we mean that institutions are associated with social controls that act in a relatively automatic fashion to encourage conformity to the convention. Nonconformity with institutions is "counteracted in a regulated fashion, by repetitively activated, socially constructed, controls" (Jepperson, 1991: 145) that can increase the costs of nonconformity in several ways: "economically (it increases risk), cognitively (it requires more thought), and socially (it reduces legitimacy and the access to resources that accompany legitimacy)" (Phillips et al., 2000: 28). Thus, institutions are differentiated

---

Box 7.1. MONEY: THE PERFECT INSTITUTION

Money may be the perfect institution. It represents a set of "humanly devised constraints," as North (1990: 97) would say, that contain and shape all sorts of social, political, and economic relationships. Furthermore, it is almost completely taken for granted by the great majority of people and they generally have no ability to even think of an option other than the use of money.

Money, like all institutions, gains the power to structure social interactions through its embeddedness in socially constructed rules and routines that provide meaning and stability to social life. Money in a real sense does not exist as anything other than an institution. Unlike some other prototypical institutions, such as marriage, money has no value or understandable existence as anything other than a set of social agreements for the purpose of facilitating and constraining economic interactions and relationships.

The history of money as an institution is a fascinating and contested one. In David Graeber's (2011) treatise on the history of debt, he argues that the dominant narrative concerning the emergence of money as evolving out of more primitive, less efficient barter economies is pure fiction. The anthropological record on the matters seems clear: "No example of a barter economy, pure and simple, has ever been described, let alone the emergence from it of money; all available ethnography suggests that there never has been such a thing" (Humphrey, 1985: 48). Instead, Graeber proposes that money is, and always has been, the maker of markets and debt, rather than the reverse; that governments create money in order to manufacture indebted citizens who must then find ways of paying back those debts (through the formation of markets and market activity). Behind the creation of money is not an invisible force seeking more efficient mechanisms for exchange, but rather "a man with a gun." Graeber (2011: 364) argues that the creation of modern money is rooted in the need for governments to finance wars, and that was true in the time of the kings and it is true today: "The creation of central banks represented a permanent institutionalization of that marriage between the interests of warriors and financiers that had already begun to emerge in Renaissance Italy, and that eventually became the foundation of financial capitalism."

This is important for understanding money as an institution, since it strips away its status as simply a solution to a technical problem and debunks the idea of economy and society as separate spheres. Money as a tool of governments to tax citizens, and through those taxes to establish a monopoly on legitimate violence in and between societies, is tied deeply and inextricably to the passions and pursuits of its creators.

from other patterns of social action in that they are subject to self-regulating controls that create pressure to act according to the convention (Phillips et al., 2004).

Institutions in Modernity and Postmodernity

Within management and organizational research, some attention has been paid to changes in how scholars conceive of institutions (see, for example, Scott (2013)), but there has been relatively little consideration of the evolution of institutions as social-symbolic objects, and particularly to how institutions have changed as societies have transitioned to modernity and to postmodernity. We argue that institutions have undergone historical changes that parallel the shifts we described in relation to the self and the organization. It is not just that our institutions have changed (which of course they have) but rather that institutions as a type of object have changed. The qualities associated with institutions as a broad class of social-symbolic objects evolved in the transition to modernity and evolved again in the transition to postmodernity.

As we argued in Chapter 2, the transition to modernity involved a shift in how people conceived of social-symbolic objects, such that they become understood as manageable, rational, and perfectible. This was a fundamental shift from premodern conceptions of social-symbolic objects as natural, inevitable, or God-given—but in any case, unchanging—and thus beyond the scope of human intervention. The transition to postmodernity brought another set of shifts in understandings of social-symbolic objects: rather than focusing on perfecting social-symbolic objects, the goals of actors conducting social-symbolic work became fragmented, so that efforts to change them might be aimed at a wide variety of potential end points. Similarly, the means to those ends shifted from the application of rationality to a plurality of possible methods, strategies, and technologies.

Institutions have been central in the transitions to modernity and postmodernity. With these transitions, institutions came to be understood first as the products of human effort and thus potentially perfectible (in modernity), and then more modestly changeable through human intervention (in postmodernity). Such a conception of institutions is in some ways obvious at this point in history, as we have myriad examples of individual and collective actors engaged in institutional work that has transformed the institutional landscapes.

But the degree to which many institutions can be changed by individuals or collective actors is still a matter of significant debate. While gender categories have become radically more fluid over the past decades, contemporary discussions of race as a social construction reveal the schisms in society (and the academy) with respect to what institutions are manipulable and which are not. More generally, institutions as a category of social-symbolic objects seem so complex and heterogeneous that making general arguments is difficult. We believe, however, that it is worthwhile considering institutions as a category of social-symbolic objects and exploring their collective history. So, to illustrate the changing nature of institutions and the historical foundations of the possibility of institutional work, we examine the history of one centrally important institution—language—and discuss the implications of its history for other institutions.

An Example: Language as an Institution

Language is, arguably, the most fundamental of social institutions. It is the foundation for all other institutions, a primary means through which all institutions are constructed, expressed, and encountered. At the same time, language—and more precisely, specific languages, language uses, and elements of language—are institutions in the same way as the institutions that language makes possible. Language is a set of conventions underpinned by relatively automatic social controls that include cognitive and normative, and occasionally regulative, mechanisms. Understanding language as an institution emphasizes a holistic conception that includes "not only rules for derivation of abstract syntactic strings but also rules specifying to whom, what, when, where and how we communicate" (Neustupný, 1974: 34).

Language represents an institution of a different order than most of the institutions examined in management and organizational research, where we more typically examine specific organizational forms, practices, or technologies, such as civil service bureaucracy, total quality management, collaborative networks, programing languages, medical treatments, or professional service firms. At first glance, language seems not to be an institution at all similar to these and consequently incomparable. From our perspective, however, this is not the case. Instead, we see language as an eminently instructive institution to consider when exploring how institutions have changed in the transitions to modernity and postmodernity.

LANGUAGE AS A MODERN INSTITUTION
Like all institutions, language has a history. Our interest in language as an institution stems from the ways in which languages have changed over time and especially the changes that occurred with the advent of modernity and the transition to postmodernity. Modern understandings of language mirror modern conceptions of the self and the organization—the products of human effort and thus manageable, potentially rational, and associated with some kind of perfectibility.

The qualities of language as a modern institution—manageable, rational, perfectible—are illustrated by what linguists refer to as "language planning," which emerged with the establishment of nation states. Language planning describes a set of formal processes intended to establish clear national borders and distinctive national identities. In France, this began with the *Académie française* in 1634—a time when European elites began to shift from Latin to local languages for formal functions. The aim of the *Académie* was to render the French language "pure, eloquent, and capable" by publishing grammars, dictionaries, and manuals of rhetoric (Nekvapil, 2011: 872).

Similar projects occurred across the emerging nation states, though with distinctive characteristics reflecting local realities. The formation of the Soviet Union, for instance, brought together more than one hundred ethnic groups, each with its own linguistic traditions, involving primarily oral languages. Unable to institutionalize Russian as the common language because of its association with oppression by the czars, early Soviet language planning involved the modernization of tens of languages through the creation of alphabets, orthography systems, textbooks, and primers (Nekvapil, 2011: 873).

In the United Kingdom, the standardization of the English language followed Anglo-Norman rule during which French was the language of regulation and administration. Although writing in English had continued during this period, it was marginalized, and so when it re-emerged as a language of formal governance, it was too heterogeneous to support a centralized state, and so the south-eastern Midland dialect used around London by the Court and merchants was chosen as the standard language for written communication.

Language as a modern institution was not, of course, solely the concern of state actors; a wide variety of individuals, groups, and organizations were preoccupied with language as manageable and improvable. As languages were modernized, an ideological turn occurred toward an understanding of language as more or less transparent (with more transparency being better). Transparency's most famous advocate was George Orwell, whose novel *1984* revolved around the relationship between truth and language. Orwell made an even more explicit plea for transparency in *Politics and the English language*, in which he urged us to "let the meaning choose the word, and not the other way about" (2013). The importance of Orwell's arguments and the more general call for transparency that marked the discourse around language use throughout much of the twentieth century is that it presumes a direct correspondence between language and the world. Efforts to shape language focused significantly on minimizing the degree to which language use obscured the "real world."

Looking across the efforts of nation states and other actors connected to the modernization of language, we see that language as a modern social-symbolic object has been understood as an object that can be shaped in ways that improve it, and that those improvements are seen as unequivocally positive. Languages are now defined as "modern" when they are homogeneous within national boundaries and complete in the sense that they can communicate all types of information (Neustupný, 1974). The modernization of language as an institution was consistent with broader shifts in the cultural understandings of institutions in the West. Across major institutional orders, including the bureaucratic state, capitalist markets, science, and representative government, there was a turn parallel to the one we have described in language, to understanding institutions as potentially perfectible products of human effort. The efforts of nation states to modernize language through large-scale, planned, educational, and administrative programs ran alongside similar efforts in these other domains. Similarly, the turn to transparency as a central priority in the evaluation of language is consistent with transformations that were occurring in relation to institutions of science, government, and commerce, which have been described as obsessed with "linear progress, machine-like efficiency, and grand, universal styles and solutions" (Hirt, 2009: 250).

LANGUAGE AS A POSTMODERN INSTITUTION
The transition of language from a modern to a postmodern institution did not involve the rejection of all modernization efforts, but rather involved problematizing the idea of language as perfectible and the potential for consensus over what constitutes improvement. While shifts in language and language use associated with postmodernity are multiple and complex, we focus on two illustrative shifts: to language as commodity, and to a pluralistic politics of language.

Beginning with language as a commodity, in the twentieth century we see a change in cultural understandings of language that allow for language use, and especially style, to move from a quality that is closer or further from a pure, unadulterated usage, to something that could be legitimately idiosyncratic, and imbued with economic value.

The potential economic value of linguistic style is illustrated by the evolution of style guides for commercial writers and editors, such as the one published by the British newspaper, *The Times*. Across its history, we see a series of revisions that reflect changes not only in the position of the newspaper, but in language use more broadly. In 1913, when *The Times* published its first formal style guide, it was simply an alphabetical list of problematic spellings and grammatical forms, and a set of instructions for listing classified advertisements (Cameron, 2012). Halfway through the century, though, *The Times* style guide declared the publication to be a "national institution" with "a special responsibility to maintain the standards of a *philologically correct, unslovenly and accurate English*" (emphasis added).

This emphasis on correctness began to shift by 1970, when the newly revised style guide noted that the "English language changes continuously and the Style Book has to be revised periodically in order to account of new forms and to change preferences that have become obsolete." The most radical change occurred in 1992 when *The Times* updated and offered the style guide for sale, announcing that "this guide is not a work of stylistic dictatorship," but rather "for enlightenment and pleasure" (Cameron, 2012). What the story of *The Times* style guide exemplifies is a turn away from language as perfectible (as potentially "philologically correct") to something shapeable but arbitrary, to the point that a commercial publication might establish idiosyncratic language use as a part of its brand identity and commodify it in the form of a purchasable guide.

As ideas of language use and style have moved away from perfection and transparency toward idiosyncrasy and commodity, so too has the relationship between language and the nation state become fractured and fractious. Where language was once an instrument of the emerging modern nation state, signaling and constructing a coherent national culture, postmodernity has witnessed a breakdown of this relationship, owing significantly to mass migration stemming from wars, famine, poverty, and political unrest, as well as increasing affluence and transnationalism in the developed West (Rassool, 1998). The impact of globalization on language is documented by the debates around the language rights of minority groups, particularly those living in advanced, Western societies. Whereas the modernization of languages meant their homogenization within nation states and the establishment of authoritative texts, postmodern language is associated with "dissonant narratives, new sets of social relations and new events to fracture previous certainties" (Rassool, 1998: 95).

With the global movement of linguistic groups through immigration, commerce, and tourism, a complex set of attitudes has emerged toward the relationship between national and minority languages. In a study of language attitudes among different ethnic minority groups in Britain, for instance, Urdu and Panjabi immigrants explained their appetite for English as a way for their children to integrate into British culture, whereas representatives from Hindi-speaking, Chinese, and Bangladeshi communities emphasized maintaining the ability of children to speak in their own languages, for its positive impact on academic achievement and to avoid the relegation of their mother tongues to the home and community (Rassool, 1998). The differing attitudes of immigrant groups toward their first languages illustrates the complex relations among institutions, motivations, and social positions. The terrain in which national language debates now play out resonate neither with modernist efforts toward unity and coherence, nor with more recent notions of multiculturalism. Instead, the interplay of language, cultural identity, and national politics represent a fluid, contested, contingent politics.

Alongside national language politics, a set of linguistic politics has developed at more local levels. These local politics have concerned individual and group identities, and the use of specific terms deemed offensive by some. For example, on one front of the "culture wars" in the United States, contests over "politically correct" language were initially advanced by feminists in the 1970s battling over terms such as chair(person/man) and the use of masculine pronouns as universal.

If we were to adopt the view that language simply reflects social life, and thus changes in language reflect social change, then the "political correctness" debates would be of little interest. But, the political correctness debates were often focused on the nature of language, rather than on issues of discrimination or sexism (Cameron, 2012). There was often little disagreement about the basic underlying principles in question, such as whether men and women were equal, or whether people of color should be treated with respect.

Instead, much of the debate turned on language itself, and whether advocates of gender neutral terms and critics of racist terms were perverting language or reading meaning into words that wasn't really there. A central question was whether language use carries with it political positions or can be neutral and simply descriptive. What those who decry "politically correct" language object to is the forced choice it brings with it: "[Y]ou can say 'Ms. A. is the chair (person)' and convey approval of feminism, or you can say 'Miss A. is the chairman' and convey a more conservative attitude," but what you cannot do is adopt a neutral position, somehow conveying nothing more than "a certain woman holds a particular office" (Cameron, 2012: 119). In this way, debates about politically correct language reveal a quintessentially postmodern institution: language is neither universal nor neutral; change does not approach perfection or an essential core, but an alignment with immediate political contests. And with this shift comes the anxiety and creativity that are associated with postmodern institutions (Lyotard, 1984).

Modern and Postmodern Institutions

We have focused on language as an institution in order to illustrate a more general phenomenon—the shifting nature of institutions from premodern, to modern, to postmodern. Language in these transitions has changed dramatically: from a local, primarily oral set of premodern institutions; to a modern set of institutions the consistency and transparency of which was enforced by the state and normative authorities such as publishers, universities, and leading authors; to a pluralistic, contested, commodified postmodern institution. Though the specifics differ, this pattern is common across a wide range of institutions rooted in science, art, markets, and the state (Gergen, 2009a; Jameson, 1991; Lyotard, 1984; Rorty, 2009).

In our brief overview of the history of institutions as social-symbolic objects we make three main claims. First, we claim that institutions as a category have a shared history, at least in the West since the advent of modernity. This may seem an uncontroversial claim, since it echoes the historian's emphasis on the interrelationships among broad social-historical shifts that cut across specific societal domains. It also echoes broad characterizations of modernity and the enlightenment, as well as postmodernity and "the sixties," that are embedded in popular and academic cultures. At the same time, it contrasts with the emphasis in management and organizational research on the idiosyncratic histories of specific institutions. Even historical studies of institutions have tended to focus on their distinctive evolutionary paths (Jones and Massa, 2013; Rao et al., 2003), rather than the common trajectory shared by institutions across different societies and societal domains. This first claim, therefore, is really a call for a shift in emphasis from focusing on institutional idiosyncrasies to commonalties.

Second, we claim that institutions as social-symbolic objects not only share a history, but have changed in specific ways. In the transition to modernity, institutions as a class of social-symbolic objects came to be understood as perfectible by actors through rational means. Then in postmodernity, they came to be understood as changeable by actors, but without a single perfect endpoint. Institutions became more arbitrary—products of human accomplishment but associated with means and motives that were driven by political, economic, and social dynamics that were specific to times and places.

Our third claim somewhat tempers the first two. The history of institutions as social-symbolic objects is—like that of selves and organizations—both coherent and fragmented. Although we see a great deal of common movement in the understanding of institutions through modernity and postmodernity, there is also significant heterogeneity with respect to which institutions came to be seen as malleable both across institutions and across segments of Western society. Thus, the "culture wars" in 1960s, 1970s, and 1980s around the status of such social-symbolic objects as gender, race, and ethnicity, and more recently the deep divides around issues of immigration and refugees, revolve significantly around the constructed versus essential nature of sets of institutions.

Conceptualizing Institutional Work

We have defined institutions as combinations of conventions and social controls that ensure conformity with respect to their meaning and use. By extension, institutional work refers to the purposeful, reflexive efforts of individuals, collective actors, and networks of actors to shape those conventions and manage the social controls that underpin them. It is social-symbolic work carried out to create, change, or maintain institutions. This, necessarily, includes a wide variety of actions, since institutions are fantastically hetero-geneous, as are the actors who might try to shape them, and the contexts in which those efforts occur.

At the same time, institutional work in no way includes all action that affects institutions, since that would include all human behavior; no behavior occurs outside of some set of institutions or occurs without affecting the institutions that shape them. Giddens' (1984) structuration theory captures this relation-ship neatly, showing how all social action at least partially reproduces institu-tions and may, intentionally or unintentionally, and often only infinitesimally, transform them. Thus, to define institutional work based on its outcomes would include all action, and thus create a meaningless concept. Instead, institutional work is defined by its aims, which involve efforts to change or maintain higher-order institutions (such as marriage, bureaucracy, or currency) or to change or maintain the local instantiation of such institutions (as in local marriage prac-tices or rules, particular organizational forms, or the ways in which currencies are used, traded, or stored) (Lawrence et al., 2009).

A wide variety of types of institutional work have been documented in management and organizational research. Lawrence and Suddaby (2006) ini-tially described seventeen types based on a review of institutional research in major management and organizational journals. They condensed the types of institutional work into three main categories—creating, maintaining, and disrupting institutions. Since then, organizational scholars have identified many variations, including institutional "dirty work" (Hirsch and Bermiss, 2009), defensive institutional work (Maguire and Hardy, 2009), narrative insti-tutional work (Zilber, 2009), contextualization work (Gond and Boxenbaum, 2013), institutional experimentation (Malsch and Gendron, 2013), and justifi-cation work (Taupin, 2013).

Scholars have also explored a range of organizational activities as forms of institutional work, including leadership as institutional work (Kraatz, 2009), standardization as institutional work (Slager et al., 2012), gender equality as institutional work (Styhre, 2013), organizing events as institutional work (Hardy and Maguire, 2010; Schüßler et al., 2014), participatory action research as institutional work (Dover and Lawrence, 2010a), and qualitative research as institutional work (Symon et al., 2008).

Dimensions of Institutional Work

Identifying types of institutional work has been useful, but does not address the more basic question of how institutional work is done—that is, its dimen-sions. As with self work and organization work, we focus on the discursive, relational, and material dimensions of institutional work, recognizing that in any instance of institutional work, all of these dimensions are present.

THE DISCURSIVE DIMENSION

As institutions are cognitive and cultural phenomena, it is not surprising that discourse is central to their construction, maintenance, and transformation (Phillips et al., 2004; Phillips and Malhotra, 2008). Moreover, scholarly interest in institutional work developed during the same period that interest in the relationship between discourse and institutions developed and was driven by some of the same philosophical concerns. As a result, discourse represents the most recognized and developed dimension of institutional work. Studies of discursive approaches to institutional work, including narratives, rhetoric, rules, and scripts, have dominated empirical studies of institutional work, with a recent review noting forty-six of fifty-four empirical studies of institutional work in major organizational journals focused on its discursive dimension (Hampel et al., 2017).

An interesting example of the importance of the discursive dimension of institutional work comes from the world of toilets. Open defecation is a serious problem in many countries, where the practice is associated with infection and disease, as well as social inequality. Nearly one billion people worldwide practice open defecation, a situation that contributes significantly to diarrhea, which is the second largest global cause of death among children under five. The negative effects of open defecation (and the associated lack of toilets) disproportionately affect women, with a large proportion of girls in sub-Saharan Africa dropping out of school when they start menstruating because of inadequate access to sanitation (Bartram and Cairncross, 2010), and women in India suffering sexual harassment and assault due to the lack of privacy and control associated with open defecation (Jadhav et al., 2016). Installing toilets might seem like a simple, effective solution. But the problem is less technological than cultural and cognitive: institutionalized beliefs have undermined attempts to shift practices even when toilets have been installed.

Where success has been achieved, it has often been through highly discursive institutional work. In rural Zambia, Chief Macha of Choma, who prefers the title "King of Shit," says, "We have to start talking about poop" (Bohn, 2014). Chief Macha went from village to village for six years campaigning on the slogan, "No shit, please! One family, one toilet." In rural India, the most famous discursive institutional work around sanitation involves a series of programs under the label, "No Toilet, No Bride." In Haryana State, this program began in 2005, with social marketing campaigns that encouraged families of marriage-age girls to demand that potential husbands' families construct a toilet as a condition of marriage. The campaign involved mass media messaging on billboards, posters, and radio advertisements, with catchphrases such as "no toilet, no bride" and "no loo, no I do" (Stopnitzky, 2017). The campaign was highly effective. As described by a local NGO leader, the program was "a bloodless coup": "When I started, it was a cultural taboo to even talk about toilets. Now it's changing. My mother used to wake up at 4am to find someplace [in the fields or rivers] to go quietly. My wife wakes up at 7am and can go safely in her home" (Stopnitzky, 2017: 271).

As the toilets story makes clear, the discursive dimension of institutional work involves an array of specific discursive strategies and tactics, often used in combination to achieve specific institutional ends. Research on management fashions, for example, has highlighted the interplay of a range of discursive activities, including defining and lobbying to achieve political ends, theorizing and mimicking (which imbues material objects with borrowed meanings) to shape technical debates, and professionalization and identity construction (Perkmann and Spicer, 2008). Similarly, research has shown the importance of the discursive dimension of institutional work in the construction the Israeli high-tech sector involving combinations of myths, stories, and other discursive activities (Zilber, 2006, 2007, 2011).

An important issue in understanding the discursive dimension of institutional work involves the role of texts, and particularly individual texts. In a series of studies of the deinstitutionalization of DDT, for example, Maguire and colleagues (Hardy and Maguire, 2010; Kisfalvi and Maguire, 2011; Maguire and Hardy, 2009) highlight the distinctive role of Rachel Carson's (1962) *Silent spring*: "Silent Spring problematized practices of DDT use—as not safe, effective, or necessary—and, in so doing, made a case for institutional change" (Maguire and Hardy, 2009: 156). Research focused on specific texts makes clear their significance in institutional work. Texts transcend the limitations associated with individual actions, which "do not easily allow for the multiple readings by multiple individuals that are necessary if ideas for organizing are to be transmitted across time and space" (Phillips et al., 2004: 638). Texts, on the other hand, do. Texts can be passed from person to person, renewed, reconstituted, and repurposed. And in this process, texts form the foundation for institutions, and as such are key intermediate products of institutional work.

Thus, an important question when considering the discursive dimension of institutional work is which texts are likely to have an impact. From a discourse perspective, the question is which texts will become embedded: which texts will be "adopted and incorporated by other organizations to become part of standardized, categorized, generalized meanings," such that it "is used as an organizing mechanism across individual situations" (Phillips et al., 2004: 643). Although a range of idiosyncratic factors may affect whether a particular text gets taken up and embedded in discourse, it is more likely to occur when the actors who produce the text have power and legitimacy

(Hardy and Phillips, 1998), the text takes the form of a recognizable genre (Bakhtin, 1986), and it is obviously connected to other texts in the discourse (Fairclough, 2001).

A particularly important form of discourse in institutional work is rhetoric. The significant relationship between rhetoric and institutions has been clear at least since Alvesson's (1993) essay connecting knowledge, myths, and rhetoric in knowledge-intensive firms (Green and Li, 2011). The significance of rhetoric to the discursive dimension of institutional work is tied to the ability of some actors, "perhaps because of their social skill and facility with varieties of capital," to employ rhetoric to affect institutions in organizations, fields, and communities (Suddaby and Viale, 2011: 434). The use of rhetoric goes beyond making rational arguments in support of altered institutional arrangements: writing on rhetoric has emphasized the important roles of pathos and egos, as well as logos, in justifying institutional change (Brown et al., 2012). A key dynamic associated with the use of rhetoric in institutional work has been the linking of local and extra-local ideas. In the London insurance market, for example, professionals connected local contingencies to universal themes to affect the institutionalized arrangements around electronic trading. Similarly, in a struggle over the legitimation of a new organizational form (a multidisciplinary partnership including both lawyers and accountants), the actors involved connected "institutional vocabularies" and "theorizations of change" to effect institutional change (Suddaby and Greenwood, 2005).

Looking across research that has highlighted the discursive dimension of institutional work, it is not surprising that its dynamics reflect the intersection of discourse and institutions. A range of studies have shown the differential use and impacts of different forms of discourse, especially highlighting the roles of narrative and rhetoric. An important, but somewhat underexamined issue in this research has been the institutionally situated and recursive nature of discursive work. The studies noted above explore how people working to affect institutional arrangements employ storytelling and persuasive language but leave aside the status of these forms of discourse as institutions in their own right. The arguments we have made previously (Phillips et al., 2004) about the potential effectiveness of individual texts—depending on their authors, their genres, and their relationships to other texts—are fundamentally recursive, in that institutions are built upon other institutions. This relationship is important to note and has implications beyond our immediate discussion of the discursive dimension of institutional work. It highlights the ways in which people engaged in institutional work are always focusing on the malleability of a small set of institutions, while bracketing the malleability of the institutions on which they rely to engage in institutional work, such as in this case institutions of storytelling and rhetoric, as well as the myriad institutions that form the backdrop for this activity. This is more than strategic action; it represents a kind of flexible and strategic bracketing where, for a time and a purpose, we treat most of the social world as fixed and taken for granted while we work to shape other parts purposefully and reflexively.

THE RELATIONAL DIMENSION

The relational dimension is central to our conception of social-symbolic work, and yet research on institutional work tends to leave this dimension implicit or overlooks it entirely. Only recently has managing relationships emerged as a matter of interest in the study of institutional work (Bertels et al., 2014; Gill and Burrow, 2018; Smets and Jarzabkowski, 2013). The relative lack of attention to this dimension may stem in part from the kinds of actors who have been the focus of research on institutional work: in their review of the empirical literature, Hampel et al. (2017) show that while studies of institutional work have moved on from the narrow focus on individual actors associated with institutional entrepreneurship research, most studies still concentrate on relatively similar groups of actors, usually with shared interests and coming from the same field, making their relationships non-problematic (e.g., Currie et al., 2012). Where the institutional work of heterogeneous actors has been examined, it nearly always focuses on conflicts among the group and the effects of these conflicts, rather than the work done to build and leverage relationships. Thus, the institutional work literature has tended to present a relatively narrow view of how relationships and relational action are involved in the efforts of actors to shape institutional arrangements.

A fascinating case of institutional work that highlights this relational dimension is offered by the Gulabi Gang—also known as the Pink Sari Brigade for the group's electric-pink sari uniform. The Gulabi Gang, based in one of the poorest regions of Uttar Pradesh, is "the world's largest existing women's vigilante group," with 20,000 members in India and a new network of members in France (Sen, 2012). The institutional work of the Gulabi Gang focuses on resisting the institutionalized oppression of women. Primarily targeting corrupt officials and violent husbands, the Gang's activities "range from beating up men who abuse their wives to shaming officials" (Dhillon, 2007). The Gulabi Gang's origins stem from an incident in which a friend of their leader, Sampat Pal, was beaten by her alcoholic husband, and the local police, known to be indifferent to violence against women, ignored her plight. Sampat tried to rescue her friend but was chased away by the inebriated husband. Refusing to give up, Sampat "gathered some neighbors, returned to her friend's house, and thrashed the abusive husband in view of the community" (Sen, 2012).

Initially, the Gang was made up of a few old friends of Sampat's, but their success in battling domestic abuse attracted dozens of female neighbors. The Gang began to train in counter-aggression techniques, including "smearing abusive men with chili powder," but their most popular drill involved the use of "lathis," the baton usually carried by local police officers when on patrol. Though not only relational, the institutional work of the Gulabi Gang revolves around its relationships to the women of its region, their families, friends, and neighbors, and especially their husbands and government officials. Moreover, the Gang's institutional work is relational at each step: it is motivated by relationships, aims to reshape relationships, and draws on other relationships as critical resources.

The relational dimension of institutional work connects to other dimensions in complex ways, potentially facilitating and constraining other facets of institutional work. This complexity is illustrated by recent research on the institutional work of The Nature Conservancy (TNC) (Bertels et al., 2014). Core to TNC's institutional work are its relationships to large corporations with access to financial resources that can be used to purchase and protect large pieces of land. But in 2003, TNC was the target of a *Washington Post* exposé that suggested, "it had developed too close a relationship with corporate America." The *Post* accused TNC of "stacking" its board with executives from environmentally unfriendly industries, including oil, chemical, auto, mining, and forestry (Bertels et al., 2014: 27). Accused of allowing corporations to "greenwash" their activities, TNC had to restructure its board, moving away from major corporations, and develop a policy to curtail any conflicts of interest. Whereas the institutional work of the Gulabi Gang seemed to be largely advanced (and triggered) by its relational dimension, the more complex interorganizational networks of US environmental movement organizations demand more responsive and potentially complicated relational work.

When considering the relational dimension of institutional work, a key issue is the role of power. Although institutional work is inherently political, the relationship between power and institutional work has been largely neglected, as it has with respect to institutions more generally (Lawrence and Buchanan, 2017). Where power is made explicit as a part of institutional work, it is often in highly contested settings. In the English NHS, for example, specialist doctors engaged in institutional work to maintain their professional dominance in the face of new nursing and medical roles (Currie et al., 2012). Motivated by threats to their professional power, the specialist doctors adopted highly relational forms of institutional work, such as delegating routine tasks and co-opting other high-status groups in ways that maintained their control over key resources and enhanced their professional status. The connection between power and institutional work may be clearest in situations of intense conflict, in which actors "seek power by creating, supporting, or modifying institutions," as in the case of the 1968 Third World Strike at San Francisco State College, where the college president, motivated by a dispute with student activists, worked to convert symbolic resources into greater authority on campus (Rojas, 2010: 1263). In Rojas' (2010: 1276) study, this process is an iterative one, in which "the authority to coerce, is tied to the creation of specific rules, which then are subject to further adjustment."

Although less well attended to than the discursive dimension of institutional work, understanding the relational dimension is critical, especially in terms of the energy that fuels institutional work, and the intended and unintended consequences of such work. The barriers to changing institutional practices and beliefs can be massive and involve significant risk for those involved. Thus, institutional work requires significant social energy, which arises in relationships that create emotions and are organized around sets of meaningful rituals (Collins, 2004; Lawrence, 2004). Once energized, institutional work remains dependent on social relations because institutions are embedded in and facilitative of those relationships, such that to affect institutions is to affect relationships—entrenching some while disrupting others and creating some anew. This is a part of what makes the outcomes of institutional work so difficult to anticipate.

THE MATERIAL DIMENSION

The final dimension of institutional work is the material dimension. This dimension is interesting both because of its obvious importance—anyone who has ever worked to affect institutional arrangements can testify to the important role of specific material objects, even if they are quite banal, such as the sheets of paper onto which memos, agendas, and letters are printed, or the buildings within which much institutional work is performed—and because it has been so overlooked in studies of institutional work. More broadly in the social sciences, there are multiple streams of research that focus on materiality and social life, but relatively little research has explored the role of material objects in institutional change, maintenance, or disruption (Jones et al., 2017).

The making of the *Oxford English Dictionary* (OED) illustrates the material dimension of institutional work. The first edition of the OED was originally proposed in 1858 and was expected to take a decade to assemble. In the end, it took nearly seventy years to complete. Understood as institutional work, constructing the OED was both institutional creation (establishing the OED itself as an institution) and institutional maintenance (preserving the meaning and history of every word in the English language). Creating the OED had an obvious discursive dimension, since the aim was to create a truly comprehensive dictionary of the English language, "from the time of the earliest records [c.AD740] down to the present day, with all the relevant facts concerning their form, sense-history, pronunciation, and etymology." This work also had an important, though less obvious, relational dimension. From the outset, the OED's creators realized that achieving this incredible objective would require a huge effort, and so a strategy from the beginning was to employ volunteer readers: "147 men (and a small number of women) who happily agreed to help find quotations showing a variety of words in contexts that the editor should find illustrated their various meanings and senses" (Winchester, 2003: 53).

Perhaps less immediately obvious when considering the making of a dictionary is the material dimension of this complex institutional work. Although the OED focuses on words and meanings, these need material expression to be captured, stored, and managed. In the 1800s, this meant a highly material solution:

> To help him in arranging the words and quotation slips—the crucially important pieces of paper that would be the project's building blocks—Coleridge had a carpenter build for him, in oak, a small suite of pigeon-holes, to hold and permit the alphabetical arrangement of the various quotation slips that his volunteers sent in. The arrangement which he designed was six square holes high, nine across—giving him a total of 54 pigeon-holes, with some 260 inches of linear space that were thought sufficient to hold comfortably between 60,000 and 100,000 of the slips. No greater number could Coleridge ever imagine his having to deal with.   (Winchester, 2003: 57)

Unfortunately for Coleridge, his estimates of necessary capacity turned out to be rather conservative, as his successors in the project ultimately collected nearly six million quotations, which made his fifty-four pigeon-holes completely insufficient.

The material dimension of institutional work can be summarized in terms of two key points. First, we can see material objects as the products of institutional work in which people embed sets of assumptions about the social world in physical form and then use the objects produced for practical purposes. This process is evident in the birth of the "Kodak Moment" (Munir and Phillips, 2005). In 1882, Kodak introduced the roll-film camera, which was far more convenient than its predecessors, but came with a loss of image quality unacceptable to professional photographers. Kodak's eventual success with this design resulted from it reshaping the institution of photography away from something done by professionals to something done by amateurs in everyday situations. This included tying photography to the notion of a holiday, and creating new roles, including the very modern "Kodak girl" who carried a camera in her handbag. Kodak thus created a material form of photography, but then needed to attach to the new kind of camera a set of beliefs and assumptions that would give it value in the world.

Second, we can see that material objects are also tools used by actors as they perform institutional work. The use of material objects as tools of institutional work involves a kind of institutional bracketing in which actors rely on certain sets of ossified assumptions and beliefs in the form of material objects, to reshape other beliefs. The Gulabi Gang, for instance, adopted the lathis (sticks) used by the police, not only as a physical instrument intended to inflict pain, but also as symbols of power and control. The impact of material objects on institutional work can also occur inadvertently, as in the case of an Italian business newspaper that integrated its online and offline news offerings with unexpected consequences: "The new technology (website) offers possibilities for action—indeed proposes action—to the journalists that differ from the action the print proposes and the journalists engage in on the newspaper" (Raviola and Norbäck, 2013: 1178–9). Here, the material dimension of institutional work takes on something of a life of its own—influencing other dimensions by allowing and even offering new possibilities for action. Material objects in this case trigger institutional work by proposing actions that cause dilemmas, constructing how these dilemmas are interpreted by framing understandings of the present and the past, and shaping action to resolve such dilemmas.

Who Does Institutional Work?

Traditional accounts of institutions and agency provide only a limited picture of the actors involved—often locating them at the center or periphery of fields (Greenwood and Suddaby, 2006; Leblebici et al., 1991), attributing both their motivations and abilities to this partial understanding of who they are in relation to the institutions that structure their lives. In contrast, research on institutional work has begun to take more seriously the idea that different people in communities and societies interact with institutions in different ways, with different resources and responsibilities, and different appreciations of the degree to which they can and should influence those institutions. Here, we consider three roles that individuals and collective actors might take on in relation to institutional arrangements—institutional entrepreneurs, institutional caretakers, and institutional troublemakers.

INSTITUTIONAL ENTREPRENEURS

Institutional entrepreneurs were the first group of actors to which institutional researchers paid significant attention. By institutional entrepreneur we mean an actor who "[leverages] resources to create new institutions or transform existing ones" (Maguire et al., 2004: 657). DiMaggio's (1988) description of how institutional entrepreneurs create new institutions brought a useful element of agency back into institutional research and inspired numerous studies that described this role and the actors that occupied it. How such actors are described has varied tremendously, from detailed narrative biographies to systematic breakdowns of the dimensions along which they can be distinguished from other actors.

Two studies by Steve Maguire and his colleagues nicely exemplify the range of approaches found in the literature. In a study of Rachel Carson, author of the environmental treatise *Silent spring*, Maguire and Kisfalvi (2011) take a psychodynamic approach to understanding institutional entrepreneurs as individuals. They argue that Carson's institutional entrepreneurship stemmed from her passions and character, which they trace to formative experiences in her life: Carson was passionate about nature, a passion that was rooted, they argue, in a desire to maintain a strong emotional link to her mother with whom she spent idyllic time in the forest.

In stark contrast to this detailed, narrative, psychodynamic approach, Maguire et al.'s (2004) examination of institutional entrepreneurs in HIV/AIDS treatment is much more "objective." To identify the individuals who were central to the establishment of the Canadian Treatment Advocates Council (CTAC) in the late 1990s, they identify a set of ten "roles and activities that contributed to the emergence and institutionalization of the new practices," including "Participated in community-based precursor to CTAC" and "Drafted discussion documents for meetings." These roles and activities form the basis for a prominent data table in which they present a matrix of twenty-nine unnamed individuals coded "yes/no" for each role and activity, and infer from this table various conclusions about the identities of the institutional entrepreneurs.

In addition to the work exploring individuals as institutional entrepreneurs, another body of work has examined how collective actors, including groups (Dorado, 2013), organizations (Garud et al., 2002), and industry associations (Greenwood et al., 2002), can act as institutional entrepreneurs. Rooted in organization studies, the attention to the institutional entrepreneurship of collective actors is important and has provided significant insights into how and when such actors are able to achieve collective agency, as well as when that agency might translate into institutional effects. An important challenge in conceptualizing organizations as institutional entrepreneurs has been the assignment of agency and intentionality; institutional entrepreneurship, and institutional work more broadly, is recognizable by its aims, which might be inferred from its accomplishments but not necessarily or non-problematically.

The study of institutional entrepreneurs and their role in institutional change brings up an enduring issue—whether it is more useful to focus on "institutional entrepreneurs" and thus explore the characteristics of individuals and organizations that might trigger and enable their efforts to shape institutions, or to focus on "institutional entrepreneurship" and thus examine the resources and capacities necessary for this kind of work. We suggest a third possibility: that the "institutional entrepreneur" represents a discrete social role, available and meaningful to actors who choose and work to take on that role for some period of time. Focusing on the idea of a role is helpful because it provides a way of locating the concept outside of identity, but also distinct from simply a set of activities or intentions (Järventie-Thesleff and Tienari, 2015).

The "institutional entrepreneur" is, we argue, a role that people, individually or collectively, step into with some awareness and reflexivity, though not necessarily before they have begun to engage in activities we would categorize as institutional entrepreneurship. Role awareness may be rooted in one's own sensemaking, triggered perhaps by noticing one's own surprising actions, or in sensegiving by others who for whatever reason wish to assign the actor to that role. The idea of institutional entrepreneurship as a role also brings up the question of its epistemological status. It suggests that for the study of institutional entrepreneurship, we need to establish a set of criteria with respect to recognizing people as institutional entrepreneurs that goes beyond simply identifying actions intended to shape institutional arrangements, but stops short of connecting institutional entrepreneurship to some essential set of personal qualities.

If we look, for instance, at the case of Rachel Carson, the perspective we are suggesting highlights the complex network of interdependencies arising from: Carson's childhood and personal history that might have predisposed her to working to change institutions; the institutional work in which she engaged (including writing *Silent spring*) that was clearly aimed at affecting institutions; and her understanding of her own role in the environmental movement. It is at the point those threads connect that we suggest the role of institutional entrepreneur sits—the point at which Carson with some awareness stepped into the role of institutional entrepreneur working to create new institutions and disrupt existing ones.

INSTITUTIONAL CARETAKERS

An important outcome of the increased scholarly interest in institutional work has been the attention paid to how actors work to maintain institutions, an issue previously assumed to be non-problematic since institutions were by definition enduring. We refer to actors who carry out this maintenance as institutional caretakers. Much of the empirical research on institutional maintenance has investigated situations of significant contest (Currie et al., 2012; Trank and Washington, 2009), where maintenance involves "defensive institutional work" (Maguire and Hardy, 2009). A smaller body of work has begun to examine the problem of institutions requiring maintenance for more mundane reasons, including simple entropy (Dover and Lawrence, 2010b), that might create the need for preservation rather than defense. It is these latter situations in which the role of the institutional caretaker is especially important.

Giraffedata is an institutional caretaker and an answer to one of the enduring mysteries of Wikipedia—who edits the entries and why? Giraffedata is one of those editors, but one with unmatched passion for a specific aim—to rid Wikipedia articles of the phrase, "comprised of." In his own words,

> I began systematically replacing "comprised of" in Wikipedia in December 2007. At that time, 11,700 articles contained the phrase. I edited about 140 a week through May 2010, totaling 18,000 ... By August 2010, I had removed every instance of "comprised of" (except the 150 or so in quotations) and entered a mode of editing the new occurrences as they were introduced.   (User, 2015)

In the real world, Giraffedata is Bryan Henderson, a software engineer from San Jose, California. In the world of Wikipedia, Giraffedata is a serious contributor, consistently placing in the top 1,000 most active editors (McMillen, 2015). More than that, however, Giraffedata is "something of a superstar among the tiny circle of people who closely monitor Wikipedia." A Wikimedia Foundation employee described Giraffedata as "one of my favorite Wikipedians of all time" (McMillen, 2015). Not only has Giraffedata singlehandedly rid Wikipedia of the scourge of "comprised of," his user page provides an elaborate description of his work, the methods he uses, the problem he is addressing, the arguments against his project, reactions to his project, and a list of his many accolades ("barnstars" in Wikipedia jargon).

Focusing on roles is particularly useful from a social-symbolic work perspective as it highlights the motivations, emotions, and routines that make up the lived experience of institutional work (Biddle, 1986). In the case of institutional caretakers, this is a lived experience largely neglected in the literature. Although Giraffedata may seem like an extreme example, his commitment to the purity of Wikipedia illustrates an important point about institutional caretakers more generally. Unlike the defensive institutional work that has been explored in depth by organizational scholars, persistent, careful effort to ensure that institutions endure, function, and live up to expectations, is much less dramatic and less obviously rewarded. Thus, the institutional caretaker may require alternative motivations and rewards that may be less obvious to the outsider.

For Giraffedata, the issue is compelling enough for him to write a 6,000-word treatise (on Wikipedia, of course) describing why the phrase is ungrammatical. More simply, though, Henderson says of his project: "I'm proud of it" (McMillen, 2015). While we might not associate the mundanity of the institutional caretaker role with high passions, it may be exactly such passions that the role requires. The study of emotions in institutional work has paid particular attention to its role in energizing institutional change (Lawrence, 2017; Voronov and Vince, 2012). Though such a connection is more obvious than its role in motivating institutional caretakers, Giraffedata's story makes clear that committing oneself to repairing and restoring an institution would be difficult without some significant emotional connection to it.

Giraffedata's approach to his role may be similarly informative. What is interesting about his actions were their routine nature, and how he worked to make them even more routine, developing technological aids and solutions to the repetitive and demanding nature of the work.

> Every Sunday night before going to bed, Henderson follows an editing routine... He begins by running a software program that he wrote himself, which sends a request to Wikipedia's server for articles containing the phrase "comprised of."... The program then compares these titles against an offline database of articles that Henderson has edited within the last six months.... Next, a simple Web page is generated on the giraffe-data.com Web server, which contains a list of links to the edit page for each remaining article. Henderson can now easily click on each entry and make the necessary changes. Finally, the program updates the database of recently edited pages. (McMillen, 2015)

While we may be used to such approaches in the world of technology, where caretakers look after physical and virtual machines, and regularly develop specialized equipment to do so, the idea of institutional caretakers developing tools to facilitate their roles seems less obvious. And yet, when we think about the complex combinations of ideational and material objects that make up some institutions this begins to make sense. Imagine complex institutions such as the corporation, currencies, markets, and regulation without specialized maintenance equipment managed by devoted institutional caretakers observing and recording compliance and non-compliance.

INSTITUTIONAL TROUBLEMAKERS

We refer to actors who work to disrupt existing institutions in some way as institutional troublemakers. Institutional troublemakers can find themselves in considerable conflict with other actors who have an interest in maintaining the status quo and who respond by undermining and even punishing actors who threaten it. In fact, the degree of resistance faced by an institutional troublemaker is a good an indicator of the degree of institutionalization of the arrangements they seek to disrupt.

A famous recent example was Aaron Swartz, who committed suicide on January 11, 2013 (for more detailed accounts, see Day, 2013; Doctorow, 2013; Madrigal, 2013). Swartz's death followed the rejection of a plea bargain by US federal prosecutors regarding his arrest on two counts of wire fraud and eleven violations of the Computer Fraud and Abuse Act. Swartz accomplished a great deal in his twenty-six years, including co-creating the RSS specification that provides a standardized format to publish blogs and news sites, and helping build Reddit. After Reddit was acquired by Wired/Conde Nast, Swartz "engineered his own dismissal and got cashed out, and then became a full-time, uncompromising, reckless and delightful shit-disturber" (Doctorow, 2013).

As recounted by his friend, blogger Cory Doctorow (2013), Swartz's "stunts were breathtaking." One such stunt involved "singlehandedly liberat[ing] 20 percent of US law": although much case law was technically in the public domain, the system (PACER) through which people could access it charged a fee for each request, and so Swartz spent "a small fortune" to download a huge amount of this data to make it freely available online to the public.

Swartz is most famous as an institutional troublemaker for the act which would ultimately lead to his arrest. On January 26, 2010, he used a laptop at the Massachusetts Institute of Technology (MIT) to rapidly download a large number of articles from JSTOR, the non-profit digital academic library. The downloading was noticed by JSTOR and MIT, which led to "a cat-and-mouse game" between Swartz and MIT: "They'd figure out a way to stop the downloads, and Swartz would come up with a way to route around the defenses" (Madrigal, 2013). This continued for a year, until in January 2011 Swartz was arrested for downloading one hundred times more articles than the rest of MIT combined during the period in question (Madrigal, 2013). Although it is not known what Swartz intended to do with the downloaded articles, he had previously written the Guerrilla Open Access Manifesto, which declared: "We need to take information, wherever it is stored, make our copies and share them with the world" (Swartz, 2008).

An important part of the Swartz story, and its implications for our understanding of institutional troublemakers, is the reaction of US federal prosecutors. After Swartz surrendered himself to authorities and was released on bail, JSTOR released a statement stating that although Swartz's actions constituted a "significant misuse" of their database, the organization "had no interest in this becoming an ongoing legal matter." In contrast, the US federal prosecutors filed felony charges. There is speculation that federal prosecutors were motivated by their inability to successfully prosecute Swartz in relation to the PACER incident, while others suggest he was simply a victim of the times: "this was a post-WikiLeaks world, where large, powerful organisations were struggling to cope with the threat posed by internet hackers who could infiltrate government records and shut down entire online systems" (Day, 2013). In either case, it seems that Swartz was prosecuted in large part for the symbolic importance of his actions, and especially due to his identity as someone who could disrupt institutions that were understood by many as important and increasingly vulnerable.

The Aaron Swartz story, and especially the reaction of the FBI to his actions, point to the importance of the institutional troublemaker role beyond the specific disruptive actions in which such an actor might engage. This is a story told repeatedly in the context of state and corporate organizations that face actors who seem to have both the ability to disrupt treasured institutions and public visibility with respect to this ability. If we think of other recent prominent institutional troublemakers—Anonymous, Chelsea Manning, WikiLeaks—the role, reputation, and moral evaluation of all of these actors have become distinct from their specific actions.

THINKING ABOUT INSTITUTIONAL ROLES

When we look across these institutional roles—institutional entrepreneur, institutional caretaker, and institutional troublemaker—two issues emerge. The first is that these roles are not simply labels to describe people engaged in particular kinds of action in relation to institutions. In fact, they are public identities that people take on, that shape their behavior, and that shape the responses of others to that behavior. This suggests the possibility of developing a more nuanced language with respect to the positions that actors hold in relation to institutions. Whereas research on institutional work has tended to focus on actors' positions in fields, often reducing them to central or peripheral, we suggest that focusing on roles associated with institutional work might allow a more elaborated conception of how actors relate to institutions. At the same time, as we suggested in relation to institutional entrepreneurs, these are not essential or even stable traits, but rather social accomplishments that people and groups achieve at particular times in particular spaces.

A second issue concerns the relationship between roles and the notions of creating, maintaining, and disrupting institutions. Each of the roles we have discussed potentially lines up with the notions of creating, maintaining, and disrupting institutions, but the stories we have used to illustrate those roles shows people engaging in all kinds of institutional work, even if the role is most obviously connected to one of the three kinds. In Swartz's story, for instance, he clearly engaged in creating institutions—helping to establish practices and transform beliefs about how information can and should be shared. Less obviously, but no less importantly, Swartz also worked to maintain institutions: he fought to maintain existing freedoms of privacy and limits on the ability of the state and corporations to pursue cases against individuals believed to have made copies of copyrighted materials. It is therefore important to maintain a distinction between roles and forms of institutional work, as the typologies associated with each is likely to both ask and answer different questions.

Summary: A Conceptualization of Institutional Work

There have been many studies, and much theorizing, of institutional work. But this literature has tended to take the concept for granted and explore its dynamics in specific contexts, focusing on how particular sets of actors engage in institutional work in response to particular sets of challenges or threats. As a consequence, there has been a relative lack of comparative studies of institutional work and relatively thin theorizing of the phenomenon.

In the last two sections, we have laid the foundation for comparative research and deeper theorizing of institutional work by outlining a set of key dimensions of institutional work (discursive, relational, and material), and a set of important institutional roles (institutional entrepreneurs, caretakers, and troublemakers). Although institutional work has primarily been studied as a discursive phenomenon (Hampel et al., 2017), our discussion also highlights the importance of attending to its relational and material dimensions. Research that only explores the discursive dimension of institutional work is in danger of producing quite simple descriptions of a complex phenomenon. Moreover, systematically engaging with institutional work as multidimensional may provide a foundation for better comparative research that can show the distinctive qualities of institutional work in different contexts. The roles we have outlined also suggest important directions for future research. Although we have touched on some of those above, there is a final point to be made in this regard. These roles may interact in interesting ways with the discursive, relational, and material dimensions of institutional work. The ability of actors to harness material resources, for instance, may be especially important in maintaining institutions: embedding ideas and relationships in material technologies, for instance, may increase their durability as well as their taken-for-grantedness.

Conclusion

In this chapter, we have explored the purposeful, reflexive efforts of individuals, collective actors, and networks of actors to shape institutions. Although the literature on institutional work is relatively well developed, our understanding of these efforts is still limited in important ways. Our discussion of the history of institutions as social-symbolic objects highlights how institutions have changed over time. Using language as an example, we argued that there were important changes in how institutions were understood as social-symbolic objects with the transitions to modernity and postmodernity—changes which echoed those we saw in relation to selves and organizations. With modernity came systematic efforts to establish languages as "pure" forms—standardizing and stabilizing language use within nation states such that languages not only facilitated communication, but also acted as symbols of the nation state. Through rational means, state and non-state organizations worked to perfect languages and language use. This shift typified the modernizing of institutions that was seen in the arts, science, and government. The transition to postmodernity involved a move away from a belief in perfection through rational means, toward a pluralism within which aesthetics and politics were recognized as key foundations for institutions.

As institutions changed, so did institutional work. "Modern" institutional work was undertaken by agencies founded on principles of rationality and progress through the application of science and logic, as seen in the academies, policy bodies, and self-appointed authorities that attempted to "govern" the evolution of language. In contrast, "postmodern" institutional work is associated with a more fragmented, contentious set of actors, whose assumptions about what institutions should be and how they should change vary widely, but hinge on the idea of institutions as products of social negotiation with significant consequences for the influence and opportunities of different actors. The evolution of money as an institution exemplifies these shifts, with the invention of portable currencies tied, at least in part, to the consolidation of power in modernity and the emergence of the nation state, and the emergence of bitcoin and other cryptocurrencies stemming from both technological capabilities and a belief in the arbitrariness of state-backed currencies.

Building on an understanding of institutions as socially constructed patterns, compliance with which is tied to relatively automatic social controls, we proposed a conception of institutional work with discursive, relational, and material dimensions. Whereas previous writing has tended to emphasize these dimensions as descriptive of "kinds" or "forms" of institutional work, we argue that all instances of institutional work contain these dimensions. The question of who does institutional work has also been underexamined. Despite attention to institutional entrepreneurs, there remains a paucity of theoretically anchored ideas about other roles connected to institutional work. In this chapter, we suggested the idea of "institutional caretakers" and "institutional troublemaker," which we believe have value in exploring the dynamics of institutional work, but there remain, of course, a tremendous potential variety of other roles to identify and explore.

Key Resources

Institutions

The concept of an institution is at the heart of much of modern social science, cutting across sociology, economics, political science, and anthropology, as well as management and organizational research. Thus, trying to grasp both its core meanings and the scope of its use is a challenge even for scholars devoted to its study. We believe it is useful to adopt a bookend approach, focusing on early treatments of the concept that have proved enduringly influential, along with recent examinations that are pushing the concept in new directions and responding to changing social conditions. Thus, we suggest starting with Berger and Luckmann's *The social construction of reality*, as also suggested as a further resource in Chapter 2, but this time focusing on the insights they provide into the basic processes through which institutions emerge out of social interaction, and the need to assign meaning to our everyday habits and routines. Despite being one of the most cited texts in the social sciences, its systematic exposition of institutional dynamics, and especially its answer to the question of what is an institution, are often overlooked. A second classic source of insight regarding institutions is Geertz's *The interpretation of cultures*, especially the first chapter. Despite not discussing institutions explicitly in this chapter, Geertz provides a wonderful introduction to thinking about institutions in a way that is consistent with, and foundational for, a social-symbolic work perspective. In lyrical, inspiring, and sometimes perplexing prose, Geertz provides such a wealth of insights into culture, method, and theory that it is worth reading and rereading many times over. The last classic text we suggest is Mary Douglas' short book on *How institutions think*. As lively as Geertz, Douglas shares the fascination with the relationship between beliefs and social order. As Douglas explains, "Half of our task is to demonstrate this cognitive process at the foundation of the social order. The other half of our task is to demonstrate that the individual's most elementary cognitive process depends on social institutions" (Douglas, 1986: 45).

Berger, P. L., and Luckmann, T. 1966. *The social construction of reality: A treatise in the sociology of knowledge*. New York: Anchor.
Douglas, M. 1986. *How institutions think*. New York: Syracuse University Press.
Geertz, C. 1973. *The interpretation of cultures: Selected essays*. New York: Basic Books.

Examples of Institutional Work

To illustrate institutional work, we suggest a pair of academic articles and a pair of movies. The articles by Hardy and Maguire explore the institutional work done in relation to the chemical DDT. In their 2009 article on "Discourse and deinstitutionalization," Hardy and Maguire explore the institutional work done by outsiders to deinstitutionalize DDT use between 1962 and 1972. Their 2010 article on "Discourse, field-configuring events, and change in organizations and institutional fields" continues to focus on the institutional work around DDT, but focuses more specifically on the discursive dimension of institutional work, carried out in the context of the

United Nations conference leading to the Stockholm Convention on Persistent Organic Pollutants. The first movie we recommend tells the story of Nelson Mandela, describing his life journey as a *Long Walk to Freedom*. Mandela's institutional work in relation to the South African apartheid state has, of course, been documented in a host of media, but this film is based on Mandela's autobiography (which we also list below), which as US President Bill Clinton describes in the book's introduction, "is more than the autobiography of a great man. It's the chronicle of a son who breaks from his family and tradition; a voice for liberty who is captured, isolated and imprisoned; a revolutionary who transcends conflict to become a peacemaker and unifier; and a rare human being who, in freeing himself of his demons, also became free to give his extraordinary leadership to his country and the world" (Mandela, 2013: ix). Finally, we recommend Ken Loach's movie, *Bread and Roses*, which stands in contrast to the story of Mandela by highlighting a much less well-known and lower-key case of institutional work, that of Los Angeles janitors who fought for better working conditions and the right to unionize.

Chadwick, J. 2013. *Mandela: Long walk to Freedom*. <http://www.imdb.com/title/tt2304771/>.

Hardy, C., and Maguire, S. 2010. Discourse, field-configuring events, and change in organizations and institutional fields: Narratives of DDT and the Stockholm Convention. *Academy of Management Journal*, 53(6): 1365–92.

Loach, K. 1994. *Bread and Roses*. <http://www.imdb.com/title/tt0212826/>.

Maguire, S., and Hardy, C. 2009. Discourse and deinstitutionalization: The decline of DDT. *Academy of Management Journal*, 52(1): 148–78.

Mandela, N. 2013. *Long walk to freedom*. London: Hachette UK.

8

Institutional Work in Management and Organizational Research

In this chapter we:

1. Examine practice work as a type of institutional work that is well established as an area of study in management and organizational research.
2. Examine category work as a type of institutional work that is emerging as an area of study in management and organizational research.

Introduction

We will now turn to the existing literature on institutional work in management and organizational research. As with self work and organization work, the literature on institutional work is organized around types of social-symbolic objects—types of institutions in this case. We begin with research on practice work, which represents the most established stream of research on institutional work. We then turn to research on category work where, despite the development of a significant literature on categories, much less research has been done on this type of institutional work. We first review their evolution as research domains, and then explore how conceptualizing them as types of social-symbolic work might influence future scholarship.

Practice Work

Practices are shared routines (Whittington, 2006) that exist as "recognized forms of activity" (Barnes, 2001: 19) and guide the behavior of actors according to the requirements of specific situations (Goffman, 1959a; Pentland and

Rueter, 1994). Practices belong to social groups, rather than to individuals: groups define the correctness of a practice, provide ways for members to learn them, and establish the social mechanisms that enforce them (Barnes, 2001; Schatzki, 2001). Thus, for an activity to be recognizable by others as an instance of a practice, it must conform to social expectations set by a specific group or community (Whittington, 2006).

An important question is whether all practices are institutions. Unfortunately, there is no simple answer to this question. Traditional institutional scholarship would have answered "no"—practices only become institutions as they diffuse across a field and gain legitimacy and taken-for-grantedness. Indeed, a common criticism of journal reviewers in response to paper submissions that examine practices as institutions is that the focal phenomena are "just practices," and not institutions at all. This kind of reaction is especially common when research examines the practices of an organization, group, or small community, rather than the practices that characterize an organizational field, industry, or society, where some scholars would argue institutions are more usefully located. An alternative understanding of institutions, and the one we adopt here, suggests that all practices are indeed institutions, or at least involve a degree of institutionalization that is independent of the size of the social group within which they are located.

Practice Work in Management and Organizational Research

Practice work has been at the core of the institutional work literature, and the literature on institutions and agency more broadly. Research on practice work can usefully be grouped using the three broad aims of institutional work articulated by Lawrence and Suddaby (2006): creating, maintaining, and disrupting.

CREATING PRACTICES
Beginning with research on institutional entrepreneurship, scholars have developed an extensive literature on the work done to create new practices and establish practices as institutions (Garud et al., 2002; Greenwood and Suddaby, 2006; Lawrence, 1999; Lawrence and Phillips, 2004; Maguire et al., 2004). The creation of new practices has provided an important point of connection between the institutional and practice-focused research traditions (Gomez and Bouty, 2011; Lounsbury and Crumley, 2007; Rao et al., 2003; Zietsma and Lawrence, 2010).

An important finding in this literature has been the interaction of projective strategic action and more immediate practical problem-solving in the emergence of new practices. The creation of "active money management" as a practice in the US mutual fund industry, for instance, involved a combination of "strategically engineered deviations" and "localized contingencies" that stemmed from increased postwar investing and fund creation (Lounsbury and Crumley, 2007: 996). The creation of new practices has also been tied to complex sequences of collaboration and competition among heterogeneous sets of actors. Creating an alternative to clear-cutting in the forestry industry, for instance, involved extended interaction among forestry firms, environmental activists, First Nations, government agencies, and large corporate consumers of forest products (Zietsma and Lawrence, 2010). This research also shows that creating a new practice depends on the availability of "subject positions" from which actors can legitimate new practices, positions which are sometimes attained through professionalization projects (Lounsbury and Crumley, 2007; Suddaby and Viale, 2011) or by moving into positions of influence (Bertels et al., 2014; Gomez and Bouty, 2011; Maguire et al., 2004).

Whereas research on new practice creation highlights the early stages of practice work, the institutional entrepreneurship literature has tended to focus on the later stages of the process, in which actors work to institutionalize practices. Studies of institutional entrepreneurship are at the core of the institutional work literature more broadly, having been a central motivating force in establishing the move to understand how and why actors work to shape institutions (DiMaggio, 1988; Lawrence and Suddaby, 2006). Hardy and Maguire (2017) organize this literature in terms of its attention to the properties and positions of institutional entrepreneurs. Like trait theories of leadership, research focused on properties suggests that institutional entrepreneurs represent an "analytically distinguished social type" (Beckert, 1999: 786) with specific cognitive and emotional capacities that allow non-compliance and creativity with respect to institutional arrangements (Kisfalvi and Maguire, 2011). In contrast, research focusing on social positions explains who does and does not act as an institutional entrepreneur in terms of people's roles in fields and organizations: Battilana (2011), for instance, showed that the social position of clinical managers in the UK NHS significantly affected their likelihood of acting as institutional entrepreneurs.

A second key dimension that divides the institutional entrepreneurship literature concerns the characteristics of fields that motivate and facilitate institutional entrepreneurship (Hardy and Maguire, 2017; Zietsma et al., 2016). This division revolves around the question of whether institutional entrepreneurship is driven by triggering events or by the state of the organizational field. The idea that events trigger institutional entrepreneurship follows the more general notion that exceptional organizational action is activated by exogenous shocks (Greenwood and Hinings, 1996; Meyer et al., 1990). Such shocks might be dramatic or emerge more gradually, as in Greenwood and Suddaby's (2006) study of institutional entrepreneurship in the Canadian accounting industry that was triggered by poor financial performance among accounting firms. In contrast to this focus on events, much of the research on institutional entrepreneurship has emphasized the degree to which fields are mature or emerging as explanatory of why institutional entrepreneurship occurs and the shape it takes (Greenwood and Suddaby, 2006; Maguire et al., 2004).

MAINTAINING PRACTICES

Although most research on practice work has examined how practices are created and institutionalized, a more recent research stream has focused on actors' efforts to maintain institutionalized practices. The need for actors to maintain practices as institutions stems from the possibility of threats to that status from institutional troublemakers and environmental jolts (Maguire and Hardy, 2009; Micelotta and Washington, 2013; Riaz et al., 2016), and from less dramatic conditions that might undermine institutional arrangements as an unintended consequence of other changes (Dover and Lawrence, 2010a; Zilber, 2009). Defensive work describes "the purposive action of individuals and organizations aimed at countering disruptive institutional work" (Maguire and Hardy, 2009: 169), and is thus triggered by the institutional work of others who are working to disrupt or displace particular institutional arrangements.

In Maguire and Hardy's (2009) study of the deinstitutionalization of DDT, for example, we see industry associations, the World Health Organization, and other powerful actors engaged in defensive institutional work in order to maintain the practice of using DDT, the legitimacy of which was threatened by environmental groups. Similarly, Riaz et al. (2016: 1533) documented the work of CEOs of large US banks immediately following the global financial crisis to maintain their positions of "epistemic authority—[their] perceived expertise and trustworthiness." In contrast to the contest and drama associated with defensive institutional work, there are also important but more mundane efforts to maintain practices from ongoing decay. Zilber (2009) suggests that such work can be carried out using narratives in organizations: her study of an Israeli rape crisis center shows how actors connected stories at the individual, organizational, and societal levels to maintain therapeutic and feminist practices. An important context in which this happened was the initial training course required of all new members: "the course structure and format [were designed] to define the core elements and beliefs according to which the center is organized and operates, and deliver them to newcomers" (Zilber, 2009: 221).

DISRUPTING PRACTICES

Alongside interest in maintaining practices as institutions, a stream of research focused on the deinstitutionalization of practices has emerged (Hiatt, Sine, and Tolbert, 2009; Maguire and Hardy, 2009; Oliver, 1992). Attention to actors working to deinstitutionalize practices began with Oliver's (1992: 563) exploration of deinstitutionalization as a process. In her influential paper, she argued that, in contrast to the then dominant view, institutionalized practices were "highly susceptible to dissipation, rejection or replacement." She followed this general insight with a discussion of the potential for actors to intentionally disrupt institutions and her ideas have been connected empirically to the maintenance work described earlier. Scholars have observed that disruption and maintenance as forms of institutional work are often found together in battles over the legitimacy of particular institutionalized practices, as illustrated in Maguire and Hardy's (2009) study of the deinstitutionalization of DDT, in which they documented both the defensive work by proponents of DDT and the disruptive work of environmental activists that resulted in the insecticide's dramatically limited global use.

Practice Work as Institutional Work

To explore practice work as a type of institutional work, we again draw on the process model introduced in Chapter 2. We have reproduced a simplified and slightly amended version of the model in Figure 8.1. The model depicts institutional work as starting from a set of motivations that leads to the employment of practices and results in intended and unintended effects. As with other forms of social-symbolic work, this process is embedded in a context we characterize in terms of the resources available to actors and the situations that trigger and shape it.

MOTIVATIONS TO PERFORM PRACTICE WORK
The literature on practice work suggests two main sets of motivations. The first involves responding to a contradiction between a situation faced by an actor

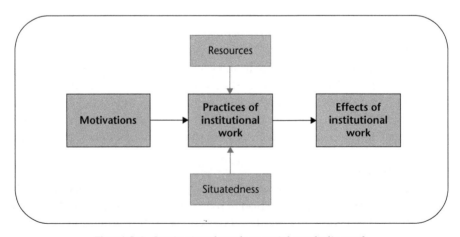

Figure 8.1. Institutional work as social-symbolic work

or actors, and the practices that are legitimately available to respond to the situation. So, for instance, Lawrence and Dover (2015) describe a situation in which growth in the size of the homeless population in a suburban neighborhood overwhelmed the repertoires of legitimate responses available to residents and community organizations, who were consequently motivated to develop and legitimate new practices that would provide shelter for the homeless and a sense of security for residents. Other examples of this kind of motivation have been documented in the context of environmental degradation (Bertels et al., 2014; Brown et al., 2009) and the outbreak of HIV/AIDS (Maguire et al., 2004). Practice work motivated by such crises is oriented toward realigning practices and situations in order to overcome or cope with those crises.

In contrast, other practice work is motivated by actors' desires for status, power, or wealth. Such work might be a part of "normal" economic competition in which firms work to shape the institutionalized practices in a competitive environment in ways that leverage their own technological competencies or market positions (Garud and Karnøe, 2003; Lawrence, 2004). These self-interested motivations are also commonly associated with attempts to increase or maintain professional status and power, in such arenas as financial and professional services (Clark and Newell, 2013; Micelotta and Washington, 2013; Riaz et al., 2016) and healthcare (Currie et al., 2012; Goodrick and Reay, 2010).

Although the motivations underpinning practice work are implicit in most studies in which they are documented, they are usually left unstated and consequently unconnected to the practices and outcomes of practice work. This is especially problematic when one considers that a central aim associated with the development of institutional work as an area of research was to move from an institution-centric view to one in which actors and agency were equally important (Lawrence et al., 2009). Recent attention to the role of emotions in institutional work (Voronov, 2014; Voronov and Vince, 2012; Wright et al., 2017) is encouraging in this regard, and points to the potential value of moving further in this direction. As we suggested in relation to strategy work, there is a broad array of concepts and a rich tradition of research from organizational behavior that could be of tremendous value in this regard: theories of ethics, conflict, collaboration, stress, decision making, and all of the literature on motivation in organizations could be employed in service of understanding why and when actors are likely to engage in effortful and potentially risky practice work.

PRACTICES OF PRACTICE WORK

Asking what practices are associated with practice work represents a seemingly circular question. Describing practice work in terms of practices seems to confuse matters, but it is a necessary step in conceptualizing practice work as a kind of institutional work and making it comparable to other kinds of social-symbolic work. All social-symbolic work involves the employment of sets of practices that are meaningful within particular communities, and this is equally the case for practice work.

What is clear is that the existing literature has focused almost exclusively on the discursive dimension of practice work despite the importance of the relational and material dimensions in the development of new practices (think of material objects like tools and special spaces as well as relationships like apprenticeships or internships). As we mentioned previously, Hampel et al.'s (2017) review of the empirical literature showed that a preponderance of research on practice work focused on discursive practices, at the expense of attention to relational and material practices; forty-six of the fifty-three studies sampled focused on the use of discursive practices, with the bulk of those relying on rhetoric and narrative. To address this limitation of the existing practice work literature will depend on not only an elaborated conceptualization of practice work, but also a significantly expanded methodological repertoire. Attending to the material and relational practices of practice work may require methods that allow greater direct observation of how material conditions contribute to practice work. This might include more use of ethnographic methods, but also the use of video and other means of directly recording action.

An important, emerging stream of research in the practice work literature focuses on indirect forms of work that set the stage for more direct forms of work, as illustrated by the study of Bertels et al. (2014) showing the ways in which relational forms of work by environmental NGOs provide the foundation for more direct practice work. As with material practices, the observation and analysis of relational practices in practice work will require conceptual and methodological creativity. Conceptually, the study of practice work will need to provide a more compelling account of the connections between institutions, agency, and relationships. At present, the empirical studies of practice work are skewed toward conceiving of agency as anchored in actors, with only a superficial acknowledgment of the relational foundations of agency. Methodologically, there needs to be a similar move to recognize the complex social chains through which practice work is accomplished. Charting complex causal chains may not be possible using traditional interview methods, but points to the potential significance of the experimental turn emerging in organization studies. This turn requires caution, though: while laboratory studies may be interesting and convenient, it is more likely that real insight will be gained from field experiments and quasi-experiments.

EFFECTS OF PRACTICE WORK

The literature on practice work suggests an array of potential effects, some of which have only been considered indirectly or occasionally. The first potential effect of practice work is its impact on the practices that are the object of such work. Although we define all social-symbolic work by its intentions, rather than its outcomes, the question of whether and how such work affects the social-symbolic objects it targets is important and tends to dominate the literature. In fact, despite repeated calls to move to a less institution-centric conception of institutional work, the literature has largely remained fixed on understanding how particular changes in practice are accomplished.

A second effect of practice work pointed to in the literature, but relatively underexplored, involves its effects on the broader political and social structures within which those practices operate. A striking example of such effects is provided by Khan et al.'s (2007) study of practice work in relation to the issue of child labor in the stitching of soccer balls in Pakistan, which prompted a "successful" chain of practice work. The study highlights, however, the broader effects of this work, which were largely overlooked by the agents of the practice work: "As far as the industry was concerned, the issue ... was self-evidently one of child labour, ... and not part of a broader issue about fair wage rates, ... gender or postcolonialism" (Khan et al., 2007: 1064).

Consequently, the practice work was undertaken in ways that excluded the most vulnerable stakeholders—the stitchers of soccer balls: while international activists and organizers regularly traveled to Pakistan, representatives of the stitchers did not have the resources necessary to fly to the International Labour Organization in Geneva. The imbalance eventually led to a situation in which child labor was eliminated from the industry, but without any real consideration of the wider consequences of this change, especially for the women stitchers. Unfortunately, the successful practice work shifted stitching out of homes and rural settings to industrial operations where effective monitoring could occur, and consequently out of reach of the poorest women who were economically dependent on stitching.

A third effect of practice work, also relatively underexamined, involves the relationships it forms, transforms, or disrupts among collaborators and competitors. This effect stems in part from the ways in which practice work is embedded in complex social networks in which actors with different skills and resources cooperate, either directly or indirectly, to effect changes in practices (Garud and Karnøe, 2003; Suddaby and Viale, 2011). These effects are evident in Lawrence's (2017) study of Insite, the first supervised injection site in North America, in which deep personal connections were formed amid the efforts to open the site. In this case, the relational impacts of practice work were tied to the emotionality of the issue and the work: people who had not previously known each other ended up working closely together, building networks of trust, compassion, and empathy that formed the foundation for collective agency that would otherwise have been impossible. The relational side-effects of practice work are important because they shape both the likelihood and the quality of subsequent practice work involving newly connected actors; the trust and sense of shared identity formed in collective practice work become the foundation for ongoing collaboration (Hardy et al., 2005).

SITUATEDNESS OF PRACTICE WORK

Research considering the context of practice work has primarily revolved around field conditions, and particularly the degree to which fields are emerging, mature, or in flux (Greenwood and Suddaby, 2006; Maguire et al., 2004). Purdy and Gray (2009), for example, examine the emerging field of alternative dispute resolution, and identify the forms of work associated with embedding logics in organizational practices. In this case, the fact that the field was emerging allowed for the proliferation of multiple sets of organizational practices allied with competing logics, rather than the dominance of a single logic as has been demonstrated in the context of mature fields (Greenwood and Suddaby, 2006; Lounsbury, 2002).

Although this focus on the status of fields has generated important insights, it has led to the neglect of the deeper situatedness of the actors involved. For collective actors, such as organizations and associations, a more complete analysis of their situatedness might involve their histories and the networks of relationships that extend well beyond the sets of practices on which the study is focused. For individuals, there may be even more complex dimensions of situatedness, including gender, race, sexuality, class, religion, family background, and occupational experience, which are important but exist at some distance from the immediate practices in question. Although fields and organizations provide much of the context of practice work, actors' backgrounds provide the lenses through which those contexts are interpreted and the repertoires of potential responses. Attending to these forms of situatedness opens up exciting new possibilities with respect to integrating concepts and theories from other literatures, such as psychoanalysis, gender studies, queer theory, postcolonialism, and Marxist theory. Integrating insights from a broader set of scholarly literatures could help broaden discussions and alleviate the self-referential tendency of much writing on practice work and institutional theory.

RESOURCES OF PRACTICE WORK

As with research on practices, research on the resources used in practice work concentrates on discursive resources at the expense of relational and material resources. At least three kinds of discursive resources have been emphasized in the literature. The first is discursive legitimacy (Hardy and Phillips, 1998). The right to speak has been shown to be a key resource, often associated with professional status (Suddaby and Viale, 2011) or with being directly affected by the practice in question (Maguire et al., 2004). The second is rhetorical and narrative skills (Suddaby and Greenwood, 2005). Brown et al. (2012), for example, demonstrate the importance of rhetorical skills in their analysis of an inquiry report that disrupted the practice of accommodating and caring for both the young disabled and frail elderly in shared facilities. Third is the availability of relevant, persuasive concepts, arguments, and other linguistic forms. For instance, in a study of institutional change in a UK school system, Ezzamel and colleagues (2007: 150) show how discourses of financial account-ability were "the key rationale for the explanations of conduct, even when informants were discussing seemingly non-financial or 'folk-based' institu-tions of accountability."

Although discursive resources dominate the practice work literature, exam-ining a concrete example of practice work illustrates the potential variety of resources that could be explored in this research. Our study of whale watching in British Columbia (Lawrence and Phillips, 2004) highlights the resources used to construct a new commercial practice. Perhaps the most obvious resources underpinning the practice work that brought commercial whale watching into existence were the array of cultural products, and especially popular films, that told stories in which whales were central characters: inspir-ing the article's title, these evolved over time from *Moby Dick* to *Free Willy*, shifting public perception along the way. Local entrepreneurs in our study relied on these popular images to legitimate whale watching as a family activity. But also key to the practice work were more proximal resources, including material elements such as the boats used for whale watching and, as described by JC (the leading entrepreneur), the networks of spotters employed to locate the whales: at first, "we were bumping into killer whales about 30% of the time. [So, we] joined up with then the only other tour operator [to] share some sighting information. Our sighting success went up to 60% of the trips that we ran. We worked on it a little harder the next year, and it went up to 80%" (Lawrence and Phillips, 2004: 700). The importance of identifying specific resources stems from their impact across the process, including shaping the motivations, practices, and effects associated with practice work. In this case, JC was motivated to launch a whale-watching company in part by his familiarity with the boats they would use and his local connections. These boats and connections also shaped the strategies in which he engaged, including locating his business in the downtown harbor, and ultimately shaped whale watching as an institutionalized practice, as competitors imitated his choice of boat and infiltrated his spotting network.

Although the article detailing the whale-watching study focused on dis-course and discursive resources, it highlights the potential value of attending to a much broader set of resources, including relational and material resources. As with other aspects of the study of practice work, systematic consideration of a broader set of resources would significantly deepen our understanding of how practice work is accomplished, and how it relates to other forms of institutional work and social-symbolic work more generally.

SUMMING UP

By exploring practice work by exploring practice work as a form of institutional work, we see important opportunities for expanding and deepening research and theoretical discussion. Many of these opportunities stem from a continued focus on the practices that are the target of an actor's work, rather than the work itself. An important theoretical move in the development of institutional work as a research domain was to reject the idea that work was only consequential in terms of its effect on institutions (Lawrence et al., 2011). Instead, the institutional work perspective was intended to highlight the experience of actors engaged in institutional work, the situations that triggered it, the efforts it required, and its unintended effects. But research on practice work, and institutional work more generally, has retained its focus on explaining changes in institutionalized practices. Our review suggests that we are again at a point where there could be tremendous value gained from broadening our interest in practice work—re-establishing it as a type of institutional work and reconnecting the study of practice work to the original work-centric agenda that was formulated a decade ago.

Category Work

Categories represent an exciting focus for research on institutional work. The concept of a category describes a "recognized type" of some phenomenon, with an important feature being an audience to whom the type is recognizable (Zuckerman, 1999). Categories are tightly tied to the concept of boundaries, and particularly "symbolic boundaries" which describe "conceptual distinctions made by social actors to categorize objects, people, practices, and even time and space" (Lamont and Molnár, 2002: 168). An important feature of categories is their use as tools for the evaluation of elements of social life: "to the extent that a community can reach consensus about [the constitution of a category]," it will "use these codes to make evaluations of future instances (e.g., products), rewarding some and penalizing others" (Kahl et al., 2010: 85). This explicitly evaluative character of categories makes them important targets of institutional work, and central to contests in which actors compete to shape categories and influence the assignment of specific objects to categories.

Key to our understanding of categories as objects of institutional work is their socially constructed nature. Put simply, categories are social-symbolic objects produced through processes of social construction. Furthermore, the social construction of categories is a "ubiquitous process that involves lumping similar things into distinct clusters, rendering them recognizable, and creating shared understandings" (Lounsbury and Rao, 2004: 969). This process creates order not only around the things being categorized, but also around the identities and interests of actors connected to those things, and the means by which audiences will evaluate those things and connected people (Kennedy et al., 2010; Lounsbury and Rao, 2004; Zuckerman, 1999). Purposeful, reflexive efforts by actors to shape categories—category work—is an important mechanism in the construction of categories.

The potential for shaping categories and gaining rewards for doing so can lead actors to engage in elaborate programs of category work, as illustrated by the birth of "nanotechnology" as a category. When the term "nanotechnology" first appeared in 1974 in a conference paper by a Japanese scientist, coupling the terms "nano" and "technology" was somewhat optimistic, as the properties of phenomena at the nano level (smaller than one ten-millionth of a meter) were not understood well enough to be employed in practical applications (Kennedy et al., 2010). But even if the category had limited practical value, it had tremendous discursive value, as illustrated by the 1986 bestseller *Engines of creation: The coming era of nanotechnology*, which paints a utopian picture of nanotechnology's potential (Kennedy et al., 2010: 378). The book's author, an MIT doctoral student at the time, went on to leverage its success to found a private think tank and preach the power of nanotechnology to a wide and influential audience.

Category Work in Management and Organizational Research

Looking across the study of category work in management and organizational research, there are three main themes: category work tied to different types of categories, the actors who engage in category work, and the characteristics of category work that distinguish it from other types of institutional work.

CATEGORY WORK AND DIFFERENT TYPES OF CATEGORIES

Two kinds of categories have dominated research on category work: categories of objects, and categories of people. In research focusing on objects, the dominant interest has been in product categories, including "light cigarettes" (Hsu and Grodal, 2015), satellite radio (Navis and Glynn, 2010), mutual funds (Lounsbury and Rao, 2004), Italian wines (Negro et al., 2011), Israeli wines, (Roberts et al., 2010), Italian spirits (Delmestri and Greenwood, 2016), and modern Indian art (Khaire and Wadhwani, 2010). All these studies share an interest in understanding the determinants of a category's commercial value, including its meaning and membership, and how interested actors worked to shape or cope with the categories through which specific products were interpreted and evaluated. In their study of the Italian spirit grappa, for instance, Delmestri and Greenwood (2016) examined the category work undertaken by a regional distiller to shift the meaning of this product category from low to high status. In a little over a decade, the distiller managed to associate grappa with a cultured Italian lifestyle by distancing it from its traditional category and presenting it in ways that connected it to higher-status categories and broader societal-level frames.

Along with objects, management and organizational researchers have spent considerable time examining category work aimed at shaping categories of people. Although one might imagine a wide variety of such categories, management and organizational research has tended to focus primarily on gender, with more recent attention to race (Acker, 2006; Nkomo, 1992), ethnicity (Essers and Benschop, 2009), age (Collien et al., 2016; Gergen and Gergen, 2003), and disability (Albrecht et al., 2001; Jammaers et al., 2016). The efforts of actors to construct gender-related categories in organizations has been the object of a great deal of feminist research, intended, at least in part, to reveal the ways in which organizational actors construct categories that enact and maintain women's oppression.

Smithson and Stokoe (2005), for instance, show how gendered categories are produced in organizational discussions of work–life balance, even when the official discourse is gender neutral. They document how actors in such a context constructed the category of "generic female parent" by excluding discussions of men or fathers and thus "implicitly assum[ing] that the mother, and not the father, is responsible for childcare" (Smithson and Stokoe, 2005: 156). As this study highlights, a key issue in studies of category work is the politics of such categories. Research in this tradition is often explicitly concerned with how some groups of people are devalued through the construction of a category, why some actors have more say in the construction of the category, and how particular individuals are placed in the resulting category.

ACTORS AND ROLES IN CATEGORY WORK

A second important theme in studies of category work has been the actors involved and their roles. Interest in the roles that different actors play stems in part from the connections between category membership and economic and social rewards. This dynamic can lead to category work that involves contests between actors benefiting from existing categories and actors who might benefit from the disruption or transformation of those categories. This tension is often described in terms of "incumbents"—"dominant firms [who] may actively seek to forestall redefinitions of product categories" (Lounsbury and Rao, 2004: 978)—and "challengers" who may be new organizations formed around the creation and exploitation of potential new categories, or existing organizations working to import categories from adjacent fields (Klepper, 2002; Navis and Glynn, 2010).

A distinctive kind of actor highlighted in category work research has been the field-level intermediary who plays an important role in defining and evaluating categories (Khaire and Wadhwani, 2010). In the world of mutual funds, for example, Lounsbury and Rao (2004: 971) show that industry media, such as trade journals, shape the symbolic environment of industries by "supplying cognitive representations such as product categories." Intermediaries shape the category boundaries and evaluate the relative value of different categories in a wide variety of contexts: in fields of cultural production, for instance, Hirsch (1972) documented the production of cultural categories by disk jockeys in the music industry, book reviewers in publishing, and film critics in the movie business.

DISTINCTIVE CHARACTERISTICS OF CATEGORY WORK
A benefit of research that focuses on particular kinds of institutions, such as categories, is the potential of this research to highlight the novel characteristics of the related form of institutional work. Research on category work has highlighted the distinctive aspects of creating categories that are tied to the cognitive characteristics of categories, and the active role of audiences in constructing categories as a sensemaking process. In a study of social categorization, for instance, Freeman (1992) shows the disconnect between how people are affiliated (how they are connected to people they interact with frequently and with positive sentiment) and how other people perceive those affiliations: whereas actual patterns of affiliation are somewhat messy, perceptions of affiliation are categorical in that people tend to assign others to discrete, non-overlapping social groups. This "need" to categorize is a ubiquitous one; the construction and use of categories is a key sensemaking strategy that cuts across much of human life. Thus, creating categories often involves an array of actors, including "producers" working to create categories that will benefit them by privileging their own products or activities, and "consumers" working to make sense of their worlds by categorizing unordered phenomena.

This dynamic highlights the importance of a range of cognitive processes including prototyping and boundary construction, as well as goal-based and causal sensemaking in regards to the boundaries around and occupants of categories (Durand and Paolella, 2013; Rosch, 1978). The kinds of category work we are interested in here do not, of course, conform neatly to these cognitive processes, but nor are they unrelated to them. To understand category work, it is important to understand it as a kind of institutional work, but one that is connected to cognitive categorization processes which give it distinctive qualities. In the emergence of different categories of jazz, for example, audiences played a crucial role in the formation of the categories, based both on the rules they understood about categorical membership and on their "concrete experiences and observations about who produces and consumes these products" (Kahl et al., 2010: 84). Similarly, creating the category of modern Indian art involved producers and consumers, but was driven by a range of other actors, including art historians, auction houses, critics, and museums (Khaire and Wadhwani, 2010).

Category Work as Institutional Work

Once again (and for the last time in this book), we explore how conceiving of a particular type of work—in this case category work—as part of a broader form of social-symbolic work (institutional work, here) might help us to understand it in new ways and influence research in this important area. We work from the framework developed in Chapter 1 (reproduced above in simplified form as Figure 8.1) to examine the existing category work literature in terms of what we know and do not know about its motivations, practices, and effects, as well as the impact of resources and situatedness.

MOTIVATIONS TO PERFORM CATEGORY WORK

The category work literature highlights the economic and social value of category membership, and thus the ways that categories shape the distribution of advantage in communities, industries, and societies. Consequently, studies of category work, even more than other research on institutional work, emphasize the importance of instrumental motivations. In category work research on product categories, for instance, a central theme has been the potential economic gains associated with controlling their definition (Hsu and Grodal, 2015; Kennedy et al., 2010; Khaire and Wadhwani, 2010; Lounsbury and Rao, 2004). These gains are tied to the economic rewards and penalties associated with the categorical imperative, which suggests that audiences reward objects that fit neatly within a single category rather than spanning multiple categories (Durand and Paolella, 2013; Zuckerman, 1999). From this perspective, category work is an extension of competitive strategy, but with a focus on shaping the rules rather than just playing the game (Lawrence, 1999).

Conceptualizing category work as institutional work is consistent with these instrumental motivations, but broadens the discussion to include not only economic gains but also political and social advantages. These broader forms of advantage are especially important when considering the categorization of people, rather than products, and have been examined in relation to social categories associated with clear patterns of advantage and disadvantage, such as gender, race, ethnicity, religion, and disability. An interesting and important emerging stream in this literature concerns the last of these—the categories and categorization associated with disability in organizations. The motivations for category work in relation to disability include both economic and social gains. Economically, a multi-billion dollar "disability business" exists in the United States that a wide range of organizations work to maintain (Albrecht, 1992). At a more micro level, individuals experience significant costs and benefits as a result of how they fit into categories of ability and disability, and are consequently motivated to shape both their relationships to these categories (as a form of self work) and the categories themselves (as a form of category work) (Jammaers et al., 2016).

PRACTICES OF CATEGORY WORK

Category work, like all types of social-symbolic work, depends on sets of practices. Category work practices may be oriented toward shaping any combination of the discursive, relational, or material aspects of a category; what is important is that they are focused on the category as a social-symbolic object. For our purposes, category work practices can be organized into four broad categories.

First, there are sets of practices associated with creating new categories. These practices are drawn on by actors as they seek to define a new category, differentiate it from existing categories, and ensure "institutional consolidation" of the new category among audiences (Hsu and Hannan, 2005: 476). This last step is necessary as new categories become "stable only when relevant audiences collectively recognize the meanings that define its identity" (Khaire and Wadhwani, 2010: 1283). A new category must be clear, different, and widely agreed to function effectively as a category.

As an example, consider the development of the category of "modern Indian art" (Khaire and Wadhwani, 2010). The actors who created this category drew on a number of practices. Art historians and critics, for instance, engaged in "problematizing," whereby they challenged existing categorizations of Indian art as either unsophisticated or derivative. Along with discursive practices, creating the category of modern Indian art depended on a range of practices focused on the relational and material aspects of the new category, such as producing catalogues, holding auctions devoted to modern Indian art, and developing networks of critics, artists, and collectors. A complex combination of different practices led to the constitution and widespread acceptance of this new category of art.

A second set of category work practices are used to manage a category's boundaries. These practices are oriented toward redefining the location of the boundary between objects inside the category and other, similar, objects that are not. Again, these practices can target the discursive, material, or relational dimensions of the category, and often a practice affects more than one dimension.

As an example, consider the category work done in relation to "light cigarettes" between 1964 and 1993. This category emerged as a distinct type of cigarette in the 1960s, as evidence for the negative health effects of traditional cigarettes become more widely accepted by the public (Hsu and Grodal, 2015). Light cigarettes as a category were initially defined by low levels of tar and nicotine which were prominently displayed in advertising. Not long after the emergence of the category, however, it became clear to tobacco companies that smokers interested in healthier cigarettes often regarded cigarettes lower in tar and nicotine as unsatisfying and lacking taste. This created a tension for tobacco companies: they had an incentive to increase the tar and nicotine of light cigarettes, but faced a potential reaction from consumers if the tar and nicotine exceeded what consumers expected from a "light cigarette." The companies' response was creative. They moved away from the category work practices initially used to define light cigarettes (associating them with low tar and nicotine), to a set of practices that allowed them to redefine the category: research to understand how consumers evaluated potential cigarettes as light or full flavor; R&D to develop filters and other features that could act as defining characteristics of light cigarettes; and extensive advertising to disassociate the category from tar and nicotine measures. Through these practices, tobacco companies moved the category boundary in a way that allowed cigarettes with significantly higher tar and nicotine to be accepted by consumers as "light cigarettes."

A third set of category work practices are associated with working to change the social evaluation of categories—the positive or negative valence that people or objects are granted by virtue of their membership in the category. Such practices are nicely illustrated in Delmestri and Greenwood's (2016) study of grappa—a traditional Italian spirit—and how it was transformed from a "course spirit" drunk by peasants and alpine soldiers to "the preferred spirit... [in] high culture social gatherings" (Delmestri and Greenwood, 2016: 508). Three broad practices were used to effect this transformation. The first was "category detachment," which involves shifting perceptions of an object away from its existing category. Second was "category emulation," in which actors work to present an object in ways that liken it to a high-status category. Third was "category sublimation," where actors work to shift the conversation around an object from local, field-specific references to broader, societal-level frames. These three sets of practices, Delmestri and Greenwood argue, were instrumental in increasing the status of grappa as a category and introducing a quality hierarchy within the category.

EFFECTS OF CATEGORY WORK

The effects of category work that have received the most attention from researchers working in this area involve the instrumental effects of categories on markets and social arenas. The effects of category work are understood primarily in terms of winners and losers in competitive markets for products and services, in which the ability to define the content and boundaries of categories carries with it a significant, usually economic, reward (Lounsbury, 2007; Navis and Glynn, 2010). The competitive effects of category work can also arise indirectly, as illustrated by the case of cost accounting in early twentieth-century American manufacturing, where cost accountants and managers reconfigured accounting categories associated with mass production in ways that facilitated organizational learning and innovation, and thus shifted the bases of competition in an array of markets to the benefit of more innovative manufacturers (Schneiberg and Berk, 2010).

A second important theme in the study of category work has been the unintended effects associated with such efforts. While not unique, this stream of work is distinctive for the emphasis that scholars have placed on exploring how working to shape a particular category can result in a range of unanticipated effects for other categories, as well as unexpected and often ironic second-order effects. This concern is prominent in research on category work aimed at social categories, as in Smithson and Stokoe's (2005) study of work to effect "genderblind" discourse that results in different but equally gendered organizational language. Similar to this is the study of age work in organizations that shows how "maintaining stereotypical age images can serve to counter age inequalities, whereas deconstructing age images can reinforce age inequalities" (Collien et al., 2016: 778).

One effect not explored is the effect on actors of working reflexively to shape categories. The categorical imperative and cognitive conceptions of categories presume a naturalness to categories that may be challenged by the experience of engaging in category work. Conceiving of categories as potentially manipulable disrupts notions of naturalness, potentially well beyond the categories in question. Category work, thus, may lead to greater agency, both for individuals and collective actors. Although agency may look different for individual and collective actors, both may gain sets of beliefs and repertoires of action that engender further institutional work.

RESOURCES FOR CATEGORY WORK
The resources on which category work studies tend to focus follow from the conception of categories as primarily cognitive/cultural objects. This has led to a focus on cognitive and discursive resources that support the possibility of shaping categories as discursive objects. Central to this stream of research are the cognitive resources of actors, such as cultural competence (Essers and Benschop, 2009; Khaire and Wadhwani, 2010) and domain expertise (Lounsbury and Rao, 2004; Schneiberg and Berk, 2010), which allow actors to imagine possible changes in the constitution of categories.

Category work research also highlights the importance of subject positions that provide actors with discursive legitimacy (Hardy and Phillips, 1998), and thus allow actors to speak on behalf of a category or make claims with respect to its content and boundaries (Eden, Donaldson, and Walker, 2006; Lounsbury and Rao, 2004). Such positions may accrue to leading actors in the field, but may also be associated with intermediaries who hold what are seen as more "objective" positions that allow them to shape categories.

Finally, the discursive nature of category work demands access to field-level mechanisms that provide for the distribution and consumption of texts. Access to this communication infrastructure goes beyond issues of discursive legitimacy, as it requires connections to specific actors, such as industry associations or consumer-focused media, through which information can be transmitted (Phillips, Lawrence, and Hardy, 2004).

Recognizing a wider range of resources involved in category work would be facilitated by a broader conceptualization of categories that recognized them as social-symbolic objects and explicitly incorporated their discursive, relational, and material dimensions. Category work shapes not only descriptions of what categories are, but also what people do with them, the social networks in which they are embedded, and their material properties. So, the resources that support category work should reflect all of these dimensions. The practical nature of categories makes category work dependent on access to the communities that legitimate those practices. The relational dimension of categories makes it important that actors gain access to social networks that often extend well beyond those directly tied to the category in question. As objects in a category are used in chains of activity, carried along as totems of meaning or practical tools, shaping that category may require access to and influence over the distributed network implicated in those activity chains.

SITUATEDNESS OF CATEGORY WORK

The last aspect of category work we explore is its situatedness, which has typically been examined in terms of the intersection of an industry, a geography, and a time period (e.g., Khaire and Wadhwani, 2010; Lounsbury, 2007; Roberts et al., 2010). Such an approach has allowed category work scholars to explore the dynamics among specific sets of competitors, consumers, intermediaries, strategies, and the categories over which competition occurs. It has also provided a basis for empirical claims regarding the status and value of particular categories, and the economic and social effects of organizations' relationships to those categories. At the same time, there has been a tendency in this work to isolate the dynamics around individual categories and category occupants, documenting the strategies and effects of actors' work but largely bracketing what is occurring outside of the focal categories.

Conceptualizing category work as a type of institutional work widens the focus, highlighting the ecologies of categories that facilitate and constrain instances of category work. Categories, like all institutions and social-symbolic objects more generally, do not exist in isolation. Their meaning and value depend on their location in networks of other social-symbolic objects, and thus the work done on them and the effects of that work are also shaped by those networks. In the case of categories, such ecologies include the relevant categories already in place, but also the networks of incumbents, challengers, and intermediaries, and the advantages and disadvantages associated with assignment to different categories. Although research on category work has attended to these ecologies as idiosyncratic "contexts," we are missing a theoretical language that might allow a comparative understanding of category ecologies and how they shape category work. Whereas institutional work has traditionally been considered in the context of fields, a focus on categories offers the opportunity to develop a more nuanced language for describing their situatedness that resonates with the distinctive qualities of categories.

So, for example, we might describe category ecologies as dense or sparse, fine-grained or coarse, centrally controlled or organic, and audience-led or producer-led. Using this kind of language, we could distinguish between some mature product markets in which there exists a great many product categories that are well understood by consumers and which evolve organically through producer experimentation and audience selection, nascent product markets in which only a few gross categories exist and evolve as a few producers develop and produce new products, and social category ecologies in which a central agency defines the relatively sparse network of categories and adjudicates individuals in relation to their fit.

SUMMING UP

The study of category work remains tied to its roots in the study of categories, which has emphasized the cognitive and discursive at the expense of other dimensions and has tended to treat categories in relative isolation from each other, at best comparing them to neighboring or directly competing categories, but failing to acknowledge their embeddedness in broader networks of categories. Conceptions of category work have followed these tendencies, focusing on the most immediate motivations, effects, and contexts, at the expense of seeing the ways in which category work is motivated by broader social and political aims, how it affects people and social systems more broadly, and its embeddedness in ecologies of categories and social networks. These limitations represent significant opportunities with respect to conceiving of category work as a type of institutional work, and more broadly as a type of social-symbolic work.

The study of category work also represents an opportunity for research on social-symbolic work to engage more directly with social-symbolic objects that are explicitly connected to the material world. Whereas most of the social-symbolic objects we have explored in this book, and most of the social-symbolic objects that have gained the attention of social scientists, are tied to actors, relationships, or communities (e.g., identity, emotions, practices), categories more obviously include material objects, such as wines, cigarettes, art, and nanotechnologies. These kinds of social-symbolic objects are important for social science in general, and especially for the social-symbolic work perspective, as they represent key features of social life, the character-istics of which may be taken for granted rather than understood as socially constructed.

Conclusion

One of the important contrasts we have made in this book is between a social-symbolic work perspective and more traditional structural and processual perspectives on organizational life. The distinctiveness of the social-symbolic work perspective is not so much the phenomena it includes, as what it moves to the foreground—actors and their purposeful, reflexive efforts to shape social-symbolic objects. A social-symbolic work perspective incorpor-ates social structure through its consideration of social-symbolic objects, and processes through the links it makes between motivations, practices, resources, situations, and effects.

As we noted in relation to practice work, however, much of the research on institutional work seems to remain significantly anchored to more traditional approaches, focused on structures and processes, and only attending to work to the extent it helps explain them. This, we believe, is a missed opportunity, not only for scholarship that could significantly broaden its attention to important facets of organizational life, but also for the potential connections that research on institutional work might make to other communities. The study of institutional work should be of value to anyone interested in systems-level change or social change, but these links are only beginning to be formed (Nilsson, 2015, In press). Similarly, there has begun to emerge a significant interest in the intersection of institutional work and a person-focused con-ception of institutions, incorporating issues of identity, emotions, and rela-tionships (Leung et al., 2014; Lok et al., 2017); these issues, however, should be far more central to research on institutional work, a change that will only occur as more institutional work research achieves a more generative balance incorporating work as much as institutions.

Key Resources

Practice Work

The study of practice work sits at the intersection of practice theory and institutional theory. Thus, our suggestions for learning more about practice work cut across these two literatures. The literature on practice theory is deep and complex, resulting in the unfortunate possibility of getting lost in abstract discussions and somewhat remote empirical observations. To avoid this, a useful place to begin is Davide Nicolini's *Practice theory, work, and organization*, which introduces the core ideas associated with this perspective, and does so (quite unusually) from the perspective of someone working in management and organizational research. Theodore Schatzki provides another, more abbreviated introduction to practice theory in the first chapter of an edited volume that has become a foundational text in this area. In "Introduction: Practice theory," Schatzki lays out some key ideas for research on practices, including what counts as a practice and what studies of practice have in common. Turning to the institutional side of practice work, Lawrence and Suddaby's chapter on "Institutions and institutional work" established the conceptual foundation that has guided much of the research on institutional work. Drawing on a review of empirical studies in major management journals, they assemble an array of kinds of work done to shape institutions in general, and organize them into three basic types—creating, maintaining, and disrupting work. Finally, Munir and Phillips illustrate the theoretical potential that exploring practice work affords in their study of "The birth of the 'Kodak Moment'"; in this study, they show how Kodak worked to shape the practice of consumer photography in order to provide a market for their technical innovations in photography.

Lawrence, T. B., and Suddaby, R. 2006. Institutions and institutional work. In S. R. Clegg, C. Hardy, T. B. Lawrence, and W. R. Nord (Eds.), *Handbook of organization studies* (2nd ed.): 215–54. London: Sage.

Munir, K. A., and Phillips, N. 2005. The birth of the "Kodak Moment": Institutional entrepreneurship and the adoption of new technologies. *Organization Studies*, 26(11): 1665–87.

Nicolini, D. 2013. *Practice theory, work, and organization: An introduction*. Oxford: Oxford University Press.

Schatzki, T. R. 2001. Introduction: Practice theory. In T. R. Schatzki, K. Knorr Cetina, and E. Von Savigny (Eds.), *The practice turn in contemporary theory*: 1–14. London: Routledge.

Category Work

The study of category work also sits at the intersection of research on the social-symbolic object and social-symbolic work—in this case categories and the institutional work that is done to produce, manage, disrupt, and shape categories. There is no better gateway to the world of category work than Bowker and Star's *Sorting things out*, which not only introduces the reader to a fascinating array of categories, ranging from ways to die and race classifications to categories of nursing practice. Their discussion also reveals the intricacies of category work, which as they point out, is often done quietly and invisibly as part of an occupational requirement. Wry et al. provide a useful complement to this extraordinary breadth by focusing on a specific set of categories in the nanotechnology industry and examining the economic costs and benefits for firms that spanned those categories. This paper is useful because it shows how categories can be the object of analysis without accepting as unequivocal the claims associated with the categorical imperative. For a contemporary study of category work in management and organizational research, we recommend starting with Khaire and Wadhwani's study of the construction of modern Indian art as a category. This study demonstrates the wide range of actors involved in work around a single category, and the complex ecologies within which this work occurs.

Bowker, G. C., and Star, S. L. 1999. *Sorting things out: Classification and its consequences.* Cambridge, MA: MIT Press.

Khaire, M., and Wadhwani, R. D. 2010. Changing landscapes: The construction of meaning and value in a new market category—modern Indian art. *Academy of Management Journal*, 53(6): 1281–304.

Wry, T., Lounsbury, M., and Jennings, P. D. 2014. Hybrid vigor: Securing venture capital by spanning categories in nanotechnology. *Academy of Management Journal*, 57(5): 1309–33.

Part III

9

Theoretical Opportunities in the Study of Social-Symbolic Work

In this chapter we:

1. Review self work, organization work, and institutional work.
2. Explore how different forms of social-symbolic work can be combined, and the implications of these combinations for the study of social-symbolic work.
3. Explore forms of social-symbolic work used to connect social-symbolic objects and the theoretical opportunities suggested by "connecting work."

Introduction

In Chapters 3–8, we focused on specific forms of social-symbolic work—self work, organization work, and institutional work—providing archaeologies of the associated social-symbolic objects, conceptualizing each form of social-symbolic work in terms of its constitutive dimensions, and examining specific types of each form of work drawn from management and organizational research.

In this chapter, we build on previous discussions to explore two sets of theoretical opportunities that arise from the social-symbolic work perspective we have developed. First, we will discuss the opportunities that arise to explore how different forms of social-symbolic work are combined in concrete situations—how actors might, for example, engage simultaneously in institutional work and organization work, and the dynamics and consequences of such a combination. Second, we will discuss the opportunities emerging from the connections between social-symbolic objects, and the efforts of actors to shape those connections. Before exploring those two opportunities, we first review the forms of social-symbolic work explored in Chapters 3–8.

Reviewing the Three Forms of Social-Symbolic Work

To explore the conceptual opportunities associated with combinations of social-symbolic work and connections between social-symbolic objects, it is important to keep in mind the contours and boundaries of self work, organization work, and institutional work. Thus, we briefly summarize these key concepts here, and highlight the aspects of each form of work that are important to remember as we begin to look at how actors use them together and the sorts of connections that exist among social-symbolic objects. The definitions of the three forms of work, examples of types of work that fall within each type drawn from the literature, and some key citations are summarized in Table 9.1.

Self Work

Self work refers to purposeful, reflexive efforts of individuals, collective actors, and networks of actors to construct a self. Self work describes all of the efforts that go into shaping an individual's place in the social world, including the roles and relationships that define their identity, their expressed and experienced emotions, and the narratives that construct their working lives. A person's relationship to self is heterogeneous, made up not only of multiple, complex elements such as identities, emotions, and careers, but also of multiple, more and less reconciled selves.

An important aspect of self work we have tried to emphasize is the variety of actors who engage in self work in relation to a particular self. Although management and organizational research has tended to focus on self work done by a focal individual (e.g., a person's own identity work), a social-symbolic work perspective highlights the distributed nature of efforts to shape any social-symbolic object, including a self. Self work is not the province of individuals, and especially not individuals *qua* individuals: instead, self work is a form of coordinated activity that we do with and in relation to others. How we describe our past, present, and future, and how we develop narratives that connect them, are done not in isolation but in a complex relationship with others who participate in those practices. Sometimes others participate only as passive audiences, but more often as co-producers of those narratives, asking questions, prompting explanations, filling in blanks, or even leading the process, as is seen in many relationships where parents, teachers, professors, counselors, lawyers, and doctors, as well as friends, lovers, siblings, and even enemies and rivals work to construct our selves in relation to us, though not always with our consent or appreciation.

More broadly, conceiving of selves as social-symbolic objects embeds them in broader social and temporal contexts, with their meaning, utility,

Table 9.1. Forms of social-symbolic work

		Definition	Contemporary cites	Foundational cites
Self work Efforts to construct a self—efforts that originate in relationship to others and exist as forms of co-action	Emotion work	Efforts "to change in degree or quality an emotion or feeling" (Hochschild, 1979: 561)	(Ashforth and Humphrey, 1993, 1993; Bolton and Boyd, 2003; Grandey, 2003; Turner and Stets, 2006)	(Fineman, 1996; Hochschild, 1979, 1983)
	Identity work	Efforts to establish, shape, and maintain one's own or another's personal identity	(Beech, 2008; Brown and Toyoki, 2013; Creed et al., 2010; Duttonet al., 2010)	(Snow and Anderson, 1987)
	Career work	Efforts to shape and leverage careers as social-symbolic objects	(Arthur and Rousseau, 2001; Chudzikowski and Mayrhofer, 2011; Duberley et al., 2006b)	(Tams and Arthur, 2010)
Organization work Efforts to construct "organizations" that incorporate sets of people, activities, goals, material arrangements, and their relationships to other individuals, groups, organizations, and societies.	Strategy work	Efforts to make, shape, and execute organizational strategies	(Jarzabkowski and Spee, 2009; Vaara and Whittington, 2012)	(Mintzberg, 1987; Mintzberg and Waters, 1985; Pettigrew, 1985)
	Boundary work	Efforts to establish, defend, disrupt, and reshape organizational boundaries	(Kreiner, Hollensbe, and Sheep, 2009; Zietsma and Lawrence, 2010), (Bechky, 2003; Carlile, 2002)	(Gieryn, 1996, 1983)
	Technology work	Efforts to shape the meaning of technologies and their place in organizational life	(Greenhalgh and Stones, 2010; Grint and Woolgar, 2013; Orlikowski, 2007; Orlikowski and Scott, 2008)	(Barley, 1986; Bijker et al., 2012; Trist, 1981)
Institutional work Efforts to construct institutions, including the shared, social understandings and the forms of social control that underpin those understandings.	Practice work	Efforts to create, transform, disrupt, maintain, diffuse, and translate recognized forms of activity that guide the behavior of actors in specific situations	(Garud et al., 2002; Gawer and Phillips, 2013; Maguire and Hardy, 2009; Maguire et al. 2004)	(Schatzki et al., 2001)
	Category work	Efforts to construct, maintain, defend, and transform categories	(Khaire and Wadhwani, 2010; Lounsbury and Rao, 2004; Negro et al., 2011; Ryen and Silverman, 2000)	(Bowker and Star, 1999; Lamont and Molnár, 2002)

and value arising out of their location in networks of social-symbolic objects. Social-symbolic objects are also embedded temporally and, thus, the universe of possible selves changes over time. It does so both exogenously as broader social and cultural currents transform understandings of what aspects of the self are changeable and how, and endogenously as actors experiment with new ways of being that expand those possibilities. The history of the self we examined in Chapter 3 highlights the ways that societal transitions to modernity and postmodernity opened up new aspects of the self to purposeful efforts to change them. This story is not, of course, simply about ever expanding opportunities to change. While there has been a broad movement in Europe and North America toward more scope for actors to manage selves, there are also many instances of the reverse where conservative actors may be successful in effecting new constraints on legitimate options for the construction of selves—regulating, for instance, the meaning of age, gender, sexuality, or occupation.

Organization Work

The second major category of social-symbolic work we explored is organization work. Organization work represents the purposeful, reflexive efforts of individuals, collective actors, and networks of actors to construct a complex social-symbolic object that incorporates a set of people, their activities, their aims, the material arrangements used in their activities, and their relationships to other individuals, groups, organizations, and societies. Organization work is the social-symbolic work that, when successful, allows us to say an organization "exists"—that there is something above and beyond the heterogeneous collection of individuals that make up its parts. That Oxford University exists as an organization is a claim that goes beyond describing sets of constituent elements and their relationships; it is a claim that says Oxford University exists as a "thing in the world" about which we can sensibly talk, and which we can relate to and differentiate both from other things in the world and from the people, places, practices, technologies, and relationships that make it up.

Our interest in organization work is clearly bounded in that we are not concerned with everything about organizing, but with how individual and collective actors shape organizations as social-symbolic objects with discursive, relational, and material dimensions. Thus, our question is not how people organize themselves to accomplish tasks (a question core to traditional organization theory), but the narrower question of how people construct organizations—how they create organizations as social-symbolic objects, with boundaries that distinguish organizations from other social objects and distinguish parts of organizations from each other, with technologies that affect organizations with routine and material presence, and with strategies that invest in organizational goals, recipes, practices, and tactics.

We emphasize this point as we believe that the articulation of organization work as a concept is an important contribution of the social-symbolic work perspective. Where institutional work, for instance, describes a form of social-symbolic work already understood as a coherent phenomenon in management and organizational research, the concept of organization work has been missing. The lack of such a concept has led, we argue, to scholars overlooking the category of activity that revolves around the social construction of organizations as social-symbolic objects. This activity, from our perspective, is distinct from the efforts of people to simply organize, and inclusive of the more specific forms of social-symbolic work already examined in organizational research, including strategy work and technology work.

Institutional Work

The concept of institutional work describes the purposeful, reflexive efforts of individuals, collective actors, and networks of actors to shape the institutions around them, sometimes creating new institutions, while at other times maintaining, transforming, or disrupting existing institutions. Although the term "institutional work" emerged only about a decade ago (Lawrence and Suddaby, 2006), the study of institutional work has been going on for much longer, embedded in studies of leadership, politics, and institutions (e.g., Selznick, 1949, 2011) and in the dynamics of organizational life (e.g., Gouldner, 1964; Hallett and Ventresca, 2006). The dominant stream of research on institutional work has focused on institutional entrepreneurship, drawing directly on DiMaggio's (1988) argument that institutions emerge out of the interested actions of resourceful individuals and groups. More recently, organizational scholars have begun to focus on institutional work that is oriented toward either disrupting (Hiatt et al., 2009; Maguire and Hardy, 2009) or maintaining institutions (Currie et al., 2012; Dacin et al., 2010; Trank and Washington, 2009).

As with self work and organization work, the defining feature of institutional work is the social-symbolic object on which it focuses—in this case, the institution. We define institutions as self-policing conventions, which exist as shared, social understandings of practices, technologies, rules, or other social structures. Institutional work, therefore, involves the efforts of actors to shape those social structures, which might include creating new ones, as well as disrupting, transforming, or maintaining existing institutions.

We believe our focus on institutions as social-symbolic objects, and on the social-symbolic work that individual and collective actors perform to change or maintain them, makes an important contribution to our thinking about institutions. First, it refocuses attention on institutions as a category rather than on particular institutions and their dynamics. While both sets of discussions are important, much of the recent work in institutional theory has focused on particular institutions with little attention paid to institutions as a kind of social-symbolic object.

Second, the focus in empirical work on particular institutions rather than institutions as a type of social-symbolic object has also resulted in a tendency to overlook the embeddedness of institutions in networks of social-symbolic objects. Institutions exist in networks of social-symbolic objects and these networks are affected by various forms of social-symbolic work. Our focus on institutions as social-symbolic objects helps to refocus attention to include these networks of social-symbolic objects and the associated forms of social-symbolic work that changes and maintains these networks. It is this latter question of how networks of social-symbolic objects are affected by different forms of work that we will examine next.

Combining Forms of Social-Symbolic Work

Up to this point, we have focused on instances of social-symbolic work intended to shape one type of social-symbolic object—a self, an organization, or an institution. While helpful for the sake of clarity, this depiction of social-symbolic work is highly simplified and unrealistic. Instead, we are more likely to encounter combinations of different forms of social-symbolic work occurring together, engaged in by various actors in ways that amplify, undermine, and transform their intended outcomes. Thus, the relationships among instances and kinds of social-symbolic work are much more complex than we have depicted so far.

This messiness, however, presents interesting, important opportunities to move beyond traditional research that has largely ignored the relationships among different social-symbolic objects and different types of social-symbolic work. Looking back at the process model of social-symbolic work we developed in Chapter 2 (applied to the literatures reviewed in Chapters 4, 6, and 8), we can imagine that combinations of different forms of social-symbolic work are likely to involve distinct motivations, practices, and effects, as well as requiring distinct sets of resources. To encourage research on these issues, we will now explore potential combinations of self work, organization work, and institutional work. We first explore three relatively simple combinations: institutional work-organization work; organization work-self work; and institutional work-self work. We then go on to examine three more general strategies that describe how actors might combine types of social-symbolic work: sequencing, aligning, and integrating. We believe this is an important research opportunity as combinations of forms of social-symbolic work also have theoretical regularities that deserve study.

Simple Combinations of Social-Symbolic Work

INSTITUTIONAL WORK AND ORGANIZATION WORK

That institutional work and organization work may occur together is not particularly surprising given the close relationship between institutions and organizations. Institutions provide the social-symbolic context for action in and around organizations, while organizations host action that intentionally, and more often unintentionally, shapes the institutional context in which they exist (Lawrence and Suddaby, 2006; Phillips et al., 2004). Institutional work and organization work describe efforts to shape institutions and organizations, but those efforts often emanate from programs of action aimed at practical outcomes, the accomplishment of which motivate, and even demand, complex combinations of both forms of social-symbolic work.

When, for example, Intel began to move from a supply chain logic to a platform logic in the 1980s and 1990s, the firm needed to engage in institutional work "to influence the process of logic change and . . . ensure that they were accepted in the role of platform leader," and organization work focused on shifting their organizational identity and practices to be consistent with the new logic (Gawer and Phillips, 2013: 1037). The firm's primary aim was to realign itself with changes at the field level, and to do so in a way that secured a dominant competitive position. This required simultaneous and mutually reinforcing institutional work and organization work reflecting the interrelations between Intel as a social-symbolic object and the institutions that populated its context.

Exploring combinations of institutional work and organization work has the potential to provide an interesting new focus for a range of areas in management and organizational research. This includes strategic management, in which the importance of institutions has been recognized (Peng, 2002), but institutional work has remained largely absent. As the Intel example illustrates, large-scale shifts in the bases of competition, often arising from technological innovations, may well require integrated attempts at institutional work and organization work. Another important area where studying this combination would be fruitful is in relation to issue management, non-market strategies, and corporate political strategy (e.g., Doh et al., 2012), all of which are concerned with the relationship between the organizations and social institutions, but which often take the organization for granted, focusing exclusively on how organizations might shape their institutional, and especially media and political, environments.

249

Across these areas of research, exploring the combination of institutional work and organization work has the potential to shine a light on how institutions shape the context within which organizational actors construct strategies that may be intended to exploit those institutions or to reshape them (Lawrence, 1999). Thus, institutional work may have profound effects on the strategies, boundaries, and technologies that are the objects of organization work by effecting, reformulating, or disrupting institutions that define the rules and rewards of competition in a domain (Hinings and Greenwood, 1988).

ORGANIZATION WORK AND SELF WORK

Organizations and selves are inextricably interconnected. One the one hand, organizations contribute directly and indirectly to the construction of selves: organizational actors work to construct the selves of their members and others, as well as providing products and services used by individuals as they construct their selves. On the other hand, organizational members' selves, including their identities, emotions, and careers, may motivate organization work, perhaps because of a tension individuals experience between their selves and their organizations (Bolton and Boyd, 2003; Zapf, 2002). Organizations as social-symbolic objects may also be influenced by the selves of one or more of their members (think, for example, of Steve Jobs and Apple). As a result of these complex interconnections, organization work and self work commonly occur together as actors try to reach objectives that require shaping or maintaining both organizations and selves as social-symbolic objects.

Combinations of organization work and self work are often seen when actors try to achieve some complex, practical outcome in organizations. For instance, when Alessi, a family-owned Italian design firm, was undergoing a leadership succession, the firm worked to construct a public narrative explaining how and why Alberto Alessi should take over from his uncle as the firm's leader (Dalpiaz et al., 2014). The firm accomplished this by engaging in self work around the identity of the new leader by developing narratives that linked the new leader to ideas such as "constructing a sense of family" and "highlighting non-family endorsement" (Dalpiaz et al., 2014: 1376). At the same time, the narratives shifted the organizational identity, focusing on the artistic element that Alberto had developed during the time he was responsible for new product development and reframing Alessi as a firm that focused on household objects as art and Alberto as the right leader for the new Alessi. This example highlights both the kind of normal organizational problems that trigger combinations of self work and organization work, and the degree to which organizational actors are aware of the need for such combinations, especially in regard to problems connected to leadership and other organizational issues that necessarily implicate the organization and selves as social-symbolic objects.

Strategies that combine self work and organization work to address organizational challenges are common in contexts where the constitution of organizations and selves as social-symbolic objects are interdependent. The Alessi example points to leadership as one such context, but organizational life is filled with situations in which this combination will play a key role. Managing organizational culture, whether preserving or changing it, involves shaping shared beliefs and values (Schein, 2016), and this implicates both the organization and selves as social-symbolic objects. Another organizational context likely to require this combination is when corporate restructuring dramatically alters an organization's structure along with the networks and routines of its members (Balogun and Johnson, 2004): in this case, organization work and self work would be necessary both to establish the changes and to help members cope with them.

INSTITUTIONAL WORK AND SELF WORK

The combination of institutional work and self work represents an interesting emerging area of concern in management and organizational research. While perhaps less obvious as a research focus than the previous two combinations, the connection between self work and institutional work is attracting increased attention as the need to change selves in order to change or maintain institutions, and conversely the need to change institutions in order to change or maintain a self, have become recognized as common situations facing actors.

An exciting turn in studies of organizational institutionalism has been the integration of the self, including a recognition of the importance of self work. This has included, for example, attention to both identity work and emotion work, though potential connections to careers and career work remain largely overlooked. Interest in the relationship between identity work and institutional work was kick-started by Creed and colleagues' (2010) study of the identity work done by LGBT ministers in response to their experience of the institutional contradictions rooted in "institutional arrangements [that] create various inconsistencies and tensions within and between social systems" (Seo and Creed, 2002: 223).

This same direction—from identity work to institutional work—is significantly extended by Leung and colleagues (2014) in their examination of a social enterprise created by Japanese middle-class housewives. The housewives paradoxically leveraged and transformed the role of "dutiful wife and nurturing mother" to become leaders and activists for social causes. This study shows how identity work can be a form of institutional work, when it involves both

251

"the endogenous process of self-constructions and the external process of changing, or maintaining, institutions" (Leung et al., 2014: 427).

A more recent integration of self work and institutional work has occurred around emotions and emotion work. Although the importance of emotions to the creation and maintenance of institutions has been recognized for some time (Lawrence, 2004; Selznick, 1996, 2011), a more recent wave of attention to this connection has emerged attending specifically to the potential connection between emotion work and institutional work (Voronov and Vince, 2012; Voronov and Weber, 2016). Voronov and Weber (2016: 456), for instance, propose a mechanism through which emotion work and institutional work can be linked in their concept of emotional competence, which they describe as "the ability to experience and display emotions that are deemed appropriate for an actor role within the institutional order" (Voronov and Weber, 2016: 457). Emotional competence bridges emotion work and institutional work by acting as a key common resource that facilitates them, and by potentially motivating both forms of work, triggered by a misalignment of emotions and institutions that undermines people's sense of self or faith in institutions.

In exploring the links between forms of social-symbolic work—emotion work and institutional work, in this case—it is critical that we make clear our conceptualization of the links, whether we are suggesting that particular sets of actions constitute both, as people engage in strategies that allow them to shape both emotions and institutions, for instance, or that these forms of work are attached to distinct activities, but are linked through some other mechanism. The concept of interaction rituals (Collins, 2004), for instance, provides an important potential link between emotion work and institutional work: interaction rituals provide a recursive process within which actors are motivated by emotions to sustain or transform institutions, and are motivated by institutions to shape their own and others' emotions (Lawrence, 2004).

Strategies for Combining Forms of Social-Symbolic Work

So far in this section, we have discussed combinations of self work, organization work, and institutional work. In each case, we have seen that these combinations are more than the sum of the individual forms of social-symbolic work—the interactions among self work, organization work, and institutional work are critical to the dynamics described and the outcomes that result. Thus, they point to new directions for theorizing and researching social-symbolic work focusing on how actors work to combine different forms of social-symbolic work, and how the different strategies for combining affect the motivations, practices, resources, and effects in play. While a great deal of theorizing and empirical work is needed to understand how this happens, a starting point for this work might be found in identifying some of the general strategies that individual and collective actors use to combine forms of social-symbolic work. To that end, we explore sequencing, aligning, and integrating as three key combining strategies.

SEQUENCING FORMS OF SOCIAL-SYMBOLIC WORK

Sequencing forms of social-symbolic work involves performing different forms of social-symbolic work in a sequence in order to achieve an objective: an actor performs one form of social-symbolic work and then another (and perhaps another), with all of the forms of work intended to address the same problem by affecting different social-symbolic objects. In some cases, the order in which the forms of work are performed may be important: the first form of social-symbolic work prepares the ground for the second, and so on. In other cases, all of the forms of social-symbolic work may be required to reach the overall objective, but the order has little impact.

Sequencing forms of social-symbolic work is illustrated by the transition from identity work to institutional work in the case of the Japanese house-wives examined by Leung and colleagues (2014). In developing the social enterprise, the Seikatsu Club Consumers' Cooperative, the founders were not initially motivated by a desire to change their identities or the institution of what it meant to be a middle-class Japanese housewife. Instead, it was their commitment to improving their role performance that led them to gradually expand their role identity, and in this process become aware of the institu-tionally prescribed constraints imposed on them. Through this process, the housewives transitioned first to engaging in identity work focused on over-coming those obstacles, and then to institutional work intended to reform their role identities in Japanese society.

This study provides a fascinating example of the potentially emergent nature of sequencing social-symbolic work, with the effects of one form of social-symbolic work (identity work in this case) motivating and shaping other forms of social-symbolic work (the institutional work of the Japanese housewives). Sequencing forms of social-symbolic work could also occur as a more explicitly planned process, where actors realize that in order to achieve some distal outcomes, they need first to engage in "indirect" social-symbolic work that provides the foundation for more direct efforts to shape social-symbolic objects (Bertels et al., 2014). Sequential combinations of social-symbolic work may also depend on distinct practices in order to successfully create a succession of forms of social-symbolic work, whereby the effects of one form of work become resources (and perhaps motivations) for another form of work. Although the Seikatsu Club example involved the same actors, sequencing could also depend on a succession of different actors. In these cases, distinctive relational practices may be required, such as "handoffs" in which responsibility and authority for a process of social-symbolic work may be passed from one set of actors to another. This might be more challenging than typical coordination processes in organizations, as sequencing social-symbolic work may often occur in novel contexts or in pursuit of complex aims which are new to the actors involved.

ALIGNING FORMS OF SOCIAL-SYMBOLIC WORK

Aligning forms of social-symbolic work involves performing different forms of social-symbolic work in parallel to achieve an objective. This strategy might be adopted because the final objective of the social-symbolic work requires change in multiple social-symbolic objects that can only be affected simultaneously, as when, for example, changing an organization's identity requires that members' identities change at the same time to avoid tension and resistance. Alternatively, aligning forms of social-symbolic work might occur when reaching a goal requires an actor to engage in multiple forms of social-symbolic work and it is more efficient for the actor to perform the forms of work simultaneously, though they would also be effective if performed sequentially.

In the Intel example discussed earlier, shifting the logic of their industry from a traditional supply chain logic to a platform logic required extensive institutional work, but Intel also needed to engage in significant organization work to become a platform leader. The study makes clear the importance of both types of social-symbolic work being performed at the same time. As the authors explain:

> At the field level, ... Intel performed external practice work and legitimacy work in order to influence the process of logic change and in order to ensure that they were accepted in the role of platform leader. Within the organization, ... the firm performed internal practice work and identity work in order to respond to the shifting logic. These different forms of institutional work did not occur in a sequential manner, but rather were simultaneous and mutually reinforcing.
>
> (Gawer and Phillips, 2013: 1037)

For Intel, an aligning strategy was required because shifting the logic of the field level also required significant changes to the organization. Although the authors described both sets of social-symbolic work as institutional work, they were, from our perspective, distinctly institutional and organization work, each focused on different social-symbolic objects and requiring different actions and resources.

As with sequencing, the possibility of aligning as a strategy to combine forms of social-symbolic work raises important issues. In particular, aligning raises the question of what resources are required to successfully follow this strategy beyond those required by the separate forms of social-symbolic work involved. One issue in aligning combinations of social-symbolic work may be the competition that parallel sets of practices create, especially if they are engaged in by the same actor or set of actors. In the case of Intel, managing the process of changing identity internally and changing practices and relationships externally was a significant challenge for Intel's management. Management time and attention was a limited resource that was stretched by this strategy.

Moreover, though each form of social-symbolic work will itself depend on certain resources, there may also be distinctive sets of resources needed to ensure that the effects of the parallel forms of work remain aligned, so that the effects are consistent and as intended. One set of resources that could be important in aligning combinations of social-symbolic work are social boundaries (and boundary spanners and boundary objects) that would be used to understand, communicate, and manage the relationship between the different forms of social-symbolic work. In the case of Intel, the key resource was again the availability of management time and attention to ensure that the two processes proceeded more or less simultaneously to avoid tensions between the sets of changes that were happening. If one set of changes got ahead of the other, significant conflict would occur as the internal and external activities become disconnected.

INTEGRATING FORMS OF SOCIAL-SYMBOLIC WORK
The last strategy we discuss—integrating forms of social-symbolic work—involves sets of actions that are intended to simultaneously affect multiple kinds of social-symbolic objects, as when an actor engages in social-symbolic work such as changing the rules that govern a social arena in order to both transform an institution and shape the selves of people connected to that institution. Integrating forms of social-symbolic work is relatively common because social-symbolic objects are often "intertwined" in ways that make shaping each dependent on shaping the others. Consider, for example, the Pussyhat Project initiated by Krista Suh and Jayna Zweiman as part of the Women's March on Washington on January 21, 2017. The pussyhats were knitted or sewn pink hats intended as a rebuke to Donald Trump's claim that women would let him "grab them by the pussy" and a satirical echo of the "Make America Great" caps prominent in Trump's presidential campaign. Thus, the Pussyhat Project was clearly an instance of institutional work, focused on disrupting the legitimacy of the newly elected president and the populist political project of which he is the figurehead. But the project was also an instance of self work: as Jayna Zweiman described, "I think it's resonating a lot because we're really saying that no matter who you are or where you are, you can be politically active." Thus, as is often seen in social movements, the same instance of social-symbolic work—making and wearing a pink

pussyhat—was intended to shape two different social-symbolic objects (the selves of the women who made and wore the hats and the political organization and project that President Trump leads and represents).

A significant issue associated with an integrating strategy to combine forms of social-symbolic work concerns its effects. We have discussed the importance of attending to the unintended effects of social-symbolic work in relation to a number of specific types of self work, organization work, and institutional work. Unintended effects may be even more likely and more consequential when actors attempt to shape multiple social-symbolic objects through one integrated set of social-symbolic work. Moreover, because integrating forms of social-symbolic work is likely to involve collaboration among a network of actors, unintended effects may stem from disparate motivations that lead actors to make conflicting decisions regarding what practices are likely to be most successful.

Connecting Social-Symbolic Objects

The final issue we consider in this chapter is how individual and collective actors connect different social-symbolic objects. As with social-symbolic work, we have to this point focused primarily on social-symbolic objects as discrete phenomena, but of course they exist in ecologies of other social-symbolic objects (and actors and actions). Social-symbolic objects are thus connected to each other in important ways: the meanings, uses, and values of social-symbolic objects are tied to those of other social-symbolic objects. These connections may emerge organically as unintended consequences of distal programs of action. But connections among social-symbolic objects may also be the result of purposeful, reflexive efforts of interested actors. Thus, the question we address now concerns this "connecting work"—how actors draw on social-symbolic objects to create or shape other social-symbolic objects. More specifically, we explore four kinds of connecting work through which actors connect different social-symbolic objects: two kinds of connecting work—enactment and abstraction—that are primarily incremental in the sense that the efforts of actors tend to reproduce the social-symbolic context; and two kinds of connecting work—translation and inversion—where the efforts of actors tend to produce more transformational effects.

Enactment

The first kind of connecting work—enactment—involves actors taking a social-symbolic object of one kind and employing it as a frame to produce a social-symbolic object of another kind. In terms of the forms of social-symbolic work on which we have focused, this might commonly involve drawing on an institution to produce an aspect of a self or organization. In such cases, institutions would provide templates for work performed to construct or shape concrete selves or organizations. A common example of enactment involves an individual drawing on a professional identity that exists as an institution—the idea of a cardiologist, airline pilot, or plumber—and bringing it to life as part of their efforts to construct a self. This might involve using the language of the profession, wearing clothing considered legitimate for members of the profession, and engaging with other people on professional terms. Through this activity, the individual moves those ideas from the realm of the institutional to the realm of the self—they take the concept of a cardiologist and create an individual who is a cardiologist.

Enactment, however, need not be done by the focal actor, or even a single actor. Although we might immediately imagine an individual working to craft her or his own self as a cardiologist, we can also imagine this work being done by a set of actors, as would occur, for example, in an educational institution where lecturers and other medical professionals work to shape a student's professional identity, emotions, and career path (Pratt et al., 2006). In fact, this kind of distributed, collective social-symbolic work is extraordinarily common with respect to enactment—engaged in by networks and communities of individual and collective actors, the combined efforts of which shape the social-symbolic object that is being produced through connecting work.

Weick (1988: 306) argues that the concept of enactment highlights the idea that "when people act, they bring events and structures into existence and set them in motion." This occurs in two steps, whereby "portions of the field of experience are bracketed and singled out for closer attention on the basis of preconceptions," and then "people act within the context of these bracketed elements, under the guidance of preconceptions, and often shape these elements in the direction of preconceptions" (Weick, 1988: 307). Thus, social-symbolic objects present themselves both as elements of a situation in need of sensemaking and as preconceived bases for interpreting those situations: selves, organizations, and institutions (and especially changes in the status of these objects, including their appearance, disappearance, or transformation) can be triggers for sensemaking while other selves, organizations, and institutions provide interpretive frames that shape responses to the situation at hand. As people and groups make sense of the situation, they produce an enacted environment. Central to this idea is the fact that enactment is not peripheral to action: "[t]he product of enactment is not an accident, an afterthought, or a byproduct. Instead, it is an orderly, material, social construction that is subject to multiple interpretations" (Weick, 1988: 307).

Abstraction

The second kind of connecting work we explore here is in some sense the inverse of enactment. Where enactment involves bringing social-symbolic objects to life, abstraction involves the construction of a social-symbolic object out of the lived experience of actors. If we take our example from above of people enacting a professional self based on an institutionalized conception of a particular profession—a surgeon constructing a self by enacting the generalized concept of a surgeon—then we can imagine the inverse where actors draw from across the lived experience of many individuals in a new profession, such as sustainability officers, to construct and institutionalize "sustainability officer" as an institution (Miller and Serafeim, 2014; Weber et al., 2009).

There exists, of course, a wide range of strategies through which people abstract from their or others' lived experience to generate social-symbolic objects. If we take a discourse-oriented view, we can understand abstraction as the construction of new concepts drawing on objects in the world (Fairclough, 1992; Hardy and Phillips, 1999). While we usually think of objects as instances of concepts (which they always are), we can also derive novel concepts from objects, usually by applying a different interpretive frame. For instance, people who do not identify as men, women, or transgendered might work to construct a particular idea of a "gender non-conforming" category by generalizing across the specific individuals who are understood to fall within this new category. Similar dynamics occur in the context of migration into new countries, whereby individuals' idiosyncratic senses of belonging (or not) can provide the concrete, lived experience that is abstracted into the "more readily understood proxy of collective identities" (Jones and Krzyżanowski, 2008: 38).

We employ the concept of abstraction to describe this process of constructing social-symbolic objects in one domain from lived experience or concrete activities in another domain. Although abstraction is often associated with formal, logical-mathematical practices and processes (Levins, 2007), our arguments regarding abstraction as social-symbolic work share more with pattern recognition in grounded theory (Glaser and Strauss, 1967). Abstraction is never a purely intellectual or direct process. It is always an iterative, social process, much like it is in grounded theory. We "notice" patterns, which involves constructing sets of likenesses across time and space; we name those patterns and ascribe emergent properties to them, try those ideas on in day-to-day life (or in our research and writing in grounded theory construction), "notice" more instances of those patterns, modify our naming and descriptions, and continue until we have a workable abstraction that is generative of action and coherent discourse (as with the development of substantive theory in grounded theory).

Translation

Translation involves the movement of social-symbolic objects across contexts. The importance of this work stems from the embeddedness of social-symbolic work: as we discussed in Chapter 2, all social-symbolic work represents a kind of embedded agency, a key feature of which is its situatedness. Agency is embedded in sets of ideas, beliefs, rules, and values that are more or less local, and always have some connection to particular times and places (Lawrence and Dover, 2015). Thus, moving social-symbolic objects across contexts—importing or exporting forms of social-symbolic objects—requires work to reshape the practices and meanings that are being moved to fit in with or leverage the selves, organizational forms, and institutions that already circulate within the new context.

To describe the efforts of actors to move social-symbolic objects across social contexts, we draw on the idea of "translation" (Callon, 1986; Callon and Latour, 1981; Latour, 1986; Sahlin and Wedlin, 2008), which has been picked up in organization studies most prominently in Scandinavian studies of how ideas circulate across organizations and societies (Boxenbaum, 2006; Boxenbaum and Strandgaard Pedersen, 2009; Sahlin and Wedlin, 2008). The attraction to translation for Scandinavian scholars was rooted in its emphasis on "the social aspects of idea circulation" (Sahlin and Wedlin, 2008: 224), and particularly the circulation of management ideas that were "translated into objects such as books, models and presentations...in the various contexts and by the many actors involved in circulating ideas" (Sahlin and Wedlin, 2008: 225).

A key finding in the study of translation has been its transformational effects on the social-symbolic objects being translated, and on the social systems into which they are imported (Boxenbaum, 2006; Lawrence, 2017; Sahlin and Wedlin, 2008). The translation of social-symbolic objects across social contexts involves the movement, not of the ideas themselves, but of "accounts and materializations" of the idea (Sahlin and Wedlin, 2008: 225), the meanings of which change "during their journey from one social context to another" (Frenkel, 2005: 279). As actors work to translate social-symbolic objects, they revise them to fit into the new context so that they are perceived as "legitimate and meaningful" (Boxenbaum, 2006: 946). Thus, translation introduces significant uncertainty with respect to what an identity, boundary, or practice might look like when introduced into a new social context.

For example, in a study of reputation management, Wæraas and Satøen (2014) show how Norwegian hospitals adapted reputation management, rooted in practices and discourse outside of Norway and outside of the hospital sector, to their context through strategies of copying, omission, and addition. Each of these strategies was applied to distinct facets of reputation management: the hospitals directly copied a concern for reputation and strategic means for expressing reputation, such as logos; in contrast, they omitted the "the type of comprehensive, soul-searching process that normally would be expected from standard reputation management thinking, in which gaps between desired and actual identity are revealed" (Wæraas and Sataøen, 2014: 248), as well as any significant attempt at differentiation among the hospitals; finally, to the institutionalized notions of reputation management portrayed in textbooks and by consultants, the Norwegian hospitals replaced a concern for differentiation with significant efforts "not to stand out from their peers or create a distinct hospital brand," but rather to be "perceived as a hospital with all its general meanings, just like any other hospital" (Wæraas and Sataøen, 2014: 250).

Inversion

The final form of connecting work we explore is "inversion," which involves the appropriation and reshaping of meaning, such that the meaning of a social-symbolic object is transformed, often in ways directly in contrast to the original meaning. A famous example is the inversion of "queer" as a label by the LGBT community. In the early twentieth century, this label came to be used pejoratively in relation to men considered effeminate or others who did not conform to gender roles and expectations (Wortham, 2016). The derogatory usage spread until the 1970s, when some activists and scholars began to invert its usage in order to claim gender and sexual identities that were distinct from a gay or lesbian identity (Butler, 1990; Sedgwick, 1985). At the 1990 Pride Parade in New York City, Queer Nation, a gay-rights group, distributed a manifesto that explained their use of "queer": "When a lot of lesbians and gay men wake up in the morning, we feel angry and disgusted, not gay. So we've chosen to call ourselves queer. Using 'queer' is a way of reminding us how we are perceived by the rest of the world" (Wortham, 2016). This public and dramatic instance of inversion illustrates core dynamics that are associated with the less visible inversion work that occurs in and around organizations as often marginalized actors engage in efforts to undermine discriminatory or exclusionary identities, boundaries, and practices.

Research on ethnic identity describes a similar process undertaken by immigrants as a "restructuring of group identities and the redefinition of social boundaries" (Massey and Sánchez, 2010: 14). Natives can attach negative meanings to immigrants that emphasize group differences and contribute to their exclusion (Barth, 1998; Lamont and Molnár, 2002; Massey and Sánchez, 2010). Immigrants learn these meanings and either embrace them or resist them—that is, "they broker the boundaries to help define the content of their ethnicity in the host society, embracing some elements ascribed to them and rejecting others, while simultaneously experiencing the constraints and opportunities associated with their social status" (Massey and Sánchez, 2010: 15). For example, boundary inversion occurred when Irish immigrants in London broke down their opportunity barriers in construction and eventually became dominant developers in the industry (Dwyer, 2015).

Conclusion

In this chapter, we have highlighted some of the opportunities for new areas of research opened up by the social-symbolic work perspective. We believe a key contribution of this perspective will be in facilitating research that explores new questions about the ways in which actors combine different forms of social-symbolic work to reach desired ends, and the kinds of social-symbolic work used to connect different kinds of social-symbolic objects. To that end, we have identified three strategies for combining forms of social-symbolic work—serial, parallel, and integrated—each of which requires different skills and resources, and is associated with distinct costs and benefits. We have also identified four forms of connecting work: enactment and abstraction, which we argue tend to reproduce the social-symbolic context; and translation and inversion, which we argue tend to produce more transformational effects.

While we have highlighted these particular strategies and forms of connecting work, they are intended to be illustrative, rather than comprehensive. Many other possibilities exist, which, along with those we have identified, provide an expansive set of opportunities for empirical research and theoretical development. The social-symbolic work perspective, by virtue of its integrative nature, provides a basis for scholars to explore the relationships between previously disparate sets of practices, processes, and structures. If taken up by other scholars, we believe that exploring these conceptual linkages may represent the most significant, long-term contribution of the social-symbolic work perspective.

10

Methodological Challenges and Choices in the Study of Social-Symbolic Work

In this chapter we:

1. Discuss strategies useful in developing a good research question for the study of social-symbolic work.

2. Consider how to identify a productive research context for a study of social-symbolic work.

3. Review a set of key questions to guide data collection in studies of social-symbolic work.

4. Explore key issues with respect to analyzing data in studies of social-symbolic work.

Introduction

Our exploration of social-symbolic work is intended not only to stimulate thinking about how actors shape the social world, but also to motivate and facilitate empirical research that examines how these processes occur in concrete contexts. We therefore now turn to considering a methodology for empirical research into social-symbolic work. Although we cannot address all of the potential methodological challenges and choices, we highlight a set of issues we believe are common to most empirical studies of social-symbolic work: developing productive research questions, identifying appropriate research contexts, collecting data on social-symbolic work and social-symbolic objects, and analyzing the data collected.

While our discussion is necessarily simplified, we believe having a "recipe" for studies of social-symbolic work is helpful, especially for new researchers, but perhaps also for experienced scholars moving into new research domains. Moreover, the steps we discuss highlight many of the important elements of a successful study and will hopefully help researchers avoid some common mistakes. At the same time, it is worth keeping in mind that these simple, linear steps become much messier and more mixed up in real life.

Before we begin, it is worth noting that the "recipe" we provide in this section is for a qualitative study of social-symbolic work. Although research on social-symbolic work might rely on quantitative methods, the history of scholarship on the forms of social-symbolic work we have reviewed point to the likely dominance of qualitative methods. This stems in part from the unavoidable focus in studies of social-symbolic work on meaning, for which qualitative methods are especially appropriate. Also, and not unimportantly, our own expertise is in qualitative methods, so we leave the exploration of quantitative methods for the study of social-symbolic work to others.

Step 1: Developing a Research Question

The first problem that needs to be addressed before beginning data collection is the development of an appropriate research question to motivate and guide a study. Although we realize that research questions inevitably evolve over the course of a study (including as it is written up and revised for publication), we believe it is still important to begin a study with a well-developed question in mind as guidance for early decisions about the research context, data collection process, and data analysis strategies.

Moreover, we have developed a theoretical framework that, if taken seriously, can change the questions we ask about traditional topics in management and organizational research, as well as providing the basis for a whole new set of research questions. In exploring how to develop good research questions for the study of social-symbolic work, we highlight two potential approaches: one that applies the social-symbolic work to existing management and organizational research topics, such as innovation and sustainability; and a second that constructs social-symbolic work itself as the focus of explanation. Before we do so, however, we think it would be useful to review the general properties associated with good research questions.

Developing a Good Research Question

As a rule of thumb, good research questions focus on understanding the relationship between two phenomena. While quantitative research is motivated by hypotheses, qualitative research is based around a clear and significant research question. The research question is important as it shapes and constrains the research study. And, perhaps most importantly, when the research question has been answered, the study is complete and, provided the research question is well located in the literature and focuses on an important topic, then the study will have made a significant and novel contribution to the literature. But developing a good research question is a significant challenge and one where potential research projects often get stuck. We will therefore provide a few ideas for developing a good research question in this section.

GAPS VERSUS PUZZLES

Identifying a potential relationship between two phenomena can be grounded primarily in either the scholarly literature or in the empirical world. These two different types of research questions are often referred to as being based on a "gap" or a "puzzle." Traditionally, the idea was that research questions would arise from a gap in the literature. For example, a researcher might notice that the literature on emotions in organizations says little about the role of technology. The researcher would then develop a research question that would motivate a study to fill this gap.

More recently, it has become increasingly common to see studies based on empirical puzzles where a researcher develops a question based on observing empirical phenomena that don't fit with the existing literature. So, for example, a researcher might notice in their everyday experience, or from media reports, that people often have highly emotional relationships with technology (both passionately engaged with and horribly frustrated by). Noticing this puzzle (what is the relationship between technology and emotion?) provides a basis for beginning to develop a research question.

These two types of research questions are, of course, rather stylized. Research questions often grow out of a combination of a gap in the literature and real-life experience. Extending our example, this combination of reading the existing literature and attending to empirical reality might lead us to form a number of research questions that relate emotions and technology in organizations: How do technologies shape emotions? How do emotions shape the use of technology in organizations? How do people use emotions to shape organizational technologies in practice?

MODERATORS AND MEDIATORS

Although research questions begin with a relationship between two phenomena, it is often the case that introducing a third phenomenon or factor into the question provides a more interesting focus for research. In quantitative research, these third variables are referred to as "moderators" (which affect the relationship between two other phenomena) and "mediators" (through which one phenomenon affects another). Although we expect studies of social-symbolic work to be primarily qualitative, keeping these basic ideas in mind can be helpful in thinking through the relationships among concepts that make up a research question.

In a qualitative study of emotions and technology, for instance, we might gain theoretical and empirical traction by introducing a "moderator" to the research question, perhaps asking how the impact of emotions on technology use varies across different professional groups. Adding the idea that membership in different professional groups might affect (moderate) the relationship between emotions and technology use would go on to shape the data we collect, how we analyze it, the findings we might present, and the theoretical claims we might make.

Similarly, introducing the idea that there exists some intermediate phenomenon (a mediator) that connects technology use and emotions might involve including in the research question some kind of cognitive phenomena. One might examine, for instance, how technology use motivates emotion work through its impact on people's confidence or efficacy, perhaps undermining or shaping that efficacy in ways that triggered emotion work on the part of people aiming to restore a positive sense of self.

CLARITY AND SPECIFICITY

As with scholarly writing more generally, a key quality we aim for with respect to crafting research questions is clarity, which in the case of research questions "hinges on adequate specificity and the correct degree of inclusiveness" (Locke and Silverman, 2007: 12). Specificity in terms of a research question means identifying the phenomena in question in a way that avoids confusion regarding the aspects of the social world under consideration. This depends on a match between the language we use and our audience. When we refer to emotions and technology in organizations, for instance, our aim is to employ language (terms such as "emotions," "emotion work," "technologies," "technology in practice") in ways that clearly signal to our readers the aspects of organizational life in which we are interested and the literatures we are drawing on to conceptualize it.

The tension that arises is that in trying to achieve clarity we might reduce simplicity: we can increase the clarity of our research question by expanding it, adding qualifiers and elaborated descriptions of the phenomena of interest, but that might diminish the overall simplicity, and hence interpretability of the question. Good research questions, thus, articulate two or three phenomena of interest and the relationships between them, but exclude references to other phenomena that while potentially connected are not the focus of the study. Moreover, they are framed in a language that makes clear what literatures they connect to, and thus the meanings of the main concepts.

SIGNIFICANCE

Along with ensuring specificity and simplicity, in developing a good research question we also need to ensure that the question we are asking is an important one, which we do in one of two main ways depending on whether the research question is based on a gap or a puzzle. If it is based on a gap, then the challenge is to show that filling the gap represents an interesting and worthwhile task. Although seemingly obvious, this can represent a real challenge for researchers. It depends on being able to argue that the answer would challenge existing perspectives or open new lines of inquiry. One powerful approach to dealing with this issue involves problematization, which involves challenging the assumptions underpinning existing research, rather than simply extending it (Alvesson and Sandberg, 2011).

If, on the other hand, our research question is based on a puzzle, then we might evaluate its importance in terms of the question's value in addressing a problem in the world. Adopting a social-symbolic work perspective when addressing a problem-based question can facilitate a broader, more integrative perspective than has traditionally been the case. In traditional problem-focused studies, scholars examined the role of a single form of social-symbolic work (such as identity work or institutional work), even though actors connected to the problem might engage in a wide range of forms of social-symbolic work targeted at a variety of social-symbolic objects. We suggest that exploring social-symbolic work more broadly and using the process model we introduced in Chapter 2 can provide a more realistic and generative approach to understanding how and why actors engage with problems in their worlds.

Applying the Social-Symbolic Work Perspective to Existing Topics

Moving from the general issue of what constitutes a good research question, to what a question would look like if it were motivated by the idea of social-symbolic work, we begin by considering research questions that apply the social-symbolic work perspective to existing management and organizational research topics, such as innovation, leadership, sustainability, or change management. In developing this kind of question, the social-symbolic work perspective provides a lens on the management and organizational topic; so we might ask, for instance, how social-symbolic work affects innovation in organizations, or what role social-symbolic work plays in organizational sustainability initiatives.

If we consider innovation in organizations, for example, we can see significant potential for research questions that apply a social-symbolic work perspective to this issue. Innovation has been described as "the successful application of new ideas" and is thus "both an outcome and a process, a fact and an act" (Dodgson et al., 2014: 5). In their review of perspectives on innovation management, Dodgson and colleagues (2014) argue that organizational actors trying to manage innovation face a number of recurrent challenges, including managing intangible assets and balancing innovation portfolios. Intangible assets are those that "cannot be seen or touched," including knowledge, intellectual property, corporate reputation, and organizational culture, all of which are critical to managing innovation in organizations. The challenge of managing these assets includes measuring them, identifying their boundaries, and establishing how and when they lead to (or stifle) innovation.

Applying a social-symbolic work perspective provides a basis for a new set of research questions to guide the exploration of the role of intangible assets in innovation. These questions start with conceptualizing intangible assets, such as culture or intellectual property, as social-symbolic objects that are therefore amenable to social-symbolic work, including its discursive, relational, and material dimensions. This conceptual move locates innovation as an intended effect of the social-symbolic work focused on shaping intangible assets in ways that would support innovation. This line of questioning starts with a relatively simple question focused on unpacking the effect of discursive, relational, or material dimensions of social-symbolic work on the ability of organizational culture or intellectual property to support innovation. Recognizing the interdependence of forms of social-symbolic work and types of social-symbolic objects then leads to more complex questions examining the potential combinations of social-symbolic work and how they can shape intangible assets (e.g., the parallel combination of technology work and boundary work in shaping intellectual property), or the potential role of connecting work (e.g., how intellectual property is translated into valuable organizational practices that could be marketable as commodities).

EXPLORING SOCIAL-SYMBOLIC WORK

One way to think about the discussion above is imagining social-symbolic work as the "independent variable" in our research—asking what the role is of social-symbolic work in an existing area of management and organizational research. We now turn to conceiving of social-symbolic work as the "dependent variable," and thus developing questions that are focused on understanding social-symbolic work and social-symbolic objects as the focus of the research. More specifically, we see this shift as leading to two broad categories of research questions: questions that focus on particular types of social-symbolic work, and questions that focus on combinations of social-symbolic work and connections between social-symbolic objects.

EXPLORING INDIVIDUAL TYPES OF SOCIAL-SYMBOLIC WORK

In Chapters 4, 6, and 8, we reviewed the literatures associated with areas of management and organizational research that we associated with self work (emotion work, identity work, career work), organization work (strategy work,

267

boundary work, technology work), and institutional work (practice work, category work). For each of these literatures, we examined how conceiving of them as forms of social-symbolic work might affect how we understand them. Here, we extend that discussion, exploring potential research questions that might emerge from such a reconceptualization. We will not do so for all these literatures; instead, we explore, as illustrative, potential research questions that might emerge from considering career work and category work as forms of social-symbolic work.

In our examination of career work as a form of self work in Chapter 4, we argued that this conceptual shift affects how we think about the motivations, practices, effects, resources, and situatedness associated with career work. With respect to motivations and practices, we noted the distributed nature of career work: rather than think of career work as limited to the individual whose career is in question, it might involve colleagues, subordinates, and bosses, as well as family, friends, and rivals. Thus, a research question that might emerge from this shift might ask when and how the motivations and practices of the career work of different actors will lead to conflict or cooperation. Such a question is interesting because it locates research on careers in the broader study of organizational power, politics, and relationships. We also noted in relation to the effects, resources, and situatedness of career work that changes in contemporary Western labor markets leading to task-based employment (the "gig economy"), rather than traditional jobs, are disrupting the boundary between careers and other facets of the self, including family and home. This change prompts research questions that focus on things like what new resources and skills are emerging as important for actors engaged in the gig economy in order for them to successfully manage these boundary disruptions. Again, this question expands the study of careers, embedding it in the study of technological disruptions and work–family boundaries.

In Chapter 8, we explored the literature on category work and highlighted the ways in which conceptualizing it as a type of institutional work might lead us to rethink the issue of motivations. The points we raised in that chapter lead to some novel research questions about the dynamics of category work. For example, we argued that thinking of category work as a type of institutional work broadens the kinds of aims that might motivate actors to engage in category work, in particular expanding existing scholarly discussions to include non-economic gains that flow from successful category work, including political and social advantage. So, a research question that would flow from this shift could ask how category work practices differ when motivated by economic, social, or political aims. Answering this question would contribute to the study of category work, which has tended to focus on isolated, rather than comparative, cases and thus failed to develop an understanding of variation in category work practices or what leads to that variation.

EXPLORING COMBINATIONS AND CONNECTIONS

The second broad category of research questions that result from placing social-symbolic work at the core of a study involves understanding combinations of types of social-symbolic work and connections between social-symbolic objects. We suggested three strategies for combining forms of social-symbolic work: sequencing, aligning, and integrating. Similarly, we explained how the relationships between social-symbolic objects occur through four kinds of connecting work: enactment, abstraction, translation, and inversion. Here, we illustrate the potential for these ideas to generate novel research questions by exploring one of each of those sets.

A basic premise of this book is that efforts to shape any complex facet of social life are likely to span multiple kinds of social-symbolic work. This is despite most management and organizational research focusing on only one, such as identity work or institutional work. As soon as we acknowledge actors' capacity to combine different kinds of social-symbolic work, the research questions we can ask become significantly more complex, and, at the same time, more grounded in the lived reality of the actors we study.

For example, if we take Gawer and Phillips' (2013) study of Intel's shift to a platform strategy that we discussed in Chapter 9, it illustrated the possibility of different forms of social-symbolic work being combined in parallel. The paper focuses on how Intel had to perform identity work inside the organization at the same time as they performed various forms of institutional work outside the organization. An extension of that study informed by a social-symbolic work perspective could look at the interaction between these forms of work and what resources and skills were needed to make this combination successful. Other studies could extend this focus on forms of work performed in parallel and examine the skills and resources needed to combine different forms of social-symbolic work, which would differ depending on the specific combinations of work. So, for instance, what resources and skills are needed to combine strategy work and technology work in parallel? We might also ask whether certain kinds of social-symbolic work tend to be combined in parallel, or under what circumstances they might be separated. So, for instance, we might ask whether strategy work and boundary work in organizations are separable, and if so under what circumstances, by what kinds of actors, and with what effects.

A second source of research questions comes from our discussion of the potential connections between social-symbolic objects, and the types of social-symbolic work through which such connections are established. If we consider enactment, for instance, it describes actors taking social-symbolic objects of one kind and employing them as a frame for the construction of a social-symbolic object of another kind, as might occur when an individual enacts a professional identity that exists as an institution. Although enactment may seem to be the most straightforward of the kinds of connecting work we have discussed, abstract ideas—such as ideal identities, emotions, boundaries, or practices—may not always be easily enacted in particular situations or contexts. This leads to research questions that ask what challenges are associated with enacting different types of social-symbolic objects in particular situations. We might ask, for instance, what challenges are associated with enacting an idealized understanding of anger as a concrete emotion in a professional work context. Or, what challenges are associated with enacting an idealized organizational form (an institution) as a concrete organization in an industry or country in which that form is unfamiliar? Alternatively, we could ask about the motivations that lead actors to enact different social-symbolic objects in particular situations. These sorts of questions have received little attention to date as different instances of enactment were not seen as being different types of the same phenomenon.

Step 2: Identifying a Context for Your Study

After developing a guiding research question, the second main issue to be faced prior to starting the study is to identify an appropriate research context— the site of social-symbolic work—in which you will explore your research question. As all experienced researchers will attest, articulating a research question and identifying a research context are inextricably linked. The question that motivates your research will guide you toward research contexts in which the dynamics you care about seem more obvious or more interesting. At the same time, the real-world contexts you observe or participate in will shape the research questions you find important or fascinating. Despite these complexities, we will for the sake of clarity discuss each as a separate challenge, while recognizing their interrelated nature and the likelihood of their ongoing evolution as your study progresses.

The problem of choosing a research site prompts a number of important questions. The first involves assessing potential sites in terms of their relationship to the ideas motivating your study. Social-symbolic work and social-symbolic objects are tremendously general concepts. Thus, on their own they don't necessarily provide a great deal of guidance with respect to what empirical contexts to study. There is one exception, however. Although all parts of the social world are made up of social-symbolic objects and involve actors engaged in social-symbolic work, the observability of that work is not evenly distributed across contexts. In some social contexts, the social-symbolic work engaged in is far more visible than in others, which is a critically important issue for the study of social-symbolic work. Highly visible social-symbolic work might be associated, for instance, with written and other records of the work, the ability of "outsiders" to observe and interpret the work, and the ability of participants to accurately recall and describe the work. In contrast, some sites host social-symbolic work that is relatively invisible, especially to outsiders, as it involves private, individual efforts that leave relatively little in terms of a public trace: imagine an individual editing technical or legal texts that define a range of social-symbolic objects, but where those edits are not recorded (in contrast to Wikipedia edits, for instance, which are all registered). While not completely invisible, observing this kind of social-symbolic work could be extremely challenging.

A second, related question concerns establishing the degree to which a site is "researchable." Researching social-symbolic work depends on finding a site that is amenable to study. This is primarily a practical question about sufficient access and the availability of data. Sometimes, researchers begin a study because they gain access to interesting data or an interesting context. In one of Nelson's studies, for example, he and his co-researcher were interviewing government officials in Canada about the refugee system when one of the officials offered to share a complete set of newspaper editorial cartoons depicting refugees over the preceding three years. The cartoons formed the foundation for a study of the construction of refugee identity in Canada—a study that would have been prohibitive in terms of time and expense without this lucky coincidence (Hardy and Phillips, 1999).

More often, however, pre-existing data do not so conveniently fall into one's lap, and so the practical problem becomes one of negotiating access. This represents an important challenge facing researchers conducting studies of social-symbolic work. The challenge of negotiating access to a site that will lead to interesting results should not be underestimated. While quantitative studies of social phenomena can, at least in some cases, draw on publicly available data, studies of social-symbolic work usually require interviews or other direct access to respondents (the ones doing the work). Therefore, access can be a major stumbling block for these studies due to the intensity of the access required.

Third, an important question to ask about empirical contexts is whether exploring them is valuable for theoretical reasons. A context is valuable for study because doing so will provide unique and distinctive insights with respect to the theoretical question that motivates our study. While data availability and access are important, it is also important that the context will yield unique and interesting insights. Simply because a context is accessible, does not make it necessarily a good context to investigate social-symbolic work. Regardless of the question that motivates your research, attempting to answer that question will be easier and more fruitful in some contexts than others.

A final question to consider in relation to studying an empirical context is whether the context itself is important or interesting. Many social-symbolic objects are of significant social, economic, cultural, or political importance, and so understanding how and why they are changing (or remaining stable) is itself of consequence, along with any potential theoretical insights that might be gleaned. Although reading common guidelines for management and organizational research would suggest that the anticipated theoretical insights should dominate our choice of empirical contexts, we are not so sure. Betting on a mundane context to provide interesting and novel insights seems to us far riskier than focusing on a context that is itself important and intrinsically interesting, since research in the latter situation is likely to provide, at a minimum, some useful practical insights about an important phenomenon and may also yield theoretical insight, whereas choosing a context strictly based on its relationship to your theoretical question may yield neither. Indeed, such a view is echoed in the growing call for management and organizational research to explore the world's grand challenges (George et al., 2016).

Step 3: Collecting Data on Social-Symbolic Work

Once you have developed a clear and interesting research question and identified an appropriate empirical setting, it is time to head out into the field and start collecting data. Although the data collection processes appropriate to the study of social-symbolic work are immensely varied, there are a number of questions to keep in mind as you begin this exciting and challenging process. While some of these questions may seem obvious, working out a convincing and compelling answer is often anything but.

How Are People Engaging in Social-Symbolic Work: What Are They Actually Doing?

Studies of social-symbolic work are, at their core, explorations of people engaged in purposeful efforts to shape social-symbolic objects. Research on social-symbolic work must therefore examine actors working in specific contexts and document what those people are doing and their intentions in doing so. The cases of social-symbolic work that we have used to illustrate this book point to the wide variety of actions that can be involved in social-symbolic work and thus the importance of data collection being sensitive to that variety and the fine-grained data necessary to capture it. Fine-grained data bring into focus the specific actions of individuals, how they engage in those actions, and the resources and skills they put to use. In Maguire and Hardy's (2009: 148) study of "defensive institutional work" in relation to the deinstitutionalization of DDT, for instance, they examined "how the actions of individuals in producing, distributing, and consuming texts can lead to radical change in an institutional field." By collecting fine-grained data, they were able to connect institutional change at the macro level with the institutional work of individuals.

An important lesson from Maguire and Hardy's (2009) study is the importance of creativity and flexibility in collecting data regarding social-symbolic work: their historical case study relied on secondary accounts of the social-symbolic work done in relation to Rachel Carson's *Silent spring*, including the book itself, a television documentary, book reviews, government reports and transcripts, interviews they performed with key actors, and archival tape recordings of interviews with actors prominent at the time of publication of *Silent spring*. This kind of triangulation is a hallmark of the best studies of social-symbolic work, which strive to assemble accurate accounts of actors' behaviors and intentions despite the challenges of retrospective biases, and idiosyncratic memories and experiences.

An alternative approach to observing the practical behaviors that make up social-symbolic work is to engage in an ethnographic research strategy. Such an approach has the advantage of avoiding, or at least minimizing, retrospection and interviewee bias. This empirical strategy is exemplified by Smets et al.'s (2012) study of "practice-driven institutional change" in UK law firms, for which they spent two weeks observing the work of professionals in each of two law firms, including sharing their offices, attending meetings, listening to phone calls, and joining in social interactions, as well as attending workshops. Observation does not, however, provide unfettered access to the social-symbolic work of actors: the corporeal limits of observers make observing the simultaneous work of actors problematic; even when behavior is directly observed, its meaning, intention, and effects may not be clear. Thus, triangulation is again important: in the Smets et al. (2012) study, for instance, the authors also relied on extensive interviews and archival material in order to document and interpret actors' behaviors.

On What Social-Symbolic Objects Are They Focusing?

The perspective we are developing revolves around the relationship between social-symbolic work and social-symbolic objects. Thus, answering these first two questions—what is the social-symbolic work and what are the social-symbolic objects?—is likely to proceed in an iterative fashion. Understanding the social-symbolic work of actors depends on understanding the social-symbolic objects on which they are focused, but being able to identify and comprehend the social-symbolic objects will likely require observing the social-symbolic work. So, research on social-symbolic work becomes an iterative sensemaking exercise, with each episode of data collection providing insights that also trigger new demands for sensemaking and thus more data collection.

This dynamic may be somewhat different from traditional studies that proceed from a narrower theoretical perspective (focused, for instance, on identity work or institutional work), which motivates the researcher to "find" particular social-symbolic objects, such as identities or institutions, because those are the focus of the theoretical perspective. From a social-symbolic work perspective, researchers may be agnostic with respect to the kinds of social-symbolic objects that might be important in understanding a phenomenon or process. This won't necessarily be the case, but a social-symbolic work perspective allows the researcher to enter the field with a broader set of conceptual lenses and a wider array of potential explanatory tools.

Ultimately, however, research from a social-symbolic work perspective demands that the relevant social-symbolic objects need to be clearly identified and defined, and their relationship to the social-symbolic work in question described. This will require a description of how changes in the social-symbolic objects are being measured, and the role of social-symbolic work explained. These challenges are both methodological and theoretical. It demands an explicit set of methodological commitments that specify the epistemological basis for the study's empirical claims, and methods that translate those commitments into concrete descriptions or measurements of specific social-symbolic objects and their place in the world. Conceptually, definitions of social-symbolic objects will generally come from existing literatures and provide a basis for research on social-symbolic work to connect to an existing body of theory (and hence the final results to have an interested audience). So, for example, identity work and emotion work represent research domains with active communities of scholars, and thus identifying identities and emotions needs to be done in ways that connect to how these concepts are already understood. This may seem obvious, but the pluralistic approach to social-symbolic objects that is implicit in the perspective we are developing may make categorizing social-symbolic objects potentially more challenging than would be the case in a more traditional, narrower, theoretical perspective.

What Resources and Skills Are Actors Using to Engage in Social-Symbolic Work?

Social-symbolic work is not only effortful and purposeful; it also demands skills and resources that translate those efforts and purposes into actions with meaningful effects for the social-symbolic objects it is intended to shape. Thus, a central question in studies of social-symbolic work concerns the resources and skills that actors are using in performing their work. This question was highlighted by Fligstein (1997: 398) when he argued that differences in actors' social skills explain why "some social actors are better at producing desired social outcomes than others." Fligstein (1997: 398) describes social skills as "the ability to motivate cooperation in other actors by providing those actors with common meanings and identities in which actions can be undertaken and justified." Although such skills are important, we can add other resources, such as status, reputation, and authority, as well as economic and material resources, to the list of things that make the social-symbolic work of some actors more successful than that of others.

The empirical challenge in dealing with resources and skills is twofold: identifying key resources, and showing how those resources affect the impact of social-symbolic work. The resources that actors draw on for their social-symbolic work vary considerably, as illustrated by our review of the different literatures associated with self work, organization work, and institutional work. They include discursive resources such as ideas and stories, relational resources such as friendships and reciprocity networks, and material resources such as spaces within which social-symbolic work can be accomplished and physical objects that help translate ideas into practical action. Although observing these kinds of phenomena is relatively straightforward, establishing their role as resources in social-symbolic work can be significantly more challenging. The problem is as much theoretical as methodological: since resources can take such a wide variety of forms, some kind of theoretical frame is needed to suggest their role as resources in social-symbolic work. In Jones and Massa's (2013) study of Frank Lloyd Wright, for example, they argue that his success in creating an architectural style that challenged the existing social-symbolic context and became "a consecrated exemplar" depended on his identity as an architect, his status and reputation, and his technical skill. Making this argument convincing depended on the authors' ability to empirically describe these discursive objects and a theory of how they might facilitate Wright's institutional work, in this case relying on the link between identities, institutions, and artifacts.

Why Are Actors Engaging in Social-Symbolic Work?

The social-symbolic work perspective assumes a purposeful relationship between social-symbolic work and social-symbolic objects. We are not suggesting that all (or even most) of the change or stability we observe in the social world stem from social-symbolic work. On this issue, our discussion of the social-symbolic work perspective has hopefully been clear. At the same time, to study social-symbolic work one needs to believe that people do sometimes work to shape their social worlds, and that they do so consciously, skillfully, and with purposes potentially available to themselves and others. Put simply, work is about people doing things with intent and studies of social-symbolic work must reflect this. Studies of social-symbolic work therefore need to include a clear concern for the intentions of the actors, but not assume any particular correspondence between intention and results.

The question of intentions is a complex one closely tied to the question of agency. The study of social-symbolic work depends on the idea that actors have intentions and the capacity to act on those intentions—they have agency. As we discussed in Chapter 2, the question of agency is a central problem in management and organizational research, the core of which asks if "structural contexts are analytically separable from (and stand over against) capacities for human agency, how is it possible for actors ever to mediate or to transform their own relationships to these context[?]" (Emirbayer and Mische, 1998: 964). The answer lies in the imperfect and conflicted nature of social structure and the ability of individuals to navigate these structures and use them in creative and innovative ways. Thus, an important aspect of data collection is developing an understanding of why actors are engaging in social-symbolic work.

The observation of intention comes with significant challenges. First, intentions are internal states, and so cannot be directly observed in the same way as actions. Intentions must be inferred by observing "markers" that provide insight into the purposes behind people's efforts. The most common method for doing so in management and organizational research is by asking people about the relationship between their work and their intentions, and so studies of social-symbolic work very often depend on interviews, which are, for the most part, retrospective. Retrospective accounts, however, raise the second challenge, which stems from the ways in which intentions and our memories of intentions change over time. People often rethink past events and reframe their involvement, making retrospective retelling potentially unreliable. Again, an important response to this problem is triangulation. The accounts of actors regarding their motivations can be buttressed or challenged if you can find other sources of data that are informative regarding those motivations. These data could include the accounts of others, archival data such as corporate reports or newspaper articles, or even physical artifacts. In a study of North America's first supervised injection site for intravenous drug users, Lawrence (2017) relied on triangulation to establish actors' motivations for actions, some of which occurred several years prior to interviewing them. Because the actions in question were of widespread interest, there existed a robust record in local and national newspapers, with many of the newspaper articles providing convincing accounts of actors' motivations.

What Are the Effects of Social-Symbolic Work?

Finally, research on social-symbolic work requires an understanding of the effects of the work being studied—changes in social reality or the maintenance of the status quo. Maguire et al. (2004), for example, explored the effects of institutional entrepreneurship in the field of HIV/AIDS treatment, and showed how a set of actors were able to create new practices and relationships among Canadian HIV/AIDS community organizations and pharmaceutical companies. There are three main challenges in demonstrating such effects.

The first challenge is to convincingly identify and demonstrate some set of effects—the creation, disruption, transformation, or maintenance of some social-symbolic objects, or their broader follow-on effects. Consider, for example, the work of various "hackers" in the 1970s and 1980s that resulted in the open-source movement that is such an important force in computing today. Their work—self work, organization work, and institutional work—established a new system of developing computer programs: volunteer programmers, a minimum of rules, little top-down control, and rapid product revisions replaced the top-down, planned, and tightly controlled traditional approach to programming in large parts of the software industry. This move from the "cathedral" to the "bazaar" as an approach to software development was the result of significant social-symbolic work focused on the institutions, organizations, and identities that populated the world of computer programming (Raymond, 2001); studying this social-symbolic work would require systematically describing and, ideally, measuring these changes in a clear and convincing way.

The second challenge stems from the unintended effects of social-symbolic work that may involve social-symbolic objects that are distant from actors' intended targets. So, for example, your research might focus on an actor engaged in self work, perhaps trying to shape their own identity or career, but that activity might have significant, unintended effects on the organization in which they work, or the institutions that surround them. Such possibilities represent, in fact, some of the most interesting effects of social-symbolic work, as profound shifts may result from social-symbolic work intended to be much more limited and local. Returning to our example of open-source programming, for instance, people like Linus Torvalds (on whose master's thesis the operating system Linux is based) were not intending to create a new programming culture when developing Linux, but work at the local level led to significant changes at the industry and broader societal levels (Torvalds and Diamond, 2002).

Third, the effects of social-symbolic work must be clearly linked to the actor and the work being investigated. Again, this is a matter of operationalization and measurement, but it also demands an explanation of the mechanisms that link social-symbolic work and putative effects. Showing that actions have had significant effects requires an explanation of the link between activities of the actor and the unintended (or only partially intended) effects. Continuing our example, the mechanism through which Linus Torvalds' creation of Linux supported the development of a new approach to computer programming was by providing a platform on top of which other people were able to produce a wide range of software. In developing Linux, Torvalds enabled the development of open-source programming and his practical work at an individual level functioned as social-symbolic work at the industry level through this mechanism.

Step 4: Back at Your Desk—Analyzing Your Data

Once you have collected sufficient data, the next challenge is to head back to your desk to analyze the data you have collected and write up the study. As we've said before, it is unlikely that you will wait until you've collected all your data, as you'll need to start making sense of it sooner rather than later, and it will likely provoke more data collection as well. In any case, analyzing your data represents a particularly challenging part of studying social-symbolic work. Exploring all possible approaches to data analysis in the study of social-symbolic work is far beyond the scope of this book, so we focus here on a two issues that are particularly important in studies of social-symbolic work: the focus of analysis in terms of the process model of social-symbolic work we presented in Chapter 1 (reproduced in simplified form in Figure 10.1); and the epistemological stance (modern or postmodern).

Elements- and Mechanisms-Focused Data Analysis

The model of social-symbolic work that we have developed suggests two possible data analytic strategies, one focused on the "boxes" (the elements

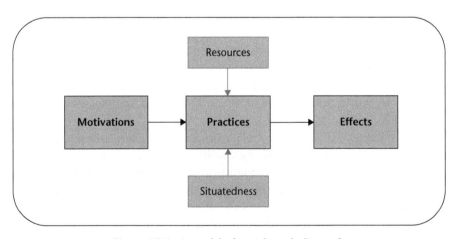

Figure 10.1. A model of social-symbolic work

of the model, including the motivations, practices, outcomes, resources, and situatedness of social-symbolic work) and one focused on the "arrows" (the connections among those elements).

ELEMENTS-FOCUSED DATA ANALYSIS

We will begin by discussing data analysis that is primarily concerned with understanding the boxes in Figure 10.1. A focus on the boxes involves asking what is inside the elements or components of social-symbolic work. This might involve, for example, developing a typology of motivations of emotion work. This approach is more likely in the early stages of studying a phenomenon, such as the early institutional work studies, for instance, which primarily documented and enumerated sets of institutional work practices (e.g., Perkmann and Spicer, 2008; Trank and Washington, 2009). This style of research is also common outside of management and organizational research, especially in anthropological studies of communities, societies, and organizations (Geertz, 1973).

Within management and organizational research, an interesting example of this kind of study comes from Barley's (1983) semiotic analysis of the social-symbolic work of funeral directors. In this analysis, based on three months of observation and interviews in a "community-oriented" funeral home, Barley (1983: 4) identifies a set of semiotic codes through which funeral directors "communicate the message of 'naturalness' through preparation of the body," with the aim of achieving a "flawless funeral." These codes, which include the "codes of posed features," "the cosmetic code," and "the clothing code" provide a fascinating look into the aims and practices of funeral directors. Theoretically, the value of such a study lies in its identification of new elements of social-symbolic work and the internal structure to these elements: in this case, Barley's identification of physical arrangements and techniques, such as the application of cosmetics, extends our understanding of semiotic codes beyond the traditional focus on linguistic codes, and shows how a set of semiotic codes together can represent a coherent "occupational perspective."

Making a contribution when focusing on the elements of social-symbolic work often depends on being able to make some kind of comparative statements about those elements, either directly or indirectly. In Barley's (1983) study, he enumerates a set of practices associated with communicating naturalness and producing a flawless funeral, and so the comparisons are within the element in question. Indirect comparative methods are common in this analytical approach, as when research focuses on the practices associated with a type of social-symbolic work particular to a context or set of actors, as in the study of identity work done by people engaged in "dirty work" occupations (Ashforth and Kreiner, 1999). A more powerful analytic strategy would involve direct comparisons of an element of social-symbolic work, either in different contexts or as associated with different types of social-symbolic work (e.g., motivations for identity work vs. emotion work, or practices of technology work vs. boundary work).

MECHANISM-FOCUSED DATA ANALYSIS

Although identifying and describing the elements of social-symbolic work is potentially valuable in and of itself, the more common analytic strategies in management and organizational research emphasize understanding the relationships between elements—how, for instance, motivations affect practices, or how practices affect outcomes. This kind of analysis leads to process or variance theories of social-symbolic work that highlight the "arrows," rather than the boxes. In management and organizational research, the most commonly employed forms of data analysis include Gioia's adaptation of grounded theory and Eisenhardt's comparative case study approach, but there exists a wide range of approaches to data analysis that are appropriate for focusing on the relationships among the elements of a form of social-symbolic work, including discourse analysis (Phillips and Hardy, 2002), process theorizing (Langley, 1999, 2007), content analysis (Duriau et al., 2007; Hoffman, 1999; Kilpatrick et al., 2012), and qualitative comparative analysis (Fiss et al., 2013; Ragin and Sedziaka, 2013). These traditions have all provided the foundation for influential publications exploring different relationships among elements of social-symbolic work.

The key to employing any of these analytic approaches in the study of social-symbolic work is describing and theorizing the mechanisms that connect the different elements of social-symbolic work, including its motivations, practices, and effects on social reality. Each of the approaches listed above is associated with particular sets of assumptions about the nature of these mechanisms and ways of describing them. An interesting example of this kind of analysis comes from Vaara et al.'s (2010) application of critical discourse analysis to a study of how a strategic plan affected the power and politics of a Finnish city. The approach they adopted assumes the idea that strategy documents are not merely representative of ideas, but rather that they have "force," which has effects in a number of ways: "they communicate socially negotiated meanings, legitimate ways of thinking and action and de-legitimate others, produce consent but may also trigger resistance, and have all kinds of political and ideological effects" (Vaara et al., 2010: 686).

In analyzing the strategic plan, Vaara et el. (2010) drew on critical discourse analysis, which they describe as a "specific discourse analytic methodology that examines the role played by language in the construction of power relationships and reproduction of domination" (Vaara et al., 2010: 688). Critical discourse analysis requires both close, detailed analysis of the texts under consideration, as well as the systematic integration of the context in which those texts were produced and consumed (Fairclough, 2003). Thus, Vaara and colleagues analyzed the textual features of the strategic plan, as well as connecting those features to the processes through which the plan was produced, "its interpretations and use by various actors" (Vaara et al., 2010: 686). The strength of the analysis in this study was in how it went beyond simply showing the power effects of the plan to linking those effects to discursive features of the plan, including "self-authorization" and "discursive innovation" (Vaara et al., 2010: 685). Although strategic plans are often cast as irrelevant exercises in bureaucracy, Vaara et al. show the implications of adopting the vocabulary of strategy in government planning, as it affected the political positions of decision-makers, and thus the outcomes of decision-making processes.

We can see from Vaara et al.'s (2010) study that for a mechanisms-focused analysis to contribute to our theoretical understanding of social-symbolic work and its role in the production of social reality, it is not enough to produce typologies of social-symbolic work; rather, such studies must also explain the interactions among elements of some form of social-symbolic work, such as how particular practices affect the social world, and explain the mechanisms through which those effects are produced. One major criticism of studies of work is that they fail to unpack and differentiate between types of work and to explain how they affect the social world in which they occur.

Modern and Postmodern Data Analysis

A final issue a researcher needs to address in developing a data analysis strategy for the study of social-symbolic work is the epistemological position they adopt in doing so. Despite the sound and fury often associated with epistemological debates in the social sciences, this is not necessarily a religious question—adopting what we will refer to as a modern or postmodern attitude toward data and analyzing data need not be understood as joining a particular camp or committing oneself to an epistemological position for the duration of your academic career. Instead, we think of these decisions as practical ones, based on the questions in which we are interested, the aims of a specific research project, and the academic community for whom we are writing.

Rather than talk in terms of positivist, realist, and social constructionist epistemologies, we adopt a more general vocabulary, drawing on the distinction we made in earlier chapters between modern and postmodern understandings of social-symbolic objects and social-symbolic work. Modern understandings, we argued, are tied to a conception of social-symbolic objects as changeable and manageable, but with essential properties that allow progress toward some kind of perfection. In contrast, postmodern understandings retain the changeability of social-symbolic objects, but move away from conceiving them as manageable and far away from the idea of essential perfectibility. Instead, a postmodern attitude toward social-symbolic objects and social-symbolic work suggests that change is unpredictable and motivated by aesthetic and political interests such that movement is toward a local ideal, rather than a universal state of perfection.

For researchers, these attitudes translate relatively easily into approaches to data analysis. A modern approach to social science—and to be clear, this is by far the dominant approach and the one that the two of us nearly always adopt—assumes that there exists some kind of essence either to social-symbolic objects or to the relationships between them (the mechanisms that link them in some causal or processual manner). This assumption allows modern social science to pursue a more perfect, rational form of explanation for any social phenomenon. This does not necessarily mean adopting a positivist epistemology; self-described social constructionist management and organizational research very often adopts a modern attitude toward data and data analysis. The work of Gioia and colleagues, and the papers that have imitated their style of data analysis and presentation, for instance, adopt an explicitly social constructionist stance: Gioia describes his work as that of a "pure interpretivist" who assumes that "the organizational world is essentially socially constructed" (Gehman et al., 2018). At the same time, Gioia and colleagues work toward producing general models of social phenomena such as strategic change and identity transformation (Gioia and Chittipeddi, 1991; Gioia and Thomas, 1996).

In our own writing, we have tended to adopt what might be described as a modern social constructionist attitude toward theory and concepts. A paper of ours that explores the relationship between discourse and institutions (Phillips et al., 2004), for instance, adopts a social constructionist and modern attitude: in it, we develop a "discursive model of institutionalization that highlights the relationships among texts, discourse, institutions, and action," and "propose a set of conditions under which institutionalization processes are most likely to occur" (Phillips et al., 2004: 635). This paper thus approaches the concepts of discourse and institutions from an explicitly social constructionist perspective, and at the same time adopts a modern attitude to the identification of relationships among social-symbolic objects that allows predictive statements and causal arguments. Not that such an approach isn't controversial, of course: this particular paper prompted a spirited debate between Lok and Willmott (2006) and ourselves (Phillips et al., 2006) in which Lok and Willmott suggested that "despite their disavowal of realism, Phillips et al. revert to a realist account of actions, texts, and discourses in their model of institutionalization" (2006: 477). They suggest our paper's shortcomings are "symptomatic of a rather timid and ambivalent explication" of our arguments (Lok and Willmott, 2006: 479). We (2006: 481) argued in response that,

Adopting a social constructionist position need neither keep us from developing theory nor entail an overly onerous reflexive position in which the socially constructed status of our concepts and theories is noted at every turn. It simply means that we accept the nature of the knowledge we produce and the inescapable role of the practices of the community within which the knowledge was produced.

For scholars engaged in the study of social-symbolic work, this debate provides an important lesson regarding the adoption of particular epistemological stances and data analytic strategies. We argue that it is entirely possible, and potentially fruitful, to engage in modern forms of data analysis and theorizing in which we seek to generate, at least somewhat, generalizable statements about the relationships among social-symbolic objects and social-symbolic work. There is also a need to recognize the potential perception of inconsistency in this approach, and (perhaps as we should have done) employ a nuanced language in describing one's arguments and making one's claims.

Shifting to the possibility of adopting a postmodern attitude toward data analysis and theorizing in the study of social-symbolic work, we suggest that doing so represents a somewhat overlooked (at least within management and organizational research), but potentially insightful and creative alternative. The question, though, is "how?"

Adopting a postmodern attitude to empirical research is complicated somewhat by the word "postmodern" describing both an epoch and an epistemology (Hassard and Parker, 1993). In this book, we have focused on the idea of postmodern as an epoch and emphasized the shifts that occurred in the mid to late twentieth century with respect to self, organizations, and institutions. These shifts have, we argue, involved a transition from an understanding of social-symbolic objects as associated with some essential qualities that made achieving perfection a possibility, to one that suggests such objects are changeable, but the direction being a matter of local, political, cultural, and aesthetic negotiations.

Hassard and Parker (1993) contrast this idea of postmodernity as an epoch with postmodernism as an epistemology, which suggests that "the world is constituted by our shared language and that we can only 'know the world' through the particular forms of discourse our language creates," and go on to argue that because "our language-games are continually in flux, meaning is constantly slipping beyond our grasp and can thus never be lodged within one term" (Hassard and Parker, 1993: 3).

The epistemological position associated with postmodernism thus creates a significant challenge for empirical research, as it seems to undermine the possibility of positive knowledge. Gergen (2009a) provides a way forward, however, in his argument that an alternative to an essentialist understanding of truth is not the absence of truth, but rather an anti-essentialist understanding that evaluates truth in terms of its support for "patterns of relationships we feel have positive rather than negative consequences for social life" (Hassard and Parker, 1993: 19). This shift is the key to adopting a postmodern attitude to analyzing social-symbolic work—focusing on the positive consequences of research for social life—and so we explore two potential ways of enacting this attitude in empirical research.

The first of these embraces an aesthetic view of social-symbolic objects and social-symbolic work, a view that highlights "the perceptions and judgements that people make about their organizational lives based especially on their sensory encounters with the world around them" (Warren, 2008: 560). Our interest in aesthetics as a foundation for postmodern studies of social-symbolic work stems from our more general conviction that the transition to postmodernity involved a profound shift in the importance of aesthetics in the evaluation of the "truth" of social-symbolic objects: as the social evaluation of social-symbolic objects moved away from essential, transcendent truth, to truth as socially negotiated; and local, aesthetic considerations moved from peripheral to central bases for the evaluation of social-symbolic objects.

Employing an aesthetic lens as an analytic strategy involves three key elements (Warren, 2008). First, it implies an object of evaluation: in our case a social-symbolic object or an instance of social-symbolic work, either of which we might consider in terms of their aesthetic qualities. Second, engaging in an aesthetic analysis depends on sensory modalities through which we encounter the focus of analysis. Aesthetic analysis involves more than "thinking"; it involves viewing, touching, tasting, smelling, and/or hearing the material dimensions of the social world (Meyer et al., 2013). Third, it depends on aesthetic judgment—"an intersubjectively constructed appraisal" (Warren, 2008: 561) of the elements of the social world under consideration (Bourdieu, 1984).

A useful example of an aesthetic approach to analyzing social-symbolic objects and social-symbolic work is provided by Carter and Jackson's (2000) analysis of the social-symbolic work of the Commonwealth War Graves Commission in creating and managing the aesthetics of war cemeteries and memorials. In this study, the authors (2000: 182) reject an understanding of aesthetics as "the science of good taste," and the associated "universal precepts of beauty." Instead, they focus on the rules and actions of the commission in creating cemeteries and memorials, including some very specific rules focused on ensuring that every plot is the same size, every headstone is of identical size and design, there is a non-hierarchical layout, there are limitations on the number of letters on any headstone (sixty), and there is no specification of the cause of death on any marker. In combination, these rules contribute to an aesthetic that produces "a feeling of solace and peace and not of depression" (Gibson and Ward, 1989: 55).

Carter and Jackson (2000: 190) build on this example to make a more general argument that in producing an aesthetic, organizations are working to elicit a positive response from their audiences, and more meaningfully to effect a "profound denial of the reality of organization(s)." In the case of the Commonwealth War Graves Commission, they argue that this denial depends on "the neatness and precision of the cemeteries and memorials . . . , compared to the utter chaos of warfare" (Carter and Jackson, 2000: 190).

What makes Carter and Jackson's study of the construction of war cemeteries such a good example of an aesthetic approach to analyzing social-symbolic work is that it focuses on the concrete efforts of an identifiable actor to shape a set of social-symbolic objects and their effects in the world, and builds on that analysis to develop more general theoretical ideas about the motivation and consequences of aesthetics-focused social-symbolic work.

The second methodological approach we think fits with a postmodern attitude to understanding social-symbolic work focuses on the potential for social-symbolic work research to effect positive social change. We have argued that truth from a postmodern perspective still exists but is a local phenomenon anchored in the social negotiations within communities. Thus, adopting a postmodern politics moves us away from research methods grounded in grand narratives of class conflict or other transcendental differences, to one concerned with local patterns of advantage and disadvantage, and the potential impacts of scholarly research on those patterns. It also moves us toward an allegiance with our studies' participants (rather than its subjects) consistent with the spirit of participatory action research methodologies.

Although there has been strikingly little connection to this point between studies of social-symbolic work and participatory action research, we believe that such a connection could provide both inspiration and direction for interesting, important new scholarship. Despite participatory action research not being used to study social-symbolic work, there are important theoretical points of connection between the approaches. At their core, they both emphasize the role of agency in social systems. Just as we have located agency at the center of studying social change, so has participatory action research. An important assumption that underpins interest in agency is that actors are "intelligent, creative, and purposive" (Dover and Lawrence, 2010b: 308). Proceeding from this assumption, participatory action research takes it further than do most research methodologies, replacing a conception of individuals and groups as objects of research, to a subject-subject relationship between researcher and research participants (Fals-Borda and Rahman, 1991).

Adopting participatory action research as an approach to studying social-symbolic work would mean engaging with research participants as competent, capable partners (McIntyre, 2008), involved in every step of the process, from identifying research question, to collecting and analyzing data, developing responses to the findings that include both practical actions and theoretical understandings. A range of practical options have emerged for scholars interested in studying social-symbolic work using participatory action research. Many of these strategies intersect with aesthetic approaches in their emphasis on creative modes of engagement such as storytelling, photography, poetry, drawing, sculpture, drama, and popular theater (Ospina et al., 2008).

One such participatory strategy is referred to as "photovoice," and depends on "participant-produced photography as a means of giving voice to marginalized persons in the community" (Bell, 2008: 34). The core of photovoice as a method involves giving cameras to community members to record images that tell the story of their community, and then coming together as a group to reflect on the photographs and what they mean. Typically, participants write "photostories"—short narratives to accompany the photographs they consider to be most important. (Bell, 2008; Wang and Burris, 1997).

The arguments for photovoice as a means of empowering research participants revolve around emphasizing problems that participants see as central to their lives, overcoming male bias in participatory research by making women visible, and including as participants those people for whom writing and speaking may not be effective means of communication (Wang and Burris, 1997). Photovoice, and other, non-traditional "postmodern" methods, offer what we think are compelling approaches to the study of social-symbolic work. Rather than depending on an understanding of truth as transcendental, achieved through objective forms of research carried out by outsiders, these methods assume that the value of research depends on whether it empowers participants by providing the foundation for their social-symbolic work through which they construct and make sense of social-symbolic objects, and in that process shape the local politics that constrain their lives.

Conclusion

In this chapter, we have presented a "recipe" for empirical research on social-symbolic work. For each of the steps in our recipe—developing a research question, identifying a research context, collecting data, analyzing data—we have examined a set of challenges and choices faced by scholars and suggested strategies for dealing with these issues. We provide a summary of our recipe in Box 10.1 by stepping through one of the studies of social-symbolic work that we have done and explaining the choices we made at each point.

Looking beyond the specifics, we also want to encourage scholars to stay close to what they genuinely find interesting as they pursue their studies. Good research happens at the intersection of scholars and the worlds that fascinate them. From our personal experience, this fascination is *the* essential

---

Box 10.1. FROM *MOBY DICK* TO *FREE WILLY*

In order to clarify the process of researching social-symbolic work, we thought it would be useful to walk through an example from our own research. In our article "From *Moby Dick* to *Free Willy*," we present the results of a study of social-symbolic work that we conducted examining how societal-level discourses and local action combined in the construction of a new organizational field (Lawrence and Phillips, 2004). The specific case we chose to investigate was the development of commercial whale watching in Victoria, on Canada's west coast.

Developing an Appropriate Research Question

Our interest in the way in which macro-cultural discourse and local action are related led us to ask two research questions. First, we focused on the role of macro-cultural discourse and asked: "what role does macro-cultural discourse play in the emergence of new institutional fields?" But we were also interested in the role of agents in this process, so we posed a second research question: "what role does institutional entrepreneurship play in the emergence of new institutional fields?"

Identifying a Context

Our choice of research context, as is often the case, emerged from the intersection of theoretical interests and practical exigencies. Theoretically, we were looking for a domain in which a new field had emerged, and in which the dynamics of the field seemed to involve both societal beliefs and assumptions, and local actors engaged in entrepreneurial activity. Whale watching as an industry seemed to be benefiting from the role of whales in popular culture, and our knowledge of the city suggested a lot of entrepreneurship on the part of local actors. Practically, the field seemed likely to be accessible and the work visible: we were interested in talking to small business owners, government regulators, and ocean scientists, all of whom had the freedom and time (we conducted interviews out of the prime whale-watching season) to speak with us.

Collecting Data on Social-Symbolic Work

What are people doing? The case study focused on the development of whale watching in Victoria, British Columbia, a city of 300,000 on Canada's west coast. We began by collecting archival data to understand as much as we could about the development of this organizational field. Based on our growing understanding we began to interview various actors who had played a role in the development of the field. Eventually we found one actor, whom we refer to as "John Cyprus" in the paper, who founded the first whale-watching business.

What are the social-symbolic objects? We identified a set of social-symbolic objects, the most important of which was the concept of the "killer whale" and the killer whales that were found in the waters around Vancouver Island. We traced the social-symbolic work done to construct the concept of a killer whale over decades of regulatory, environmental, and pop culture discourses, and the work done locally to construct the local whales, for instance, as "urban whales."

What resources and skills are they using? We identified discursive, relational, and material resources: discursive resources included scientific descriptions of whales, as

(continued)

Box 10.1. CONTINUED

---

well as movies and stories about killer whales; relational resources included networks of whale spotters, and the collaborative relationships between commercial operators and scientists studying whale behavior; material resources included the "small, fast boats" that operators used to take tourists out on the water, as well as the physical space in downtown Victoria from which operators ran their businesses.

What are their intentions? Although we interviewed a range of actors, we focused much of our analysis on John Cyprus. His initial intention was not to create a whale-watching company, but rather one that would take tourists on "adventure coastal tours." This evolved into the first whale-watching business in response to customer desire to see whales. Thus, his intentions and the effects of his actions were only partially aligned, and unpacking the relationship between the two was a central point of the paper.

What are the effects? We trace two sets of effects in this paper. We argue that changes in the three macro-cultural discourses all have an effect through the social-symbolic work of interested actors, including whaling companies, environmentalists, and movie producers, and led to the social construction of killer whales as "no longer resources to be harvested or even species to be saved, but rather individuals to be appreciated and respected . . . [with] almost human behaviors and . . . mythical properties" (Lawrence and Phillips, 2004: 698).

The second set of effects, and those that we focus on, stem from Cyprus' efforts to launch his venture. These included the direct effects of initiating whale watching as a local tourist activity, but also included a set of unintended effects, whereby the decisions he made regarding the size of boats, launch schedules, and networks of spotters became standards for the new organizational field.

Analyzing Data on Social-Symbolic Work

This study is a useful example of the use of multiple methods to investigate social-symbolic work across multiple levels of analysis. In this case, the data analysis involved two separate methodologies. At the macro level, we used discourse analysis to understand how perceptions of whales had changed over time. In particular, we studied three discourses—the regulatory discourse, the anti-whaling discourse, and the popular culture discourse—and were able to show a dramatic change in the perception of whales from dangerous monsters and a resource to be harvested to "individuals to be appreciated and respected" (Lawrence and Phillips, 2004: 698).

At the same time, at the micro level we traced the relationships between intentions, practices, and effects associated directly with the development of whale watching in Victoria. For this part of the study we applied traditional coding techniques to the interview transcripts, combined with insights drawn from archival data, to understand the dynamics of the process that led to the creation of this industry.

---

ingredient in any successful study. All management and organizational research is challenging, and the perspective we are proposing might often make it even more so, as the breadth of forms of work and types of objects make the complexity greater than traditional approaches. As a result, a genuine fascination with the topic of research becomes even more important to sustaining the long-term commitment and enthusiasm that a scholar embarking on a study of social-symbolic work requires.

11

Conclusions: Understanding the Implications of a Social-Symbolic Work Perspective for Scholars, Change-Makers, and Citizens

In this chapter we:

1. Discuss the implications of a social-symbolic work perspective for scholarship by considering what assumptions in social science are challenged by the perspective.

2. Explore the implications of a social-symbolic work perspective for practical action, focusing on social innovation, managing workforce diversity, and entrepreneurship.

3. Examine the implications of a social-symbolic work for understanding the world around us, including tribalism in contemporary politics, technology and the sharing economy, and the Anthropocene.

Introduction

This book grew out of the observation that management and organizational research had become fascinated by "work," but not traditional forms of labor. Instead, organizational scholars were focusing on forms of work that were aimed at changing or maintaining aspects of organizational life that might once have been understood as beyond the scope of purposeful efforts to shape them. What made forms of work like emotion work, identity work, and category work interesting was their immediate resonance with people's day-to-day lives, and their contrast with previous scholarship on emotions, identities, and categories. Despite the growing interest in these types of work, however, there remained a lack of recognition that they might form some kind of family. Beginning to explore the commonalties among these types of work led us to a further observation that each was studied as something of an anomaly against a background of structural and processual theories that dominate management and organizational research. Work was everywhere, but fragmented and conceptually homeless.

In response, we have introduced the social-symbolic work perspective, which revolves around the relationship between social-symbolic work and social-symbolic objects. To explore this relationship, we have examined three broad forms of social-symbolic work—self work, organization work, and institutional work—and prominent streams of management and organizational research associated with each. In this chapter, we move on to a broader set of questions concerning the potential importance of a social-symbolic work perspective for different communities. In particular, we explore the implications of the social-symbolic work perspective for scholars analyzing the social world, change-makers trying to make it better, and citizens trying to understand and cope with its roaring currents of change.

Implications for Scholarship

In this section, we explore how the social-symbolic work perspective shifts our understanding of the social world, and how such a shift might influence the kinds of questions we ask and the kinds of research in which we engage. To explore these issues, we draw on Murray Davis' (1971) article, "That's interesting," which has profoundly influenced scholarly thinking about what makes research impactful. Davis (1971: 309) argued that the impact of social scientific theories was not due to their accuracy, but by the degree to which they are "interesting"—the degree to which they "*deny* certain assumptions of their audience."

We believe the social-symbolic work perspective is "interesting." More specifically, we think it challenges commonly held assumptions regarding the nature of social life and thus provides a foundation for novel research directions. Along with Davis' general observations, he also offered a set of specific characteristics of theories that make them interesting—the "Index of the Interesting"—which we draw on to explore some of the ways in which the social-symbolic work perspective might be interesting for scholars.

Things We Thought Were Different Are Actually the Same

We begin with the notion of composition, which highlights the relationship between parts and wholes. The social-symbolic work perspective is interesting in terms of composition because it suggests that "what seem to be assorted heterogeneous phenomena are in reality composed of a single element"

(Davis, 1971: 315). In this case, a core assertion of our perspective on social-symbolic work is that seemingly diverse forms of action are all instances of a single phenomenon. Indeed, our initial interest in developing the concept of social-symbolic work was triggered by the intuition that there was something common across forms of action that were being conceptualized and studied as forms of work within separate streams of organizational research.

The implications for organizational scholars of this basic argument are, we believe, profound. They begin with our own identities and the categories we employ to organize our profession. Organization studies, especially in North America, is routinely divided into "micro" and "macro" variants, with major academic bodies, such as the Academy of Management, mirroring that split with micro (Organizational Behavior) and macro (Organization and Management Theory) divisions, and individual scholars primarily affiliating with one or the other. If we take seriously the idea that self work (primarily examined by "micro" scholars), institutional work (primarily a topic for "macro" scholars), and organization work (which has been studied by strategy scholars and technology scholars, as well as by "macro" organizational scholars), are all instances of social-symbolic work, then the traditional divisions come into question. In fact, they may be dysfunctional with respect to the study of social-symbolic work.

Moreover, many of the topics in organizational research, such as leadership, change, regulation, negotiations, and innovation, involve self, organization, and institutional work, but are often pigeon-holed within our broad academic groups (so that leadership, for instance, is far more often examined by micro scholars than by those who identify as macro, and organizational change is more often studied by macro organizational researchers). To the extent that these organizational phenomena, such as leadership and change, involve a wide variety of forms of social-symbolic work, this creates serious problems for our understanding of these organizational phenomena. Adopting a social-symbolic work perspective on leadership, for example, would lead scholars to examine its social-symbolic facets that involve the self, organizations, and institutions, including identity work, emotion work, boundary work, strategy work, category work, and practice work, all of which can easily be recognized as important to effective organizational leadership.

The implications of this complex combination of processes for organizational scholars are clear. What are traditionally thought of as different areas of study share forms of social-symbolic work, and our understanding of the social-symbolic objects on which these areas of study focus can be increased by recognizing and researching the role of various kinds of social-symbolic work in the creation, change, and maintenance of the phenomenon being studied. Thus, working from a social-symbolic work perspective may challenge researchers to be more phenomenon focused and less theory driven and will, we believe, lead to theoretical developments with important practical implications.

Things We Thought Were at One Level of Analysis Are Actually at Another

A second dimension along which social-symbolic work is interesting concerns what Davis calls "abstraction"—the ways in which phenomena that seem to be individualistic are collective, and vice versa. The classic example he cites of a theory being interesting in this way is Durkheim's assertion that suicide is not an individual phenomenon, but rather a collectively determined one. While the assumption up to that point was that suicide was intensely personal and hence individual, Durkheim showed that he could predict the total number of suicides that were likely to occur in France in the following year. In doing so, he showed that suicide was not simply an individual-level phenomenon, but also a societally determined one.

For us, this dimension of interestingness points to the relationship between forms of social-symbolic work and the different levels of analysis at which they occur. If we take self work as an example, it can easily be viewed as a kind of work undertaken by individuals in relation to their own selves, or perhaps other selves, but it can also involve groups, organizations, and networks engaging in collective efforts to shape particular selves. In an organizational context, routine socialization processes, including but not limited to induction, are squarely focused on shaping the selves of individual members. Less routinely, but still often, groups, organizations, and communities work to shape the selves of particular members, such as leaders whose identities they might try to craft in ways that reflect positively on the individual and the community (Meindl et al., 1985), as well as on outcasts whose identities are collectively constructed as toxic or impure (Goffman, 1963). At the same time, research on institutional and organization work has shown that such efforts are undertaken by communities and organizations, but also by individuals and small groups (Lawrence and Phillips, 2004; Maguire et al., 2004).

The implications of this complex combination of processes for organizational scholars concerns the ways in which we define the boundaries and focus of our studies: the potential roles of individuals, groups, organizations, and communities in self work, organization work, and institutional work suggest that we need to accommodate unexpected causal paths in our research so that we do not overlook effects that cut across levels of analysis in surprising ways. In doing so, the social-symbolic work perspective is a useful way to bridge the gap between micro and macro perspectives in social theory, something that has long been considered problematic (Ritzer, 1990).

What Seems to Be a Local Phenomenon Is Really a General One

The third way in which social-symbolic work is interesting is in terms of "generalization," which concerns whether a phenomenon only occurs in some limited context or whether it is something that is more general. Freud, for example, discussed how the "sexual impulse" was not something that occurred only in adults, but also occurs in children. This assertion was interesting because it suggested that something that was thought to be limited to one part of the population (adults) is actually more general (in adults and children).

Social-symbolic work is doubly interesting along this dimension. First, our arguments suggest that where previous research on specific forms of social-symbolic work has often implied that they were the work of particular kinds of individuals, such as leaders (Selznick, 2011), institutional entrepreneurs (Kisfalvi and Maguire, 2011), or bill collectors (Rafaeli and Sutton, 1991), the diverse kinds of social-symbolic work and contexts we have explored suggest it may be a much more universal part of organizational life, involving all kinds of organizations and organizational members. Thus, social-symbolic work is a more general phenomenon than might initially be imagined. If we take this idea seriously—that social-symbolic work can involve a wide range of actors at different times and in different ways—then we begin to ask different questions. We are, for instance, no longer interested in "institutional entrepreneurs" as special individuals carrying out institutional work, but as roles that can be taken on and abandoned by different actors in different ways in different contexts.

At the same time, the concept of social-symbolic work highlights a second interesting issue of generalization that runs in the opposite direction. Often, social-symbolic objects such as emotions, categories, boundaries, practices, and technologies are treated as universal phenomena, their characteristics and dynamics unconnected to local contexts or processes. In contrast, the concept of social-symbolic work denaturalizes such phenomena, pointing to their locally constituted nature, and highlighting their variation across space and time. Thus, the localness of phenomena previously understood as universal, such as emotions and cognitive processes, will motivate studies that both document that localness through cross-cultural and historical research (Henrich et al., 2010) and, of special interest for us, studies that explore the work done to establish and naturalize local variants of those processes.

An important and largely missing focus in organizational and management research is the simultaneous examination of cross-cultural and cross-temporal variation in social-symbolic objects and of the social-symbolic work that underpins that variation. Although we have numerous studies that are either cross-cultural/temporal or focused on social-symbolic work within a particular culture/time frame, we have very little comparative research on social-symbolic work that would examine both the different constructions of social-symbolic objects, such as emotions, careers, categories, and practices, and the kinds of work done in different places or at different times to achieve that variation. The combination of these two shifts—in how we understand the generality of social-symbolic work across actors, and the localness of the social-symbolic objects on which they work—implies an important corrective to much organizational research that has tended to rely on the opposite combination.

Something that is Understood to Function Ineffectively is in Reality Effective

Social-symbolic work is also interesting in terms of "function," which describes the degree to which a phenomenon that is understood to function ineffectively as a means to an end in reality functions effectively. In scholarly and practical discussions of management and organizations, there is a long history of underemphasizing the social and symbolic dimensions of work, while highlighting the material and technical. The social and symbolic have often been cast as superficial, ephemeral, or epiphenomenal. Such arguments are associated with technological determinism, but also with Marx and other positions that suggest some kind of "real" base to reality that the social and symbolic are built upon. Such normative conceptions are also commonplace in lay and popular discourse, where social connections and impression management are sometimes understood as unsavory routes to economic success that come at the expense of adding real value to the world.

In contrast, our conceptualization of social-symbolic work highlights the potential value for individuals, organizations, and communities of producing and maintaining social-symbolic objects. Such a conception opens up the opportunity for scholars to engage in research that examines the social and economic value of social-symbolic work. This line of research has tremendous potential in helping move management and organizational research toward policy- and practice-relevancy and to connecting scholars to important societal problems that have not traditionally been the focus of research in our field.

The implications of this for scholars are significant. Simply put, it challenges scholars to question the practical effects of forms of work. This means uncovering and measuring the practical effects of forms of work that have been assumed to have little practical effect. The focus on the practical effects of social-symbolic work has real potential to ground organization and management research in important practical questions and to develop theory with much greater relevance and deeper practical implications.

Unrelated Phenomena Are in Reality Correlated

Whereas the first part of Davis' Index of the Interesting focuses on how we characterize a single phenomenon, the second part focuses on relationships among phenomena. Two aspects of such relationships are germane to our discussion of social-symbolic work: co-relation and causation. The idea of co-relation points to situations in which seemingly unrelated (independent) phenomena are in reality correlated (interdependent).

For the study of social-symbolic work, this form of interestingness is related to the issue of holism, discussed earlier. There is more here, though, since we are not only arguing that forms of social-symbolic work represent instances of a unitary category, but also that different forms of work trigger, facilitate, and undermine other forms of work. For instance, identity work might contribute to or undercut institutional work to the extent that the institutional work is dependent on the achieved identities of particular actors. The question of co-relations among forms of social-symbolic work is a critical one for scholars interested in leveraging our arguments to advance studies of specific forms of social-symbolic work. Institutional work scholars, for instance, could gain significant theoretical and empirical traction by exploring how it is connected to kinds of organization work and self work.

These connections have begun to be explored by institutional scholars interested in identity (Creed et al., 2010) and emotions (Voronov and Vince, 2012), but these connections represent a vast unexplored territory, the mapping of which could underpin studies of institutional work for a significant length of time. Similarly, scholars currently focusing on forms of self work, such as emotion work and career work, could benefit tremendously from integrating conceptions of institutional work and organization work into their research. Examining the reciprocal impacts of these other kinds of work could, we argue, enliven more "micro" research and produce sets of findings with greater social and economic significance than has been associated with the studies focused exclusively on self work.

What Seems to be the Independent Phenomenon is in Reality Dependent

The final form of interestingness that is relevant to our discussion concerns "causation," and specifically the possibility that "[w]hat seems to be the independent phenomenon ... in a causal relation is in reality the dependent phenomenon." This inversion is foundational to the study of institutional work: the concept of social-symbolic work inverts the traditional understandings that suggest human behavior is caused by social-symbolic objects (e.g., our emotions drive our behavior, organizational boundaries shape behavior in organizations, or institutions constrain thought and behavior). Instead, the concept of social-symbolic work highlights how people shape those social-symbolic objects.

This causal relationship is at the heart of the study of social-symbolic work, but it needs to be interpreted carefully. It is not that we are suggesting that the status of social-symbolic objects is completely under the control of actors who can shape them and use them in whatever ways they wish, unconstrained by the social context. Rather, it is the possibility of shaping social-symbolic objects, and actors' awareness of that possibility, that underpins the study of social-symbolic work. Thus, we are interested in how actors engage in social-symbolic work that affects social-symbolic objects in intended ways, but we are just as interested in the unintended effects, the experience of engaging in social-symbolic work, and the situations and events that motivate it.

In other words, the causal inversion associated with social-symbolic work is interesting in part as an explanation of why and how social-symbolic objects come to exist as they do, but it opens up a wide range of questions beyond that. Our approach to social-symbolic work is work-centric, rather than object-centric: our aim is less to explain social-symbolic objects (which are reasonably the focus of much research), but rather to understand the work that is connected to those objects—the motivations, skills, experiences, and effects associated with that work.

What's Interesting about Social-Symbolic Work?

Davis (1971) provides a practical framework for thinking about what makes academic research interesting. We have selectively drawn on his framework to explore what makes a social-symbolic work perspective "interesting." Looking across the ways in which theory might be interesting, we see that the social-symbolic work perspective challenges a range of assumptions about the social world that have tended to steer management and organizational research. These challenges provide important opportunities for scholars to reexamine existing research and develop new research questions and empirical studies. We have summarized our discussion of social-symbolic work and Davis' Index of the Interesting in Table 11.1.

It is worth emphasizing that we are not suggesting scholars abandon existing approaches and methods. We are simply presenting social-symbolic work as an alternative way of researching the social world that highlights a number of its aspects that are often under-researched and currently play a limited role in our theories. The social-symbolic work perspective seeks to rebalance the emphasis among structure, process, and purposeful action in a way that makes theory more complete and more practical. Incorporating purposeful, reflexive efforts provides a foundation for theories with the potential to facilitate

Table 11.1. Social-symbolic work and the Index of the Interesting

Form of interestingness	Applicability to social-symbolic work	Potential research implication
1. Composition What seem to be assorted heterogeneous phenomena are in reality composed of a single element.	The concept of social-symbolic work asserts that seemingly diverse forms of action are all instances of a single phenomenon—the purposive efforts of individuals and groups to shape their social-symbolic worlds or to manage meaning and relationships in their organizational life.	The argument that different forms of social-symbolic work constitute a class of phenomena, or even instances of a single phenomenon, raises questions regarding our disciplinary boundaries. Where, for instance, does leadership belong, when it involves all kinds of social-symbolic work, including institutional work, organization work, and self work.
2. Abstraction What seems like an individual phenomenon is in reality a holistic phenomenon (sociologizing).	An important insight afforded by the social-symbolic work perspective is the potential for both intended and unintended cross-level effects of work, such that the self is the object of work for individuals, but also for groups, organizations, and networks. The same is true of institutions that cut across fields, industries, communities, and societies.	These cross-level dynamics raise important questions about how, why, and when they occur. In particular, this kind of abstraction leads us to investigate how and when larger collective actors work to shape social-symbolic objects at finer levels of analysis, such as when communities work to shape the identities of their leaders, or organizations shape the emotions of their employees.
What seems like a holistic phenomenon is in reality an individual phenomenon (psychologizing).	Same as above. One implication of the fact that social-symbolic work is interesting in both ways is that it may require a different set of ontological premises, especially regarding the notion of scale. It may require a "flat" ontology.	The impact of individuals on organizations and institutions has been examined in studies of leadership and institutional entrepreneurship, where the questions concern the work of individuals and groups to shape organizations and institutions.
3. Generalization What seems to be a local phenomenon is in reality a general phenomenon.	Whereas previous research suggests that the manipulation of social-symbolic objects was the work of particular kinds of individuals, such as leaders, institutional entrepreneurs, sales people, and bill collectors, the diverse kinds of social-symbolic work and context we have explored suggest it may be universal part of organizational life.	Studies that, for example, are no longer interested in "institutional entrepreneurs" as individuals but as identities that can be gained and lost by different actors in different ways.
What seems to be a general phenomenon is in reality a local phenomenon.	There is a sense in which social-symbolic work denaturalizes the social-symbolic objects on which it focuses. Identities, for instance, are no longer natural inevitable universal phenomena, but locally achieved.	Comparative research on social-symbolic work that examines both the different constructions of social-symbolic objects, such as emotions, careers, categories, and practices, and the kinds of work done in different places or at different times to achieve that variation.

(continued)

Table 11.1. Continued

Form of interestingness	Applicability to social-symbolic work	Potential research implication
4. Function What seems to be a phenomenon that functions ineffectively as a means for the attainment of an end is in reality a phenomenon that functions effectively.	There is a long history of downplaying the social and symbolic dimensions of work in contrast to the material and technical, which have been seen as more "real" and important. This is found in technological determinism, but also in Marx and other positions that suggest some kind of real base to reality that the social and symbolic are built upon. Lay arguments are often made that denigrate the symbolic nature of products, relationships, etc., suggesting that they are not the real or important elements, and in fact may obscure or undermine the real. In contrast, social-symbolic work highlights the real value in producing and maintaining social and symbolic phenomena in organizations and society.	Research that examines the social and economic value of social-symbolic work. This line of research could be immensely important in helping move organization studies toward policy- and practice-relevancy.
5. Co-relation What seem to be unrelated (independent) phenomena are in reality correlated (interdependent) phenomena.	There is a sense in which different forms of work have not only been treated as separate classes of phenomena, but also independent phenomena. We see, however, that different forms of work trigger, facilitate, and undermine other forms of work. So, for instance, identity work might contribute to or undercut institutional work to the extent that the institutional work is dependent on the achieved identities of particular actors.	Exploring these interrelationships could enliven many specific streams of social-symbolic work research. Institutional work scholars, for instance, could gain significant theoretical and empirical traction by exploring how it is connected to kinds of organization work and self work. Studies of self work, such as emotion work and career work, could benefit tremendously from integrating conceptions of institutional work and organization work. Examining the reciprocal impacts of these other kinds of work could produce findings with greater social and economic significance than has been associated with studies focused exclusively on self work.
6. Causation What seems to be the independent phenomenon (variable) in a causal relation is in reality the dependent phenomenon (variable).	The general notion of social-symbolic work and all of its forms invert the traditional understandings that suggest that human behavior is caused by/shaped by social-symbolic objects (e.g., our emotions drive our behavior; organizational boundaries shape behavior in organizations; institutions constrain thought and behavior). Instead, social-symbolic work highlights how people shape those objects.	This dimension of interestingness underpins the whole study of social-symbolic work, but our aim is less to explain social-symbolic objects (which are reasonably the focus of much of social science), but rather to understand the work that is connected to those objects—the motivations, skills, experiences, and outcomes associated with that work.

action: it is the practical utility of the social-symbolic work perspective to which we turn in the next section.

Implications for Practical Action

The social-symbolic work perspective provides a map of the social world that is practical, and thus potentially useful for actors working to effect organizational change, respond to serious social problems, manage complex systems, or establish new business ventures. In this section, we explore some of the practical implications of the social-symbolic work perspective, focusing in particular on its implications for social innovation, managing diversity, and entrepreneurship.

A Social-Symbolic Work Perspective on Social Innovation

In 1998, Mark Richardson and Paul Harrod founded Aspire—a UK-based retail business with a mission to fight homelessness (see Tracey et al., 2011). Richardson and Harrod believed that the solution to homelessness was not to provide housing, but to give the homeless decent jobs. Aspire was thus created to provide employment for homeless people while making a profit that could be reinvested in growing the business and putting on programs to help the homeless workers build skills. In creating Aspire, Richardson and Harrod sought to bridge two different logics—those of for-profit retail and non-profit homelessness support. Novel at the time, their aim was to create a new kind of social-purpose organization that would not require ongoing financial support from the government or from external donors. Unfortunately, Richardson and Harrod turned out to be better innovators than managers: the jobs they provided were of tremendous benefit to their employees but Aspire failed to make profits sufficient to support the social enterprise. As a business it was a failure, but as a case of social innovation it was a success: the Aspire experiment, the work that Richardson and Harrod did communicating their vision, and their collaboration with government inspired a number of other charities to add for-profit business to their activities in the homeless sector.

Social innovation represents the creation of novel solutions to pressing social problems. Proponents of social innovation argue it has emerged as an important response to social problems because "existing structures and policies have found it impossible to crack some of the most pressing issues of our times" (Murray et al., 2010: 3). Traditionally, responses to social problems have come from government or markets, both of which have serious limitations when facing complex social problems: the "policies and structures of

299

government have tended to reinforce old rather than new models," whereas the "market...lacks the incentives and appropriate models to solve many of these issues" (Murray et al., 2010: 3–4).

In contrast, social innovation is associated with (often small) organizations built or repurposed to create, distribute, and institutionalize new approaches to serious problems, often in ways that cut across traditional sectoral boundaries (Seelos and Mair, 2005). Aspire represented exactly such an organization: motivated by the failure of the market to address the needs of homeless people, its founders attempted to create an organization in which the incentives of all parties were aligned to allow self-sufficiency on the part of both the organization and its employees.

SOCIAL INNOVATION AS SOCIAL-SYMBOLIC WORK

To see how the social-symbolic work perspective we are developing might be useful to social innovators, we first unpack the definition of social innovation in social-symbolic work terms, focusing in particular on the idea of a social problem, and what makes for an effective, and innovative response.

A focus on social problems is a widely shared anchor for understanding social innovation and its aims. In a much cited review of social innovation research, Phills et al. (2008: 3) argue that social problems represent a coalescing point—although stakeholders often argue about the best courses of action, there "tends to be greater consensus within societies about what constitutes a social need or problem." While this observation may reflect common tendencies, it also shows little awareness that the identification and description of problems might itself be the contentious outcome of processes of social construction. Writing on social innovation tends to ignore conflict around the definition of social problems, instead citing examples such as poverty that seem to evoke a consensus on the need to act. But even poverty as a social problem is contentious (its boundaries, its roots, its relationship to race, ethnicity, and gender), let alone issues such as sexual and reproductive rights, or the unequal distribution of global financial resources. Despite the centrality of social problems to discussions of social innovation, actors in this arena have left relatively unexplored questions such as how certain problems come to dominate other issues, how problems are defined and understood, and how focusing on certain problems might come at the cost of not examining other issues (Loseke, 2003).

How social problems are identified and evaluated is an important point of connection between social innovation and social-symbolic work. If what constitutes a social problem is socially negotiated in ways that reflect the norms, values, and beliefs of those involved, as well as the power relations among them (Lawrence et al., 2013), then the constitution of social problems depends on forms of social-symbolic work. Institutional work, for instance, is core to defining social problems: if we take homelessness as an example, defining the category of "homeless" is centrally important to understanding the problem and responding to it. At its most restrictive, the concept describes people who are not "buying or paying mortgage or rent on a primary residence and living in it regularly" (Bogard, 2001: 107). But Shelter (the advocacy NGO) argues for a much more inclusive definition, counting people as homeless if they are "staying with friends or family; staying in a hostel, night shelter or B&B; squatting...; at risk of violence or abuse in your home;... [or] living apart from your family because you don't have a place to live together" (Shelter, 2018). Clearly, which of these definitions prevails will have a massive impact on how much of a problem it is considered to be (since far more people would "count" as homeless under the Shelter definition), and a much wider array of resources might be employed in response.

Self work is also important to the definition of social problems, particularly when definitions connect social problems and individual failings. Some of the most contentious debates of our time revolve around the role of choice in contributing to individual suffering, and consequently whether and how that suffering constitutes a "social problem." Global variation in approaches to drug use and addiction highlight the centrality of socially constructed selves in understanding social problems: the US-based "war on drugs" has at its core a conceptualization of drug users as immoral and criminal; in contrast, "harmreduction" approaches in Europe, Canada, and Australia are based on an understanding of drug users as suffering from a chronic health condition rooted in social structures and systems, and hence require interventions that minimize the health, social, and economic harms of drug use. These conceptualizations are more than abstract categories; they are applied to individuals at the local level, with immediate and profound consequences for those individuals.

Moving from the social problem to the response to that problem, social innovation continues to involve significant social-symbolic work. Despite ongoing disagreements over the nature of social innovation, the idea that social innovation creates systemic change in social systems has received considerable support (Murray et al., 2010; Nilsson, 2003). Westley and Antadze (2010: 2), for example, distinguish between "social inventions" and social innovation on the basis that the latter effects, or is at least intended to effect, transformational change in social systems, potentially challenging "the very institutions that created the social problem which they address."

The distinction between social invention and social innovation provides a useful basis for understanding the importance of social-symbolic work in this area. Whereas social inventions might be fundamentally technological, such as clean-burning stoves, social innovation involves efforts to shape the social-symbolic objects that constitute the context in which those inventions are employed. Drawing on our own work (Lawrence and Dover, 2015), a wet weather mat program in a suburban neighborhood might represent a social invention, providing shelter to those without housing. But the process through which its creators challenged the assumptions and beliefs about homelessness in that neighborhood, created social connections among a range of organizations and individuals, and shifted the values of a community represents a significant social innovation.

Thus, we would argue that at its core, social innovation *is* social-symbolic work. Social innovation describes the efforts of actors to achieve positive social change by effecting transformational change in social systems. It begins with the self, organization, and institutional work of defining important social problems and goes on to include all those kinds of work in effecting systemic social change. Consequently, we argue that this perspective has value for social innovators trying to create positive social change in the world.

THE VALUE OF A SOCIAL-SYMBOLIC WORK PERSPECTIVE FOR DOING SOCIAL INNOVATION

For social innovators, the value of a social-symbolic work perspective is tied to how it can help shift behaviors and beliefs—their own, the people who work with them (and against them), and the populations they serve. We have already discussed the importance of institutional work and self work in defining social problems and focusing on systemic change as the outcome of social innovation. Along with these forms of social-symbolic work, social innovators need to engage in organization work to establish durable social mechanisms that respond to the problems they care about. Achieving systemic change, we argue, depends on social innovators engaging in strategy work that establishes a robust, compelling narrative that will engender the enduring support from stakeholders necessary for the organization to effect the intended change, and adapt to the inevitable, unexpected consequences of and responses to its actions. Social innovators also need to engage in boundary work in order to corral needed resources and create boundary objects that allow them to coordinate across organizational and sectoral boundaries. Finally, social innovation depends on technology work, and not only in relation to the digital creations that garner so much popular attention, but also to effect much more prosaic material responses, which are often at the heart of effective, cost-efficient solutions.

We see the concept of social-symbolic work as potentially valuable to social innovators primarily as a lens on the needs of their project or organization, including the self work, organization work, and institutional work needed to accomplish some goal. In the time- and resource-pressured world of social innovators, there may be a tendency to focus on what gets asked for (especially by resource providers, such as a funder), which may not be aligned with the diffuse and complex requirements associated with managing the emotions, identities, and careers of employees and clients, the boundaries, technologies, and strategies of the social innovation organization, and the categories and practices that may ultimately resolve or maintain the social problem that motivates the whole enterprise. Moreover, social innovators, like all of us, have histories. They have lives filled with personal and professional experiences that sensitize them to some facets of social reality while leaving them relatively ignorant of or apathetic about other parts. The holistic and integrative character of social-symbolic work as a concept is, therefore, a valuable addition to a social innovator's toolkit to the extent that it helps them overcome some of those blinders and soften some of those biases.

A Social-Symbolic Work Perspective on Managing Diversity in Organizations

A central challenge for organizational managers today is responding to work-force diversity—expanding it, leveraging it, and coping with it.[1] Managers of organizations, and especially large organizations, are facing a far more diverse and complex social landscape that stems from shifts in global migration patterns, the increased political power of women and visible minorities, identity rights movements including those attached to more expansive conceptions of gender and sexuality, and calls from consumers for products and services that suit specific lives and identities. Although a significant body of practice-focused research and writing has emerged in response to these challenges, it tends toward a view of diversity that takes for granted existing categories, social boundaries, and identities, rather than scrutinizing the work that may go into fashioning those social divisions and attachments. A social-symbolic work perspective provides a basis for recognizing and understanding that work, and thus may have significant utility for those trying to shape organizations with respect to diversity, as managers, employees, or activists.

MANAGING DIVERSITY AS SOCIAL-SYMBOLIC WORK
The common theme that runs across the dominant definitions of workforce diversity in management and organization research is its focus on the differences among people at work. This idea can be traced to the *Workforce 2000* report (Johnston and Packer, 1987) that predicted a more heterogeneous US labor force by the year 2000, with increasing proportions of women, racial/ ethnic minorities, and immigrants relative to "native" white men. The concept of diversity from this perspective describes an objectively observable

[1] Thanks very much to Stephanie Creary for all her insights and inspiration in linking social-symbolic work to managing workforce diversity.

303

pattern of differences among individuals in organizations (Cox and Blake, 1991; Ely, 1995). Moreover, diversity from this perspective is not neutral: it is seen as an organizational good with beneficial effects on organizational performance (Roberson et al., 2017) that stem from the potential for organizations to draw on a wider range of perspectives and experiences in decision making (Reis et al., 2007; van Knippenberg and Schippers, 2007).

A social-symbolic work perspective reconceptualizes workforce diversity. Rather than consider diversity a description of some objective characteristics of organizations, such that they are more or less diverse, with greater or lesser advantages flowing from that diversity, a social-symbolic work perspective conceives of workforce diversity as a social accomplishment—a social-symbolic object with important discursive, relational, and material dimensions.

The discursive dimension is fundamental to workforce diversity as a social-symbolic object. This dimension emphasizes the location of diversity in the ideational sphere—the "ideas, categories, relationships, and theories through which we understand the world and relate to one another" (Hardy and Phillips, 1999: 3). The discursive dimension of workforce diversity describes a set of ideas constituted in text, talk, and other forms of discourse: these ideas describe what differences we notice among people, what social categories are relevant to the notion of workforce diversity (e.g., race and gender, but not usually height or eye color), how we assign people to these categories, how we understand our own social categories, and how social categories are represented and enacted in the wide range of practices that implicate diversity. From this perspective, diversity is a social-symbolic object, as well as a discourse that incorporates a whole array of social-symbolic objects.

The relational dimension of workforce diversity highlights the ways in which people occupy organizations as members of informal cliques and social networks inside the organization, as well as broader social networks, some of which emphasize social characteristics, such as race, gender, ethnicity, religion, and sexuality, that are immensely important in understanding and managing workforce diversity. All of these attachments and connections are vital to understanding the dynamics of workforce diversity. The relational dimension problematizes the idea of workforce diversity as a unitary dimension of organizations that we might measure and assess in some straightforwardly comparable manner. The relational dimension of workforce diversity as a social-symbolic object is more than simply an added complication to its objective description. Instead, it suggests that what workforce diversity is will vary across organizational contexts, as it is constituted in networks of negotiated similarity and difference among interested actors, who will be differentially advantaged and disadvantaged by particular definitions of diversity. Of course, this is where the relational and discursive dimensions of workforce diversity intersect, and why incorporating both dimensions is so critical.

Finally, workforce diversity has an immensely important material dimension. The human body is the most obvious part of the material dimension of workforce diversity: the shapes, sizes, colors, and abilities of people in the organization are pivotal to the construction of diversity. The body is, however, only one part of the material dimension, and from a social-symbolic work perspective neither more nor less fundamental than other material aspects. Spaces and places are also important to workforce diversity. Some are more obvious, such as gendered (or not) washrooms, and the existence (or not) of prayer rooms. But the material dimension of workforce diversity also includes the physical locations, layouts, and arrangements of offices, factories, and warehouses that facilitate or hinder workforce participation by particular populations due to the ease or difficulty with which members of those populations can access those locations, experience safety and comfort in those layouts, and work productively in those arrangements.

THE VALUE OF A SOCIAL-SYMBOLIC WORK PERSPECTIVE FOR MANAGING DIVERSITY

Our conception of workforce diversity as a social-symbolic object broadens how we think about diversity. Similarly, for organizational actors seeking to manage workforce diversity, a key contribution of social-symbolic work is a broadening of possible strategies. In this section, we explore a few such possibilities, focusing on how managing workforce diversity might employ boundary work and practice work in organizations.

An important potential type of social-symbolic work for managing workforce diversity involves shaping the social boundaries in organizations. Social boundaries are of considerable importance for managing workforce diversity because they translate into "unequal access to and unequal distribution of resources (material and nonmaterial) and social opportunities" (Lamont and Molnár, 2002: 168). They play critical roles in shaping the diversity landscape in organizations: while there may exist formal rules that prohibit gender- or race-based discrimination, for example, there may also exist social boundaries in the organization that limit inclusion and participation on those very bases. Such boundaries may shape workforce diversity by fostering active exclusionary processes such as discrimination driven by out-group antipathy, or by facilitating "opportunity hoarding" based on in-group preference (Tilly, 1998).

These dynamics make social boundaries an important target of social-symbolic work intended to shape workforce diversity. Boundary work in this case might involve establishing inclusive networking and professional development events to disrupt social boundaries that would otherwise control participation in such events, and the access to networks and resources that go along with them. Boundary work focused on shaping diversity might also involve establishing new social boundaries, perhaps building communities within an organization that help shield minority employees from less "inclusive" professional or departmental groups (Humberd et al., 2015). Boundary work to this end could also involve efforts to shape the consequences of social boundaries, as when members work to mitigate the harmful effects of demographic "faultlines" in teams (Lau and Murnighan, 2005) by creating clear, shared objectives among group members (van Knippenberg et al., 2011).

A second important type of social-symbolic work for shaping workforce diversity is practice work. As discussed in Chapter 8, practices describe the shared routines that organize the social world (Whittington, 2006). Practices are organized by cognitive and discursive rules that operate as informal schema and guidelines, or as more formal routines, and procedures that enable and constrain shared routines. For example, organizations establish rules regarding recruitment and hiring practices intended to attract members of particular groups, as well as methods through which organizations assemble counts of "minority" employees (Kalev et al., 2006). Practices related to workforce diversity in organizations are often tied to professional networks through which diversity managers develop routines intended to establish and maintain a diverse workforce (Kelly and Dobbin, 1998).

Practice work focused on workforce diversity, thus, could focus on shaping the rules attached to practices or the social networks through which workforce diversity is constructed in an organization. Practice work focused on shaping rules might include the creation of specific organizational roles charged with setting diversity goals, establishing plans to achieve those diversity goals, and monitoring implementation and effectiveness (Kalev et al., 2006). Practice work can also focus on the concepts "inside" practices, such as working to legitimate a definition of "immigrant" that makes underrepresentation more visible, or revising the definition of "underrepresented minority" in the workplace so as to include transgender men and women in mentoring programs. Practice work could also focus on practices of accounting for workforce diversity in an organization. This might involve, for example, implementing and enforcing the use of "diversity scorecards" to monitor the representation of employees from minority groups in managerial positions (Hubbard, 2004). A common form of practice work in many organizations is the promotion and establishment of diversity training programs, which tackle issues of unconscious bias and cultural sensitivity, despite the evidence that such programs may have negative effects on the diversity of organizations (Dobbin and Kalev, 2017).

A Social-Symbolic Work Perspective on Entrepreneurship

In exploring the implications of a social-symbolic work perspective for entrepreneurship, we start from a classic definition of entrepreneurship as "combining...resources in novel ways so as to create something of value" (Aldrich and Waldinger, 1990: 112). Along with this general statement, most conceptions of entrepreneurship link it to the founding of a new venture of some kind (Gartner, 1990). Another important facet of entrepreneurship, as separate from business or management more generally, is the role of the entrepreneur: whereas the novel combination of resources through the establishment of a new business could just as easily describe a corporate spin-off or acquisition, the focal role of the entrepreneur—nearly always understood as an individual or a small set of individuals—is a distinctive characteristic of entrepreneurship. Thus, a general conceptualization of entrepreneurship would describe the efforts of an individual or small set of individuals to combine resources in a novel manner through the establishment of a firm with the aim of creating economic value. This understanding of entrepreneurship provides a powerful foundation for understanding how a social-symbolic work perspective might contribute to entrepreneurship and entrepreneurs.

ENTREPRENEURSHIP AS SOCIAL-SYMBOLIC WORK

To examine the potential contribution of a social-symbolic work perspective to entrepreneurship as a practical activity, we first explore what entrepreneurship looks like when viewed through the lens of social-symbolic work. For us, entrepreneurship provides a powerful illustration of the integration of self work, organization work, and institutional work.

Patrick and John Collinson grew up in Dromineer, an isolated village in rural Ireland, where they did a great deal of self work that laid the foundation for Stripe—their hugely successful startup that has democratized online payments (Armstrong, 2018). Bored by school, the brothers had nine computers at home by the time they were in their early teens, and were smuggling science and history books into class to overcome the tedium. After winning Ireland's annual school student science competition for creating a new programing language at sixteen, Patrick went to study at MIT, and was followed shortly by his younger brother John. There, they launched a software platform for eBay power users and an offline copy of Wikipedia. Although their parents had both run and started businesses, the brothers saw themselves as something different: "they were just starting a business—they weren't entrepreneurs, so we had no-one to ask about what we were doing." For Patrick and John Collinson, entrepreneurship was more than starting a business—it was about constructing a life as entrepreneurs.

The impetus for the organization work they engaged in to found Stripe was their own frustration as digital entrepreneurs trying to deal with online payments. Despite the advent of PayPal, the brothers found the process of accepting payment online extraordinarily complex, especially in contrast to the simplicity of online communication, where anyone could easily sign up for a WhatsApp or Skype account and be in immediate contact with friends around the world. In response, they began developing APIs that would allow online vendors to embed the Stripe payment system into their websites with just a few lines of code. To help fund their startup, the brothers approached an unlikely source—the founders of PayPal, Peter Thiel and Elon Musk, who had allegedly solved the online payments problem with their own massively successful venture. Thiel led a US$2 million round of funding for Stripe, which allowed the startup to scale in a way that led to deals with a raft of major internet vendors, including Lyft, Facebook, Deliveroo, *The Guardian*, Boohoo, Salesforce, and Shopify.

The social-symbolic work of these entrepreneurs went well beyond shaping their selves and their organization: in the next phase of their efforts, they established the Stripe Atlas platform, intended to help entrepreneurs start a business from anywhere by enabling them to incorporate as a US company in business-friendly Delaware for only US$500. The Stripe Atlas platform illustrates the potential for entrepreneurship to involve significant institutional work, shaping global business practices by lowering the costs for other entrepreneurs to organize and establishing a financial framework that can facilitate funding and scaling. Just being able to accept US dollars as payment has opened greater market opportunities for small businesses located in countries in which currency fluctuations and political instability might otherwise frighten off clients. As Patrick Collinson described it, most of the growth in internet commerce will be coming from emerging markets and developing economies, which amounts to "about 6.2 billion people we don't reach yet, and that's a huge missed opportunity" (Armstrong, 2018).

The story of Stripe is a story of entrepreneurship as social-symbolic work. The brothers invested immense effort in developing the human and social capital necessary to start the business. They educated themselves, moved continents, experimented with smaller ventures, and connected themselves to prominent organizations and individuals. Their organization work involved establishing a technology, a business, a brand, funding, connections, deals, and an overarching narrative that made sense of all those pieces. The institutional work of Stripe is ongoing, as it works to shape the rules and routines of global internet commerce. What we hope is clear from this example is that a social-symbolic work perspective provides a novel and more integrated way for researchers to conceptualize and research entrepreneurs and entrepreneurship.

THE VALUE OF A SOCIAL-SYMBOLIC WORK PERSPECTIVE FOR ENTREPRENEURS

We believe that the perspective we have developed is also valuable for entrepreneurs. To explore this potential value, we concentrate on one facet of the social-symbolic work perspective: the connecting forms of social-symbolic work—enactment, abstraction, translation, and inversion. The importance for entrepreneurs of assembling resources in novel, valuable ways suggests to us that these connecting forms of work might provide inspiration and guidance for entrepreneurs as they seek to develop new offerings and new business models.

From a social-symbolic work perspective, enactment describes taking a social-symbolic object of one kind and employing it as a frame to produce a social-symbolic object of another kind. The most obvious way this might happen is when actors draw on an institution, such as a practice or category, to enact some facet of a self or an organization, such as a professional identity or a generic strategy. From an entrepreneur's perspective, enactment represents a basic but important opportunity to produce novel, valuable combinations of resources. Although the popular image of entrepreneurship may be akin to the Stripe story of young, tech-minded disruptors, most successful entrepreneurs are older individuals who launch firms in industries where they are already experienced and established (Azoulay et al., 2018). The success of these older, experienced entrepreneurs is tied to their ability to see the potential value in drawing on existing patterns of commercial activity and enacting new instances that meet unmet demands or exploit unused resources. While opening a machine shop or insurance broker may not make it into the pages of Fast Company, such prosaic business foundings are core to what entrepreneurship, especially successful entrepreneurship, really looks like. Thus, if we consider the education, finance, and other programs that governments and universities establish in support of entrepreneurship, we should ensure that there is a significant emphasis on enactment as a key strategy that entrepreneurs understand and appreciate.

Whereas enactment involves creating a social-symbolic object based on some more general concept, abstraction represents the inverse: it involves constructing an idea or concept based on concrete activities and experiences. Like enactment, though, abstraction can be a key strategy for entrepreneurs trying to imagine new and valuable ways of combining resources. Abstraction as an entrepreneurial strategy involves developing a concept or idea that itself represents a valuable resource that can be exploited by the entrepreneur. So, for instance, the development of a brand might depend on abstraction, whereby an entrepreneur articulates the shared, common values or beliefs associated with a group of people, an activity, or a set of objects.

An entrepreneurial story of abstraction comes from New York in the early 1960s, where the concept of vintage clothing as a commercial product was born in the United States. As part of the 1960s cultural rebellion, teenagers and young adults cultivated an aesthetic of "calculated grubbiness" (Calhoun, 2017), which included messy hair, and used and worn-out clothing. The style was meant to be both environmentally friendly and abhorrent to their parents' generation. In New York's East Village, a set of entrepreneurs noticed this trend and opened used-clothing stores, the most famous of which was Marty Freedman's store, Limbo. Freedman noticed that hippies were into army surplus wear:

> "I found out where I could get them," says Freedman. "We called them at the time rag dealers—big warehouses where they shipped old clothes mostly to places like Nigeria and Afghanistan. . . . They were selling it for pennies a pound. We'd load up my Volkswagen. We called it 'carefully selected dead man's clothing.' "
>
> (Calhoun, 2017)

Limbo's most famous entrepreneurial innovation was introducing distressed jeans to the market, when faded and ripped jeans were the markers of the working class and the impoverished. Freedman bought used jeans from Mormon families in Utah, gave them to local East Village artists who would further distress them and adorn with decorative sewing, and sell them for $200 when new jeans were selling for $2.50. Taking as inspiration (and economic motivation) the everyday habits of hippies and beatniks, these East Village entrepreneurs created American Vintage.

From a social-symbolic work perspective, translation involves the movement of social-symbolic objects across social contexts. Translation represents an important entrepreneurial strategy whereby entrepreneurs recognize in some other context a potentially valuable practice, object, or service, and bring it into a new context in which it was previously unavailable. The embeddedness of social-symbolic objects means that moving them across contexts always requires work to reshape them in ways that fit with and are valuable in the new context. A key ability in this regard is recognizing what features of the object can be moved intact and what features need to be reworked.

A classic, entrepreneurial example of translation is provided by Howard Schultz's work to bring Italian café culture to the United States. Schultz's translation efforts were sparked by a trip to Italy in 1983, where he was impressed by the skilled baristas and sense of community in Italian coffee bars (Schultz, 2011). A few years later, Schultz acquired Starbucks and transformed it from a regional coffee wholesaler to a national, and then international, translation of those Italian coffee bars, complete with skilled baristas and physical and social arrangements designed to encourage customers to treat their local Starbucks as a place to gather with friends and work colleagues. No one would mistake a Starbucks for a coffee bar in Rome, but that's the point—translation is not about simply importing a social-symbolic object from another place, but transforming that object to fit the new environment (Tracey et al., 2018).

The final form of connecting work we examine in relation to entrepreneurship is inversion, which describes the appropriation and reshaping of meaning, such that the meaning of a social-symbolic object is transformed in ways that contrast with the original meaning. In Chapter 9, we illustrated inversion with the example of the LGBT community inverting the concept of "queer" in the 1970s, shifting its meaning from a derogatory epithet to a proud declaration of difference. While this example is compelling, inversion also provides opportunities to entrepreneurs who might want to invert the meaning or use of a social-symbolic object for commercial, rather than ideological, reasons.

While there are many examples of inversion by entrepreneurs, some of the most compelling are found in the world of fashion. For example, fashion house Balenciaga has developed a handbag with a striking resemblance to the iconic blue IKEA Frakta shopping bag that retails at £1,705 instead of the £0.40 that IKEA charges for the Frakta (Morby, 2017). The creative director at Balenciaga who has come up with the design is famous for previous use of inversion at edgy brand Vetements, where he designed T-shirts with a DHL logo that sell for more than £800.

SOCIAL-SYMBOLIC WORK AND PRACTICAL ACTION

Our aim in this section has been to examine the practical value of a social-symbolic work perspective by exploring its value for social innovation, managing diversity, and entrepreneurship. Although our primary aspiration for this book has been to develop a set of concepts and arguments with scholarly value, we also believe that a social-symbolic work perspective can provide significant insights, inspiration, and guidance to actors engaged in practical concerns. The practical value of a social-symbolic work perspective stems from its dual focus on the concrete activities of actors and the social-symbolic objects that make up social systems: this combination provides a repertoire of potential strategies through which actors can engage with the social world, and a way of understanding the social world that breaks it down into potential targets for social-symbolic work. This combination looks different when applied to social innovation, workforce diversity, and entrepreneurship, but what is common across these domains is the importance of being able to step back from taken-for-granted objects, see them as social constructions that are potentially shapeable through social-symbolic work, and recognize the potential social and economic value that social-symbolic work might create.

Social-Symbolic Work and the World Around Us

We have argued that the importance of social-symbolic work stems in part from broader changes in society that have made us more aware of it as a phenomenon and elevated its role in societal dynamics: social movements that have undermined long-standing beliefs about the naturalness of the social order; technologies that have disrupted assumptions about time and space; the emergence of global corporations that challenge our understandings of statehood and sovereignty; widespread opportunities for long-distance travel that break up routines based on local relationships and beliefs. These dynamics and more like them reveal the ubiquity and power of others' social-symbolic work in everyday life, as well as the necessity of our own.

In this section, we revisit these connections to explore the implications of the concept of social-symbolic work for people as citizens, rather than as scholars or change-makers. We do so by exploring social-symbolic work in relation to three "worlds" and a contemporary issue that illustrates each one: the social (tribalism), the technological (the sharing economy), and the natural (the Anthropocene).

Social-Symbolic Work and the Social World: Modern Tribalism

It is perhaps most obvious that the concept of social-symbolic work might inform our understanding of the social world. The concept is anchored in the social and our arguments have focused on relationships within the social world, especially the world of organizations. What we find interesting, though, is how the concept of social-symbolic work provides a useful lens on phenomena and issues that while obviously social, can seem beyond the "work" of actors—social dynamics that seem to be evolving under a logic of their own, out of reach of any individual or group of actors.

An important example of such a phenomenon is the tension between globalism and tribalism—one of the defining issues of our day. Although some commentators have declared the triumph of globalism (Friedman, 2007), the history of international relations since the collapse of the Soviet Union, along with recent political dynamics in the United States and Europe, suggest otherwise. At its simplest, tribalism describes people's possession of cultural or ethnic identities that separate members of a group from members of other groups, and motivate efforts to protect group members at the expense of other groups. While this can sound innocuous, tribalism is the basis of extreme nationalism, racism, football hooliganism, various forms of religious fundamentalism, and other vicious forms of identity politics.

Tribalism as it is understood in contemporary international politics had its resurgence following the collapse of the Soviet Union, and the conflicts that ensued. With all of its problems, the Soviet Union provided a certain stability that overrode traditional, tribal differences. In an editorial from the time, Jacques Attali, a prominent French civil servant, argued that: "Unless we take action I fear that [the civil war in] Yugoslavia will only be a beginning.

A new variant of the domino theory will be upon us. But the dominoes will fall not this time towards communism, not even towards nationalism, but towards tribalism" (Attali, 1992). Attali's prediction seems particularly prescient today, and the impacts he predicted are occurring far beyond the reaches of the former Soviet Union. Tribalism is implicated in violence in nearly every part of the world, from genocides in Rwanda, to shootings and bombings in Paris, to mass murders in Asia, Europe, and America.

For us, the concept of social-symbolic work provides a helpful (though obviously partial) lens on tribalism: how it can be understood, and how it might be addressed. From a social-symbolic work perspective, tribalism involves a set of interconnected social-symbolic objects that have been created and maintained by interested actors, and that jointly support partisan action by groups. No single form of social-symbolic work can adequately describe, let alone explain, tribalism, but together they can provide a helpful map of its contours.

From an institutional work perspective, tribalism involves the establishment and institutionalization of boundaries that separate groups. These boundaries, like all social boundaries, are neither natural nor inevitable. They are the product of interested actors engaged in boundary work that valorizes those inside the boundary and demonizes those outside of it. As so many civil wars have shown, those boundaries can be incredibly powerful, even when the differences between tribes seems slight to those outside the conflict.

In the spring of 2016, a vivid example of these dynamics played out in Libya, where five years earlier, in the "Arab Spring" of 2011, the Gaddafi government was ousted after forty-two years in power by a combination of local opposition and an international coalition that supported the rebels with airstrikes. Like many of the events following the Arab Spring, the complexities of Libyan politics since then have turned out to be far more convoluted than was anticipated in the glow of overthrowing a cruel, dictatorial regime.

By the time of the five-year anniversary of the revolution's success, Libya was a political mess, enmeshed in civil war that broke out shortly after the Arab Spring, with territories controlled by at least five different sets of actors, including the Islamist group ISIL that was spawned in part by the revolution five years earlier. At this point, the United Nations and a coalition of nations, led by France, Britain, and the US, were searching desperately for solutions. The civil war, and a UN arms embargo preventing weapons being transferred to either the Tobruk or Tripoli governments, gave ISIL fighters a distinct advantage. Whereas a one-state solution had been the aim of the coalition, the conflict made clear the importance of the traditional, tribal boundaries. The separate, warring governments in Tobruk and Tripoli reflected the division of Libya in the early twentieth century, and the corresponding "inability of the rival factions to accept the concept of shared governance over the country," or "even genuinely recognize the notion that Libya is a country" (Luft, 2015). Stability in the region may yet be dependent on recognizing the legitimacy of those divisions and building new institutions that reflect them.

The first step in thinking about how to apply a social-symbolic work perspective to the problem of tribalism begins with a recognition that the violence and other harms that result from tribalism emanate not from tribal boundaries per se, but from the clash between tribal identities and global interests that fail to recognize the importance of those identities. Thus, reducing the negative consequences through institutional work involves a complex set of strategies that disrupt tribal boundaries—undermining their moral or political meanings—and proposing alternative, less explosive boundaries around which social action might revolve. This is, of course, not a simple matter, in part because the meaningfulness of these boundaries is deeply rooted in social and cultural practices, and because the unintended consequences of disrupting social boundaries have been amply demonstrated, including by the violence and suffering that followed the collapse of the Soviet Union. Alternatively, it may involve recognizing and valorizing those tribal boundaries and developing institutions that account for them, allowing members to enact historical identities in ways that somehow fit into global relations.

Resolving the challenges of the clash of tribalism and globalism plays out as much through organization work as through institutional work. In 2016, the world was facing one of the worst refugee crises since World War II. According to the UN High Commissioner for Refugees, there were approximately sixty million people displaced by war. From Syria, alone, there were four million refugees, with another seven million internally displaced. Although much of the media coverage of this crisis focused on nations (those in crisis and those accepting or refusing to accept refugees) and individuals (refugees and "heroic" individuals who stepped up to offer shelter or aid), the crisis was just as much an organizational one. Crises, such as the Syrian refugee crisis, spawn a plethora of organization work that involves new organizations forming and existing organizations re-evaluating their boundaries, technologies, and strategies. A *Huffington Post* article on the Syrian refugee crisis, for instance, described organizations "You might not have heard of": the Syrian American Medical Society, which provided medical treatment on the ground in southern Syria; the Karam Foundation, which operated out of Turkey to raise funds for rebuilding schools in Syria; Sunrise USA, which delivered food, supports education, and established trauma-care facilities in Syria; and Islamic Relief USA, which provided food, clothing, housing necessities and medicine for Syrian refugees in neighboring countries.

Equally importantly, the tribal–global divide is not about large-scale divisions, but about the geography of the self. It is about how people identify and feel attached to particular sets of concepts that tie them either to the local and specific or the global and universal. Tribal and global divides are not about the occupation of places by people so much as the occupation of people by places. Self work, therefore, plays a central role in shaping how tribalism and globalism are understood and enacted, as individuals, collective actors, and networks of actors work to push people's identities and emotions toward either tribal or global affinities. These dynamics are most obviously present in families and schools where young people are taught the importance of valorizing and protecting their ethnic or religious traditions, and how their traditions relate to those of others, but equally play out in the media as leaders argue for constructions of self for members of their tribe.

Tribalism, like many issues, plays out around us in ways that often feel beyond our control—shaping global and local politics, alternately inciting violence and compassion, and connecting and dividing communities and countries. Our discussion of tribalism from a social-symbolic work perspective highlights the ways in which it is shaped by the purposeful, reflexive efforts of individuals, organizations, and networks of actors, and thus potentially within reach of our own efforts to influence at least our local experience of its dynamics. Recognition and analysis of this possibility are important, as they provides a basis to combat political apathy and frustration.

Social-Symbolic Work and the Technological World: The Sharing Economy

In Chapter 6, we explored technology work as a type of organization work. Our main concern in that discussion was how organizational actors might engage with and shape technology to achieve organizational goals. In contrast, when we think about technology from the perspective of an individual consumer or citizen, our questions about technology shift to trying to understand how we can best use or cope with the seemingly relentless changes in the technologies that structure our day-to-day lives. How we entertain ourselves, manage our financial lives, shop, and communicate with each other—these are not just changing, but going through wave after wave of transformation. These changes not only challenge our competencies and routines, but our senses of privacy, control, and security. How then does a social-symbolic work perspective help us understand the extraordinarily dynamic world of technology?

From a social-symbolic work perspective, technologies exist as social-symbolic objects characterized not only by their physical and technical properties, but also by the meanings attached to them and the relationships in which they are embedded. This more expansive understanding of technology provides a basis for consumers and citizens to engage with technology with greater agency, since even if they lack the skills or knowledge to shape its technical features, they may be able to influence how a technology is understood and its role in their life. For entrepreneurs and innovators comfortable with the technical aspects of technology, it also points to the importance of managing the symbolic and social facets of technology as a way of opening up new opportunities for value creation.

As an example, consider couchsurfing.com. Founded in 2004, couchsurfing.com provides an online forum for members to arrange to "surf" on a host's couch, offer to host travelers who want to "surf" on their couch, or join an event to make new friends. Members create an online profile that describes them, their interests, their favorite books and movies, and anything else that might help identify appropriate hosts or guests. In 2016, the site had grown to over four million members and was arranging 400,000 visits each year, all the time strictly forbidding payment among members.

Couchsurfing.com is interesting for us both because of how it provides a foundation for social-symbolic work by its many members, and because of the social-symbolic work that was required to create it. The site was the brainchild of Casey Fenton, who bought a cheap ticket to Iceland while in university but didn't have enough money for a hotel for his visit. On a lark, he e-mailed 1,500 university students in Reykjavik asking if anyone would like an American guest for a few days and was surprised by more than fifty positive responses. This experience led him to create a website to facilitate this sort of sharing and to create a community of like-minded people who would facilitate each other's travel. "We popularized the term and gave it an adventurous association," Fenton said. "We changed the context so there was a community aspect" (Marx, 2012). In other words, Fenton performed extensive social-symbolic work.

The story of couchsurfing.com highlights the recursive cycle that exists among technical inventions, innovations that leverage those inventions in unexpected ways, and shifts in the identities of individuals and in broader institutional norms. In this case, the internet was developed as a technical foundation for communication among university scientists. The world wide web was developed as a set of technical standards on top of the internet that included peer-to-peer sharing as a core technology. The relative simplicity of setting up websites and the distributed responsibility that came with peer-to-peer technologies led to widespread illegal file-sharing, most famously facilitated by Napster and Pirate Bay. Although both of these sites were long under siege by copyright owners and regulators, the young people who used them got a taste of what it was like to have access to everything while owning nothing. And with those technologies and temptations grew the foundation for sharing as a technologically facilitated revolution in commerce and culture.

What fueled that cycle of technology and culture change was a wide variety of social-symbolic work by a range of actors. If we go back to couchsurfing.com, for instance, the organization was initially established as a not-for-profit: groups of volunteers, referred to as "Collectives," formed to support the development of the website. In addition, there were "Ambassadors" who volunteer to act as resource people for new members in their local area. So, in addition to the work of the founder and his team, there were a number of groups and individuals supporting and developing couchsurfing.com as a technology and, even more importantly, a community. Thus, by focusing on the role of work, we can identify the actors responsible, unpack their intentions and motivations, and better understand the actions they performed that shaped the technology and the associated social structures and processes.

We believe that one of the most valuable features of a social-symbolic work perspective is its potential for empowering people in relation to features of social life they might otherwise conceive of as beyond their ability to influence. Technology is a prime example. All too often, people see technology as determining their lives and possibilities, rather than the reverse. In contrast, a social-symbolic work perspective helps people understand technology as an object that is very much the result of complex social processes that they can shape, and provides a set of tools to explore how things can be changed in positive ways when technologies begin to have negative effects on individuals, groups, or societies. By focusing on purposeful, reflexive efforts, our framework encourages social-symbolic work that moves technology and its social enactment in a positive direction.

More generally, this discussion of technology highlights an important feature of the social-symbolic work perspective. Its focus on the role of agency in shaping social life points to the importance of both radical, transformational efforts we might associate with social movements, disruptive innovators, and high-profile politicians, but it also recognizes the importance of much more modest efforts to change or maintain social-symbolic objects in everyday life, as carried out by managers, teachers, and parents, as well as custodians, shopkeepers, and technicians.

Social-Symbolic Work and the Natural World: Constructing the Anthropocene

The final topic we will consider in this section is the natural environment. Whereas the social and technological worlds are built by people and thus more obviously connected to the social-symbolic work perspective, the natural environment seems to stand apart from humanity, perhaps affected by our behaviors, but not "constructed" in the sense we have been using the term. In fact, it is this exact issue that is at the heart of contemporary debates

317

around the natural environment, including those focused on climate change. To explore the relevance and potential utility of a social-symbolic work perspective for understanding the natural environment, we focus on one relatively recent and controversial issue—the Anthropocene: "The Anthropocene is a proposed epoch that begins when human activities started to have a significant global impact on Earth's geology and ecosystem" (Wikipedia, 2016a).

The idea of the Anthropocene is a powerful one. It suggests the earth has entered a new epoch, which sounds dramatic and is in many ways, but it is also an extraordinarily esoteric idea the significance of which could easily be relegated to particular academic specializations. Wikipedia (2016b) defines an epoch as "a subdivision of the geologic timescale that is longer than an age and shorter than a period," which, like "other geochronological divisions, . . . are normally separated by significant changes in the rock layers to which they correspond." For most of us, our interest in the Anthropocene has just been cut short—we don't usually care about changes in the rock layers of the earth. And yet, earnest and even passionate discussions of the Anthropocene are found in *Nature* (Crutzen, 2002), the *New York Times*—including an article on "Learning how to die in the Anthropocene" (Scranton, 2013)—in literary journals where scholars ask "What are the novels of the Anthropocene?" (Marshall, 2015), and, of course, in management and organizational scholarship (Hoffman and Jennings, 2015).

The energetic conversations around what might be a spectacularly esoteric topic point to its significance for us as an illustration of the relationship between social-symbolic work and nature in at least two ways. The first way in which the construction of the Anthropocene involves social-symbolic work involves its translation into a diverse set of existing conversations around people, society, and the natural environment. These translations are sparked by the Anthropocene's radical disruption of traditional assumptions about the separation of humanity and nature. The Anthropocene suggests there "is no more nature that stands apart from human beings. There is no place or living thing that we haven't changed," and thus, "The question is no longer how to preserve a wild world from human intrusion; it is what shape we will give to a world we can't help changing" (Purdy, 2015).

This shift opens up a range of possibilities with respect to how people construct their selves, organizations, and institutions in relation to a nature that is no longer a backdrop to those constructions, but rather an integral part. An example of the institutional work that this shift facilitates is that of Peter Kareiva, chief scientist of TNC, who describes "environmentalism as philosophically naïve and politically backward" (Purdy, 2015), and argues that "[i]nstead of scolding capitalism, conservationists should partner with corporations in a science-based effort to integrate the value of nature's benefits into their operations and cultures" (Kareiva et al., 2012). Thus, the Anthropocene becomes a powerful discursive tool in the institutional work of "re-branding" (Purdy, 2015) both capitalism and environmentalism in ways that might seem rather beneficial to TNC's corporate partners, including Dow, Monsanto, Goldman Sachs, and Rio Tinto.

In stark contrast, Purdy (2015), a professor of law, suggests that the idea of the Anthropocene has the potential to lead in a very different direction, toward a more radical reconstruction of global relations, or at least an acknowledgment of the interpenetration of nature, society, and inequality. Purdy's argument starts from the observation that the impacts of nature are highly dependent on the wealth of those affected. Focusing on the United States, Purdy argues that the intensive and extensive engineering of modern life in the US, including vast canal and irrigation systems, and nearly ubiquitous air conditioning, turn droughts and heatwaves that would be disasters elsewhere into merely bad news. The Anthropocene, Purdy (2015) argues, will "amplify the inequalities that sort out those who get news from those who get catastrophes; but these inequalities, arising as they do from a post-natural nature, will feel as if they were built into the world itself."

So, the idea of the Anthropocene acts as a catalyst for social-symbolic work. It provides a foundation for people to either bring into question or maintain existing sets of selves (environmentalists, capitalists), organizational forms, and institutions. But the Anthropocene is also itself a target of substantial social-symbolic work; in this case, institutional work. First coined in the 1980s, the term has been the subject of ongoing debate, in part about its meaning and scope, but more profoundly about its very existence. The reality of geological epochs depends in a significant way on their ratification by scholarly bodies. A proposal, for example, was made in 2008 to the Stratigraphy Commission of the Geological Society of London to make the Anthropocene a formal unit of geological epoch divisions. Perhaps reasonably, however, a decision to alter the geological time scale does not occur rapidly, with working groups and committees established to investigate the reasonableness of the proposal and the specific characteristics of the epoch should it be institutionalized.

For our purposes, the Anthropocene illustrates the potential importance of self, organization, and institutional work in relation to nature. On the one hand, it highlights a potential ontological imperative: if we accept even the basic premise of the Anthropocene, it points to nature as a social construction, not in the usual way we use the term but in a more material way. The Anthropocene as a concept rests on the premise that the social activities of humanity shape the earth such that the division between the natural and social worlds collapses. In a less dramatic fashion, the activity around the concept of the Anthropocene highlights forms of self, organization, and institutional work that together construct nature, selves that exist with and in nature, and sets of organizations that mediate that relationship. We see from the work of TNC leadership the attempt to leverage the idea of the Anthropocene to reformulate identities, including environmentalist and capitalist, so that entrepreneurs and business managers might be seen as partners that would engage in "science-based effort to integrate the value of nature's benefits into their operations and cultures" (Kareiva et al., 2012). We see significant organization work, which includes technologies, boundaries, and strategies, in the formation of a number of Anthropocene journals by for-profit publishers, such as Elsevier's *Anthropocene* and Sage's *The Anthropocene Review*. And most obviously we see widespread institutional work, with actors trying to establish new practices that cross fields, sectors, and nations, as well as social and symbolic boundaries that define the Anthropocene.

Conclusion

In this chapter, we have suggested that the implications of the social-symbolic work perspective for scholars, change-makers, and citizens are many and varied. For scholars, the social-symbolic work perspective challenges many assumptions that have traditionally guided social science research. For change-makers, it provides a valuable lens on society that points to new opportunities for innovation and a diverse set of strategies to take advantage of those opportunities. For citizens and consumers, the social-symbolic work perspective is an empowering one: it highlights the possibilities for agency in relation to the social, technological, and natural worlds, when so many features of those worlds can seem to be acting on us, rather than for us or by us.

Stepping back further, this book has been an attempt to develop a way of understanding and analyzing how actors engage in constructing organizational life. The perspective we have developed emphasizes the role of agency and the complex set of actors, motivations, practices, resources, and effects that go with it. In Chapter 1, we described the intellectual roots of our argument as emerging from the writing of Berger and Luckmann, Foucault, and contemporary sociology and psychology. Our perspective, thus, sits at the intersection of social construction and human agency—it emphasizes the socially constructed nature of social reality, but points to the role of purpose and reflection in guiding the efforts on which social construction depends. Unlike the caricature that is sometimes depicted by skeptics, the idea of social construction does not imply simply wishing into existence any reality we choose. Constructing organizational life is tremendously effortful, full of risks and uncertainties, dependent on scarce resources, and immensely important. It also represents a fascinating, exciting, confusing, and enduring topic for scholarly investigation. If you made it to the end of this book, you likely agree, and so we wish you much luck in your own investigations into social-symbolic work.

References

Abbott, A. 1983. Professional ethics. *American Journal of Sociology*, 88(5): 855–85.

Acker, J. 2006. Inequality regimes: Gender, class, and race in organizations. *Gender & Society*, 20(4): 441–64.

Agranoff, R., and McGuire, M. 2005. Managing in network settings. *Review of Policy Research*, 16(1): 18–41.

Ahmedani, B. K. 2011. Mental health stigma: Society, individuals, and the profession. *Journal of Social Work Values and Ethics*, 8(2): 4–1.

Åkerström, M. 2002. Slaps, punches, pinches—but not violence: Boundary-work in nursing homes for the elderly. *Symbolic Interaction*, 25(4): 515–36.

Albert, S., and Whetten, D. A. 1985. Organizational identity. In B. M. Staw (Ed.), *Research in organizational behavior*, vol. 7: 263–95. Greenwhich, CT: JAI Press.

Albrecht, G. L. 1992. *The disability business: Rehabilitation in America*. London: SAGE.

Albrecht, G. L., Seelman, K. D., and Bury, M. 2001. *Handbook of disability studies*. London: SAGE.

Aldrich, H. E., and Waldinger, R. 1990. Ethnicity and entrepreneurship. *Annual Review of Sociology*, 16: 111–35.

Aldrich, H., and Herker, D. 1977. Boundary spanning roles and organization structure. *Academy of Management Review*, 2(2): 217–30.

Allan, H., and Barber, D. 2005. Emotional boundary work in advanced fertility nursing roles. *Nursing Ethics*, 12(4): 391–400.

Allen, D. 2001. Narrating nursing jurisdiction: "Atrocity stories" and "boundary-work." *Symbolic Interaction*, 24(1): 75–103.

Alstyne, M. W. V., Parker, G. G., and Choudary, S. P. 2016. Pipelines, platforms, and the new rules of strategy. *Harvard Business Review*, 94(4): 54–62.

Altman, Y., and Baruch, Y. 2010. The organizational lunch. *Culture & Organization*, 16(2): 127–43.

Alvesson, M. 1993. Organizations as rhetoric: Knowledge-intensive firms and the struggle with ambiguity. *Journal of Management Studies*, 30(6): 997–1015.

Alvesson, M. 1994. Talking in organizations: Managing identity and impressions in an advertising agency. *Organization Studies*, 15(4): 535–63.

Alvesson, M., and Sandberg, J. 2011. Generating research questions through problematization. *Academy of Management Review*, 36(2): 247–71.

Alvesson, M., and Willmott, H. 2002. Identity regulation as organizational control: Producing the appropriate individual. *Journal of Management Studies*, 39(5): 619–44.

Anderson, L. 2011. Demystifying the Arab Spring: Parsing the differences between Tunisia, Egypt, and Libya. *Foreign Affairs*, 90(3): 2–7.

References

Ansari, S., and Phillips, N. 2011. Text me! New consumer practices and change in organizational fields. *Organization Science*, 22(6): 1579–99.

Anteby, M. 2013. *Manufacturing morals: The values of silence in business school education*. Chicago, IL: University of Chicago Press.

Armstrong, S. 2018, October 5. The untold story of Stripe, the secretive $20bn startup driving Apple, Amazon and Facebook. *Wired UK*. <https://www.wired.co.uk/article/stripe-payments-apple-amazon-facebook>.

Aron, A., and Nardone, N. 2011. Self and close relationships. In M. R. Leary and J. P. Tangney (Eds.), *Handbook of self and identity* (2nd ed.): 520–41. New York: The Guilford Press.

Arthur, M. B., and Rousseau, D. M. 2001. Introduction: The boundaryless career as a new employment principle. In M. B. Arthur and D. M. Rousseau (Eds.), *The boundaryless career: A new employment principle for a new organizational era*: 1–17. Oxford: Oxford University Press.

Ashcraft, K. L. 2005. Resistance through consent? Occupational identity, organizational form, and the maintenance of masculinity among commercial airline pilots. *Management Communication Quarterly*, 19(1): 67–90.

Ashforth, B. E., and Humphrey, R. H. 1993. Emotional labor in service roles: The influence of identity. *Academy of Management Review*, 18(1): 88–115.

Ashforth, B. E., and Kreiner, G. E. 1999. "How can you do it?": Dirty work and the challenge of constructing a positive identity. *Academy of Management Review*, 24(3): 413–34.

Ashforth, B. E., Kreiner, G. E., and Fugate, M. 2000. All in a day's work: Boundaries and micro role transitions. *Academy of Management Review*, 25(3): 472–91.

Ashforth, B. E., and Mael, F. 1989. Social identity theory and the organization. *The Academy of Management Review*, 14(1): 20–39.

Ashforth, B. E., and Saks, A. M. 1996. Socialization tactics: Longitudinal effects on newcomer adjustment. *The Academy of Management Journal*, 39(1): 149–78.

Atewologun, D., Sealy, R., and Vinnicombe, S. 2016. Revealing intersectional dynamics in organizations: Introducing "intersectional identity work." *Gender, Work & Organization*, 23(3): 223–47.

Attali, J. 1992. Hope borne on a trade wind: Jacques Attali believes there is one way to stop Europe's descent into tribalism. *The Guardian*, September 8.

Avant, D. 2000. From mercenary to citizen armies: Explaining change in the practice of war. *International Organization*, 54(1): 41–72.

Azoulay, P., Jones, B., Kim, J. D., and Miranda, J. 2018. *Age and high-growth entrepreneurship*. no. WP-18–11, Evanston, IL: Northwestern Institute for Policy Research.

Bakhtin, M. M. 1986. *Speech genres and other late essays*. (M. Holquist and C. Emerson, Eds., V. W. McGee, Trans.) Austin, TX: University of Texas Press.

Balogun, J., and Johnson, G. 2004. Organizational restructuring and middle manager sensemaking. *Academy of Management Journal*, 47(4): 523–49.

Bansal, P., and Knox-Hayes, J. 2013. The time and space of materiality in organizations and the natural environment. *Organization & Environment*, 26(1): 61–82.

Barley, S. R. 1983. The codes of the dead: The semiotics of funeral work. *Journal of Contemporary Ethnography*, 12(1): 3–31.

Barley, S. R. 1986. Technology as an occasion for structuring: Evidence from observations of CT scanners and the social order of radiology departments. *Administrative Science Quarterly*, 31(1): 78–108.

Barley, S. R. 1989. Careers, identities, and institutions: The legacy of the Chicago School of Sociology. In M. B. Arthur, D. T. Hall, and B. S. Lawrence (Eds.), *Handbook of career theory*: 41–65. Cambridge: Cambridge University Press.

Barley, S. R., Bechky, B. A., and Milliken, F. J. 2017. The changing nature of work: Careers, identities, and work lives in the 21st century. *Academy of Management Discoveries*, 3(2): 111–15.

Barley, S. R., and Kunda, G. 2011. *Gurus, hired guns, and warm bodies: Itinerant experts in a knowledge economy*. Princeton, NJ: Princeton University Press.

Barnard, C. I. 1968. *The functions of the executive* (30th Anniversary). Cambridge, MA: Harvard University Press.

Barnes, B. 2001. Practice as collective action. In T. R. Schatzki, K. Knorr Cetina, and E. Von Savigny (Eds.), *The practice turn in contemporary theory*: 17–28. London: Routledge.

Barney, J. B. 1986. Organizational culture: Can it be a source of sustained competitive advantage? *Academy of Management Review*, 11(3): 656–65.

Barry, D., and Elmes, M. 1997. Strategy retold: Toward a narrative view of strategic discourse. *The Academy of Management Review*, 22(2): 429–52.

Barsade, S. G., and O'Neill, O. A. 2014. What's love got to do with it? A longitudinal study of the culture of companionate love and employee and client outcomes in a long-term care setting. *Administrative Science Quarterly*, 59(4): 551–98.

Bartel, C. A. 2001. Social comparisons in boundary-spanning work: Effects of community outreach on members' organizational identity and identification. *Administrative Science Quarterly*, 46(3): 379–413.

Barth, F. 1998. *Ethnic groups and boundaries: The social organization of culture difference*. Long Grove, IL: Waveland Press.

Bartram, J., and Cairncross, S. 2010. Hygiene, sanitation, and water: Forgotten foundations of health. *PLOS Medicine*, 7(11): e1000367.

Bartunek, J. M. 1984. Changing interpretive schemes and organizational restructuring: The example of a religious order. *Administrative Science Quarterly*, 29(3): 355–72.

Battilana, J. 2006. Agency and institutions: The enabling role of individuals' social position. *Organization*, 13(5): 653–76.

Battilana, J. 2011. The enabling role of social position in diverging from the institutional status quo: Evidence from the UK National Health Service. *Organization Science*, 22(4): 817–34.

Battilana, J., and D'Aunno, T. A. 2009. Institutional work and the paradox of embedded agency. In T. B. Lawrence, R. Suddaby, and B. Leca (Eds.), *Institutional work: Actors and agency in institutional studies of organizations*: 31–58. Cambridge: University of Cambridge Press.

Battilana, J., Leca, B., and Boxenbaum, E. 2009. How actors change institutions: Towards a theory of institutional entrepreneurship. *Academy of Management Annals*, 3: 65–107.

Bauman, Z. 2000. *Modernity and the Holocaust*. Ithaca, NY: Cornell University Press.

Baumeister, R. F. 1987. How the self became a problem: A psychological review of historical research. *Journal of Personality and Social Psychology*, 52(1): 163–76.

Bechky, B. A. 2003. Object lessons: Workplace artifacts as representations of occupational jurisdiction. *American Journal of Sociology*, 109(3): 720–52.

Beckert, J. 1999. Agency, entrepreneurs, and institutional change: The role of strategic choice and institutionalized practices in organizations. *Organization Studies*, 20(5): 777–99.

Beech, N. 2008. On the nature of dialogic identity work. *Organization*, 15(1): 51–74.

Belk, R. W. 1988. Possessions and the extended self. *Journal of Consumer Research*, 15(2): 139–68.

Bell, S. E. 2008. Photovoice as a strategy for community organizing in the central Appalachian coalfields. *Journal of Appalachian Studies*, 14(1/2): 34–48.

Benford, R. D., and Snow, D. A. 2000. Framing processes and social movements: An overview and assessment. *Annual Review of Sociology*, 26: 611–39.

Berger, P. L., and Luckmann, T. 1966. *The social construction of reality: A treatise in the sociology of knowledge*. New York: Anchor.

Berger, P. L., and Luckmann, T. 1967. *The social construction of reality: A treatise in the sociology of knowledge*. New York: Anchor.

Bertels, S., Hoffman, A. J., and DeJordy, R. 2014. The varied work of challenger movements: Identifying challenger roles in the US environmental movement. *Organization Studies*, 35(8): 1171–210.

Berthon, P. R., Pitt, L. F., McCarthy, I., and Kates, S. M. 2007. When customers get clever: Managerial approaches to dealing with creative consumers. *Business Horizons*, 50(1): 39–47.

Biddle, B. J. 1986. Recent developments in role theory. *Annual Review of Sociology*, 12(1): 67–92.

Bijker, W. E. 2012. The social construction of Bakelite: Toward a theory of invention. In W. E. Bijker, T. P. Hughes, and T. J. Pinch (Eds.), *The social construction of technological systems: New directions in the sociology and history of technology* (Anniversary): 155–82. Cambridge, MA: MIT Press.

Bijker, W. E., Hughes, T. P., and Pinch, T. J. 2012a. *The social construction of technological systems: New directions in the sociology and history of technology* (Anniversary). Cambridge, MA: MIT Press.

Bijker, W. E., Hughes, T. P., and Pinch, T. J. 2012b. Preface to the anniversary edition. In W. E. Bijker and T. P. Hughes (Eds.), *The social construction of technological systems: New directions in the sociology and history of technology* (Anniversary). Cambridge, MA: MIT Press.

Bogard, C. J. 2001. Advocacy and enumeration: Counting homeless people in a suburban community. *American Behavioral Scientist*, 45(1): 105–20.

Bohn, L. 2014. It's time to start giving a shit about toilets. *Foreign Policy*. <https://foreignpolicy.com/2014/11/20/its-time-to-start-giving-a-shit-about-toilets/>.

Boje, D. M. 1991. The storytelling organization: A study of story performance in an office- supply firm. *Administrative Science Quarterly*, 36(1): 106–26.

Boje, D. M. 1995. Stories of the storytelling organization: A postmodern analysis of Disney as "Tamara-land." Academy of Management Journal, 38(4): 997–1035.

Bolton, S. C., and Boyd, C. 2003. Trolley dolly or skilled emotion manager? Moving on from Hochschild's managed heart. *Work, Employment & Society*, 17(2): 289–308.

Bourdieu, P. 1977. *Outline of a theory of practice*. Cambridge: Cambridge University Press.

Bourdieu, P. 1980. *The logic of practice*. Stanford, CA: Stanford University Press.

Bourdieu, P. 1984. *Distinction: A social critique of the judgement of taste*. Cambridge, MA: Harvard University Press.

Bourque, N., and Johnson, G. 2008. Strategy workshops and "away days" as ritual. In G. P. Hodgkinson and W. H. Starbuck (Eds.), *The Oxford handbook of organizational decision making*: 522–64. Oxford: Oxford University Press.

Bowker, G. C., and Star, S. L. 1999. *Sorting things out: Classification and its consequences*. Cambridge, MA: MIT Press.

Boxenbaum, E. 2006. Lost in translation: The making of Danish diversity management. *American Behavioral Scientist*, 49(7): 939–48.

Boxenbaum, E., and Strandgaard Pedersen, J. 2009. Scandinavian institutionalism: A case of institutional work. In T. B. Lawrence, R. Suddaby, and B. Leca (Eds.), *Institutional work: Actors and agency in institutional studies of organization*: 178–204. Cambridge: Cambridge University Press.

Bracker, J. 1980. The historical development of the strategic management concept. *Academy of Management Review*, 5(2): 219–24.

Brann, N. L. 1981. *The Abbot Trithemius (1462–1516): The renaissance of monastic humanism*. Leiden: Brill.

Brewis, J., and Linstead, S. 2000. "The worst thing is the screwing": Consumption and the management of identity in sex work. *Gender, Work & Organization*, 7(2): 84–97.

Brotheridge, C. M., and Grandey, A. A. 2002. Emotional labor and burnout: comparing two perspectives of "people work." *Journal of Vocational Behavior*, 60(1): 17–39.

Brown, A. D. 2015. Identities and identity work in organizations. *International Journal of Management Reviews*, 17(1): 20–40.

Brown, A. D. 2017. Identity work and organizational identification. *International Journal of Management Reviews*, 19(3): 296–317.

Brown, A. D., Ainsworth, S., and Grant, D. 2012. The rhetoric of institutional change. *Organization Studies*, 33(3): 297–321.

Brown, A. D., and Toyoki, S. 2013. Identity work and legitimacy. *Organization Studies*, 34(7): 875–96.

Brown, H. S., de Jong, M., and Lessidrenska, T. 2009. The rise of the Global Reporting Initiative: A case of institutional entrepreneurship. *Environmental Politics*, 18(2): 182–200.

Brown, J. S., and Duguid, P. 1991. Organizational learning and communities-of-practice: Toward a unified view of working, learning, and innovating. *Organization Science*, 2(1): 40–57.

Brown, J. S., and Duguid, P. 2000. *The social life of information*. Boston, MA: Harvard Business School Press.

Buckingham, D., and Willett, R. 2013. *Digital generations: Children, young people, and the new media*. London: Routledge.

Budgeon, S. 2003. Identity as an embodied event. *Body & Society*, 9(1): 35–55.

References

Burawoy, M. 1979. *Manufacturing consent: Changes in the labor process under monopoly capitalism*. Chicago, IL: University of Chicago Press.

Burgelman, R. A., Floyd, S. W., Laamanen, T., Mantere, S., Vaara, E., et al. 2018. Strategy processes and practices: Dialogues and intersections. *Strategic Management Journal*, 39 (3): 531–58.

Burt, R. S. 2009. *Structural holes: The social structure of competition*. Cambridge, MA: Harvard University Press.

Butler, J. 1990. *Gender trouble: Feminism and the subversion of identity*. London: Routledge.

Cabantous, L., Gond, J.-P., and Johnson-Cramer, M. 2010. Decision theory as practice: Crafting rationality in organizations. *Organization Studies*, 31(11): 1531–66.

Calhoun, A. 2017. The birthplace of American Vintage: How East Village shop Limbo made secondhand clothes cool. *New York Magazine*, November 22. <https://www.thecut.com/2017/11/the-new-york-origins-of-vintage-shopping.html>.

Callon, M. 1986. Some elements of a sociology of translation: Domestication of the scallops and the fishermen of St. Brieuc Bay. *Power, Action, and Belief: A New Sociology of Knowledge*, 32: 196–223.

Callon, M., and Latour, B. 1981. Unscrewing the big leviathan: How actors macrostructure reality and how sociologists help them to do so. In K. Knorr Cetina and A. V. Cicourel (Eds.), *Advances in social theory and methodology: Toward an integration of micro and macro-sociologies*: 277–303. Boston, MA: Routledge and Kegan Paul.

Cameron, D. 2012. *Verbal Hygiene*. London: Routledge.

Carlile, P. R. 2002. A pragmatic view of knowledge and boundaries: Boundary objects in new product development. *Organization Science*, 13(4): 442–55.

Carlile, P. R., Nicolini, D., Langley, A., and Tsoukas, H. (Eds.). 2013. *How matter matters: Objects, artifacts, and materiality in organization studies*. Oxford: Oxford University Press.

Carlsen, A. J., Clegg, S., and Gjersvik, R. 2012. *Idea work: Lessons of the extraordinary in everyday creativity*. Oslo: Cappelen Damm.

Carlson, A. 1991. When is a woman not a woman? *Women's Sports and Fitness*, 13: 24–9.

Carson, R. 1962. *Silent spring*. New York: Houghton Mifflin.

Carter, P., and Jackson, N. 2000. An-aesthetics. In S. Linstead and H. J. Höpfl (Eds.), *The aesthetics of organization*: 181. London: SAGE.

Cash, D. W., Clark, W. C., Alcock, F., Dickson, N. M., Eckley, N., et al. 2003. Knowledge Systems for Sustainable Development. *Proceedings of the National Academy of Sciences of the United States of America*, 100(14): 8086–91.

Caza, B. B., Moss, S., and Vough, H. 2018. From synchronizing to harmonizing: The process of authenticating multiple work identities. *Administrative Science Quarterly*, 63(4): 703–45.

Chudzikowski, K., and Mayrhofer, W. 2011. In search of the blue flower? Grand social theories and career research: The case of Bourdieu's theory of practice. *Human Relations*, 64(1): 19–36.

Clark, C. E., and Newell, S. 2013. Institutional work and complicit decoupling across the U.S. capital markets: The work of rating agencies. *Business Ethics Quarterly*, 23(1): 7–36.

Clegg, S. R., and Kornberger, M. (Eds.). 2006. *Space, organizations and management theory*. Copenhagen: Copenhagen Business School Press.

Coleman, J. S. 1974. *Power and the structure of society* (1st ed.). New York: Norton.

Coleman, J. S. 2000. Social capital in the creation of human capital. In E. L. Lesser (Ed.), *Knowledge and social capital*: 17–41. Boston, MA: Butterworth-Heinemann.

Collien, I., Sieben, B., and Müller-Camen, M. 2016. Age work in organizations: Maintaining and disrupting institutionalized understandings of higher age. *British Journal of Management*, 27(4): 778–95.

Collins, R. 2004. *Interaction ritual chains*. Princeton, NJ: Princeton University Press.

Cooper, R., and Foster, M. 1971. Sociotechnical systems. *American Psychologist*, 26(5): 467–74.

Corn, J. J. 1979. Making flying "thinkable": Women pilots and the selling of aviation, 1927–1940. *American Quarterly*, 31(4): 556–71.

Cox, T. H., and Blake, S. 1991. Managing cultural diversity: Implications for organizational competitiveness. *The Executive*, 45–56.

Crary, M. 1987. Managing attraction and intimacy at work. *Organizational Dynamics*, 15 (4): 27–41.

Creary, S. J., Caza, B. B., and Roberts, L. M. 2015. Out of the box? How managing a subordinate's multiple identities affects the quality of a manager–subordinate relationship. *Academy of Management Review*, 40(4): 538–62.

Creed, W. E. D., DeJordy, R., and Lok, J. 2010. Being the change: Resolving institutional contradiction through identity work. *Academy of Management Journal*, 53(6): 1336–64.

Crutzen, P. J. 2002. Geology of mankind. *Nature*, 415(6867): 23.

Curchod, C., Patriotta, G., and Neysen, N. 2014. Categorization and identification: The identity work of "business sellers" on eBay. *Human Relations*, 67(11): 1293–320.

Currie, G., Lockett, A., Finn, R., Martin, G., and Waring, J. 2012. Institutional work to maintain professional power: Recreating the model of medical professionalism. *Organization Studies*, 33(7): 937–62.

Dacin, M. T., Munir, K., and Tracey, P. 2010. Formal dining at Cambridge colleges: Linking ritual performance and institutional maintenance. *Academy of Management Journal*, 53(6): 1393–418.

Dahl, R. A. 1973. *Polyarchy: Participation and opposition*. New Haven, CT: Yale University Press.

Dale, K., and Burrell, G. 2008. *The spaces of organisation and the organisation of space: Power, identity and materiality at work*. Basingstoke: Palgrave Macmillan.

Dalpiaz, E., Tracey, P., and Phillips, N. 2014. Succession narratives in family business: The case of Alessi. *Entrepreneurship Theory and Practice*, 38(6): 1375–94.

Davidson, S. 2013. *A new era in U.S. health care: Critical next steps under the Affordable Care Act*. Stanford, CA: Stanford University Press.

Davis, G. F. 2016. *The vanishing American corporation: Navigating the hazards of a new economy*. Oakland, CA: Berrett-Koehler.

Davis, M. 1971. That's interesting: Towards a phenomenology of sociology and a sociology of phenomenology. *Philosophy of the Social Sciences*, 1(4): 309–44.

Day, E. 2013. Aaron Swartz: hacker, genius . . . martyr? *The Guardian*, June 2. <http://www.theguardian.com/technology/2013/jun/02/aaron-swartz-hacker-genius-martyr-girlfriend-interview>.

de Certeau, M. 2011. *The practice of everyday life*. University of California Press.

de Raeve, L. 2002. The modification of emotional responses: A problem for trust in nurse–patient relationships? *Nursing Ethics*, 9(5): 466–71.

Delmestri, G., and Greenwood, R. 2016. How Cinderella became a queen: Theorizing radical status change. *Administrative Science Quarterly*, 61(4): 507–50.

Demetry, D. 2017. Pop-up to professional: Emerging entrepreneurial identity and evolving vocabularies of motive. *Academy of Management Discoveries*, 3(2): 187–207.

Denis, J.-L., Lamothe, L., and Langley, A. 2001. The dynamics of collective leadership and strategic change in pluralistic organizations. *Academy of Management Journal*, 44(4): 809–37.

Desanctis, G., and Poole, M. S. 1994. Capturing the complexity in advanced technology: Adaptive structuration theory. *Organization Science*, 5(2): 121–47.

Desrochers, S., and Sargent, L. D. 2004. Boundary/border theory and work–family integration. *Organization Management Journal*, 1(1): 40–8.

Dhillon, A. 2007. Pretty in pink, female vigilantes also handy with an axe. *theage.com. au.*, December 14. <http://www.theage.com.au/news/world/pretty-in-pinkfemale-vigilantes-also-handy-with-an-axe/2007/12/14/1197568262475.html>.

DiMaggio, P. J. 1988. Interest and agency in institutional theory. In L. G. Zucker (Ed.), *Institutional patterns and organizations: Culture and environment*: 3–21. Cambridge, MA: Ballinger.

Dobbin, F., and Kalev, A. 2017. Are diversity programs merely ceremonial? Evidence-free institutionalization. In R. Greenwood, C. Oliver, T. B. Lawrence, and R. E. Meyer (Eds.), *Handbook of organizational institutionalism* (2nd ed.): 808–28. London: SAGE.

Dobrow, S. R., and Higgins, M. C. 2005. Developmental networks and professional identity: A longitudinal study. *Career Development International*, 10(6/7): 567–83.

Doctorow, C. 2013. RIP, Aaron Swartz. *Boing Boing*, January 12. <http://boingboing.net/2013/01/12/rip-aaron-swartz.html>.

Dodgson, M., Gann, D. M., and Phillips, N. 2014. Perspectives on innovation management. In M. Dodgson, D. M. Gann, and N. Phillips (Eds.), *The Oxford Handbook of Innovation Management*: 3–25. Oxford: Oxford University Press.

Dodgson, M., Gann, D., and Salter, A. 2008. *The management of technological innovation: Strategy and practice*. Oxford: Oxford University Press.

Doh, J. P., Lawton, T. C., and Rajwani, T. 2012. Advancing nonmarket strategy research: Institutional perspectives in a changing world. *Academy of Management Perspectives*, 26(3): 22–39.

Dorado, S. 2013. Small groups as context for institutional entrepreneurship: An exploration of the emergence of commercial microfinance in Bolivia. *Organization Studies*, 34(4): 533–57.

Dourish, P. 2003. The appropriation of interactive technologies: Some lessons from placeless documents. *Computer Supported Cooperative Work (CSCW)*, 12(4): 465–90.

Dover, G., and Lawrence, T. B. 2010a. Technology, institutions and entropy: Understanding the critical and creative role of maintenance work. *Technology and organization: Essays in honour of Joan Woodward*, vol. 29: 259–64. Bingley: Emerald Group.

Dover, G., and Lawrence, T. B. 2010b. A gap year for institutional theory: Integrating the study of institutional work and participatory action research. *Journal of Management Inquiry*, 19(4): 305–16.

Drucker, P. 1954. *The practice of management*. New York: Harper & Brothers.

Drucker, P. F. 2011. *The age of discontinuity: Guidelines to our changing society*. New Jersey: Transaction Publishers.

Duberley, J., Cohen, L., and Mallon, M. 2006a. Constructing scientific careers: Change, continuity and context. *Organization Studies*, 27(8): 1131–51.

Duberley, J., Mallon, M., and Cohen, L. 2006b. Exploring career transitions: Accounting for structure and agency. *Personnel Review*, 35(3): 281–96.

Dunlap, E., Johnson, B. D., and Manwar, A. 1994. A successful female crack dealer: Case study of a deviant career. *Deviant Behavior*, 15(1): 1–25.

Durand, R., and Paolella, L. 2013. Category stretching: Reorienting research on categories in strategy, entrepreneurship, and organization theory. *Journal of Management Studies*, 50(6): 1100–23.

Duriau, V. J., Reger, R. K., and Pfarrer, M. D. 2007. A content analysis of the content analysis literature in organization studies: Research themes, data sources, and methodological refinements. *Organizational Research Methods*, 10(1): 5–34.

Dutton, J. E. 2006. *Energize your workplace: How to create and sustain high-quality connections at work*. Oxford: John Wiley and Sons.

Dutton, J. E., and Heaphy, E. D. 2003. The power of high-quality connections. In K. S. Cameron, J. E. Dutton, and R. E. Quinn (Eds.), *Positive organizational scholarship: Foundations of a new discipline*, vol. 3: 263–78. San Francisco, CA: Berrett-Koehler.

Dutton, J. E., Roberts, L. M., and Bednar, J. 2010. Pathways for positive identity construction at work: Four types of positive identity and the building of social resources. *Academy of Management Review*, 35(2): 265–93.

Dwyer, E. 2015. We Built This City: Film celebrates Irish influence in London. *The Irish Times*. <http://www.irishtimes.com/life-and-style/abroad/generation-emigration/we-built-this-city-film-celebrates-irish-influence-in-london-1.2296118>.

Dyer, J. H., and Nobeoka, K. 2000. Creating and managing a high-performance knowledge-sharing network: The Toyota case. *Strategic Management Journal*, 21(3): 345–67.

Dyer, S., McDowell, L., and Batnitzky, A. 2008. Emotional labour/body work: The caring labours of migrants in the UK's National Health Service. *Geoforum*, 39(6): 2030–8.

Eden, S., Donaldson, A., and Walker, G. 2006. Green groups and grey areas: Scientific boundary-work, nongovernmental organisations, and environmental knowledge. *Environment and Planning A*, 38(6): 1061–76.

Elfenbein, H. A. 2007. Emotion in organizations: A review and theoretical integration. *Academy of Management Annals*, 1: 315–86.

Elsbach, K. D. 2003. Relating physical environment to self-categorizations: Identity threat and affirmation in a non-territorial office space. *Administrative Science Quarterly*, 48(4): 622.

Eltantawy, N., and Wiest, J. B. 2011. The Arab Spring: Social media in the Egyptian revolution: Reconsidering resource mobilization theory. *International Journal of Communication*, 5: 1207–24.

Ely, R. 1995. The power in demography: Women's social constructions of gender identity at work. *Academy of Management Journal*, 38(3): 589–634.

Emirbayer, M. 1997. Manifesto for a relational sociology. *American Journal of Sociology*, 103(2): 281–317.

Emirbayer, M., and Mische, A. 1998. What is agency? *American Journal of Sociology*, 103(4): 962–1023.

Ensher, E. A., and Murphy, S. E. 1997. Effects of race, gender, perceived similarity, and contact on mentor relationships. *Journal of Vocational Behavior*, 50(3): 460–81.

Essers, C., and Benschop, Y. 2009. Muslim businesswomen doing boundary work: The negotiation of Islam, gender and ethnicity within entrepreneurial contexts. *Human Relations*, 62(3): 403–23.

Evetts, J. 1992. Dimensions of career: Avoiding reification in the analysis of change. *Sociology*, 26(1): 1–21.

Ezzamel, M., Robson, K., Stapleton, P., and McLean, C. 2007. Discourse and institutional change: "Giving accounts" and accountability. *Management Accounting Research*, 18(2): 150–71.

Ezzy, D. 2000. Illness narratives: Time, hope and HIV. *Social Science & Medicine*, 50(5): 605–17.

Fairclough, N. 1992. *Discourse and social change*. Cambridge: Polity Press.

Fairclough, N. 2001. *Language and power* (2nd ed.). Harlow: Longman.

Fairclough, N. 2003. *Analysing discourse: Textual analysis for social research*. London: Routledge.

Fairhurst, G. T. 2008. Discursive leadership: A communication alternative to leadership psychology. *Management Communication Quarterly*, 21(4): 510–21.

Fals-Borda, O., and Rahman, M. A. 1991. *Action and knowledge: Breaking the monopoly with participatory action research*. New York: Apex Press.

Faulkner, P., and Runde, J. 2009. On the identity of technological objects and user innovations in function. *Academy of Management Review*, 34(3): 442–62.

Fauré, B., and Rouleau, L. 2011. The strategic competence of accountants and middle managers in budget making. *Accounting, Organizations and Society*, 36(3): 167–82.

Fausto-Sterling, A. 2008. *Sexing the body: Gender politics and the construction of sexuality*. New York: Basic Books.

Felin, T., and Powell, T. C. 2016. Designing organizations for dynamic capabilities. *California Management Review*, 58(4): 78–96.

Fenton, C., and Langley, A. 2011. Strategy as practice and the narrative turn. *Organization Studies*, 32(9): 1171–96.

Fine, G. A. 1992. Agency, structure, and comparative contexts: Toward a synthetic Lnteractionism. *Symbolic Interaction*, 15(1): 87–107.

Fine, G. A. 1996. Justifying work: Occupational rhetorics as resources in restaurant kitchens. *Administrative Science Quarterly*, 41(1): 90–115.

Fine, G. A. 2003. Crafting authenticity: The validation of identity in self-taught art. *Theory and Society*, 32(2): 153–80.

Fineman, S. 1996. Emotion and organizing. In S. Clegg, C. Hardy, and W. Nord (Eds.), *Handbook of organization studies*: 543–64. Thousand Oaks, CA: SAGE.

Fiol, C. M. 1989. A semiotic analysis of corporate language: Organizational boundaries and joint venturing. *Administrative Science Quarterly*, 34(2): 277–303.

Fiss, P. C., Cambre, B., and Marx, A. 2013. *Configurational theory and methods in organizational research*. Bingley: Emerald Group.

Fleming, D. 2001. Narrative leadership: Using the power of stories. *Strategy & Leadership; Chicago*, 29(4): 34–6.

Fleming, P., and Spicer, A. 2004. "You can checkout anytime, but you can never leave": Spatial boundaries in a high commitment organization. *Human Relations*, 57(1): 75–94.

Fligstein, N. 1997. Social skill and institutional theory. *American Behavioral Scientist*, 40(4): 397–405.

Fligstein, N. 2001. Social skill and the theory of fields. *Sociological Theory*, 19(2): 105–25.

Fonner, K. L., and Stache, L. C. 2012. All in a day's work, at home: Teleworkers' management of micro role transitions and the work-home boundary. *New Technology, Work & Employment*, 27(3): 242–57.

Forrester, I., McClellan, J., Anderson, K., Charman-Anderson, S., Thompson, B., et al. 2011. *Hacking the BBC: A backstage retrospective*. London: BBC.

Foucault, M. 1979. *Discipline and punish: The birth of the prison*. (A. Sheridan, Trans.) New York: Vintage Books.

Frank, A. W. 1997. *The wounded storyteller: Body, illness, and ethics*. Chicago, IL: University of Chicago Press.

Freeman, L. C. 1992. Filling in the blanks: A theory of cognitive categories and the structure of social affiliation. *Social Psychology Quarterly*, 55(2): 118–277.

Frenkel, M. 2005. The politics of translation: How state-level political relations affect the cross-national travel of management ideas. *Organization*, 12(2): 275–301.

Friedman, R. A., and Podolny, J. 1992. Differentiation of boundary spanning roles: Labor negotiations and implications for role conflict. *Administrative Science Quarterly*, 37(1): 28–47.

Friedman, T. L. 2007. *The world is flat 3.0: A brief history of the twenty-first century*. New York: Macmillan.

Fukuyama, F. 1989. The end of history? *The National Interest* (16): 3–18.

Fulk, J. 1993. Social construction of communication technology. *Academy of Management Journal*, 36(5): 921–50.

Gamble, C., Gowlett, J., and Dunbar, R. 2014. *Thinking big: How the evolution of social life shaped the human mind*. London: Thames and Hudson Ltd.

Gartner, W. B. 1990. What are we talking about when we talk about entrepreneurship? *Journal of Business Venturing*, 5(1): 15–28.

Garud, R., Jain, S., and Kumaraswamy, A. 2002. Institutional entrepreneurship in the sponsorship of common technological standards: The case of Sun Microsystems and Java. *Academy of Management Journal*, 45(1): 196–214.

Garud, R., and Karnøe, P. 2003. Bricolage versus breakthrough: Distributed and embedded agency in technology entrepreneurship. *Research Policy*, 32(2): 277–300.

Gawer, A., and Phillips, N. 2013. Institutional work as logics shift: The case of Intel's transformation to platform leader. *Organization Studies*, 34(8): 1035–71.

Geels, F. W. 2004. From sectoral systems of innovation to socio-technical systems. *Research Policy*, 33(6–7): 897–920.

Geertz, C. 1973. *The interpretation of cultures: Selected essays*. New York: Basic Books.

Gehman, J., Glaser, V. L., Eisenhardt, K. M., Gioia, D., Langley, A., et al. 2018. Finding theory–method fit: A comparison of three qualitative approaches to theory building. *Journal of Management Inquiry*, 27(3): 284–300.

Gehman, J., Trevino, L., and Garud, R. 2013. Values work: A process study of the emergence and performance of organizational values practices. *Academy of Management Journal*, 56(1): 84–112.

George, G., Howard-Grenville, J., Joshi, A., and Tihanyi, L. 2016. Understanding and tackling societal grand challenges through management research. *Academy of Management Journal*, 59(6): 1880–95.

Gergen, K. J. 1977. The social construction of self-knowledge. In T. Mischel (Ed.), *The self: Psychological and philosophical issues*: 139–69. Lanham, Maryland: Rowman & Littlefield.

Gergen, K. J. 1991. *The saturated self: Dilemmas of identity in contemporary life*. New York: Basic Books.

Gergen, K. J. 2009a. *An invitation to social construction* (2nd ed.). London: SAGE.

Gergen, K. J. 2009b. *Relational being: Beyond self and community*. New York: Oxford University Press.

Gergen, M., and Gergen, K. J. 2003. Positive aging. In J. F. Gubrium and J. A. Holstein (Eds.), *Ways of aging*: 203–24. Malden, MA: Wiley-Blackwell.

Giardini, A., and Frese, M. 2006. Reducing the negative effects of emotion work in service occupations: Emotional competence as a psychological resource. *Journal of Occupational Health Psychology*, 11(1): 63–75.

Gibson, A. 2015. On being #transracial, or the arrogance of white privilege and cultural appropriation. *For Harriet*, June 15. <http://www.forharriet.com/2015/06/on-being-transracial-or-arrogance-of.html>.

Gibson, M. E., and Ward, G. K. 1989. *Courage remembered: The story behind the construction and maintenance of the Commonwealth's military cemeteries and memorials of the wars of 1914–18 and 1939–45*. London: HMSO.

Giddens, A. 1984. *The constitution of society: Outline of the theory of structuration*. Cambridge: Polity Press.

Giddens, A. 1991. *Modernity and self-identity: Self and society in the late modern age*. Cambridge: Polity Press.

Gieryn, T. 1996. Policing STS: A boundary-work souvenir from the smithsonian exhibition on "science in American life." *Science, Technology, & Human Values*, 21(1): 100–15.

Gieryn, T. F. 1983. Boundary-work and the demarcation of science from non-science: Strains and interests in professional ideologies of scientists. *American Sociological Review*, 48(6): 781–95.

Gieryn, T. F. 2000. A space for place in sociology. *Annual Review of Sociology*, 26: 463–96.

Gieryn, T. F. 2002. What buildings do. *Theory and Society*, 31(1): 35–74.

Gill, M. J., and Burrow, R. 2018. The function of fear in institutional maintenance: Feeling frightened as an essential ingredient in haute cuisine. *Organization Studies*, 39(4): 445–65.

Gilligan, C. 1982. *In a different voice: Psychological theory and women's development*. Cambridge, MA: Harvard University.

Gimlin, D. 2007. What is "body work"? A review of the literature. *Sociology Compass*, 1(1): 353–70.

Gimlin, D. L. 2002. *Body work: Beauty and self-image in American culture*. Berkeley, CA: University of California Press.

Gioia, D. A., and Chittipeddi, K. 1991. Sensemaking and sensegiving in strategic change initiation. *Strategic Management Journal*, 12(6): 433–48.

Gioia, D. A., and Thomas, J. B. 1996. Identity, image and issue interpretation: Sensemaking during strategic change in academia. *Administrative Science Quarterly*, 41(3): 370–403.

Glaser, B. G., and Strauss, A. L. 1967. *The discovery of grounded theory: Strategies for qualitative research*. Chicago, IL: Aldine.

Glynn, M. A. 2000. When cymbals become symbols: Conflict over organizational identity within a symphony orchestra. *Organization Science*, 11(3): 285–98.

Goffman, E. 1959a. *The presentation of self in everyday life*. Garden City, NY: Anchor Doubleday.

Goffman, E. 1959b. The moral career of the mental patient. *Psychiatry*, 22(2): 123–42.

Goffman, E. 1963. *Stigma: Notes on the management of spoiled identity*. Englewood Cliffs, NJ: Prentice Hall.

Gomez, M.-L., and Bouty, I. 2011. The emergence of an influential practice: Food for thought. *Organization Studies*, 32(7): 921–40.

Gond, J.-P., and Boxenbaum, E. 2013. The glocalization of responsible investment: Contextualization work in France and Québec. *Journal of Business Ethics*, 115(4): 707–21.

Goodrick, E., and Reay, T. 2010. Florence Nightingale endures: Legitimizing a new professional role identity. *Journal of Management Studies*, 47(1): 55–84.

Gorman-Murray, A. 2008. Reconciling self: Gay men and lesbians using domestic materiality for identity management. *Social and Cultural Geography*, 9(3): 283–301.

Gouldner, A. W. 1964. *Patterns of industrial bureaucracy*. New York: Free Press.

Graeber, D. 2011. *Debt: The first 5,000 years*. Brooklyn, NY: Melville House.

Grandey, A. A. 2003. When "the show must go on": Surface acting and deep acting as determinants of emotional exhaustion and peer-rated service delivery. *Academy of Management Journal*, 46(1): 86–96.

Grandey, A. A., Rafaeli, A., Ravid, S., Wirtz, J., and Steiner, D. D. 2010. Emotion display rules at work in the global service economy: The special case of the customer. *Journal of Service Management*, 21(3): 388–412.

Granovetter, M. 1973. The strength of weak ties. *American Journal of Sociology*, 78(6): 1360–80.

Granqvist, N., and Gustafsson, R. 2016. Temporal institutional work. *Academy of Management Journal*, 59(3): 1009–35.

Grant, A. M. 2013. Rocking the boat but keeping it steady: The role of emotion regulation in employee voice. *Academy of Management Journal*, 56(6): 1703–23.

Gray, W. E. 1992. *Prussia and the evolution of the reserve army: A forgotten lesson of history*. no. ACN 92050, Carslisle, PA: Strategic Studies Institute, US Army War College. <http://www.dtic.mil/docs/citations/ADA257661>.

Green, S. E. J., and Li, Y. 2011. Rhetorical institutionalism: Language, agency, and structure in institutional theory since Alvesson 1993. *Journal of Management Studies*, 48(7): 1662–97.

Greenhalgh, T., and Stones, R. 2010. Theorising big IT programmes in healthcare: Strong structuration theory meets actor-network theory. *Social Science & Medicine*, 70(9): 1285–94.

Greenwood, R., and Hinings, C. r. 1996. Understanding radical organizational change: Bringing together the old and the new institutionalism. *Academy of Management Review*, 21(4): 1022–54.

Greenwood, R., and Suddaby, R. 2006. Institutional entrepreneurship in mature fields: The Big Five accounting firms. *Academy of Management Journal*, 49(1): 27–48.

Greenwood, R., Suddaby, R., and Hinings, C. R. 2002. Theorizing change: The role of professional associations in the transformation of institutionalized fields. *Academy of Management Journal*, 45(1): 58–80.

Grint, K., and Woolgar, S. 2013. *The machine at work: Technology, work and organization*. Oxford: John Wiley and Sons.

Gubrium, J. F., and Holstein, J. A. 1994. Grounding the postmodern self. *The Sociological Quarterly*, 35(4): 685–703.

Gunn, R., and Williams, W. 2007. Strategic tools: An empirical investigation into strategy in practice in the UK. *Strategic Change*, 16(5): 201–16.

Hackett, E. J., Amsterdamska, O., Lynch, M., and Wacjman, J. (Eds.). 2008. *The handbook of science and technology studies* (3rd ed.). Cambridge, MA: MIT Press and the Society for the Social Studies of Science.

Haidt, J. 2001. The emotional dog and its rational tail: A social intuitionist approach to moral judgment. *Psychological Review*, 108(4): 814–34.

Haidt, J. 2007. The new synthesis in moral psychology. *Science*, 316(5827): 998–1002.

Haidt, J. 2012. *The righteous mind: Why good people are divided by politics and religion*. New York: Random House Digital, Inc. <http://www.contentreserve.com/TitleInfo.asp?ID={93A5D3EB-2DF4-4F12-BB68-5BD7983B898A}andFormat=410>.

Hall, D. T. 2001. *Careers in and out of organizations*. Thousand Oaks, CA: SAGE.

Hallett, T., and Ventresca, M. J. 2006. Inhabited institutions: Social interactions and organizational forms in Gouldner's "Patterns of industrial bureaucracy." *Theory and Society*, 35(2): 213–36.

Hampel, C. E., Lawrence, T. B., and Tracey, P. 2017. Institutional work: Taking stock and making it matter. In R. Greenwood, C. Oliver, T. B. Lawrence, and R. E. Meyer (Eds.), *SAGE handbook of organizational institutionalism* (2nd ed.): 558–90. London: SAGE.

Handy, C. 2012. *The age of unreason*. New York: Random House.

Haner, U.-E. 2005. Spaces for creativity and innovation in two established organizations. *Creativity and Innovation Management*, 14(3): 288–98.

Haraway, D. J. 1985. A manifesto for cyborgs: Science, technology, and socialist feminism in the 1980s. *Socialist Review*, 80(March–April): 65–107.

Hardy, C., Lawrence, T. B., and Grant, D. 2005. Discourse and collaboration: The role of conversations and collective identity. *Academy of Management Review*, 30(1): 58.

Hardy, C., and Maguire, S. 2008. Institutional entrepreneurship. In R. Green, C. Oliver, K. Sahlin, and R. Suddaby (Eds.), *SAGE handbook of organizational institutionalism*: 198–217. London: SAGE.

Hardy, C., and Maguire, S. 2010. Discourse, field-configuring events, and change in organizations and institutional fields: Narratives of DDT and the Stockholm Convention. *Academy of Management Journal*, 53(6): 1365–92.

Hardy, C., and Maguire, S. 2017. Institutional entrepreneurship and change in fields. In R. Greenwood, C. Oliver, T. B. Lawrence, and R. E. Meyer (Eds.), *SAGE Handbook of organizational institutionalism* (2nd ed.). London: SAGE.

Hardy, C., and Phillips, N. 1998. Strategies of engagement: Lessons from the critical examination of collaboration and conflict in an interorganizational domain. *Organization Science*, 9(2): 217–30.

Hardy, C., and Phillips, N. 1999. No joking matter: Discursive struggle in the Canadian refugee system. *Organization Studies*, 20(1): 1–24.

Hargrave, T. J., and Van de Ven, A. H. 2006. A collective action model of institutional innovation. *Academy of Management Review*, 31(4): 864–88.

Harvey, D. 1989. *The condition of postmodernity: An enquiry into the origins of cultural change*. Oxford; Cambridge, MA: Blackwell.

Hassard, J., and Parker, M. (Eds.). 1993. Postmodernism and organizational analysis: An overview. In *Postmodernism and organizations*: 1–23. London; Newbury Park, CA: SAGE.

Hatch, M. J. 1997. *Organization theory: Modern symbolic and postmodern perspectives*. Oxford: Oxford University Press.

Heehs, P. 2013. *Writing the self: Diaries, memoirs, and the history of the self*. New York: Bloomsbury Academic.

Hendry, J. 2000. Strategic decision making, discourse, and strategy as social practice. *Journal of Management Studies*, 37(7): 955–78.

Hendry, K. P., Kiel, G. C., and Nicholson, G. 2010. How boards strategise: A strategy as practice view. *Long Range Planning*, 43(1): 33–56.

Henrich, J., Heine, S. J., and Norenzayan, A. 2010. The weirdest people in the world? *Behavioral and Brain Sciences*, 33(2–3): 61–83.

Hernes, T. 2004. *The spatial construction of organization*. Amsterdam: John Benjamins.

Hiatt, S. R., Sine, W. D., and Tolbert, P. S. 2009. From Pabst to Pepsi: The deinstitutionalization of social practices and the creation of entrepreneurial opportunities. *Administrative Science Quarterly*, 54(4): 635–67.

Hinings, C. R., and Greenwood, R. 1988. The normative prescription of organizations. In L. G. Zucker (Ed.), *Institutional patterns and organizations: Culture and environment*: 53–70. Cambridge, MA: Ballinger.

Hirsch, P. M. 1972. Processing fads and fashions: An organization-set analysis of cultural industry systems. *American Journal of Sociology*, 77(4): 639–59.

Hirsch, P. M., and Bermiss, Y. S. 2009. Institutional "dirty" work: Preserving institutions through strategic decoupling. In T. B. Lawrence, R. Suddaby, and B. Leca (Eds.), *Institutional work: Actors and agency in institutional studies of organizations*: 262–83. Cambridge: University of Cambridge Press.

Hirt, S. A. 2009. Premodern, modern, postmodern? Placing new urbanism into a historical perspective. *Journal of Planning History*, 8(3): 248–73.

Hochschild, A. R. 1979. Emotion work, feeling rules, and social structure. *American Journal of Sociology*, 85(3): 551–75.

Hochschild, A. R. 1983. *The managed heart: Commercialization of human feeling*. Berkeley, CA: University of California Press.

Hoffman, A. J. 1999. Institutional evolution and change: Environmentalism and the U.S. chemical industry. *Academy of Management Journal*, 42(4): 351–71.

Hoffman, A. J., and Jennings, P. D. 2015. Institutional theory and the natural environment research in (and on) the Anthropocene. *Organization & Environment*, 28(1): 8–31.

Hoppe, R. 2010. *Lost in translation? A boundary work perspective on making climate change governable.* <http://works.bepress.com/cgi/viewcontent.cgi?article=1012&context=robert_hoppe1>.

Hotho, S. 2008. Professional identity: Product of structure, product of choice. *Journal of Organizational Change Management*, 21(6): 721–42.

Hsu, G., and Grodal, S. 2015. Category taken-for-grantedness as a strategic opportunity: The case of light cigarettes, 1964 to 1993. *American Sociological Review*, 80(1): 28–62.

Hsu, G., and Hannan, M. T. 2005. Identities, genres, and organizational forms. *Organization Science*, 16(5): 474–90.

Hubbard, E. E. 2004. *The diversity scorecard: Evaluating the impact of diversity on organizational performance*. Abingdon: Butterworth-Heinemann.

Hughes, E. C. 1958. *Men and their work*. Glencoe, IL: Free Press.

Hughes, T. P. 1986. The seamless web: Technology, science, etcetera, etcetera. *Social Studies of Science*, 16(2): 281–92.

Humberd, B. K., Clair, J. A., and Creary, S. J. 2015. In our own backyard: When a less inclusive community challenges organizational inclusion. *Equality, Diversity and Inclusion: An International Journal*, 34(5): 395–421.

Humphrey, C. 1985. Barter and economic disintegration. *Man*, 20(1): 48–72.

Hunter, B. 2005. Emotion work and boundary maintenance in hospital-based midwifery. *Midwifery*, 21(3): 253–66.

Huy, Q. N. 2011. How middle managers' group-focus emotions and social identities influence strategy implementation. *Strategic Management Journal*, 32(13): 1387–410.

Ibarra, H. 1999. Provisional selves: Experimenting with image and identity in professional adaptation. *Administrative Science Quarterly*, 44(4): 764–91.

Ibarra, H., and Barbulescu, R. 2010. Identity as narrative: Prevalence, effectiveness, and consequences of narrative identity work in macro work role transitions. *Academy of Management Review*, 35(1): 135–54.

Ibarra, H., and Deshpande, P. 2007. Networks and identities: Reciprocal influences on career processes and outcomes. In H. Gunz and M. Peiperl (Eds.), *Handbook of career studies*: 268–82. Los Angeles, CA: SAGE.

Idrissou, L., Aarts, N., Leeuwis, C., Leeuwis, C., and Paassen, A. V. 2016. Identity dynamics and conflict in collaborative processes: The case of participatory management of protected areas in Benin. *Journal of Environmental Protection*, 7: 1981–2008.

Inkson, K., Dries, N., and Arnold, J. 2014. *Understanding careers: Metaphors of working lives* (2nd ed.). London: SAGE.

Jacobs, J. 1961. *The death and life of great American cities*. New York: Vintage.

Jadhav, A., Weitzman, A., and Smith-Greenaway, E. 2016. Household sanitation facilities and women's risk of non-partner sexual violence in India. *BMC Public Health*, 16: 1139.

Jameson, F. 1991. *Postmodernism, or, the cultural logic of late capitalism*. Durham, NC: Duke University Press.

Jammaers, E., Zanoni, P., and Hardonk, S. 2016. Constructing positive identities in ableist workplaces: Disabled employees' discursive practices engaging with the discourse of lower productivity. *Human Relations*, 69(6): 1365–86.

Jarratt, D., and Stiles, D. 2010. How are methodologies and tools framing managers' strategizing practice in competitive strategy development? *British Journal of Management*, 21(1): 28–43.

Järventie-Thesleff, R., and Tienari, J. 2015. Roles as mediators in identity work. *Organization Studies*, 37(2): 237–65.

Jarzabkowski, P. 2004. Strategy as practice: Recursiveness, adaptation, and practices-in-use. *Organization Studies*, 25(4): 529–60.

Jarzabkowski, P. 2005. *Strategy as practice: An activity-based approach*. London; Thousand Oaks, CA: SAGE.

Jarzabkowski, P., and Balogun, J. 2009. The practice and process of delivering integration through strategic planning. *Journal of Management Studies*, 46(8): 1255–88.

Jarzabkowski, P., Balogun, J., and Seidl, D. 2007. Strategizing: The challenges of a practice perspective. *Human Relations*, 60(1): 5–27.

Jarzabkowski, P., Burke, G., and Spee, P. 2015. Constructing spaces for strategic work: A multimodal perspective: constructing spaces for strategic work. *British Journal of Management*, 26: S26–47.

Jarzabkowski, P., and Kaplan, S. 2014. Strategy tools-in-use: A framework for understanding "technologies of rationality" in practice. *Strategic Management Journal*, 36(4): 537–58.

Jarzabkowski, P., and Spee, A. P. 2009. Strategy-as-practice: A review and future directions for the field. *International Journal of Management Reviews*, 11(1): 69–95.

Jepperson, R. L. 1991. Institutions, institutional effects, and institutionalism. In W. W. Powell and P. J. DiMaggio (Eds.), *The new institutionalism in organizational analysis*: 143–63. Chicago: University of Chicago Press.

Jermier, J. M., Knights, D., and Nord, W. R. (Eds.). 1994. *Resistance and power in organizations*. London: Routledge.

Johnson, G., Melin, L., and Whittington, R. 2003. Micro strategy and strategizing: Towards an activity-based view. *Journal of Management Studies*, 40(1): 3–22.

Johnston, W. B., and Packer, A. E. 1987. *Workforce 2000: Work and workers for the 21st century*. Indianapolis, IN: Hudson Institute.

Jones, C., and Massa, F. G. 2013. From novel practice to consecrated exemplar: Unity Temple as a case of institutional evangelizing. *Organization Studies*, 34(8): 1099–136.

Jones, C., Meyer, R. E., Jancsary, D., and Höllerer, M. A. 2017. The material and visual basis of institutions. In R. Greenwood, C. Oliver, T. B. Lawrence, and R. E. Meyer (Eds.), *The SAGE handbook of organizational institutionalism*, vol. 2: 621–46. London: SAGE.

Jones, M. 2014. A matter of life and death: Exploring conceptualizations of socio-materiality in the context of critical care. *MIS Quarterly*, 38(3): 895–A6.

Jones, M. R., and Karsten, H. 2008. Giddens's structuration theory and information systems research. *MIS Quarterly*, 32(1): 127–57.

Jones, P., and Krzyżanowski, M. 2008. Identity, belonging and migration: Beyond constructing "others." In G. Delanty, R. Wodak, and P. Jones (Eds.), *Identity, belonging and migration*: 38–53. Liverpool: Liverpool University Press.

Kahl, S., Kim, Y.-K., and Phillips, D. J. 2010. Identity sequences and the early adoption pattern of a jazz canon, 1920–1929. In G. Negro, G. Hsu, and Ö. Koçak (Eds.), *Categories in markets: Origins and evolution*, vol. 31: 81–113. Bingley: Emerald Group.

Kahneman, D. 2011. *Thinking, fast and slow*. London: Penguin.

Kahneman, D., and Tversky, A. 1984. Choices, values, and frames. *American Psychologist*, 39(4): 341–50.

Kalev, A., Dobbin, F., and Kelly, E. 2006. Best practices or best guesses? Assessing the efficacy of corporate affirmative action and diversity policies. *American Sociological Review*, 71(4): 589–617.

Kallinikos, J., Leonardi, P. M., and Nardi, B. A. 2012. The challenge of materiality: origins, scope, and prospects. In P. M. Leonardi, B. A. Nardi, and J. Kallinikos (Eds.), *Materiality and organizing: social interaction in a technological world*: 3–22. Oxford: Oxford University Press.

Kanter, R. M. 1983. The architecture of culture and strategy change. In R. M. Kanter (Ed.), *The Change Masters*: 278–306. New York: Simon & Schuster.

Kanter, R. M. 2008. *Men and women of the corporation* (new ed.). New York: Basic Books.

Kaplan, R. S. 1997. *Mobil USM&R (A): Linking the balanced scorecard*. Boston, MA: Harvard Business School.

Kaplan, S. 2008. Framing contests: Strategy making under uncertainty. *Organization Science*, 19(5): 729–52.

Kaplan, S. 2010. Strategy and PowerPoint: An inquiry into the epistemic culture and machinery of strategy making. *Organization Science*, 22(2): 320–46.

Kaplan, S., and Orlikowski, W. J. 2013. Temporal work in strategy making. *Organization Science*, 24(4): 965–95.

Kareiva, P., Marvier, M., and Lalasz, R. 2012. Conservation in the Anthropocene: Beyond solitude and fragility. *The Breakthrough*, Winter. <http://thebreakthrough.org/index.php/journal/past-issues/issue-2/conservation-in-the-anthropocene>.

Keller, B. 2013. Obamacare: The rest of the story. *The New York Times*, October 13. <http://www.nytimes.com/2013/10/14/opinion/keller-obamacare-the-rest-of-the-story.html>.

Kellogg, K. C. 2009. Operating room: Relational spaces and microinstitutional change in surgery. *American Journal of Sociology*, 115(3): 657–711.

Kelly, E., and Dobbin, F. 1998. How affirmative action became diversity management: Employer response to antidiscrimination law, 1961 to 1996. *American Behavioral Scientist*, 41(7): 960–84.

Kennedy, M. T., Lo, J., Yu-C., and Lounsbury, M. 2010. Category currency: The changing value of conformity as a function of ongoing meaning construction. In G. Negro, G. Hsu, and Ö. Koçak (Eds.), *Categories in markets: Origins and evolution*, vol. 31: 369–97. Bingley: Emerald Group.

Khaire, M., and Wadhwani, R. D. 2010. Changing landscapes: The construction of meaning and value in a new market category—modern Indian art. *Academy of Management Journal*, 53(6): 1281–304.

Khan, F. R., Munir, K. A., and Willmott, H. 2007. A dark side of institutional entrepreneurship: Soccer balls, child labour and postcolonial impoverishment. *Organization Studies*, 28(7): 1055–77.

Kilpatrick, K., Lavoie-Tremblay, M., Ritchie, J. A., Lamothe, L., and Doran, D. 2012. Boundary work and the introduction of acute care nurse practitioners in healthcare teams. *Journal of Advanced Nursing*, 68(7): 1504–15.

King, B. G. 2015. Organizational actors, character, and Selznick's theory of organizations. In M. S. Kraatz (Ed.), *Institutions and ideals: Philip Selznick's legacy for organizational studies*: 149–74. Bingley: Emerald.

King, Z. 2004. Career self-management: Its nature, causes and consequences. *Journal of Vocational Behavior*, 65(1): 112–33.

Kisfalvi, V., and Maguire, S. 2011. On the nature of institutional entrepreneurs: Insights from the life of Rachel Carson. *Journal of Management Inquiry*, 20(2): 152–77.

Kiss, J. 2011. BBC Backstage: The end of five years of hackery, mischief—and true innovation. *The Guardian*, January 5. <http://www.theguardian.com/technology/pda/2011/jan/05/bbc-backstage>.

Klepper, S. 2002. The capabilities of new firms and the evolution of the US automobile industry. *Industrial & Corporate Change*, 11(4): 645–66.

Kling, R. 1991. Computerization and social transformations. *Science, Technology, & Human Values*, 16(3): 342–67.

Knights, D., and Morgan, G. 1990. The concept of strategy in sociology: A note of dissent. *Sociology*, 24(3): 475–83.

Knights, D., and Morgan, G. 1991. Corporate strategy, organizations, and subjectivity: A critique. *Organization Studies*, 12(2): 251–73.

Knights, D., and Willmott, H. 1989. Power and subjectivity at work: From degradation to subjugation in social relations. *Sociology*, 23(4): 535–58.

Kohn, L. T., Corrigan, J., and Donaldson, M. S. (Eds.). 2000. *To err is human: Building a safer health system*. Washington, DC: National Academy Press.

Kondra, A. Z., and Hinings, C. R. 1998. Organizational diversity and change in institutional theory. *Organization Studies*, 19(5): 743–67.

Kornberger, M., and Brown, A. D. 2007. "Ethics" as a discursive resource for identity work. *Human Relations*, 60(3): 497–518.

Kornberger, M., and Clegg, S. 2011. Strategy as performative practice: The case of Sydney 2030. *Strategic Organization*, 9(2): 136–62.

Kossek, E. E., Lautsch, B. A., and Eaton, S. C. 2006. Telecommuting, control, and boundary management: Correlates of policy use and practice, job control, and work–family effectiveness. *Journal of Vocational Behavior*, 68(2): 347–67.

Kraatz, M. S. 2009. Leadership as institutional work: A bridge to the other side. In T. B. Lawrence, R. Suddaby, and B. Leca (Eds.), *Institutional work: Actors and agency in institutional studies of organizations*: 59–91. Cambridge: University of Cambridge Press.

Krackhardt, D., and Hanson, J. R. 1993. Informal networks: The company behind the chart. *Harvard Business Review* (July/August): 104–11.

Kreiner, G. E., Hollensbe, E. C., and Sheep, M. L. 2006. Where is the "me" among the "we"? Identity work and the search for optimal balance. *Academy of Management Journal*, 49(5): 1031–57.

Kreiner, G. E., Hollensbe, E. C., and Sheep, M. L. 2009. Balancing borders and bridges: Negotiating the work–home interface via boundary work tactics. *Academy of Management Journal*, 52(4): 704–30.

Kwok, R. 2017. Flexible working: Science in the gig economy. *Nature*, 550(7676): 419–21.

Kyratzis, A. 1999. Narrative identity: Preschoolers' self-construction through narrative in same-sex friendship group dramatic play. *Narrative Inquiry*, 9(2): 427–55.

Laabs, J. J. 1992. American Airlines: A profile in employee involvement. *Personnel Journal*, 71(8): 63–3.

Lachmann, R. 1988. Graffiti as career and ideology. *American Journal of Sociology*, 94(2): 229–50.

Lainer-Vos, D. 2013. Boundary objects, zones of indeterminacy, and the formation of Irish and Jewish transnational socio-financial networks. *Organization Studies*, 34(4): 515–32.

Lamont, M., and Molnár, V. 2002. The study of boundaries in the social sciences. *Annual Review of Sociology*, 28: 167–95.

Langley, A. 1999. Strategies for theorizing from process data. *Academy of Management Review*, 24(4): 691–710.

Langley, A. 2007. Process thinking in strategic organization. *Strategic Organization*, 5(3): 271–82.

Latour, B. 1986. The powers of association. In J. Law (Ed.), *Power, action, and belief: A new sociology of knowledge?* 264–80. London: Routledge & Kegan Paul.

Latour, B. 1990. Technology is society made durable. *The Sociological Review*, 38(S1): 103–31.

Latour, B. 1999. *Pandora's hope: Essays on the reality of science studies*. Cambridge, MA: Harvard University Press.

Lau, D. C., and Murnighan, J. K. 2005. Interactions within groups and subgroups: The effects of demographic faultlines. *Academy of Management Journal*, 48(4): 645–59.

Lawrence, T. B. 1999. Institutional strategy. *Journal of Management*, 25(2): 161–87.

Lawrence, T. B. 2004. Rituals and resistance: Membership dynamics in professional fields. *Human Relations*, 57(2): 115–43.

Lawrence, T. B. 2017. High-stakes institutional translation: Establishing North America's first government-sanctioned supervised injection site. *Academy of Management Journal*, 60(5): 1771–800.

Lawrence, T. B., and Buchanan, S. 2017. Power, institutions and organizations. In R. Greenwood, C. Oliver, T. B. Lawrence, and R. E. Meyer (Eds.), *SAGE handbook of organizational institutionalism* (2nd ed.): 477–506. London: SAGE.

Lawrence, T. B., and Dover, G. 2015. Place and institutional work: Creating housing for the hard-to-house. *Administrative Science Quarterly*, 60(3): 371–410.

Lawrence, T. B., Dover, G., and Gallagher, B. 2013. Managing social innovation. In M. Dodgson, D. M. Gann, and N. Phillips (Eds.), *The Oxford handbook of innovation management*: 316–34. Oxford: Oxford University Press.

Lawrence, T. B., and Phillips, N. 2004. From *Moby Dick* to *Free Willy*: Macro-cultural discourse and institutional entrepreneurship in emerging institutional fields. *Organization*, 11(5): 689–711.

Lawrence, T. B., Phillips, N., and Hardy, C. 1999. Watching whale watching: Exploring the discursive foundations of collaborative relationships. *Journal of Applied Behavioral Science*, 35(4): 479–502.

Lawrence, T. B., and Suddaby, R. 2006. Institutions and institutional work. In S. R. Clegg, C. Hardy, T. B. Lawrence, and W. R. Nord (Eds.), *Handbook of organization studies* (2nd ed.): 215–54. London: SAGE.

Lawrence, T. B., Suddaby, R., and Leca, B. 2009. Introduction: Theorizing and studying institutional work. In T. B. Lawrence, R. Suddaby, and B. Leca (Eds.), *Institutional work: Actors and agency in institutional studies of organizations*: 1–27. Cambridge: University of Cambridge Press.

Lawrence, T. B., Suddaby, R., and Leca, B. 2011. Institutional work: Refocusing institutional studies of organization. *Journal of Management Inquiry*, 20(1): 52–8.

Leary, M. R., and Tangney, J. P. 2003. The self as an organizing construct in the behavioral and social sciences. In M. R. Leary and J. P. Tangney (Eds.), *Handbook of self and identity* (2nd ed.): 1–18. New York: The Guilford Press.

Leblebici, H., Salancik, G. R., Copay, A., and King, T. 1991. Institutional change and the transformation of interorganizational fields: An organizational history of the U.S. radio broadcasting industry. *Administrative Science Quarterly*, 36(3): 333–63.

Leifer, R., and Delbecq, A. 1978. Organizational/environmental interchange: A model of boundary spanning activity. *Academy of Management Review*, 3(1): 40–50.

Leonardi, P. M., and Barley, S. R. 2008. Materiality and change: Challenges to building better theory about technology and organizing. *Information and Organization*, 18(3): 159–76.

Leonardi, P. M., and Barley, S. R. 2010. What's under construction here? Social action, materiality, and power in constructivist studies of technology and organizing. *Academy of Management Annals*, 4(1): 1–51.

Leonardi, P. M., Nardi, B. A., and Kallinikos, J. 2012. *Materiality and organizing: Social interaction in a technological world*. Oxford: Oxford University Press.

Leung, A., Zietsma, C., and Peredo, A. M. 2014. Emergent identity work and institutional change: The "quiet" revolution of Japanese middle-class housewives. *Organization Studies*, 35(3): 423–50.

Levi, K. 1981. Becoming a hit man: Neutralization in a very deviant career. *Journal of Contemporary Ethnography*, 10(1): 47.

Levins, R. 2007. Strategies of abstraction. *Biology and Philosophy*, 21(5): 741–55.

Lindner, M. 2009. What people are still willing to pay for. *Forbes*, January 15. <http://www.forbes.com/2009/01/15/self-help-industry-ent-sales-cx_ml_0115selfhelp.html>.

Liu, F., and Maitlis, S. 2014. Emotional dynamics and strategizing processes: A study of strategic conversations in top team meetings. *Journal of Management Studies*, 51(2): 202–34.

Llewellyn, S. 1998. Boundary work: Costing and caring in the social services. *Accounting, Organizations and Society*, 23(1): 23–47.

Locke, L. F., and Silverman, S. J. 2007. *Proposals that work: A guide for planning dissertations and grant proposals*. London: SAGE.

Lok, J., Creed, W. E. D., DeJordy, R., and Voronov, M. 2017. Living institutions: Bringing emotions into organizational institutionalism. In R. Greenwood, C. Oliver, T. B. Lawrence, and R. E. Meyer (Eds.), *The SAGE handbook of organizational institutionalism* (2nd ed.): 591–620. London: SAGE.

Lok, J., and Willmott, H. 2006. Institutional theory, language, and discourse analysis: A comment on Philips, Lawrence, and Hardy. *Academy of Management Review*, 31(2): 477–80.

Loseke, D. R. 2003. *Thinking about social problems* (2nd ed.). Brunswick, NJ: Aldine Transaction.

Lounsbury, M. 2001. Institutional sources of practice variation: Staffing college and university recycling programs. *Administrative Science Quarterly*, 46(1): 29–56.

Lounsbury, M. 2002. Institutional transformation and status mobility: The professionalization of the field of finance. *Academy of Management Journal*, 45(1): 255–66.

Lounsbury, M. 2007. A tale of two cities: Competing logics and practice variation in the professionalizing of mutual funds. *Academy of Management Journal*, 50: 289–307.

Lounsbury, M., and Crumley, E. T. 2007. New practice creation: An institutional perspective on innovation. *Organization Studies*, 28(7): 993–1012.

Lounsbury, M., and Glynn, M. A. 2001. Cultural entrepreneurship: Stories, legitimacy, and the acquisition of resources. *Strategic Management Journal*, 22(6/7): 545–64.

Lounsbury, M., and Rao, H. 2004. Sources of durability and change in market classifications: A study of the reconstitution of product categories in the American mutual fund industry, 1944–1985. *Social Forces*, 82(3): 969–99.

Luft, G. 2015. Plan B for Libya. *Middle East Forum*, October 1. <http://www.meforum.org/5534/partition-libya>.

Lyotard, J.-F. 1984. *The postmodern condition: A report on knowledge*. Minneapolis, MN: University of Minnesota Press.

Mackenzie, D. 2008. *An engine, not a camera: How financial models shape markets*. Cambridge, MA: MIT Press.

MacKenzie, D. 2012. Missile accuracy: A case study in the social processes of technological change. In W. E. Bijker, T. P. Hughes, and T. J. Pinch (Eds.), *The social construction of technological systems* (Anniversary): 189–216. Cambridge, MA: MIT Press.

Madrigal, A. C. 2013. Editor's note to Quinn Norton's account of the Aaron Swartz investigation—technology—the Atlantic. *The Atlantic*, March 3. <http://www.theatlantic.com/technology/print/2013/03/editors-note-to-quinn-nortons-account-of-the-aaron-swartz-investigation/273666/>.

Magnavita, J. J. 2000. *Relational therapy for personality disorders*. Hoboken, NJ: John Wiley & Sons.

Maguire, S., and Hardy, C. 2009. Discourse and deinstitutionalization: The decline of DDT. *Academy of Management Journal*, 52(1): 148–78.

Maguire, S., Hardy, C., and Lawrence, T. B. 2004. Institutional entrepreneurship in emerging fields: HIV/AIDS treatment advocacy in Canada. *Academy of Management Journal*, 47(5): 657–79.

Mahoney, J. T., and Pandian, J. R. 1992. The resource-based view within the conversation of strategic management. *Strategic Management Journal*, 13(5): 363–80.

Maitlis, S. 2004. Taking it from the top: How CEOs influence (and fail to influence) their boards. *Organization Studies*, 25(8): 1275–311.

Maitlis, S. 2009. Who am I now? Sensemaking and identity in posttraumatic growth. In L. M. Roberts and J. E. Dutton (Eds.), *Exploring positive identities and organizations: Building a theoretical and research foundation*: 47–76. Mahwah, NJ: Lawrence Erlbaum.

Maitlis, S., and Lawrence, T. B. 2003. Orchestral manoeuvres in the dark: Understanding failure in organizational strategizing. *Journal of Management Studies*, 40(1): 109–39.

Malsch, B., and Gendron, Y. 2013. Re-theorizing change: Institutional experimentation and the struggle for domination in the field of public accounting. *Journal of Management Studies*, 50(5): 870–99.

Mandela, N. 2013. *Long Walk to Freedom: The Autobiography of Nelson Mandela*. Boston: Little, Brown and Co.

Mann, S., and Cowburn, J. 2005. Emotional labour and stress within mental health nursing. *Journal of Psychiatric and Mental Health Nursing*, 12(2): 154–62.

Mansell, R., Avgerou, C., Silverstone, R., and Quah, D. 2007. *The Oxford handbook of information and communication technologies*. Oxford: Oxford University Press.

Mantere, S., and Vaara, E. 2008. On the problem of participation in strategy: A critical discursive perspective. *Organization Science*, 19(2): 341–58.

March, J. G. 2006. Rationality, foolishness, and adaptive intelligence. *Strategic Management Journal*, 27(3): 201–14.

Marcus, G. 1990. *Lipstick traces: A secret history of the twentieth century*. Cambridge, MA: Harvard University Press.

Marrewijk, A. van, and Yanow, D. 2010. *Organizational spaces: Rematerializing the workaday world*. Cheltenham: Edward Elgar.

Marshall, K. 2015. What are the novels of the Anthropocene? American fiction in geological time. *American Literary History*, 27(3): 523–38.

Martínez-Patiño, M. J. 2005. Personal account: A woman tried and tested. *The Lancet*, 366(Supplement 1): S38.

Marx, P. 2012. You're welcome: Couch-surfing the globe. *The New Yorker*, 16(4): 2012.

Mason, J. 2004. Personal narratives, relational selves: Residential histories in the living and telling. *The Sociological Review*, 52(2): 162–79.

Massey, D. S., and Sánchez, M. 2010. *Brokered boundaries: Creating immigrant identity in anti-immigrant times*. New York: Russell Sage Foundation.

McGivern, G., Dopson, S., Ferlie, E., Fischer, M., Fitzgerald, L., et al. 2018. The silent politics of temporal work: A case study of a management consultancy project to redesign public health care. *Organization Studies*, 39(8): 1007–30.

McIntyre, A. 2008. *Participatory action research*. London: SAGE.

McMillen, A. 2015. Meet the ultimate Wikignome. *Medium*, February 3. <https://medium.com/backchannel/meet-the-ultimate-wikignome-10508842caad>.

McQueen, A. C. H. 2004. Emotional intelligence in nursing work. *Journal of Advanced Nursing*, 47(1): 101–8.

Meindl, J. R., Ehrlich, S. B., and Dukerich, J. M. 1985. The romance of leadership. *Administrative Science Quarterly*, 30(1): 78–102.

Melucci, A. 1996. Individual experience and global issues in a planetary society. *Social Science Information*, 35(3): 485–509.

Meyer, A. D., Brooks, G. R., and Goes, J. B. 1990. Environmental jolts and industry revolutions: Organizational responses to discontinuous change. *Strategic Management Journal*, 11: 93–110.

Meyer, R. E., Höllerer, M. A., Jancsary, D., and van Leeuwen, T. 2013. The visual dimension in organizing, organization, and organization research: Core ideas, current developments, and promising avenues. *Academy of Management Annals*, 7(1): 489–555.

Meyer, S. 1981. *The Five Dollar Day: Labor management and social control in the Ford Motor Company, 1908–1921*. Albany, NY: State University of New York Press.

Micelotta, E. R., and Washington, M. 2013. Institutions and maintenance: The repair work of Italian professions. *Organization Studies*, 34(8): 1137–70.

Miles, R. E., and Snow, C. C. 1978. *Organizational strategy, structure, and process*. New York: McGraw-Hill Book Co.

Miller, D. 1988. *Material culture and mass consumption*. Oxford: Basil Blackwell.

Miller, K., and Serafeim, G. 2014. Chief sustainability officers: Who are they and what do they do? *Harvard Business School Working Paper* (15-011).

Miller, K. D. 2009. Organizational risk after modernism. *Organization Studies*, 30(2–3): 157–80.

Miller, P. J., Potts, R., Fung, H., Hoogstra, L., and Mintz, J. 1990. Narrative practices and the social construction of self in childhood. *American Ethnologist*, 17(2): 292–311.

Mintzberg, H. 1973. *The nature of managerial work*. New York: Harper and Row.

Mintzberg, H. 1987. Crafting strategy. *Harvard Business Review*, 65(4): 66–75.

Mintzberg, H., and Waters, J. A. 1985. Of strategies, deliberate and emergent. *Strategic Management Journal*, 6(3): 257–72.

Mitchell, A. M., Jones, G. B., and Krumboltz, J. D. 1979. *Social learning and career decision making*. Cranston, RI: Carroll Press.

Mitchell, R. K., Agle, B. R., and Wood, D. J. 1997. Toward a theory of stakeholder identification and salience: Defining the principle of who and what really counts. *Academy of Management Review*, 22(4): 853–86.

Moore, G. L. 2018. Who will step up and save The Denver Post? *The Denver Post*, April 6. <https://www.denverpost.com/2018/04/06/who-will-step-up-and-save-the-denver-post/>.

Morby, A. 2017. Balenciaga sells £1,705 version of IKEA's blue tote bag worth 40p. *Dezeen*, April 19. <https://www.dezeen.com/2017/04/19/balenciaga-luxury-version-iconic-blue-ikea-fakta-tote-bag-fashion-design/>.

Mumby, D. K., and Clair, R. 1997. Organizational discourse. In T. A. van Dijk (Ed.), *Discourse as structure and process: Discourse studies*, vol. 2: 181–205. London: SAGE.

Munir, K. A., and Phillips, N. 2005. The birth of the "Kodak Moment": Institutional entrepreneurship and the adoption of new technologies. *Organization Studies*, 26(11): 1665–87.

Murray, R., Caulier-Grice, J., and Mulgan, G. 2010. *The open book of social innovation*. London: Young Foundation.

Nag, R., Hambrick, D. C., and Chen, M.-J. 2007. What is strategic management, really? Inductive derivation of a consensus definition of the field. *Strategic Management Journal*, 28(9): 935–55.

Nakamoto, S. 2008. Bitcoin: A peer-to-peer electronic cash system. *Satoshi Nakamoto Institute*, October 31. <http://nakamotoinstitute.org/bitcoin/>.

Navis, C., and Glynn, M. A. 2010. How new market categories emerge: Temporal dynamics of legitimacy, identity, and entrepreneurship in satellite radio, 1990–2005. *Administrative Science Quarterly*, 55(3): 439–71.

Negro, G., Hannan, M. T., and Rao, H. 2011. Category reinterpretation and defection: Modernism and tradition in Italian winemaking. *Organization Science*, 22(6): 1449–63.

Nekvapil, J. 2011. The history and theory of language planning. In E. Hinkel (Ed.), *Handbook of research in second language teaching and learning*, vol. 2: 871–87. London: Routledge.

Neustupný, J. V. 1974. The modernization of the Japanese system of communication. *Language in Society*, 3(1): 33–50.

Nicolini, D., and Monteiro, P. 2017. The practice approach: For a praxeology of organizational and management studies. In H. Tsoukas and A. Langley (Eds.), *The SAGE handbook of process organization studies*: 110–26. London: SAGE.

Nilsson, W. 2015. Positive institutional work: Exploring institutional work through the lens of positive organizational scholarship. *Academy of Management Review*, 40(3): 370–98.

Nilsson, W. O. 2003. *Social innovation: An exploration of the literature*. Montreal, QC: McGall-Dupont Social Innovation Initiative.

Nilsson, W. O. In press. Social innovation as institutional work. In G. George, T. Baker, P. Tracey, and J. Havoshi (Eds.), *Handbook of inclusive innovation: The role of organizations, markets and communities in social innovation*. Cheltenham: Edward Elgar.

Nippert-Eng, C. 1996. Calendars and keys: The classification of "home" and "work." *Sociological Forum*, 11(3): 563–82.

Nkomo, S. M. 1992. The emperor has no clothes: Rewriting "race in organizations." *Academy of Management Review*, 17(3): 487–513.

Noddings, N. 2003. *Caring : A feminine approach to ethics and moral education* (2nd ed.). Berkeley, CA: University of California Press.

North, D. C. 1990. *Institutions, institutional change and economic performance*. Cambridge: Cambridge University Press.

Nyström, M., Dahlberg, K., and Carlsson, G. 2003. Non-caring encounters at an emergency care unit—a life-world hermeneutic analysis of an efficiency-driven organization. *International Journal of Nursing Studies*, 40(7): 761–9.

OED. 2004. Organization, n. *OED Online*, September. Oxford: Oxford University Press. <http://www.oed.com/view/Entry/132452>.

OED. 2016. Strategy, n. *OED Online*, December. Oxford: Oxford University Press. <http://www.oed.com/view/Entry/191319>.

Ohmae, K. 1982. *The mind of the strategist*. London: Penguin.

Oliver, C. 1992. The antecedents of deinstitutionalization. *Organization Studies*, 13(4): 563–88.

Oluo, I. 2017. The heart of whiteness: Ijeoma Oluo interviews Rachel Dolezal, the white woman who identifies as black. *The Stranger*, April 19. <https://www.thestranger.com/features/2017/04/19/25082450/the-heart-of-whiteness-ijeoma-oluo-interviews-rachel-dolezal-the-white-woman-who-identifies-as-black>.

Orlikowski, W. J. 1992. The duality of technology: Rethinking the concept of technology in organizations. *Organization Science*, 3(3): 398–427.

Orlikowski, W. J. 2000. Using technology and constituting structures: A practice lens for studying technology in organizations. *Organization Science*, 11(4): 404–28.

Orlikowski, W. J. 2007. Sociomaterial practices: Exploring technology at work. *Organization Studies*, 28(9): 1435–48.

Orlikowski, W. J., and Baroudi, J. J. 1991. Studying information technology in organizations: Research approaches and assumptions. *Information Systems Research*, 2(1): 1–28.

Orlikowski, W. J., and Scott, S. V. 2008. Sociomateriality: Challenging the separation of technology, work and organization. *Academy of Management Annals*, 2(1): 433–74.

Orwell, G. 2013. *Politics and the English language*. London: Penguin.

Ospina, S., Dodge, J., Foldy, E. G., and Hofmann-Pinilla, A. 2008. Taking the action turn: Lessons from bringing participation to qualitative research. In P. Reason and H Bradbury (Eds.), *The SAGE handbook of action research: participative inquiry and practice*: 420–34. London: SAGE.

Ovadia, S. 2003. Suggestions of the postmodern self: Value changes in American high school students, 1976–1996. *Sociological Perspectives*, 46(2): 239–56.

Oyserman, D., Elmore, K., and Smith, G. 2012. Self, self-concept, and identity. In M. R. Leary and J. P. Tangney (Eds.), *Handbook of self and identity*, vol. 2: 69–104. New York: The Guilford Press.

Parker, I. 2014. *Discourse dynamics: Critical analysis for social and individual psychology* (Psychology revivals). London: Routledge.

Parkhe, A. 1993. Strategic alliance structuring: A game theoretic and transaction cost examination of interfirm cooperation. *Academy of Management Journal*, 36(4): 794–829.

Peng, M. W. 2002. Towards an institution-based view of business strategy. *Asia Pacific Journal of Management*, 19(2–3): 251–67.

Pentland, B. T., and Rueter, H. H. 1994. Organizational routines as grammars of action. *Administrative Science Quarterly*, 39(3): 484–510.

Perkmann, M., and Spicer, A. 2008. How are management fashions institutionalized? The role of institutional work. *Human Relations*, 61(6): 811–44.

Perlow, L. A. 2012. *Sleeping with your smartphone: How to break the 24/7 habit and change the way you work*. Cambridge, MA: Harvard Business Press.

Perrow, C. 1967. A framework for the comparative analysis of organizations. *American Sociological Review*, 32(2): 194–208.

Perrow, C. 1986. *Complex organizations: A critical essay* (3rd ed.). New York: McGraw-Hill.

Peterson, G. W., Sampson, J. P., and Reardon, R. C. 1991. *Career development and services: A cognitive approach*. Pacific Grove, CA: Brooks/Cole.

Peterson, R. A. 2005. In search of authenticity. *Journal of Management Studies*, 42(5): 1083–98.

Petriglieri, G., Petriglieri, J. L., and Wood, J. D. In press. Fast tracks and inner journeys: Crafting portable selves for contemporary careers. *Administrative Science Quarterly*. <https://doi.org/10.1177/0001839217720930>.

Pettigrew, A. M. 1985. *The awakening giant: Continuity and change in Imperial Chemical Industries*. Oxford: Blackwell.

Pettigrew, A. M. 1992. The character and significance of strategy process research. *Strategic Management Journal*, 13(Winter special issue): 5–16.

Pfeffer, J., and Salancik, G. R. 1978. *The external control of organizations: A resource dependence perspective*. New York: Harper and Row.

Phelan, M. P., and Hunt, S. A. 1998. Prison gang members' tattoos as identity work: The visual communication of moral careers. *Symbolic Interaction*, 21(3): 277–98.

Philipkoski, K. 2005. Furniture causes FedEx fits. *WIRED*, August 11. <http://archive.wired.com/culture/lifestyle/news/2005/08/68492>.

Phillips, N., and Brown, J. L. 1993. Analyzing communication in and around organizations: A critical hermeneutic approach. *Academy of Management Journal*, 36(6): 1547–76.

Phillips, N., and Hardy, C. 2002. *Discourse analysis: Investigating processes of social construction*. Thousand Oaks, CA: SAGE.

Phillips, N., Lawrence, T. B., and Hardy, C. 2000. Inter-organizational collaboration and the dynamics of institutional fields. *Journal of Management Studies*, 37(1): 23–43.

Phillips, N., Lawrence, T. B., and Hardy, C. 2004. Discourse and institutions. *Academy of Management Review*, 29(4): 635–52.

Phillips, N., Lawrence, T. B., and Hardy, C. 2006. Discussing "Discourse and institutions": A reply to Lok and Willmott. *Academy of Management Review*, 31(2): 480–3.

Phillips, N., and Malhotra, N. 2008. Taking social construction seriously: Extending the discursive approach in institutional theory. In R. Greenwood, C. Oliver, K. Sahlin, and R. Suddaby (Eds.), *SAGE handbook of organizational institutionalism*: 702–20. London: SAGE.

Phillips, N., and Oswick, C. 2012. Organizational discourse: Domains, debates, and directions. *Academy of Management Annals*, 6(1): 435–81.

Phills, J. A. J., Deiglmeier, K., and Miller, D. T. 2008. Rediscovering social innovation. *Stanford Social Innovation Review* (Fall): 34–43.

Pickering, A. 2010. *The mangle of practice: Time, agency, and science*. Chicago, IL: University of Chicago Press.

Pinch, T. J. 2008. Technology and institutions: Living in a material world. *Theory and Society*, 37(5): 461–83.

Pinch, T. J., and Bijker, W. E. 1984. The social construction of facts and artefacts: Or how the sociology of science and the sociology of technology might benefit each other. *Social Studies of Science*, 14(3): 399–441.

Pinch, T. J., and Bijker, W. E. 2012. The social construction of facts and artifacts: Or how the sociology of science and the sociology of technology might benefit each other. In W. E. Bijker, T. P. Hughes, and T. J. Pinch (Eds.), *The social construction of technological systems: New directions in the sociology and history of technology* (Anniversary): 11–40. Cambridge, MA: MIT Press.

Polkinghorne, D. E. 1991. Narrative and self-concept. *Journal of Narrative and Life History*, 1(2): 135–53.

Pondy, L. R., Frost, P. J., Morgan, G., and Dandridge, T. C. (Eds.). 1983. *Organizational symbolism*. Greenwich, CT: JAI Press.

Poole, M. S., and Van de Ven, A. H. (Eds.). 2004. *Handbook of organizational change and innovation*. New York: Oxford University Press.

Porter, M. E. 1980. *Competitive strategy: Techniques for analyzing industries and competition*. New York: The Free Press.

Porter, R. 1997. Introduction. In R. Porter (Ed.), *Rewriting the self: Histories from the middle ages to the present*. London: Routledge.

Pratt, M. G. 2000. The good, the bad, and the ambivalent: Managing identification among Amway distributors. *Administrative Science Quarterly*, 45(3): 456–93.

Pratt, M. G., and Rafaeli, A. 1997. Organizational dress as a symbol of multilayered social identities. *Academy of Management Journal*, 40(4): 862–98.

Pratt, M. G., Rockmann, K. W., and Kaufmann, J. B. 2006. Constructing professional identity: The role of work and identity learning cycles in the customization of identity among medical residents. *Academy of Management Journal*, 49(2): 235–62.

Puranam, P., Alexy, O., and Reitzig, M. 2014. What's "new" about new forms of organizing? *Academy of Management Review*, 39(2): 162–80.

Purdy, J. 2015. Anthropocene fever. *Aeon*, March 31. <https://aeon.co/essays/should-we-be-suspicious-of-the-anthropocene-idea>.

Purdy, J. M., and Gray, B. 2009. Conflicting logics, mechanisms of diffusion, and multilevel dynamics in emerging institutional fields. *Academy of Management Journal*, 52(2): 355–80.

Putnam, R. D. 2001. *Bowling alone*. New York: Simon and Schuster.

Rafaeli, A., and Pratt, M. G. (Eds.). 2013. *Artifacts and organizations: Beyond mere symbolism*. Malwah, NJ: Lawrence Erlbaum.

Rafaeli, A., and Sutton, R. I. 1987. Expression of emotion as part of the work role. *Academy of Management Review*, 12(1): 23–37.

Rafaeli, A., and Sutton, R. I. 1990. Busy stores and demanding customers: How do they affect the display of positive emotion? *Academy of Management Journal*, 33(3): 623–37.

Rafaeli, A., and Sutton, R. I. 1991. Emotional contrast strategies as means of social influence: Lessons from criminal interrogators and bill collectors. *Academy of Management Journal*, 34(4): 749–75.

Ragin, C. C., and Sedziaka, A. A. 2013. QCA and fuzzy set applications to social movement research. In *The Wiley-Blackwell encyclopedia of social and political movements*. Oxford: Wiley-Blackwell. https://doi.org/10.1002/9780470674871.wbespm482.

Rao, H., Monin, P., and Durand, R. 2003. Institutional change in Toque Ville: Nouvelle cuisine as an identity movement in French gastronomy. *American Journal of Sociology*, 108(4): 795–843.

Rao, H., Morrill, C., and Zald, M. N. 2000. Power plays: How social movements and collective action create new organizational forms. *Research in Organizational Behavior*, 22: 237–82.

Rassool, N. 1998. Postmodernity, cultural pluralism and the nation-state: Problems of language rights, human rights, identity and power. *Language Sciences*, 20(1): 89–99.

Raviola, E., and Norbäck, M. 2013. Bringing technology and meaning into institutional work: Making news at an Italian business newspaper. *Organization Studies*, 34(8): 1171–94.

Raymond, E. S. 2001. *The cathedral and the bazaar: Musings on Linux and open source by an accidental revolutionary*. Cambridge, MA: O'Reilly Media.

Reis, C. R. D. A. D., Castillo, M. Á. S., and Dobón, S. R. 2007. Diversity and business performance: 50 years of research. *Service Business*, 1(4): 257–74.

Riaz, S., Buchanan, S., and Ruebottom, T. 2016. Rhetoric of epistemic authority: Defending field positions during the financial crisis. *Human Relations*, 69(7): 1533–61.

Rigg, C., O'Dwyer, B., and O'Dwyer, B. 2012. Becoming an entrepreneur: Researching the role of mentors in identity construction. *Education + Training*, 54(4): 319–29.

Ritzer, G. 1990. Micro-macro linkage in sociological theory: Applying a metatheoretical tool. In G. Ritzer (Ed.), *Frontiers of social theory: The new syntheses*: 347–70. New York: Columbia University Press.

Roberson, Q., Holmes IV, O., and Perry, J. L. 2017. Transforming research on diversity and firm performance: A dynamic capabilities perspective. *Academy of Management Annals*, 11(1): 189–216.

Roberts, L. M., and Creary, S. J. 2013. Navigating the self in diverse work contexts. In J. T. Jost, A. C. Kay, and H. Thorisdottir (Eds.), *Oxford handbook of diversity and work*: 73–97. Oxford: Oxford University Press.

Roberts, P. W., Simons, T., and Swaminathan, A. 2010. Crossing a categorical boundary: The implications of switching from non-kosher wine production in the Israeli wine market. In G. Hsu, G. Negro, and Ö. Koçak (Eds.), *Categories in markets: Origins and evolution*, vol. 31: 153–73. Bingley: Emerald Group.

Robinson, S. K., and Kerr, R. 2009. The symbolic violence of leadership: A critical hermeneutic study of leadership and succession in a British organization in the post-Soviet context. *Human Relations*, 62(6): 875–903.

Rojas, F. 2010. Power through institutional work: Acquiring academic authority in the 1968 Third World Strike. *Academy of Management Journal*, 53(6): 1263–80.

Roos, J., Victor, B., and Statler, M. 2004. Playing seriously with strategy. *Long Range Planning*, 37(6): 549–68.

Rorty, R. 1967. *The linguistic turn: Essays in philosophical method*. Chicago, IL: University of Chicago Press.

Rorty, R. 2009. *Philosophy and the mirror of nature* (30th Anniversary). Princeton, NJ: Princeton University Press.

Rosch, E. 1978. Principles of categorization. In E. Rosch and B. B. Lloyd (Eds.), *Cognition and categorization*, vol. 189: 27–48. Hillsdale, NJ: Erlbaum.

Rouleau, L. 2005. Micro-practices of strategic sensemaking and sensegiving: How middle managers interpret and sell change every day. *Journal of Management Studies*, 42(7): 1413–41.

Ruebottom, T. 2013. The microstructures of rhetorical strategy in social entrepreneurship: Building legitimacy through heroes and villains. *Journal of Business Venturing*, 28(1): 98–116.

Rutgers, M. R. 1999. Be rational! But what does it mean? A history of the idea of rationality and its relation to management thought. *Journal of Management History*, 5(1): 17–35.

Ryen, A., and Silverman, D. 2000. Marking boundaries: Culture as category work. *Qualitative Inquiry*, 6(1): 107–28.

Sahlin, K., and Wedlin, L. 2008. Circulating ideas: Imitation, translation and editing. In R. Green, C. Oliver, K. Sahlin, and R. Suddaby (Eds.), *SAGE handbook of organizational institutionalism*: 219–42. London: SAGE.

Salmon, F. 2013. The Bitcoin bubble and the future of currency. *Medium*, November 26. <https://medium.com/@felixsalmon/the-bitcoin-bubble-and-the-future-of-currency-2b5ef79482cb>.

Samra-Fredericks, D. 2005. Strategic practice, "discourse" and the everyday interactional constitution of "power effects." *Organization*, 12(6): 803–41.

Santos, F. M., and Eisenhardt, K. M. 2005. Organizational boundaries and theories of organization. *Organization Science*, 16(5): 491–508.

Sarbin, T. 1986. The narrative as a root metaphor for psychology. In T. Sarbin (Ed.), *Narrative psychology : The storied nature of human conduct*: 3–21. New York: Praeger.

Saussure, F. de. 1983. *Course in general linguistics*. Duckworth.

Scandura, T. A. 1992. Mentorship and career mobility: An empirical investigation. *Journal of Organizational Behavior*, 13(2): 169–74.

Schatzki, T. R. 2001. Introduction: Practice theory. In T. R. Schatzki, K. Knorr Cetina, and E. Von Savigny (Eds.), *The practice turn in contemporary theory*: 1–14. London: Routledge.

Schatzki, T. R., Knorr Cetina, K., and Von Savigny, E. 2001. *The practice turn in contemporary theory:* London: Routledge.

Schein, E. H. 1996. Career anchors revisited: Implications for career development in the 21st century. *Academy of Management Executive*, 10(4): 80–8.

Schein, E. H. 2016. *Organizational culture and leadership* (5th ed.). Hoboken, NJ: Wiley.

Schendel, D. E., and Hofer, C. W. 1979. *Strategic management: A new view of business policy and planning*. Boston, MA: Little, Brown.

Schneiberg, M., and Berk, G. 2010. From categorical imperative to learning by categories: Cost accounting and new categorical practices in American manufacturing, 1900–1930. In G. Negro, G. Hsu, and Ö. Koçak (Eds.), *Categories in markets: Origins and evolution*, vol. 31: 255–92. Bingley: Emerald Group.

Schultz, H. 2011. *Onward: How Starbucks fought for its life without losing its soul*. Chichester: John Wiley & Sons.

Schüßler, E., Dobusch, L., and Wessel, L. 2014. Backstage: Organizing events as proto-institutional work in the popular music industry. *Schmalenbach Business Review (SBR)*, 66: 415–37.

Scott, W. R. 2003. *Organizations: Rational, natural, and open systems* (5th ed). Upper Saddle River, NJ: Prentice Hall.

Scott, W. R. 2013. *Institutions and organizations: Ideas, interests and identities* (4th ed.). London: SAGE.

Scranton, R. 2013. Learning how to die in the Anthropocene. *New York Times*, November 10. <http://opinionator.blogs.nytimes.com/2013/11/10/learning-how-to-die-in-the-anthropocene/>.

Sedgwick, E. K. 1985. *Between men: English literature and male homosocial desire*. New York: Columbia University Press.

Seelos, C., and Mair, J. 2005. Social entrepreneurship: Creating new business models to serve the poor. *Business Horizons*, 48(3): 241–6.

Selznick, P. 1949. *TVA and the grass roots: A study of politics and organization.* Berkeley, CA: University of California Press.

Selznick, P. 1996. Institutionalism "old" and "new." *Administrative Science Quarterly*, 41(2): 270–7.

Selznick, P. 2011. *Leadership in administration: A sociological interpretation* (Digital). New Orleans, LA: Quid Pro.

Sen, A. 2012. Women's vigilantism in India: A case study of the Pink Sari Gang. In *Online encyclopedia of mass violence*, December 20. Paris: Mass Violence and Resistance—Research Network. <http://www.massviolence.org/Article?id_article=574>.

Seo, M.-G., and Creed, W. E. D. 2002. Institutional contradictions, praxis, and institutional change: A dialectical perspective. *Academy of Management Review*, 27(2): 222–47.

Seron, C., and Ferris, K. 1995. Negotiating professionalism: The gendered social capital of flexible time. *Work and Occupations*, 22(1): 22–47.

Shelter. 2018. What is homelessness? *Shelter England*, April 3. <http://england.shelter.org.uk/housing_advice/homelessness/rules/what_is_homelessness>.

SIOP. 2018. *What are SIOP and I-O psychologists?* <http://www.siop.org/media/what.aspx#>.

Slager, R., Gond, J.-P., and Moon, J. 2012. Standardization as institutional work: The regulatory power of a responsible investment standard. *Organization Studies*, 33(5–6): 763–90.

Smets, M., and Jarzabkowski, P. 2013. Reconstructing institutional complexity in practice: A relational model of institutional work and complexity. *Human Relations*, 66(10): 1279–309.

Smets, M., Morris, T., and Greenwood, R. 2012. From practice to field: A multilevel model of practice-driven institutional change. *Academy of Management Journal*, 55(4): 877–904.

Smith, G. D., and Winchester, H. P. M. 1998. Negotiating space: Alternative masculinities at the work/home boundary. *Australian Geographer*, 29(3): 327–39.

Smith, R. 1997. Self-reflection and the self. In R. Porter (Ed.), *Rewriting the self: Histories from the middle ages to the present*: 49–57. London: Routledge.

Smith, W. K., and Besharov, M. L. 2017. Bowing before dual gods: How structured flexibility sustains organizational hybridity. *Administrative Science Quarterly*, 64(1): 1–44.

Smithson, J., and Stokoe, E. H. 2005. Discourses of work–life balance: Negotiating "genderblind" terms in organizations. *Gender, Work & Organization*, 12(2): 147–68.

Snow, C. C., Miles, R. E., and Coleman, J., Henry J. 1992. Managing 21st century network organizations. *Organizational Dynamics*, 20(3): 4–20.

Snow, D. A., and Anderson, L. 1987. Identity work among the homeless: The verbal construction and avowal of personal identities. *American Journal of Sociology*, 92(6): 1336–71.

Sommers, B. D., and Bindman, A. B. 2012. New physicians, the affordable care act, and the changing practice of medicine. *JAMA*, 307(16): 1697–8.

Spee, A. P., and Jarzabkowski, P. 2009. Strategy tools as boundary objects. *Strategic Organization*, 7(2): 223–32.

References

Spreitzer, G., Sutcliffe, K., Dutton, J., Sonenshein, S., and Grant, A. M. 2005. A socially embedded model of thriving at work. *Organization Science*, 16(5): 537–49.

Stahl, G., and Mendenhall, M. (Eds.). 2005. *Mergers and acquisitions: Managing culture and human resources*. Stanford, CA: Stanford Business Books.

Stanovich, K. E., and West, R. F. 2000. Advancing the rationality debate. *Behavioral and Brain Sciences*, 23(05): 701–17.

Star, S. L., and Griesemer, J. R. 1989. Institutional ecology, "translations" and boundary objects: Amateurs and professionals in Berkeley's Museum of Vertebrate Zoology, 1907–39. *Social Studies of Science*, 19(3): 387–420.

Steinberg, R. J., and Figart, D. M. 1999. Emotional labor since *The Managed Heart*. *The Annals of the American Academy of Political and Social Science*, 561(1): 8–26.

Stopnitzky, Y. 2017. No toilet no bride? Intrahousehold bargaining in male-skewed marriage markets in India. *Journal of Development Economics*, 127: 269–82.

Strupp, H. H., Butler, S. F., and Rosser, C. L. 1988. Training in psychodynamic therapy. *Journal of Consulting and Clinical Psychology*, 56(5): 689–95.

Styhre, A. 2013. Gender equality as institutional work: The case of the Church of Sweden. *Gender, Work & Organization*. <https://doi.org/10.1111/gwao.12024>.

Suddaby, R., and Greenwood, R. 2005. Rhetorical strategies of legitimacy. *Administrative Science Quarterly*, 50(1): 35–67.

Suddaby, R., and Viale, T. 2011. Professionals and field-level change: Institutional work and the professional project. *Current Sociology*, 59(4): 423–42.

Sullivan, S. E., and Baruch, Y. 2009. Advances in career theory and research: A critical review and agenda for future exploration. *Journal of Management*, 35(6): 1542–71.

Suominen, K., and Mantere, S. 2010. Consuming strategy: The art and practice of managers' everyday strategy usage. In J. A. C. Baum and J. Lampel (Eds.), *The globalization of strategy research*: 211–45. Bingley: Emerald Group.

Sutton, R. I., and Rafaeli, A. 1988. Untangling the relationship between displayed emotions and organizational sales: The case of convenience stores. *Academy of Management Journal*, 31(3): 461–87.

Svejenova, S. 2005. "The path with the heart": Creating the authentic career. *Journal of Management Studies*, 42(5): 947–74.

Sveningsson, S., and Alvesson, M. 2003. Managing managerial identities: Organizational fragmentation, discourse and identity struggle. *Human Relations*, 56(10): 1163–93.

Swartz, A. 2008. *Guerilla open access manifesto*. Eremo, Italy. <http://archive.org/details/GuerillaOpenAccessManifesto>.

Symon, G., Buehring, A., Johnson, P., and Cassell, C. 2008. Positioning qualitative research as resistance to the institutionalization of the academic labour process. *Organization Studies*, 29(10): 1315–36.

Talusan, M. 2015. There is no comparison between transgender people and Rachel Dolezal. *The Guardian*, June 12. <http://www.theguardian.com/commentisfree/2015/jun/12/comparison-transgender-people-rachel-dolezal>.

Tams, S., and Arthur, M. B. 2010. New directions for boundaryless careers: Agency and interdependence in a changing world. *Journal of Organizational Behavior*, 31(5): 629–46.

Taupin, B. 2013. The more things change... Institutional maintenance as justification work in the credit rating industry. *M@n@gement*, 15(5): 529–62.

Taylor, F. W. 1914. *The principles of scientific management*. New York: Harper.

Taylor, J. R., and Every, E. J. V. 1993. *The vulnerable fortress: Bureaucratic organization and management in the information age*. Toronto, ON: University of Toronto Press.

Taylor, S., and Spicer, A. 2007. Time for space: A narrative review of research on organizational spaces. *International Journal of Management Reviews*, 9(4): 325–46.

The Free Dictionary. 2015. Institution. *The Free Dictionary*.

Tilly, C. 1998. *Durable inequality*. Berkeley, CA: University of California Press.

Torvalds, L., and Diamond, D. 2002. *Just for fun: The story of an accidental revolutionary*. New York: HarperCollins.

Tracey, P., Dalpiaz, E., and Phillips, N. 2018. Fish out of water: Translation, legitimation, and new venture creation. *Academy of Management Journal*, 61(5): 1627–66.

Tracey, P., and Phillips, N. 2016. Managing the consequences of organizational stigmatization: Identity work in a social enterprise. *Academy of Management Journal*, 59(3): 740–65.

Tracey, P., Phillips, N., and Jarvis, O. 2011. Bridging institutional entrepreneurship and the creation of new organizational forms: A multilevel model. *Organization Science*, 22(1): 60–80.

Trank, C. Q., and Washington, M. 2009. Maintaining an institution in a contested organizational field: The work of AACSB and its constituents. In T. B. Lawrence, R. Suddaby, and B. Leca (Eds.), *Institutional work: Actors and agency in institutional studies of organizations*: 236–61. Cambridge: University of Cambridge Press.

Trist, E. L. 1981. *The evolution of socio-technical systems: Occasional paper No. 2*. Toronto, ON: Quality of Working Life Centre.

Trist, E. L., and Bamforth, K. W. 1951. Some social and psychological consequences of the longwall method of coal-getting: An examination of the psychological situation and defences of a work group in relation to the social structure and technological content of the work system. *Human Relations*, 4(1): 3–38.

Tseëlon, E. 1992. Is the presented self sincere? Goffman, impression management and the postmodern self. *Theory, Culture & Society*, 9(2): 115–28.

Tuan, Y.-F. 1975. Place: An experiential perspective. *Geographical Review*, 65(2): 151–65.

Tuan, Y.-F. 1977. *Space and place: The perspective of experience*. Minneapolis, MN: University of Minnesota Press.

Tucker, K. 1998. *Anthony Giddens and modern social theory*. London: SAGE.

Turner, J. H., and Stets, J. E. 2006. Sociological theories of human emotions. *Annual Review of Sociology*, 32: 25–52.

Tushman, M. L., and Scanlan, T. J. 1981. Characteristics and external orientations of boundary spanning individuals. *Academy of Management Journal*, 24(1): 83–98.

Tyler, J. R., Wilkinson, D. M., and Huberman, B. A. 2005. E-mail as spectroscopy: Automated discovery of community structure within organizations. *The Information Society*, 21(2): 143–53.

Tyler, M., and Cohen, L. 2010. Spaces that matter: Gender performativity and organizational space. *Organization Studies*, 31(2): 175–98.

User:Giraffedata/comprised of. 2015. *Wikipedia*, February 6. <http://en.wikipedia.org/w/index.php?title=User:Giraffedata/comprised_ofandoldid=645884255>.

Uys, L. R. 1980. Towards the development of an operational definition of the concept "therapeutic use of self." *International Journal of Nursing Studies*, 17(3): 175–80.

Vaara, E., Sorsa, V., and Pälli, P. 2010. On the force potential of strategy texts: A critical discourse analysis of a strategic plan and its power effects in a city organization. *Organization*, 17(6): 685–702.

Vaara, E., and Whittington, R. 2012. Strategy-as-practice: Taking social practices seriously. *Academy of Management Annals*, 6(1): 285–336.

Valve Software. 2012. *Valve: Handbook for new employees*. Bellevue, WA: Valve Corporation. <https://assets.sbnation.com/assets/1074301/Valve_Handbook_LowRes.pdf>.

Van de Ven, A. H. 1992. Suggestions for studying strategy process: A research note. *Strategic Management Journal*, 13(Summer special issue): 169–88.

Van Kleef, G. A., Homan, A. C., Beersma, B., and van Knippenberg, D. 2010. On angry leaders and agreeable followers: How leaders' emotions and followers' personalities shape motivation and team performance. *Psychological Science*, 21(12): 1827–34.

Van Kleef, G. A., Homan, A. C., and Cheshin, A. 2012. Emotional influence at work: Take it EASI. *Organizational Psychology Review*, 2(4): 311–39.

van Knippenberg, D., Dawson, J. F., West, M. A., and Homan, A. C. 2011. Diversity faultlines, shared objectives, and top management team performance. *Human Relations*, 64(3): 307–36.

van Knippenberg, D., and Schippers, M. C. 2007. Work group diversity. *Annual Review of Psychology*, 58(1): 515–41.

van Knippenberg, D., van Knippenberg, B., De Cremer, D., and Hogg, M. A. 2004. Leadership, self, and identity: A review and research agenda. *The Leadership Quarterly*, 15(6): 825–56.

Van Maanen, J., and Barley, S. R. 1984. Occupational communities: Culture and control in organizations. *Research in Organizational Behavior*, 6: 287–365.

Vergne, J.-P., and Wry, T. 2014. Categorizing categorization research: Review, integration, and future directions. *Journal of Management Studies*, 51(1): 56–94.

Vines, G. 1992. Last Olympics for the sex test? *New Scientist*, 135(1828): 39–42.

von Neumann, J., and Morgenstern, O. 1944. *Theory of games and economic behavior*. Princeton, NJ: Princeton University Press.

Voronov, M. 2014. Toward a toolkit for emotionalizing institutional theory. *Emotions and the Organizational Fabric*, vol. 10: 167–96. Bingley: Emerald Group.

Voronov, M., and Vince, R. 2012. Integrating emotions into the analysis of institutional work. *Academy of Management Review*, 37(1): 58–81.

Voronov, M., and Weber, K. 2016. The heart of institutions: Emotional competence and institutional actorhood. *Academy of Management Review*, 41(3): 456–78.

Wæraas, A., and Sataøen, H. L. 2014. Trapped in conformity? Translating reputation management into practice. *Scandinavian Journal of Management*, 30(2): 242–53.

Wallace, B. 2011. The rise and fall of Bitcoin. *WIRED*, November 23. <http://www.wired.com/2011/11/mf_bitcoin/>.

Walsham, G. 1995. The emergence of interpretivism in IS research. *Information Systems Research*, 6(4): 376–94.

Wang, C., and Burris, M. A. 1997. Photovoice: Concept, methodology, and use for participatory needs assessment. *Health Education and Behavior*, 24(3): 369–87.

Ward, J., and Winstanley, D. 2005. Coming out at work: Performativity and the recognition and renegotiation of identity. *The Sociological Review*, 53(3): 447–75.

Warhurst, C., and Nickson, D. 2009. "Who's got the look?" Emotional, aesthetic and sexualized labour in interactive services. *Gender, Work & Organization*, 16(3): 385–404.

Warren, S. 2008. Empirical challenges in organizational aesthetics research: Towards a sensual methodology. *Organization Studies*, 29(4): 559–80.

Watson, T. J. 2008. Managing identity: Identity work, personal predicaments and structural circumstances. *Organization*, 15(1): 121–43.

Watson, T. J. 2009. Entrepreneurial action, identity work and the use of multiple discursive resources: The case of a rapidly changing family business. *International Small Business Journal*, 27(3): 251–74.

Weber, M. 1958. The three types of legitimate rule. *Berkeley Publications in Society and Institutions*, 4(1): 1–11.

Weber, M. 2001. *The Protestant ethic and the spirit of capitalism.* (T. Parsons, Trans.). London: Routledge.

Weber, S., Bookhart, D., and Newman, J. 2009. Research and solutions: Institutionalizing campus-wide sustainability: a programmatic approach. *Sustainability: The Journal of Record*, 2(3): 173–8.

Weick, K. E. 1988. Enacted sensemaking in crisis situations. *Journal of Management Studies*, 25(4): 305–17.

Weitzer, R. 2009. Sociology of sex work. *Annual Review of Sociology*, 35(1): 213–34.

Wenzel, J. 2018. @johnwenzel, April 6. <https://t.co/beQqUqEv63>.

Wernerfelt, B. 1984. A resource-based view of the firm. *Strategic Management Journal*, 14: 4–12.

Westley, F., and Antadze, N. 2010. Making a difference: Strategies for scaling social innovation for greater impact. *The Innovation Journal: The Public Sector Innovation Journal*, 15(2): Article 2.

Whitaker, M. C. 2005. *Race work: The rise of civil rights in the urban west.* Lincoln, NB: University of Nebraska Press.

Whittington, R. 1996. Strategy as practice. *Long Range Planning*, 29(5): 731–5.

Whittington, R. 2006. Completing the practice turn in strategy research. *Organization Studies*, 27(5): 613–34.

Whittington, R. 2015. The massification of strategy. *British Journal of Management*, 26(S1).

Whittington, R., Molloy, E., Mayer, M., and Smith, A. 2006. Practices of strategising/organising: Broadening strategy work and skills. *Long Range Planning*, 39(6): 615–29.

Whyte, W. H., Jr. 1956. *The organization man.* New York: Simon and Schuster.

Wikipedia. 2016a. Anthropocene. *Wikipedia*, February 29. <https://en.wikipedia.org/w/index.php?title=Anthropoceneandoldid=707596377>.

Wikipedia. 2016b. Epoch (geology). *Wikipedia*, April 4. <https://en.wikipedia.org/w/index.php?title=Epoch_(geology)andoldid=713550752>.

Wilf, E. 2012. Sincerity versus self-expression: Modern creative agency and the materiality of semiotic forms. *Cultural Anthropology*, 26(3): 462–84.

Williams, G. 2008. Review of *The Wounded Storyteller* by Arthur Frank. *Sociology of Health and Illness*, 18(5): 714–15.

Williamson, O. E. 1985. *The economic institutions of capitalism: Firms, markets, relational contracting*. New York: Free Press.

Winchester, S. 2003. *The Meaning of Everything: The Story of the Oxford English Dictionary*. Oxford: Oxford University Press.

Wittgenstein, L. 2009. *Philosophical investigations*. Oxford: John Wiley & Sons.

Woodward, J. 1958. *Management and technology: Problems and progress in technology. 3*. London: Her Majesty's Stationery Office.

Wortham, J. 2016. When everyone can be "queer," is anyone? *The New York Times Magazine*, July 17: MM13.

Wright, A., Zammuto, R., and Liesch, P. 2017. Maintaining the values of a profession: Institutional work and moral emotions in the emergency department. *Academy of Management Journal*, 60(1): 200–37.

Wrzesniewski, A., and Dutton, J. E. 2001. Crafting a job: Revisioning employees as active crafters of their work. *Academy of Management Review*, 26(2): 179–201.

Wrzesniewski, A., Dutton, J. E., and Debebe, G. 2003. Interpersonal sensemaking and the meaning of work. *Research in Organizational Behavior*, 25: 93–135.

Yanow, D. 1998. Space stories: Studying museum buildings as organizational spaces while reflecting on interpretive methods and their narration. *Journal of Management Inquiry*, 7(3): 215–39.

Young, E. 1989. On the naming of the rose: Interests and multiple meanings as elements of organizational culture. *Organization Studies*, 10(2): 187–206.

Zaheer, S. 1995. Overcoming the liability of foreignness. *Academy of Management Journal*, 38(2): 341–63.

Zapf, D. 2002. Emotion work and psychological well-being: A review of the literature and some conceptual considerations. *Human Resource Management Review*, 12(2): 237–68.

Zapf, D., and Holz, M. 2006. On the positive and negative effects of emotion work in organizations. *European Journal of Work and Organizational Psychology*, 15(1): 1–28.

Zapf, D., Vogt, C., Seifert, C., Mertini, H., and Isic, A. 1999. Emotion work as a source of stress: The concept and development of an instrument. *European Journal of Work and Organizational Psychology*, 8(3): 371–400.

Zbaracki, M. J. 1998. The rhetoric and reality of total quality management. *Administrative Science Quarterly*, 43(3): 602–36.

Zelizer, V. A. 2000. The purchase of intimacy. *Law & Social Inquiry*, 25(3): 817–488.

Zelizer, V. A. 2012. How I became a relational economic sociologist and what does that mean? *Politics & Society*, 40(2): 145–74.

Zerubavel, E. 1981. *Hidden rhythms*. Chicago, IL: University of Chicago Press.

Ziegler, C. 2011. Nokia CEO Stephen Elop rallies troops in brutally honest "burning platform" memo? (update: it's real!). *Engadget*, August 2. <https://www.engadget.com/2011/02/08/nokia-ceo-stephen-elop-rallies-troops-in-brutally-honest-burnin/>.

Zietsma, C., Groenewegen, P., Logue, D., and Hinings, C. R. 2016. Field or fields? Building the scaffolding for cumulation of research on institutional fields. *Academy of Management Annals*.

Zietsma, C., and Lawrence, T. B. 2010. Institutional work in the transformation of an organizational field: The interplay of boundary work and practice work. *Administrative Science Quarterly*, 55(2): 189–221.

Zilber, T. B. 2006. The work of the symbolic in institutional processes: Translations of rational myths in Israeli high tech. *Academy of Management Journal*, 49(2): 281–303.

Zilber, T. B. 2007. Stories and the discursive dynamics of institutional entrepreneurship: The case of Israeli high-tech after the bubble. *Organization Studies*, 28(7): 1035–54.

Zilber, T. B. 2009. Institutional maintenance as narrative acts. In T. B. Lawrence, R. Suddaby, and B. Leca (Eds.), *Institutional work: Actors and agency in institutional studies of organizations*: 205–35. Cambridge: University of Cambridge Press.

Zilber, T. B. 2011. Institutional multiplicity in practice: A tale of two high-tech conferences in Israel. *Organization Science*, 22(6): 1539–59.

Zuckerman, E. W. 1999. The categorical imperative: Securities analysts and the illegitimacy discount. *American Journal of Sociology*, 104(5): 1398–438.

Author Index

General Index